The Realm of Rights

The Realm of Rights

Judith Jarvis Thomson

Harvard University Press
Cambridge, Massachusetts
London, England

Library of Congress Cataloging-in-Publication Data
Thomson, Judith Jarvis.
The realm of rights / Judith Jarvis Thomson.
p.   cm.
Includes bibliographical references.
ISBN 0-674-74948-0 (alk. paper)
1. Law and ethics. I. Title. II. Title: Rights.
BJ55.T46   1990
170—dc20   90-31045
CIP

In Memory of

James F. Thomson
Theodore R. Jarvis

Acknowledgments

I am deeply indebted to Michael Hardimon and David Brink for helpful criticism of large parts of the semifinal draft.

An earlier draft of parts of the manuscript was helpfully criticized by the members of my seminar on moral philosophy at MIT (fall 1988). The members were: Ann Bumpus, Susan Dwyer, David Galloway, Richard Heck, Eric Lormand, Michael Picard, Paul Pietroski, Hugh Sansom, Robert Stainton, and Ed Stein. Parts of a still earlier draft benefited from criticism by my students at the Yale Law School; I am grateful to Deans Harry Wellington and Guido Calabresi and their faculty for inviting me to make a series of visits there.

Jonathan Bennett, Mary Mothersill, Derek Parfit, and Mary C. Potter (among others) commented on an early draft of the Introduction. A later draft was presented at a conference on the foundations of moral and political philosophy at the Social Philosophy and Policy Center, Bowling Green State University; I thank the participants for their comments. The conference papers appear in *Social Philosophy and Policy*, 7 (fall 1989).

The Introduction and Chapters 1–4 were helpfully criticized by the members of Thomas Nagel's and Ronald Dworkin's seminar in philosophy and law (fall 1988) at the New York University Law School.

Part of Chapter 3 benefited from comments by Ruth Marcus.

I am grateful to Mary C. Potter for suggestions about the cases discussed in Chapter 7 and for criticism of my successive attempts to understand them. I am grateful also to Joshua Cohen for comments on an early draft of Chapter 7 and for advice about the literature on slavery—this material was helpful background for the issues dealt with in Chapter 8.

Part of Chapter 8 was presented as the John Dewey Lecture at the University of Chicago Law School (spring 1989).

Thomas M. Scanlon gave me helpful suggestions about Chapter 13.

The first complete draft of the manuscript was written during the academic years 1986–87 and 1987–88; I thank the National Endowment for the Humanities and the John Simon Guggenheim Memorial Foundation for successive fellowships during those two years. I owe thanks also to MIT for a sabbatical leave during the first of them and a leave of absence during the second.

But I am most indebted to the members of the Society for Ethical and Legal Philosophy, who have given me over the years some of the most enjoyable and profitable experiences of my academic life. I can only hope that I have not helped myself to more of their ideas than is permitted among friends.

Contents

Introduction and Metaethical Remarks   1

PART I   Rights: What They Are

1   Claims, Privileges, and Powers   37

2   Duties   61

3   Ought   79

4   Enforcing Claims   105

5   Value   123

6   Tradeoffs   149

7   The Trolley Problem   176

PART II   Rights: Which They Are

8   Trespass and First Property   205

9   Harm   227

10   Distress and Harm   249

11   Liberty   272

12   Giving One's Word   294

13   Second Property   322

14   Ceasing To Have a Right   348

Index   375

The Realm of Rights

Introduction and Metaethical Remarks

1. We take ourselves to have rights. We often say to each other, and to those who govern us, not "It would be a bad thing if you did such and such", not even "You ought not do such and such", but rather "I have a *right* that you not do such and such". What I wish to do is to work out how these ideas we have about our rights hang together.

For they do hang together. We do not arbitrarily fasten on one or another concern of ours and declare a right that it be met or satisfied; there are general principles behind the attributions of rights that we make to ourselves and to others. I think it an enterprise of great interest to ask what they are.

I should say straightway, however, that the enterprise I am inviting you to engage in is not a study of the law. Our law is rich in declarations about who has rights against whom to what, and certain very general ideas in and about law will be of much use to us. But our enterprise is not legal, it is moral. Some of the rights we have against each other we do have only because our legal system assigns them to us. For example, I have a right against my neighbors that they not leave their garbage on the sidewalk in front of my house, except on Wednesdays, and I have that right against them only because of our town's regulations governing garbage collection. For our purposes, the interesting question such examples raise is not which rights the law assigns us, but how and why government action can make a person have (or lack) a right—when it can. That is not a legal question, but a moral one.

Moreover, while many of the rights we have against each other are assigned to us by our legal system, some of them we do not have *merely* because our legal system assigns them to us: we would have them even if our legal system did not assign them to us. For

1

example, I have a right against you that you not break my nose. The criminal law assigns me that right against you in that it proscribes nose-breaking, but I would have that right even if there were no law proscribing acts of that kind. For our purposes, the interesting question such examples raise is not what is the content of our criminal law, but what it is about us that makes us have rights that we would have even if the law did not assign them to us. That too is not a legal question, but a moral one.

Those rights that we would have even if our legal system did not assign them to us are in a sense prior to law: it is not law, or anyway it is not law *alone,* that makes us have them.

Indeed, some of those rights are in yet another sense prior to law: a legal system would be defective if it did not assign them to those governed by it. A legal system that does not assign to anyone governed by it a right to not be killed by others is perhaps not even an imaginable legal system. A legal system that does not assign Jews or blacks the right to not be killed by others is all too easily imaginable, and grossly defective for its failure.

For a person's having a right has consequences. I have a right against you that you not break my nose, and much follows from the fact that I do. Other things being equal, for example, you ought not break my nose. Other things being equal, it is morally permissible for me to defend myself against an attempt at nose-breaking by you. If you break my nose, then other things being equal, you ought to pay my medical costs for the repair of it. Other things being equal, there ought to be laws dealing with nose-breaking and with the ways in which the victim of such an act is to be compensated for it, and if there are not, then other things being equal we ought to pass some. And so on. Having a right is having a valuable moral status precisely because it has these consequences, and asserting the right is demanding that people act as these consequences say they ought to act. It would be no wonder if people who think government a mere creature of the governed, and each member of the governed the equal of every other, spoke to their government and each other in the words "I have a right!"

The consequences of a person's having a right, however, are moral, and may be merely moral. I might truly say to my government, or to another person, "I have a right", and my government, or that other person, might pay no attention to me. In that I have the right, it follows that others ought to do a variety of different things. But they might not in fact do them. Having a right is not the same as, and does not even include, being accorded what one has a right to.

What does it include? I have a right against you that you not break my nose, and I said that it follows from that, for example, that *other things being equal* you ought not break my nose. Why did I not say, simply, that it follows that you ought not break my nose?—why did I qualify by use of the words "other things being equal"? On some views, the qualification is not necessary in that all rights are in a sense 'absolute': that is, if X has a right against Y that Y do something, then Y ought to do it, whatever the circumstances and whatever Y's doing it might cost Y or Z or still others. On other views, some rights at least are not absolute: that is, it might be the case that X has a right against Y that Y do something, and that Y nevertheless need not do it in light of the circumstances and the costs of doing it. We will have to look into this more closely.

More generally, the concept of a right is only one among many moral concepts, and understanding what it is to have a right requires us to get a sense of how that concept is related to the others. How it is related in particular to the concept of what a person ought to do, for it is in the bearing of a person's rights on what he or she[1] or others ought or ought not do that the importance of rights and the value of having them are to be found. We might think of morality as a continent and of rights as a territory or realm somewhere in it; understanding what is within the realm of rights requires getting a sense of where in the continent it lies.

---

1. Until very recently it seemed to me that those who object to the use of the masculine "he" to refer to a person chosen at random were merely being tiresome. Not so now. On the other hand, "she" is no better. Indeed, it is in two ways worse. In the first place, prose should be transparent, like a pane of glass through which one sees the thoughts behind it; the use of "she" for these purposes is like a smudge on the pane—it captures the attention. In the second place, those who now use "she" in this way are making a moral point in doing so, a moral point I think entirely right; but it is annoying to have that moral point introduced (with the back of the hand, as it were) into matters it has no connection with—one feels nagged. All the same, "he or she" very soon yields impossible clutter. I therefore adopt two clutter-reducing conventions. Unless I indicate otherwise, "A", "B", "C", and so on, are dummy names for men (you might think of them as short for "Alfred", "Bert", and so on); and a character named "Bloggs", who will turn up from time to time, is also male. "X", "Y", and "Z", however, are variables ranging over things generally, whether male or female, human or non-human. "Does alpha", "does beta", and so on, are dummy verb phrases.

In fact we shall have to look into this question before we ask what general principles lie behind such attributions of rights as we make to ourselves and others: we cannot expect to become clear what those principles are until we are clear what the phenomenon is that they are supposed to be the principles *of*.

So we will begin with the question where, within morality, does the realm of rights lie? Without the metaphor: what is the moral significance of having a right? That will be the topic of Part I. We will then be in a position to ask which rights we have, and why. That will be the topic of Part II.

2. But it might be well to begin by saying something about the method I will be using. Those who find methodological discussion uninteresting, and those who think it better to see a method at work before looking at a defense of it (not a bad idea actually), are cordially invited to pass on straightway to Chapter 1. But there may be those who expect something I will not try to provide, and a warning is therefore called for. In short, and to shift metaphor, I take much of the stuff of morality as given: I do not offer a recipe for constructing it out of elementary particles.

For example, I will often say such things as "But surely A ought to do such and such" or "Plainly it is morally permissible for B to do so and so", and I will not even try to prove that those things are true. I will say, for example, "But surely B ought to give A a banana" in circumstances in which (as I will invite you to imagine) B has freely promised A he would give A a banana, and can easily do so, and has in no way committed himself to anyone else to not doing so, and will cause no harm by doing so—quite to the contrary, will cause harm if he fails to do so. I hope you will agree that it is true to say in those circumstances that B ought to give A a banana; but I will not try to prove that it is.

Moreover, I will not merely say such things; I will rest weight on them. I do not wish merely to produce a list of moral judgments that we (I hope) will agree to be true; I will draw conclusions from the supposition that those judgments are true, conclusions, in particular, about people's rights. They will serve as *data* for the theory of rights to be presented. If you think them false, then you have as serious a ground for objection to what goes on as you have if you find a mistake in my reasoning from them.

Yet there are people who would reply that I am not entitled to rest any weight at all on those judgments. They would say, not that the judgments are false, but that there is no reason to believe them true. They would say, more generally, that there is no reason to think of any moral judgment that it is true. It is that idea I want to attend to here; I will call it the No-Reason Thesis. If this thesis is correct, then the enterprise I am inviting you to engage in with me is pointless, and in two ways at that: on the one hand, the premises on which I rest my conclusions are judgments there is no reason to think true, and on the other hand the conclusions are themselves judgments of a kind that no premises could give reason for. So the No-Reason Thesis has to be taken seriously—if there is reason to think it is itself true.

Is there? Some philosophers think not merely that there is reason to think the No-Reason Thesis true, but that it *is* true. Many of them credit Hume with the insight that lies behind it. Hume said, in a well-known passage,[2]

> In every system of morality, which I have hitherto met with, I have always remark'd, that the author proceeds for some time in the ordinary way of reasoning, and establishes the being of a God, or makes observations concerning human affairs; when of a sudden I am surpriz'd to find, that instead of the usual copulations of propositions, *is,* and *is not,* I meet with no proposition that is not connected with an *ought,* or an *ought not.* This change is imperceptible; but is, however, of the last consequence. For as this *ought,* or *ought not,* expresses some new relation or affirmation, 'tis necessary that it shou'd be observ'd and explain'd; and at the same time that a reason should be given, for what seems altogether inconceivable, how this new relation can be a deduction from others, which are entirely different from it. (p. 469)

That is, moralists begin by telling us that the world is this way and is not that way. They then say "So people ought to do this and ought not do that". But the conclusion they draw "expresses some new relation or affirmation"; and it seems "altogether inconceivable" that it should be deducible from what preceded it, which is "entirely different from it".

There has been dispute as to what Hume actually intended, and it is arguable that he did not mean what he has in our century been

2. David Hume, *A Treatise of Human Nature,* ed. L. A. Selby-Bigge (London: Oxford University Press, 1973). Page references in parentheses after quotations from Hume are to this edition.

taken to have meant; what matters for our purposes is what the passage seemed to say, and indeed seemed to be right in saying: namely that no statement to the effect that a person ought or ought not do a thing can be "a deduction from" any statement about what is in fact the case. Or, as I shall put the point: no statement to the effect that a person ought or ought not do a thing *is entailed by* any statement about what is in fact the case.

I should perhaps stop to say a word about my use of the phrases "is entailed by" and (in the active mode) "entails". I will throughout say that a statement Q is entailed by a statement P (and that P entails Q) if and only if, if P is true, then so must Q also be true.[3]

And why merely "ought" and "ought not"? Why not also "right" and "wrong", "good" and "bad", and so on? Are these not also "new relations or affirmations"? So it seemed right to say, more generally, that no moral judgment at all is entailed by any statement about what is in fact the case. We might call this the Fact-Value Thesis.

The Fact-Value Thesis says (in the active mode) that no statement of fact entails any moral judgment. The No-Reason Thesis certainly appears to be considerably stronger: it says that there is no reason at all to think any moral judgment true. How is one to get from the Fact-Value Thesis to the No-Reason Thesis? One popular route (more popular some years ago than it is nowadays) passes through a certain diagnosis of the source of the Fact-Value Thesis. You begin with the fact that you have already shown *that* the Fact-Value Thesis is true. (How did you show this? By appeal to Hume, by pointing in one or another way to the fact that, as Hume put it, a moral concept "expresses some new relation or affirmation".[4]) Then what you do is to ask *why* the Fact-Value Thesis is true—what explains its being a truth. And you offer the following answer: having a moral belief is merely having an attitude, and making a moral assertion is merely displaying that attitude (as a smile is a display of an attitude); moral 'judgments' therefore have no truth-value (as smiles have no truth-

3. I think it arguable that this is how Hume meant us to understand "a deduction from". Whatever precisely Hume may have had in mind in the passage quoted above, it is surely plain that he did not mean to be drawing our attention merely to the fact that "ought" is not obtainable from "is" within first-order logic. See note 14 below.

4. See, for example, G. E. Moore's 'open question argument' in *Principia Ethica* (London: Cambridge University Press, 1966), pp. 15–16. A similar argument is in A. J. Ayer *Language, Truth and Logic*, 2nd ed. (New York: Dover Publications, 1952), ch. 6.

value). Certainly if that answer is correct, then its being correct would explain why the Fact-Value Thesis is true, for if moral 'judgments' have no truth-value, then *a fortiori* no statement of fact entails a moral judgment.

Moreover, if that is why the Fact-Value Thesis is true, then the No-Reason Thesis is also true, for if moral 'judgments' have no truth-value, then *a fortiori* nothing really is reason to think them true. So that diagnosis of the source of the Fact-Value Thesis takes us all the way to the No-Reason Thesis.

This is not the only possible route along which a philosopher might think to get from the Fact-Value Thesis to the No-Reason Thesis, but it was, as I say, a popular one. In the first place, moral beliefs (if they can properly be called beliefs) plainly do connect with attitudes: people who believe people ought not do a thing do typically (always?) have an unfavorable attitude toward the doing of it. Second, what property could it be thought that we ascribe to a person or to a kind of act when we say that the person ought not engage in an act of that kind? There seems to be nothing discoverable by looking, as the presence of redness is discoverable by looking, or by listening, as the presence of sounds is discoverable by listening, or by any other form of perception, which wrongness could be thought to consist in. (If there were, then moral judgments would be entailed by statements of fact, which the Fact-Value Thesis denies.) But then doesn't a hard-headed empiricist do better to say that there is no such property as wrongness?—and thus that 'ascriptions of wrongness' are not *really* ascriptions of anything? And if they are not ascriptions of anything, what more plausible than to think that they are mere displays of attitudes?

All this has been very abstract. Consider the disputes about capital punishment. I say "disputes", since there are several of them. Many people argue that we ought to make it impermissible for the death penalty to be imposed on anyone for any crime, even for murder, even for a particularly despicable murder, even for a second commission of a particularly despicable murder. Others disagree. Now some of those arguments issue from disagreements as to the facts. One side believes it wrong to impose the death penalty *because* they believe it does not deter more effectively than long prison terms; the other side believes it acceptable to impose the death penalty *because* they believe it does deter more effectively than long prison terms. In the case of these arguments, one is inclined to think that the difference of opinion on the moral matter would end if the two sides came to agreement on the facts.

But in the case of other disputes about capital punishment, that is not so. We may imagine that A believes that we ought to make it impermissible for the death penalty to be imposed on anyone for any crime, even for murder, even for a particularly despicable murder, even for a second commission of a particularly despicable murder, and this *not* because he has a belief of fact of the kind I mentioned above: A believes this because he believes that a community (like an individual) must never intentionally kill a person who is in captivity, and who thus currently constitutes no threat to others, and who can be kept from constituting a threat to others by less drastic means than killing. B, by contrast, believes it permissible for the death penalty to be imposed on those who are properly convicted of particularly despicable crimes in that he thinks they deserve death for their crimes and that, by executing them, the community demonstrates its respect for their victims and its commitment to the belief that the crimes in question really are particularly despicable. Indeed, we may suppose B to believe that the community's failure to execute them (on proper conviction) would precisely show a lack of respect for their victims and a lack of commitment to its moral beliefs. It is plausible to think that *this* dispute about capital punishment is purely moral: we may plausibly think that A and B are in complete agreement on all the relevant matters of fact while nevertheless disagreeing as to the moral permissibility of capital punishment.

It is worth noticing in passing that it was not necessary to invent people with wild or crazy moral views in order to invent what looks for all the world like a purely moral dispute. We did not even need to look across cultures; A and B are our neighbors here at home.

How is the dispute between A and B to be settled? Friends of the Fact-Value Thesis say it cannot be settled by convicting either one of the parties to the dispute of an inconsistency between his beliefs of fact on the one hand and his moral belief about capital punishment on the other hand, for if the Fact-Value Thesis is true, then no statement reporting all of the relevant matters of fact believed by both A and B entails that capital punishment is, or entails that it is not, permissible. And isn't that plausible?

One who takes the step from the Fact-Value Thesis to the No-Reason Thesis says that the dispute between A and B cannot be settled at all. A thinks capital punishment impermissible, B thinks it permissible, but neither has any reason at all for thinking this, for, as the No-Reason Thesis says, there is no reason to think of any moral judgment that it is true. And isn't that plausible too? For if the No-Reason Thesis is true, it would be no wonder that our deepest differences over capital punishment have proved so resistant to settlement.

There are of course a great many moral judgments that are not at all in dispute among our neighbors here at home, judgments for example to the effect that it is on the whole not a good thing to lie and cheat, maim people and cause them pain. But mightn't it occur to us that agreement on those matters would also be no wonder, given our common background and education? Perhaps we need to invent a person with wild or crazy moral views if we are to invent a purely moral dispute about our most favored moral views. But can't we?

It is a good question whether the procedure for getting from the Fact-Value Thesis to the No-Reason Thesis that I described above really does get us there. That procedure is suspect, in a number of ways. More generally, I know of no clear way of *proving* that if the Fact-Value Thesis is true, then so also is the No-Reason Thesis.

On the other hand, I am inclined to think, myself, that if the Fact-Value Thesis is true, then we would be right to be suspicious of the idea that there is reason to believe some moral judgment is true. After all, if no statement of fact P entails a moral judgment Q, then even a statement of fact P that is a 'complete' report of all of the facts of our world does not entail Q; and that means that the totality of all of the facts of our world is compatible with Q's not being true. What, then, is supposed to be the reason to think Q really is true?

I suggest that we bypass the question whether one can get from the Fact-Value Thesis to the No-Reason Thesis, and if so how. Many (I think most) philosophers who accepted the Fact-Value Thesis did take that step, and we can at least understand why they thought they were entitled to. Moreover, what we will focus on below is the Fact-Value Thesis itself. If the Fact-Value Thesis is false, then it matters not a bit how one might pass from it to the No-Reason Thesis. Indeed, if the Fact-Value Thesis is false, then the No-Reason Thesis is also false, and we need not attend to any of the many considerations brought forward in support of it.

3. I hope it will be clear that I have not been trying to prove the No-Reason Thesis or even the Fact-Value Thesis. I wanted only to bring

out what lies behind them and to do this as convincingly as I could. For I think Hume was entirely right to be struck by the sudden shift from "is" to "ought" in the writings of the moralists, and that he made a major contribution to philosophy in showing it to us. I think, moreover, that his modern followers also made a major contribution to philosophy in bringing out, explicitly, the threat to moral confidence that lurks in what Hume showed us. At the very least, the burden of proof nowadays lies on the defender of moral confidence. One way in which that burden has been assumed comes out as follows.

Disputes about capital punishment are in a number of ways particularly well suited to the purposes of one who wishes to make us feel in sympathy with the Fact-Value Thesis and the No-Reason Thesis. In the first place, there are ongoing unsettled disputes about capital punishment, and it is plausible to think that some of them really are purely moral.

Second, and more important, the considerations that people bring to bear in support of their views about capital punishment are relatively easy to divide into the factual on the one hand and the moral on the other.[5]

But a number of people have entirely rightly drawn attention to the fact that much of our moral thinking is neither purely factual nor purely moral;[6] and some have offered that fact as an objection to the Fact-Value Thesis. Philippa Foot, for example, invited us to take note of such predicates as "rude". She said:

> I think it will be agreed that in the wide sense in which philosophers speak of evaluation, 'rude' is an evaluative term . . . it expresses disapproval, is meant to be used when action is to be discouraged, implies that other things being equal the behavior to which it is applied will be avoided by the speaker, and so on.[7]

It seems right to think that saying about Bloggs that he behaved rudely is making an unfavorable moral judgment about him. On the other

5. This is not true of many other current moral disputes, such as those about abortion. The question whether the fetus is a person—which most participants take seriously—is neither straightforwardly factual nor straightforwardly moral.

6. A kind of 'straddle' judgment (a judgment neither purely factual nor purely moral) that is different from what we are about to look at was pointed out by Arthur N. Prior in "The Autonomy of Ethics", reprinted in his *Papers in Logic and Ethics* (Amherst: University of Massachusetts Press, 1976).

7. See her "Moral Arguments", reprinted in her *Virtues and Vices* (Oxford: Basil Blackwell, 1978). My quotations are all from p. 102.

hand, a bit of behavior is rude if it meets certain conditions of fact. Foot suggests that a bit of behavior is rude just in case it "causes offence by indicating lack of respect"; whether or not that is correct as an account of what rudeness *is,* it does seem right to think that if Bloggs interrupted a lecture at a scholarly meeting with an insult, then it follows that he acted rudely. In short, Foot says, some moral judgments are entailed by some statements of fact, namely those moral judgments to the effect that someone has been rude.

There is a range of concepts here, of which the concept 'rude' is only one. Bernard Williams helpfully gives them the name "thick ethical concepts".[8] Among the examples he gives are 'treachery', 'brutality', 'courage', and 'cowardice'. It seems right to think that saying about Bloggs that he behaved treacherously is making a moral judgment about him. On the other hand, a bit of behavior is treachery if it meets certain conditions of fact. Treachery is breach of trust, and it does seem right to think that if Bloggs sold his country's secrets to the enemy during wartime, then it follows that he acted treacherously. Similar points hold for ascriptions of brutality, courage, and cowardice. So anyone who agrees with Foot about rudeness will very likely want to say that here are further moral judgments which are entailed by statements of fact.

Williams gives two further examples of thick ethical concepts which seem to me different, namely the concepts 'promise' and 'lie'. It does seem right to think that saying about Bloggs that he behaved rudely or treacherously or brutally, and so on, is making a moral judgment about him; does it seem right to think that saying about him that he made (or broke) a promise, or that he told a lie, is making a moral judgment about him? That is less clear. To borrow Foot's language, these do not seem to be evaluative terms, they do not seem to express disapproval. Certainly if I merely say Bloggs *made* a promise, I express no disapproval; and even though disapproval may well be in place where Bloggs broke a promise or lied, to say he broke a promise or lied does not seem to have already expressed that disapproval.

Nevertheless it is arguable that Foot's concept 'rude' and all of Williams' sample thick ethical concepts (including 'promise' and lie') do have something important in common, a something in virtue of which they all yield countercases to the Fact-Value Thesis. What I

8. Bernard Williams, *Ethics and the Limits of Philosophy* (Cambridge: Harvard University Press, 1985), pp. 129, 140.

have in mind is hinted at in the passage by Foot quoted above (notice her use of the phrase "other things being equal") and comes out as follows. It seems right to think that there are statements of fact about A's current circumstances (as it might be: lecturer, scholarly meeting, serious faces all round) that entail

(1) A will be acting rudely if he shouts "Boo!"

(1) does not entail "A ought not shout 'Boo!' ", for as Foot says, "there are occasions when a little rudeness is in place"; but it seems right to think that (1) entails

(2) Other things being equal, A ought not shout "Boo!"

And isn't (2) a moral judgment? No doubt "Other things being equal, A ought not shout 'Boo!' " is a weak moral judgment—weaker by far than "A ought not shout 'Boo!' ". All the same, if an author "proceeded for some time in the ordinary way of reasoning", telling us about what is in fact the case, and then suddenly said "So other things being equal, one ought not do such and such", should we not be as much struck by the appearance of a "new relation or affirmation" as Hume told us we should be if our author had suddenly said the stronger "So one ought not do such and such"? But if (2) is a moral judgment, then since (2) is entailed by (1) and (1) is entailed by a statement of fact, there are moral judgments that (by transitivity) are entailed by statements of fact, and the Fact-Value Thesis is false.

This little argument does not presuppose that (1) is itself a moral judgment: where one draws the line between fact and value does not matter to this argument—indeed, it is among the central points that those struck by the thick ethical concepts want to make by appeal to them precisely that there is a continuum between fact and value.

And a similar argument is constructable for each of Williams' sample thick ethical concepts, including 'promise' and 'lie'. It seems right to think that

(1′) B promised to pay Smith five dollars

is entailed by some statements of fact. (1′) does not entail "B ought to pay Smith five dollars", for B might already have paid. Or B might not already have paid, but might desperately need the five dollars to buy food for his starving wife, child, dog, or cat. And so on. But it seems right to think that (1′) entails

(2′) Other things being equal, B ought to pay Smith five dollars.

No doubt (2′) is not as strong a moral judgment as "B ought to pay Smith five dollars", but (2′) surely is a moral judgment all the same. If so, then since (2′) is a moral judgment and is entailed by (1′), and (1′) is entailed by some statements of fact, there are moral judgments that (by transitivity) are entailed by statements of fact;[9] and we now have a second demonstration that the Fact-Value Thesis is false. And this whether or not (1′) is, itself, a moral judgment.

What should we make of these arguments? Four things call for attention. In the first place, consider

(1″) If C rings D's doorbell he will thereby cause D pain.

(Think of poor D as wired up to his own doorbell.) There really is no better reason to think (1) entails (2) and (1′) entails (2′) than there is to think (1″) entails

(2″) Other things being equal, C ought not ring D's doorbell.

If (2) and (2′) are moral judgments, so surely is (2″). But (1″) is not merely entailed by some statement of fact—it is, on any view, *itself* a statement of fact. 'Causes a person pain' is not a thick ethical concept, for surely it is not an ethical concept at all. Thus we need not have attended to the thick ethical concepts in order to find countercases to the Fact-Value Thesis[10]: countercases to that thesis lie ready to hand in considerably simpler moral considerations.

But second, if we are to take these ideas seriously, hadn't we better take a closer look at that phrase "other things being equal"? What role does it play in (2), (2′), and (2″)? People do very often use "other things being equal" in moral discourse, and such discourse would be

9. Compare John Searle's route from fact to value in his "How to Derive 'Ought' from 'Is' ", *Philosophical Review,* 73 (1964), 43–58. Searle begins with what is on any view a statement of fact, "Jones uttered the words 'I hereby promise to . . .' " and at the end arrives at what is on any view a moral judgment, "Jones ought to. . . ." He breaks the step from premise to conclusion into a series of substeps. It is certainly plausible to think that by the time we reach "Other things being equal, Jones ought to . . ." we have already reached a moral judgment. I should say, however, that I do not agree with Searle's account of what makes those substeps acceptable. We will look at what makes promises binding in Chapter 12.

10. And the fact that the thick ethical concepts lend themselves to this kind of argument against the Fact-Value Thesis is not a fact about them by means of which they can be distinguished from concepts—such as 'causes a person pain'— which are not ethical concepts at all and *a fortiori* are not thick ethical concepts.

the poorer if this phrase were not available to us. But what exactly do we mean by it?

It seems to me that there are two ways in which the phrase is used in moral discourse. One is epistemic and relatively weak. Take, for example, something rather more general than what we have looked at so far:

(3″) Other things being equal, one ought not cause others pain.

On the epistemic, relatively weak, way of using "other things being equal", (3″) means something like

If one would cause a person pain by doing a thing, then there is reason to think one ought not do it.

Or, slightly stronger,

The fact that one would cause a person pain by doing a thing is itself reason to think one ought not do it.

I say this is relatively weak since, while it reports an evidential connection, it leaves open what the source of the evidential connection is.

A second (and I think more common) way in which the phrase is used in moral discourse is metaphysical and relatively strong. On this second way of using it, (3″) means something that can be expressed as follows:

'Causes a person pain' is a wrong-making feature of an act.

I say this is relatively strong since, while it entails the weaker reading, it in addition purports to point to the source of the evidential connection. I say only that it "purports" to do this since we lack an account of what exactly it is for a feature of an act to be a wrong-making feature; but as I see it, that is not so much an objection to reading (3″) in this way as rather a philosophical problem to be solved.[11] I will bypass that problem here and suppose that what (3″) says is

---

11. The notion at work here is presumably the obverse of Ross' 'prima facie duty'. See W. D. Ross, *The Right and the Good* (Oxford: Clarendon Press, 1930), ch. 2. Nobody regards Ross as having made that notion satisfactorily clear; everyone, I think, has a sense of what notion he was trying to make clear.

An act's being an instance of 'causes a person pain' is favorably relevant to its being wrongful,

leaving open how precisely that relevance is to be understood.

Let us turn back now to

(2″) Other things being equal, C ought not ring D's doorbell.

I will suppose, analogously, that what this says is

Something that is the case is favorably relevant to its being the case that C ought not ring D's doorbell.

But doesn't

(1″) If C rings D's doorbell he will thereby cause D pain

entail that? How *could* it be that if C rings D's doorbell he will thereby cause D pain, and yet that there is nothing at all that is favorably relevant to the truth of "C ought not ring D's doorbell"?

Another way to put the point comes out as follows,

(3″) Other things being equal, one ought not cause others pain

is surely true: an act's being an instance of 'causes a person pain' *is* favorably relevant to its being wrongful. An act's being an instance of 'causes a person pain' is not conclusive proof that it is wrongful, for surely it could be, and in some cases is, permissible to cause pain (as, for example, where the victim will die if not caused pain and prefers pain to death). But that fact about an act is certainly favorably relevant to its being wrongful.

More strongly, (3″) is surely a necessary truth: it not merely is but could not have failed to be the case that an act's being an instance of 'causes a person pain' is favorably relevant to its being wrongful. Some people like to express such claims as follows: there is no possible world in which an act's being an instance of 'causes a person pain' is irrelevant to the question whether it is wrongful. (Perhaps you think of a possible world in which people like pain? I doubt that there can be such a world, in light of what pain is. If there is, then you are invited to replace "pain" by "excruciating pain" throughout: there certainly is no possible world in which people like excruciating pain. No doubt people on occasion welcome excruciating pain, for example because they want to do penance for past sins. But supplying oneself with some excruciating pain would not constitute doing penance if excruciating pain were not a pretty awful business—and thus if it were not the case that an act's being an instance of 'causes a person excruciating pain' was favorably relevant to its being wrongful.)

But if (3″) is a necessary truth, then (1″) really does entail (2″). I do not say merely that if (3″) is a necessary truth, then the conjunction of (1″) with (3″) entails (2″); the conjunction of (1″) with (3″) entails (2″) whether or not (3″) is a necessary truth. What I say is that if (3″) is a necessary truth, then (1″), by itself, entails (2″). But that is surely right. If (3″) is a necessary truth, then it really could not be the case that C would cause D pain by ringing his doorbell, though there is nothing at all that is favorably relevant to its being wrongful for C to do this.

Similarly for the arguments we looked at that involve thick ethical concepts. That B promised to pay Smith five dollars is favorably relevant to its being the case that he ought to do this, and could not have failed to be.

> (3′) Other things being equal, one ought to do what one promised

is not merely a truth, it could not have failed to be a truth. To promise is to bind, or commit, oneself to another to do a thing; how could the fact that you bound yourself to do a thing fail to be favorably relevant—merely favorably relevant!—to its being the case that you ought to do it? If so, then (1′) entails (2′). Again, that A would be acting rudely if he shouted "Boo!" is favorably relevant to its being the case that he ought not do this, and could not have failed to be.

> (3) Other things being equal, one ought not act rudely

is not merely a truth, it could not have failed to be a truth. Rudeness is of less moral moment than causing pain and breach of promise, but it is not nothing, and could not have failed to be something. (We distort the content of morality if we think it concerns itself only with evils.) If so, then (1) entails (2).

Skepticism about morality issues from a worry about whether morality can be thought to mesh with the world *at all*. I have suggested that there are necessary connections between facts on the one hand and weak moral judgments on the other hand—where weak moral judgments are judgments to the effect that there is something that is favorably relevant to the truth of a strong moral judgment to the effect that someone ought or ought not do a thing. If that is true, then morality really does mesh with the world. For some reason people do not generally ask whether it is true. We tend to feel that morality had better be simple, so that morality is suspect if we can't go the whole way from facts to strong moral judgments in one step. But this feeling wants diagnosis rather than succumbing to.

There remains a moral question how morality meshes with the world, and we will be looking at some of the ways in which it does. There also remains a metaphysical question why it does, though I suspect that our sense that this is a deep question issues as much as anything from our unclarity about what the question asks for. Yet another question that remains is how strong moral conclusions to the effect that someone ought or ought not do a thing can be arrived at by the weighing of the various considerations that are favorably or unfavorably relevant to their truth. But this is in some ways less interesting because—as we forget when we are doing ethics—we are familiar from other areas of investigation with models of the weighing of considerations. There is no reason for suspicion of ethics on the ground that it too calls for weighing.

I said earlier that four things call for attention. The first was that if arguments involving the thick ethical concepts yield countercases to the Fact-Value Thesis, so also do arguments involving concepts such as 'causes a person pain' that are not ethical concepts at all and *a fortiori* are not thick ethical concepts. The second was that we needed an account of the role played by "other things being equal" in the sentences we have been looking at. The third is that once we take seriously the possibility that some statements of fact really do entail some moral judgments, we can surely find even simpler candidates than the ones we have been looking at: we not only need not have attended to the thick ethical concepts, we need not have restricted ourselves to weak moral judgments of the form "Other things being equal, one ought (or ought not) do such and such". Consider

(1‴) E plans to torture a baby to death for fun.

Surely that entails

(2‴) E ought not do what he plans to do.

(1‴) is a statement of fact, and (2‴) is not merely a moral judgment, it is—unlike (2), (2′), and (2″)—a strong moral judgment. But how *could* it fail to be the case that E will do something he ought not do if he proceeds to torture a baby to death for fun?

We might have put the point in another way. Consider

    (3‴) One ought not torture babies to death for fun.

Surely (3‴) is true. It is not merely true that other things being equal one ought not torture babies to death for fun; one just plain ought not do it, no matter what the circumstances. Indeed, (3‴) is surely a necessary truth. How on earth could it fail to be the case that a person who has tortured a baby to death for fun has acted impermissibly in doing so? Suppose we made the amazing discovery that torturing a baby to death for fun actually causes the crops to improve. (You are invited to invent the causal mechanism.) Would that incline us to think that perhaps we live in a world in which (3‴) is false? We certainly would not ignore this amazing discovery, but we would also certainly not meet it by thinking we had been mistaken about the moral status of torturing babies to death for fun: we would instead try to figure out how to short-circuit the causal mechanism, so as to be able to obtain the same effect from a different cause. But of course if (3‴) is a necessary truth, then we can easily produce a very simple countercase to the Fact-Value Thesis, for if (3‴) is a necessary truth, then (1‴) entails (2‴).

Overheated examples in ethics are tiresome (one feels one's lapels are being clutched), and I apologize for this one. Still, if what is wanted is places where morality meshes with the world, then melodrama is useful: it supplies places where facts mesh directly with strong moral judgments to the effect that a person ought or ought not do a thing.

The fourth and last thing I wished to call attention to comes out as follows. I suggested that (1), (1′), (1″), and (1‴) entail (2), (2′), (2″), and (2‴). Saying so comes to the same as saying that certain rather more general statements, such as

    (3″) Other things being equal, one ought not cause others pain

and

    (3‴) One ought not torture babies to death for fun,

are necessary truths; and I have suggested that these *are* necessary truths—they not only are true but could not have failed to be. But people who take a certain view of what makes a truth be a necessary truth are sure to find this objectionable. The view I have in mind is that a statement is a necessary truth if and only if it is 'analytic':

roughly, true by virtue of the meanings of the words used to make it. If that view is correct, then necessary truths must surely be trivial. But how could a triviality license a step from facts to value, that being a step which is surely anything but trivial?[12]

Again, the likes of (3″) and (3‴) certainly appear to be, themselves, moral judgments. But a moral judgment is not a triviality. How then can it be a necessary truth?

What we should think of the view that a statement is a necessary truth only if it is analytic is a larger issue than I can deal properly with here, perhaps a larger issue than I am competent to deal properly with anywhere. But this much is certainly plausible: a truth T can be a necessary truth even if T cannot be certified as a truth by looking in a dictionary, and even if T is nontrivial. "All bachelors are unmarried" can be certified as a truth by appeal to a dictionary, and is trivial. So presumably also for "Whatever is red is colored". But this is not so of any of the candidate necessary truths that are of interest to philosophers (or of those that are of interest to mathematicians). Kripke argues, very convincingly, that a great many statements one might not have thought necessary truths—such as "Water is H_2O", "Gold is the element with atomic number 79", and "The table in my attic was made out of a chunk of wood" [the table in my attic was in fact made out of a chunk of wood]—really are necessary truths, and one cannot conclude that he is mistaken on the ground that they are not trivial and not certifiable as truths by appeal to a dictionary.[13]

In any case, the fourth and last thing I wished to call attention to is that, in saying that the sample arguments we looked at really are countercases to the Fact-Value Thesis, I am committing myself to the view that there are necessary truths that are nontrivial—the likes of (3″) and (3‴), for example. Since it seems to me that the likes of (3″) and (3‴) are moral judgments, I am also committing myself to the

12. See, for example, R. M. Hare, *The Language of Morals* (Oxford: Clarendon Press, 1952). Hare says, for example, that "to hold that an imperative conclusion can be derived from purely indicative premises leads to representing matters of substance as if they were verbal matters" (pp. 46–47).

13. See Saul A. Kripke, *Naming and Necessity* (Cambridge: Harvard University Press, 1972). Other interesting examples and further discussion appear in Jerrold J. Katz, *Cogitations* (Oxford: Oxford University Press, 1986).

view that there are moral judgments that are nontrivial necessary truths.[14] But these things seem to me to be right.[15]

4. We certainly act as if we thought of many of our moral beliefs as necessary truths; and we often respond to moral proposals as if they were intended to have the status of necessary truths, and think ourselves entitled to reject them when they do not. When I put

(3''') One ought not torture babies to death for fun

to my students (who are rightly suspicious of moralizing), they do not ask me whether I have examined all actual past instances of people who tortured babies to death for fun; what they do is to try to invent

14. I should think it could be said not merely that (3) through (3''') are moral judgments that are nontrivial necessary truths, but also that it is not at all clear how their negations could be accommodated into what would be recognizable as a moral code.

In passing, that there are moral judgments that are nontrivial necessary truths is arguably something Hume would have denied. As I said in note 3 above, it is surely plain that Hume was not, in the well-known passage quoted, drawing our attention merely to the fact that "ought" is not obtainable from "is" within first-order logic; it is arguable that he would have denied that there is *any* necessary connection between "ought" and "is". Hume went on to say: "But as authors do not commonly use this precaution, I shall presume to recommend it to the readers; and am persuaded, that this small attention wou'd subvert all the vulgar systems of morality, and let us see, that the distinction of vice and virtue is not founded merely on the relations of objects, nor is perceiv'd by reason" (*Treatise*, pp. 469–470). Statements whose truth is "perceiv'd by reason" are statements whose truth we can come to know of *a priori*, and—following Kripke (in *Naming and Necessity*)—we nowadays distinguish between the *a priori* and the necessary. But it is arguable that Hume did not.

15. It might be worth drawing attention to the fact that my sample moral judgments which are nontrivial necessary truths—(3'') and (3''')—are relatively specific, as opposed to general. This is because I think the more general the moral judgment, the more likely it is that either we are unclear about exactly what we are committed to if we accept it or we are able to find countercases to it. (What I will call the Central Utilitarian Idea, and discuss at length in Chapter 5, is a good example.) Unless, that is, it is carefully qualified. T. M. Scanlon proposes that "An act is wrong if its performance under the circumstances would be disallowed by any system of rules for the general regulation of behavior which no one could reasonably reject as a basis for informed, unforced general agreement," all of the qualifications being essential. See his "Contractualism and Utilitarianism", in Amartya Sen and Bernard Williams, eds., *Utilitarianism and Beyond* (Cambridge: Cambridge University Press, 1982). It is arguable that this—like (3'') and (3''')—really is a necessary truth. But see note 19 below.

a possible scenario, an imaginary, even a contra-causal scenario, in which someone tortured a baby to death for fun and yet was not acting wrongly in doing so. When (to provoke discussion) I tell my students that lying is wrong, they tell me I am mistaken; but no one feels a need to draw my attention to an instance of nonwrongful lying last week in New Jersey—they feel it enough to refute me if they can invent a possible instance of nonwrongful lying, as of course they can.

That is not true of our attitudes toward all of our moral beliefs, and it is not true of our responses to just any moral proposal. If I were to put the following moral judgment to my students

Bloggs acted wrongly this morning

they would not invent scenarios in which Bloggs did not act wrongly this morning. They would rightly view me as having made an assertion that rests heavily on the truth of an array of suppositions of fact, facts in particular about what Bloggs did this morning; and they would ask what those facts are.

Similarly for some moral judgments that are markedly more general than "Bloggs acted wrongly this morning". I might think, and there-fore tell my students, that engaging in a certain activity K is morally quite all right, and I am not moved to give up that view by invented scenarios—I am moved to give up that view only when a student brings home to me that as a matter of fact engaging in K causes harm, a fact I had not been aware of.

Moreover, some moral judgments are given a different status by different people. We took note earlier of the fact that a person, say Bloggs, might believe that capital punishment is permissible because of its being (as he thinks) a more effective deterrent than long prison terms, and would give up that moral belief if he were convinced that this is not so. We might put it that Bloggs gives his moral belief that capital punishment is permissible the status of a contingent truth.

As we also imagined, however, B believes capital punishment per-missible on quite different grounds: *he* believes on the one hand that those who commit particularly despicable crimes deserve the death penalty and, on the other, that the community that does not impose the death penalty fails to display respect for the victims of those crimes and also fails to display an appropriately strong commitment to its own moral beliefs. Should we say that B gives his moral belief that capital punishment is permissible the status of a necessary truth? It depends. We need to hear more about B before we can say that about him. For example, would he give up his belief about capital punishment if he became convinced that people do not react to a failure to impose that penalty in the way in which he takes them to react?

It pays to take note of this possibility because it reminds us that the bearing of facts on moral beliefs may be relatively indirect. As we know, some people believe capital punishment permissible because they believe it a more effective deterrent than long prison terms; in their case, there is a question of fact—about deterrence—that has an immediate and direct bearing on their moral belief about capital punishment. But a question of fact might have a less direct bearing on a person's moral belief about capital punishment. If B would give up his moral belief if he were convinced that attitudes toward capital punishment are not what he takes them to be, then there is a question of fact—about attitudes—that has a bearing on his moral belief about capital punishment, but only through its having a bearing on his moral beliefs about what communities ought to do to display an appropriately strong commitment to their own moral beliefs.

And it pays to be reminded of this because what it issues from is very important indeed, namely that moral judgments do not face the facts one by one. What each of us confronts the world of facts with is a battery of interconnected moral beliefs. It is because of this that a discovery of fact may bear on a moral belief indirectly, by virtue of bearing on another, linked, moral belief. We will come back to this in the following section.

On the other hand, it might be that B would not give up his belief about capital punishment if he became convinced that people do not react to a failure to impose that penalty in the way in which he takes them to react—it might be that he would reply that this just shows people do not react as they ought to react. And it might be, more generally, that he neither is nor would be moved by any discovery of fact. Then he does give his moral belief that capital punishment is permissible the status of a necessary truth. In this respect he differs from Bloggs, who gives his the status of a contingent truth.

From the point of view of whether capital punishment is permissible, of course, it makes no difference whether Bloggs or B or anyone else gives his or her moral belief about it the status of a necessary truth. That one or the other side in disputes about capital punishment do give their moral belief this status does not show that they are right to do so. It does not even show that their belief is true, and *a fortiori* does not show that their belief is a necessary truth.

How *is* it to be decided which view on this matter is true?

5. Is capital punishment permissible? To ask that question is to be asking what we should believe.

Some people think capital punishment is permissible if and only if it is a more efficient deterrent than a life sentence. This raises two questions. Is capital punishment a more efficient deterrent than a life sentence? That is a question of fact. It has turned out to be a peculiarly difficult question to answer, but it is not of interest for our purposes. The second question is markedly more interesting. Is capital punishment permissible if and only if it is a more efficient deterrent than a life sentence? That is a moral question.

We know that many people would say no in answer to this moral question. Here is B, for example. B would say that it does not matter whether capital punishment does (or does not) deter more efficiently than a life sentence. How so? B would reply that those who commit particularly despicable crimes deserve the death penalty, whether or not they would have been (and whether or not anyone else would be) deterred by the prospect of its imposition. And he would add that the community that does not impose the penalty fails to display respect for the victims of those despicable crimes and also fails to display an appropriately strong commitment to its own moral beliefs.

We know that A would reject this: A, we imagined, believes capital punishment impermissible on the ground that a community (like an individual) must never intentionally kill a person who is in captivity, and who thus currently constitutes no threat to others and who can be kept from constituting a threat to others by less drastic means than killing him. So A would say that B is right to think that it does not matter whether capital punishment does (or does not) deter more efficiently than a life sentence; but he would argue that B's reasons for believing that capital punishment is permissible are not good enough reasons for believing it permissible.

Should we agree with A? Should we agree with B? Or should we instead think that the question whether capital punishment is permissible *is* settled by the answer to the question how efficiently it deters—and thus think that maybe A is right that capital punishment is impermissible, maybe B is right that capital punishment is permissible, but that both are mistaken in the reasons they have for thinking this? And there are other possibilities for us too.

For my part, I agree with A and B that the question whether capital punishment is permissible is not settled by the answer to the question how efficiently it deters, but I am on the fence about their reasons for the conclusions they draw. One thing that is plain, however, is that whether we are on or off the fence, we have a pretty good idea how both A and B would argue if they came to argument with each other. I said earlier that it was plausible to think that the dispute between them is a purely moral dispute.[16] But to have reached a point at which it has become clear that a dispute between two people is a purely moral dispute is by no means to have arrived at a point after which there is nothing more to be done. I also said earlier that the disputes about capital punishment are particularly well suited to the purposes of one who wishes to convince us of the truth of the Fact-Value Thesis, and from there of the truth of the No-Reason Thesis. But in one way they are ill suited to those purposes, for purely moral disputes about capital punishment are disputes in which there is a considerable amount of room for good and bad reasoning *inside morality itself.*

For example, A is likely to zero in on the concept 'deserving something' and try to bring out that B's views about it are incoherent. He is also likely to accuse B of condoning a state's using people as means by which to express its attitudes. B is likely to respond that there is no more incoherence in the idea of deserving death than there is in the idea of deserving a term in jail, and ask why imposing a term in jail is any the less a use of a person. What the parties to a purely moral dispute do is to search for common moral ground, for something that is in both their 'moral codes', that can be brought to bear on the issue in hand to settle it. The options here are vastly richer than one might think from an examination of the arguments for the No-Reason Thesis.

---

16. I said this because I am inclined to think it rare that disputants on this issue disagree because they disagree about whether human acts have causes. If a pair of disputants on this issue do disagree because they disagree about whether human acts have causes, then although their dispute presumably cannot be settled by appeal to evidence about human acts (or anything else), the dispute between them is not purely moral. But it is, I think, far more common for disputants about capital punishment to agree that acts have causes, and to disagree only about the moral significance to be attached to that fact.

Let me first bring out what I mean by a person's moral code. Each of us who has grown to the status of adult has a battery of moral beliefs, many of them more or less loosely stitched together by nonmoral beliefs. Most of us, I should think, believe that it is, other things being equal, wrong to break promises, lie, cheat, cause harm, and so on. We might (or might not) in addition have the nonmoral belief that lying very often causes harm, and we might (or might not) therefore have the further moral belief that when lying is wrong it is wrong because it causes harm. We might also have the nonmoral belief that Bloggs kicked his little brother for fun this morning, and we might therefore have the further moral belief that Bloggs did something he ought not have done this morning. But I suspect that no one's moral beliefs are more than *very* loosely stitched together in the ways I point to here.

A person, say Bloggs, knows that he believes P_1, P_2, . . . , for a great many propositions P; indefinitely many further propositions follow from them, and in the case of a great many of them, say Q_1, Q_2, . . . , Bloggs does not know that they follow from P_1, P_2, ... Should we choose to say that what Bloggs believes includes all and only those propositions Bloggs knows he believes? Or should we instead choose to say that what Bloggs believes includes also all those propositions that follow from the propositions Bloggs knows he believes? This is a matter for choice: there is no theoretically interesting ground for choosing one way or the other. Let us make the former choice: let us so use "believes" that what Bloggs believes includes all and only those propositions he knows he believes. So, for example, if Bloggs knows he believes that he has no sisters or half-sisters, and that his first cousins are all doctors, and that Alice is a daughter of his paternal grandmother's only daughter, then all the same it remains an open question whether Bloggs believes that Alice is a doctor. For while that follows from what he knows he believes, he could simply have failed to notice that it does; and we are so using "belief" that if Bloggs does not know he believes that Alice is a doctor, then he does not believe that she is.

How could Bloggs have failed to draw the conclusion that Alice is a doctor? There is range of phenomena we might call "failing to connect".[17] One species of it is failing to notice that propositions one

17. The term comes from E. M. Forster's *Howard's End* (Harmondsworth: Penguin Books, 1941).

knows one believes commit one to the truth of others. This is very common when the deduction is complex, as where proving the conclusion from the premises would be difficult. (It really does take a minute or two to see that what Bloggs knows he believes does commit him to Alice's being a doctor.) But it is also common where the deduction is simple but one has strong motives for failing to draw the conclusion, and we might in such cases speak not merely of failing to connect, but of positive "walling off". A man might know he believes that blacks are human beings, and therefore possessed of all such rights as are possessed by human beings, but refuse (typically unconsciously) to draw the conclusion that certain discriminatory practices he himself engages in are impermissible. The more profitable it is to a man that he keep certain of his beliefs walled off from the conclusions that follow from them (if only to avoid internal discomfort), the harder it is to get him to see that's what he's doing.

A second species of failing to connect is failing to notice the possibility that propositions one knows one believes have something in common. Three subspecies are familiar to all of us. First, Bloggs might know he believes that one ought not eat bananas, that one ought not eat apples, and that one ought not eat pears, but never have asked himself whether the prohibition extends to all kinds of fruit. This would be failure to notice the possibility of generalizing. Again, second, Bloggs might know he believes that one ought not torture babies, that one ought not torture little children, and that one ought not torture the mentally retarded, but never have asked himself whether that is because one ought not torture the innocent. This would be failure to notice the possibility of explaining. Third, Bloggs might know he believes that he owes Jones five dollars, and know he believes that he ought to pay Jones the five dollars, but not have asked himself whether owing someone something just is its being the case that one ought to supply it. This would be failure to notice the possibility of simplifying. These three subspecies obviously overlap, for some generalizations explain and some explanations simplify. And here too there might be positive walling off: a failure to generalize, explain, or simplify—like a failure to draw conclusions—might be motivated.

My examples of failing to connect have included failing to draw a moral conclusion, failing to connect one moral belief with another, and failing to connect a moral belief with a nonmoral belief. Let us refer to the totality of a person's moral beliefs as that person's "moral code". We may fail to connect within our moral code; we may also fail to connect across the boundary of our moral code.

Now, as I said, what the parties to a purely moral dispute try to do is to search for common moral ground: something that is in both their moral codes, that can be brought to bear on the issue in hand to settle it. That means that what X tries to do is to convict Y of failing to connect, either within Y's own moral code or across its boundary. It is because there is the possibility of success in doing this that one side can surprise the other and that one side can learn from the other, even if discovery of fact is not in question. Moreover, it is because there is the possibility of success in doing this that one side can be persuaded by the other and that moral arguments can be settled.

It must of course be granted that if one of the parties, X, does succeed in demonstrating that the other party, Y, failed to connect, either within or across the boundary of Y's moral code, this would not show that any particular given belief of Y's is false: it would show only that Y's totality of beliefs as a whole is defective. What it will strike Y as right to revise in his or her beliefs would remain to be seen—it will turn on such matters as the relative weights Y had attached, or now thinks it right to attach, to the different beliefs. And if X is not satisfied with the revision offered by Y, it would be up to X to begin the process all over again.

6. It is largely because there is such a thing as failing to connect that there is such a thing as moral progress.

People's views about capital punishment, for example, have changed over several generations. There was a time (not all that long ago) when it was widely thought appropriate to attach the death penalty to what we now regard as relatively minor crimes, such as petty theft, and when it was widely thought appropriate for the criminal to be executed in public. Even those who favor capital punishment nowadays do not favor attaching the death penalty to theft and do not favor public executions.[18]

---

18. Nor do they favor execution by ghastly means. But that, I fancy, is due more to a change in conception of how much pain and humiliation may be caused in the name of a public purpose than to a change in conception of what warrants killing.

No doubt these changes have a complex variety of sources. Among them, however, is surely this: an increase in the value placed on a human life and of the respect due to it. But this is nothing new. Such changes can easily be seen as a product of the recognition that there had been a failure to connect.

I said only "largely", however, since truly dramatic changes in moral beliefs across generations probably issue from matters of fact as well as from recognition that there was a failure to connect. I have in mind here changes in the facts themselves as well as changes that consist in discoveries of fact—as where resources expand or where technology makes new activities possible. A dramatic change, however, is not one that consists in replacement of an old code by an entirely new one. (How is 'an entirely new moral code' supposed to differ from an old one? How would we recognize that it is a moral code? What could possibly make us think it true?) A dramatic change in moral beliefs is one that involves a major reorganization in moral thinking, which may involve an expanding or a shrinking or both, but which finds its justification in parts of the moral thinking that preceded it.

It will be noticed that I said only "changes" in moral beliefs across generations: I did not say "progress". There is no *a priori* reason why such changes should be for the better. Consider a tribe whose moral code consists in the belief that one ought to do whatever the gods enjoin, together with such consequences as they believe follow from that in light of their beliefs about what in fact the gods do enjoin. We now convince them that, as a matter of fact, there are no gods. This will provoke a deep change in their moral code, but there are any number of possibilities. They might retain some of their moral beliefs—for example, that one ought not eat bananas—while either retaining them as a mere clutter, or supplying some new common source or sources for them. Or again they might take the view that morality permits everything. Indeed, they might not undergo a *change* in moral code, for they might instead reject morality altogether. We might plausibly view some of these possible changes as progress, but not just any.

What then does mark such a change as progress? Whatever marks such a change in an individual as progress. Suppose that B were convinced by A that B should give up his belief that capital punishment is permissible. Would that be progress in B? To ask this is to ask whether B should make this shift. And to ask that is to ask for the kind of discussion I described in the preceding section.

7. And a discussion of that kind *may* end in stalemate. Sometimes it ends in stalemate for an entirely uninteresting reason: one of the parties demonstrates that the other really is misrepresenting the facts or is failing to connect, but the other party cannot be got to see this. Sometimes the discussion ends in stalemate for a more interesting reason: neither party is able to demonstrate that the other is misrepresenting the facts or is failing to connect. Are there moral disputes in which the discussion ends in stalemate for the most interesting reason?—that is, not only can neither of the parties demonstrate one of these failings in the other, but there is no such failing in either? This seems to be a real possibility. The dispute between A and B about capital punishment may itself be an example. In light of the history of moral beliefs about capital punishment, that is, in light of the direction of the changes in moral belief about it that have taken place over time, I think this exceedingly unlikely to be the case, but it might be.

Very well, suppose it is. What does that show? We would have to grant that there are at least two moral codes, one containing that capital punishment is permissible, the other that it is not, such that there is no more reason to choose one than there is to choose the other.

But that does not for a moment show there is something suspect about morality generally. In particular, it does not lend support to the No-Reason Thesis or even to the Fact-Value Thesis. That there are equally well-supported moral codes (if there are) does not show there is no reason to believe about any given moral judgment that it is true. For some moral judgments could not have been false; and others flow from them in complex ways that we learn of when we recognize that we had been failing to connect.

8. The method of argument that consists in an attempt to get others either to represent the facts correctly or to connect in ways they had been failing to connect in, or (perhaps more typically) both, is the method of moral theory. In serious moral dispute we all use it, and we are more or less likely to convince our opponents in proportion as we use it well or ill.

A moral dispute in ordinary life is typically a dispute about what we might call an object-level moral judgment, which says that such and such is good or bad, right or wrong, other things being equal good or bad, other things being equal right or wrong, and so on. "Capital punishment is wrong" and "Other things being equal, capital punishment is wrong" are object-level moral judgments.

A moral theory contains object-level moral judgments, though typically they are relatively general—for example, "Intentional killing of those who constitute no threat to others is wrong" rather than "Capital punishment is wrong". Dispute about the acceptability of the theory typically includes dispute about those very general object-level moral judgments; but however general they may be, the method by which they are defended is the same.

But a moral theory contains more than object-level moral judgments. At the heart of every moral theory there lie what we might call explanatory moral judgments, which explicitly say that such and such is good or bad, right or wrong, other things being equal good or bad, other things being equal right or wrong, and so on, *because* it has feature F—for example, "Capital punishment is wrong *because* it is intentional killing of those who constitute no threat to others". These are moral judgments too, and are defended by the same method as object-level moral judgments. Dispute about the acceptability of a moral theory typically includes dispute about both kinds of moral judgments. But it is worth mention that dispute about the acceptability of a moral theory may consist entirely in dispute about its explanatory moral judgments, for both parties to the dispute may agree on its object-level moral judgments.[19]

It is a good question why people go in search of a moral theory. As I said, each of us who has grown to the status of adult has a battery of moral beliefs, only very loosely stitched together: they form

19. I said in note 15 that Scanlon's (object-level) 'contractualist principle' is arguably a necessary truth. What seems to me doubtful is the explanatory judgment Scanlon invites us to accept as well; namely that an act that is wrong is wrong *because* it meets the condition laid out in the principle. For my own part, I cannot bring myself to believe that what *makes* it wrong to torture babies to death for fun (for example) is that doing this "would be disallowed by any system of rules for the general regulation of behavior which no one could reasonably reject as a basis for informed, unforced general agreement". My impression is that explanation goes in the opposite direction—that it is the patent wrongfulness of the conduct that explains why there would be general agreement to disallow it. (We will return to contractualist ideas in Chapter 7 below.)

a mere clutter. But what is wrong with that? It is surely possible to lead a blameless life, indeed a life of moral excellence, without ever once engaging in moral theorizing. The Ten Commandments are a mere clutter of object-level moral judgments; but one who lives in accord with them, and with a handful of others as well (for there are areas of the moral life they do not reach), does as well in life as anyone needs to do.

Mightn't one make moral mistakes for lack of theory? Certainly. But that possibility cannot be the whole of what impels us to theorize about morality. We do not merely want to have true moral beliefs; we want to know what makes them true. For example, I suggested earlier that many of our moral beliefs—such as "One ought not torture babies to death for fun"—are necessary truths and *a fortiori* are truths. All the same, we want to know what makes them be truths. We want to know what the explanatory moral judgments are that tell us why they are truths.

Socrates invented the enterprise of moral theory, and what led him to do so was something theoretical, something deep: the quite general idea that while a clutter of beliefs may be a clutter of true beliefs, may even be a clutter of beliefs some or all of which are necessarily true beliefs, *knowledge* that they are true requires knowledge of what makes them true. We sometimes feel the need of a moral theory when we feel stymied for lack of one in midstream of a moral dispute. But I suspect that this is relatively rare. For the most part, it is in our reflective moments alone that we wonder how and why our moral beliefs hang together.

What makes it so hard to get a grip on this theoretical and deep idea, however, is that explanatory judgments, whether moral or non-moral, are no more secure than are the object-level judgments they bring together into a theory, for explanatory judgments entail the object-level judgments that serve in them as explanans and explanandum, and hence are true only if they are true. Why is it so satisfying to learn that the one explains the other?

In any case, what is central to any moral theory are the explanatory moral judgments contained in it. Participants in a moral dispute in ordinary life do rely on certain explanatory assumptions in arguing as they do, but they rarely make those assumptions explicit, and assessment of them is never the aim of the enterprise.

Indeed, it is from the differences between the aims of the enterprises that there flow all of the differences between moral dispute in ordinary life, on the one hand, and dispute about the acceptability of a moral theory on the other—for it is from the difference in aims that there flows a difference in what anchors the process of argument. Participants in moral dispute in ordinary life aim only at convincing each other and are therefore content to take as data what is in fact agreed between them, even if they are aware that what is agreed between them might well be rejected by third parties. Theorists aim at convincing the universe and therefore try to be sure that what they take as data would be accepted by all. For preference, what could not have been false.[20] It is most unlikely that a very general moral theory, one that tries to answer all moral questions, could be defended only by appeal to such data. (How, for example, is the theory's stand on capital punishment to be defended?) But there is no reason why a theory could not be more modest, taking no stand, or taking a stand while leaving it open for the universe to disagree, on what the theorist cannot defend in that way. The extent of what can be defended in that way may be surprisingly large, however, since connecting is a creative activity whose results can greatly surprise us.

9. What we will be concerned with in this book is not morality generally: it is a theory of rights that we will be in search of. The method remains the same. As I said in section 2, I will often say such things as "But surely A ought to do such and such" or "Plainly it is morally permissible for B to do so and so". I will feel free to do this insofar as I think you would agree with me that these things are clearly true. I said that I would be taking much of the stuff of morality as given. I will, for example, assume you believe that, other things being equal, it is wrong to break promises, lie, cheat, and cause pain. Much of this Introduction has aimed at bringing out that I am entitled to do so, for it has aimed at bringing out that the No-Reason Thesis is false and that such judgments as these show that it is.

But I will not be taking all of the stuff of morality as given. For example, I will not assume that you think capital punishment permissible or that you think it impermissible. I will only assume that

20. The method of moral theory I have been describing is like the process Rawls describes as the effort to reach "reflective equilibrium", with this proviso: on Rawls' account of the matter, everything is provisional, everything is open to revision, whereas I am suggesting that some moral judgments are plausibly viewed as necessary truths and hence not open to revision. See John Rawls, *A Theory of Justice* (Cambridge: Harvard University Press, 1971), pp. 20, 48–51.

you believe a certain moral judgment true if I find it hard to understand how you could possibly believe it false. As I said earlier, if I make a mistake about what you take to be clear moral truths, you have as much ground for objection to what goes on as you have if you find a mistake in my reasoning from them.

More important, second, I will not *assume* the truth of any ascriptions of rights. I did not mention this in section 2, but I will also often say such things as "It is plausible to think that so and so has such and such a right". That the person does have the right is something I invite you to suppose, provisionally, until we see whether his or her having it can be accommodated in a theory of rights. But I will do this only where I think you would agree that it is anyway plausible to think his or her having it should be accommodated in a theory of rights.

I will suggest that rights reduce, in a certain way, to what—other things being equal—people ought or ought not do, and may or may not do. We will have to see first, in Part I, what that complex constraint on behavior consists in; showing, in Part II, that a person has a certain right will then involve showing that others are subject to that complex constraint on behavior. I will also make suggestions about why we have such rights as we do. All theorizing is theorizing from a body of data; my data will throughout be moral judgments that I think you would take to be clear moral truths.

I should say also that the theory that emerges is not compact and does not aspire to completeness. It is in my view an important fact about morality in general, and even about the realm of rights in particular, that there is no one or set of three or six principles that governs it all. What I have hoped for is not so much a system as something more open-ended, a way of looking at rights. I think that way of looking at them will help us to understand those I discuss; I hope that it would also help us to understand those I may have overlooked.

PART I

Rights: What They Are

Chapter 1

Claims, Privileges, and Powers

1. Among the rights we take ourselves to have are rights to life, liberty, and property.[1] Every right is a right *to* something; what exactly are these rights rights to? What in particular is the right to life a right to? Perhaps the right to life is the right to not be killed. Or anyway perhaps it is the right to not be killed unjustly, for there might be occasions on which it was no infringement of any right possessed by A to kill him—if, for example, A is villainously attacking another person whose life cannot be saved unless A is himself killed. Or perhaps we should say, more precisely, that the right to life *includes* the right to not be killed unjustly, for the right to life presumably includes other rights as well, such as the right to try to preserve one's life against attacks on it. The right to life is on any view complex.

I should think that this is also true of the rights to liberty and property. To have a right to liberty is presumably to have, among other rights, a right to do such and such if one wishes, a right to do so and so if one wishes, and so on—though there no doubt are limits on the such and such and so and so which having a right to liberty

1. Why didn't I say "rights to life, liberty, and the pursuit of happiness"? It is clear enough why Jefferson did not include the right to property among his examples in writing the Declaration of Independence: his were to be examples of inalienable rights. But why bother to mention the right to pursue happiness? What do you add if, having mentioned rights to life and liberty, you go on to say "*and* the right to pursue happiness"? The right to pursue happiness is certainly not plausibly viewable as a right to happiness itself; and isn't the right to *pursue* happiness included in the right to liberty? Garry Wills gives a helpful account of why Jefferson took the right to pursue happiness seriously; see his *Inventing America* (New York: Vintage Books, 1979). But Wills does not speak to the question what Jefferson thought was the relation between the right to liberty and the right to pursue happiness.

is having a right to do. Moreover, the right to liberty presumably also includes rights to noninterference with the doing of some of those things. The right to property is surely even more complex. The person who has a right to property presumably has rights to each of the particular things he or she in fact owns, such as chairs and tables and shoes; and ownership is presumably itself a complex of rights, arguably a different complex for each thing owned.

We do best, I think, to begin with a simpler kind of right, a kind of right for which we have no trouble saying what the right is a right to. The rights I have in mind are those a person has against a person that a certain quite particular state of affairs shall obtain; in the case of those rights, what the right is a right to is precisely the obtaining of that state of affairs.

Suppose that A owns a piece of land. We might therefore think that A has a right against B that B stay off it. Suppose A does have this right. Then here is a right for which—by contrast with the rights to life, liberty, and property—it is quite clear, and easy to say, what the right is a right to: A's right is a right to the obtaining of the state of affairs that consists in B's staying off A's land.

It does not follow from the fact that A owns the land that A has this right. A might have given B permission to enter his land. Or A might have rented his land to B. Several things might have made it the case that although A owns the land, A nevertheless does not have a right against B that B stay off it. Which exactly are they? That is a good question. (Another good question is how A could have come to own the land in the first place.) But we cannot settle whether A does have the right until we have first answered the question what it would be for A to have it if he had it. We will turn in Part II to the question which rights we have; in Part I, we take up the prior question what rights are.

To have a right is to have a kind of moral status. What kind of moral status? To ask that is to ask what the moral significance of having a right is. So this gives us another way of characterizing the question to be dealt with in Part I: in Part I, we take up the question what the moral significance of having a right is.

Let us begin with our simple example. It is intuitively plausible to think that some people do own bits of land, and that some among them have rights against some others that those others stay off the land; and we can for the time being suppose that A is among those owners, and that B is among the others against whom A has the right.

Well, so what if A has it? Why, and in what way, is his having it of moral interest to anybody? In short, what is the moral significance of his having it?

2. A particularly interesting answer to the question "What is the moral significance of A's having a right against B that B stay off A's land?" is suggested in a classic article by Wesley Newcomb Hohfeld.[2] I think that this article is a work of major importance and that it pays us to be clear about what goes on in it. Some readers are already familiar with it; I apologize to them, for in light of its importance I will assume that none are.

Hohfeld said that a right is the "correlative" of a duty—by which he meant that X's having a right against Y to the obtaining of a certain state of affairs is equivalent to Y's being under a duty toward X, namely the duty that Y discharges if and only if the state of affairs does obtain.[3]

We must be a little more careful, however. Hohfeld said:

> the term "rights" tends to be used indiscriminately to cover what in a given case may be a privilege, a power, or an immunity, rather than a right in the strictest sense . . . (p. 36)

And it is only rights "in the strictest sense" that we are to take to be correlative with duties.

---

2. "Some Fundamental Legal Conceptions as Applied in Judicial Reasoning", *Yale Law Journal*, 23 (1913). This article and a second with the same name, *Yale Law Journal*, 26 (1917), were reprinted in Wesley Newcomb Hohfeld, *Fundamental Legal Conceptions*, ed. Walter Wheeler Cook (New Haven: Yale University Press, 1919). My page references to both articles are to the Cook edition. Hohfeld was a professor of law, not of moral philosophy, and what he was interested in was, as his titles put it, fundamental legal conceptions—not fundamental moral conceptions. I pretend otherwise throughout Chapter 1; we will come back to this point in Chapter 2, section 4.

3. Hohfeld's words were: "if X has a right against Y that he shall stay off the former's land, the correlative (and equivalent) is that Y is under a duty toward X to stay off the place" (p. 38). The careful reader will have noticed that I do not say that (on Hohfeld's view) X's having a right against Y to the obtaining of a certain state of affairs is equivalent to Y's being under a duty toward X, namely the duty that Y discharges if and only if Y *makes* the state of affairs obtain. Y's duty is discharged so long as the state of affairs does obtain and thus whether or not Y, or anybody else, or anything at all, *makes* the state of affairs obtain. The importance for us of this point will come out in Chapter 12.

What are privileges, powers, and immunities? And how do they differ from rights in the strictest sense? Which in fact *are* the rights in the strictest sense? Hohfeld says:

> Recognizing, as we must, the very broad and indiscriminate use of the term "right," what clue do we find, in ordinary . . . discourse,[4] toward limiting the word in question to a definite and appropriate meaning? That clue lies in the correlative "duty," for it is certain that even those who use the word and the conception "right" in the broadest possible way are accustomed to thinking of "duty" as the invariable correlative. (p. 38)

No doubt people use the term "right" broadly and indiscriminately, but (Hohfeld says) even those who use it most broadly and indiscriminately are accustomed to thinking of rights as having duties as correlatives. This suggests that the feature 'having a duty as a correlative' is in some way central to our notion of a right; so (Hohfeld says) let us mark off a subclass of rights—to be thought of as the rights in the strictest sense—which are all and only those rights that do have this feature, that is, they are all and only those rights that have duties as correlatives.

Of course if we do mark off in this way the subclass of rights that are rights in the strictest sense, then it would be no wonder if Hohfeld's assertion that rights in the strictest sense are correlative with duties were true. No matter. We have had our attention drawn to a subclass of rights that is in some way central, and all of whose members are correlative with duties.

To avoid confusion with privileges, powers, and immunities (what they are will begin to come out shortly), Hohfeld suggests that we call rights in the strictest sense "claims". This seems to me a good idea: we do well to mark the difference Hohfeld will be drawing our attention to, and the term he suggests is in some ways well chosen. Not in every way, unfortunately. Talk of X's claims hints at X's actually having made some claims (as a person—say Bloggs—does if he announces that he has such and such rights or, more strongly, demands that they be accorded him). We have to remember that Hohfeld has none of this in mind in using, and inviting us to use, the term "claim". He means merely: right in the strictest sense, thus right

---

4. What Hohfeld actually wrote was not "ordinary discourse" but "ordinary legal discourse". As I said, I am here ignoring the fact that it was law, not morality, that he was interested in.

that is the correlative of a duty. On balance, his choice of the term seems to me a good one, and I will adopt it in what follows.

We can construct a compact way of showing how, following Hohfeld, I will be using the word "claim". By definition, one who ascribes a claim ascribes a right in the strictest sense. In light of Hohfeld's way of marking off the class of rights in the strictest sense, therefore, one who says something of the form

> X has a claim against Y that p,

where "p" is replaced by any sentence you like, says something equivalent to the result of writing that same sentence in for "p" in

> Y is under a duty toward X, namely the duty that Y discharges if and only if p.

Let us abbreviate[5] these expressions, respectively, as

> $C_{X, Y}\, p$

and

> $D_{Y, X}\, p$.

Then we can display the terminological practice I will be following in this way:

> (H₁) $C_{X, Y}\, p$ is equivalent to $D_{Y, X}\, p$.

I give this thesis the name "(H₁)" since it is the first of a series of theses that we will extract from Hohfeld's article.

It pays to take explicit note of one consequence of this decision about usage. What I have in mind is that, given this decision, every claim is a right that an entity *has against an entity*. One cannot have a claim that is a claim against nothing—a claim out into the blue, as it were. This issues from the fact that we have decided so to use "claim" that a claim is a right in the strictest sense, and thus that X's having a claim is equivalent to Y's being under a duty, from which

---

5. Hohfeld calls claims and duties (also privileges, powers, and immunities) "relations". I think it better to reconstruct his ideas about claims and duties (also privileges) by use of modal operators, since the entailment relations between ascriptions of rights are the more easily characterizable in that way. Thus, for example, I should think that "$C_{X,Y}p$ & $C_{X,Y}q$" entails "$C_{X,Y}r$", wherever the conjunction of p and q entails r; and it is (to say the least) not easy to see how this generalization is to be expressed if claims are relations.

it follows that there had better be a Y that is under a duty to accord X what X has a claim to, and thus a Y against which X has the claim, if X really is to have the claim.

Of course this leaves it entirely open to us to say, if we wish, that there are other rights, rights that are not rights in the strictest sense and that are thus not claims, that are had but not *had against* anything. We will come back to this later.

It pays to take explicit note also of two things that are *not* consequences of this decision about usage. I said in the Introduction that I would take the variables "X" and "Y" to range over whatever there is, and *a fortiori* over things that are not human beings as well as over things that are human beings. But accepting (H₁) does not commit us to supposing that things that are not human beings have claims and that claims are had against things that are not human beings. Many people do think that some nonhuman things (such as animals) have rights and that some rights are had against nonhuman things (such as governments and other kinds of institutions). Accepting (H₁) does not commit us to agreeing with these ideas. (Nor, of course, does it commit us to rejecting them.) It commits us only to agreeing that a thing X does have a claim against a thing Y if and only if Y is under the relevant duty toward X, which is compatible with, but does not entail, that nonhuman things have claims and that things have claims against nonhuman things.

A second point is this: accepting (H₁) does not commit us to supposing that people (or things of any other kind) have claims only against others. I am sure that when we look more closely at claims we will not find ourselves wanting to say that a person has claims against himself or herself, but (H₁) takes no stand on the matter. You are invited to insert the same name in for "X" and "Y" in (H₁) if you like, "Bloggs" perhaps; what the result of making this insertion tells us is only that Bloggs has the claim against himself if and only if he is under the duty toward himself, and that is compatible with its being the case that Bloggs has no claims at all against himself.

I have spoken of (H₁) as a thesis and an assertion, but strictly speaking it is merely a display of the way in which the term "claim" is going to be used. Now for something substantive. Consider the right we are supposing A to have against B. As I said, this is a right that a certain state of affairs, namely B's staying off A's land, shall obtain. We say something substantive about that right if we say it is a claim. But that seems very plausible. For suppose someone ascribes that right to A. It is very plausible to think that what he or she says is equivalent to

> B is under a duty toward A, namely the duty that B discharges if and only if B stays off A's land,

or, less long-windedly, to

> B is under a duty toward A to stay off A's land.

After all, B accords A what A has a right to—namely B's staying off A's land—if and only if B actually does stay off A's land. But if all this is true, then the right *is* a claim.

Moreover, we do now have an answer to the question "What is the moral significance of A's having that right against B?" For the right being a claim, the moral significance of A's having it is that B is under a duty toward A to stay off A's land.

We do not of course have an answer to the quite general question "What is the moral significance of having a right?" What we need to do is to turn to rights of other kinds, rights that are not rights in the strictest sense and thus are not claims.

3. The example of A and B and the land is Hohfeld's; here is another of his examples. Suppose that C owns some salad but that he gave D permission to eat it. It is intuitively plausible to think that C thereby gave D a right as regards C, a right to eat the salad. (It is intuitively plausible to think that some people own bits of land and that they have rights against some others that those others stay off the land; so also is it intuitively plausible to think one gives others rights by giving them permission to do this or that with one's property.) This right of D's is different from A's, and it is important to see how.

A's right is a right he has against B that a certain state of affairs, namely B's staying off A's land, shall obtain. So B accords A what A's right is a right to if and only if that state of affairs does obtain, thus if and only if B stays off A's land. It seems correct, for that reason, to think that A's right against B is correlative with a duty in B, a duty that B discharges if and only if B stays off A's land.

Consider D's right. We *can* say that D's right is a right he has 'against' C, though to mark the difference I wish to draw attention to I propose we say instead that D's right is a right he has 'as regards'

C. Moreover, we *can* say that D's right is a right that a certain state of affairs, namely D's eating the salad, shall obtain. But we could hardly say that C accords D what D's right is a right to if and only if that state of affairs does obtain, thus if and only if D eats the salad. When you give a man permission to eat your salad, and thereby give him a right to eat it, you surely cannot be thought to have failed to accord him what he had a right to if for any of a number of possible reasons—such as his developing a sudden lack of interest in salad—he simply decides not to eat it and therefore does not eat it. D's right as regards C therefore is quite certainly not correlative with a duty in C which C discharges if and only if D eats the salad. D has the right, but C has no such duty.

It is a substantive thesis about D's right—a thesis Hohfeld thinks true—that D's right is what Hohfeld wishes us to call a "privilege". A privilege, Hohfeld tells us, "is the mere negation of a *duty*," but "a duty having a content or tenor precisely *opposite* to that of the privilege in question" (p. 39). Thus on his view, for D to have that right just is for D to *not* be under a duty toward C to *not* eat C's salad.

"Privilege" hints at a special social status (as a man has if he holds high rank in an aristocracy); so we have to remember that Hohfeld has none of this in mind in using, and inviting us to use, the term "privilege". He means merely: negation of a duty of opposite "content". On balance, his choice of the term seems to me a good one, and I will adopt it in what follows.

Let us construct a compact characterization of the way in which, following Hohfeld, I will be using the word "privilege".

A preliminary move will be helpful. It seems correct to say that for X to have a privilege as regards Y is for X to have, as regards Y, a privilege of letting a certain state of affairs obtain. (So for D to have a privilege as regards C of eating C's salad is for D to have, as regards C, a privilege of letting it be the case that D eats C's salad.)

Now we can proceed as follows. Suppose a person, say Bloggs, ascribes a privilege to someone; suppose he says something that (in light of our preliminary move) is of the form

X has as regards Y a privilege of letting it be the case that p,

where "p" is replaced by any sentence you like. What he says is equivalent to *the negation of* the result of writing that same sentence in for "p" in

X is under a duty toward Y, namely the duty that X discharges if and only if not-p.

Let us abbreviate these expressions, respectively, as

$P_{X, Y} \, p$

and

$D_{X, Y} \, Not\text{-}p$.

Then we can characterize the terminological practice I will be following in this way:

(H₂) $P_{X, Y}$ is equivalent to $Not\text{-}(D_{X, Y} \, Not\text{-}p)$.

And if Hohfeld's substantive thesis about D's right is true—if D's right as regards C really is a privilege—then we have an answer to a further question we might have asked: "What is the moral significance of D's having that right as regards C?" For the right being a privilege, the moral significance of D's having it is that D is not under a duty toward C to not eat C's salad.

4. Privileges have three interesting, connected features because of the way in which the term was defined.

In the first place, many privileges are in a certain way *relative*. I here and now have a privilege as regards you of trampling Bloggs' roses, for I am under no duty toward *you* to not trample Bloggs' roses. But I do not have a privilege as regards *Bloggs* of trampling Bloggs' roses. Relative to you I have the privilege; relative to him I do not.

That many privileges are relative in this way certainly does not make privileges unique among rights, for many claims too are relative in this way. For example, A has a claim against B that B stay off A's land, but A has no claim against *you* that B stay off A's land.

But, in the second place, many privileges are not relative in this way, and all claims are. As I shall put it: many privileges, but no claims, are *extensive*. What I have in mind is this. There is nothing in the universe toward which I am now under a duty to not pinch my own nose. In light of

(H₂) $P_{X, Y} \, p$ is equivalent to $Not\text{-}(D_{X, Y} \, Not\text{-}p)$

we may conclude that I now have a privilege as regards everything in the universe of pinching my nose. It might be perspicuous to express this fact as follows:

Whatever thing X you choose, $P_{I, x}$ I pinch my nose.

One may have a privilege as regards this thing and not as regards that thing; but one may also have a privilege (indeed, I am sure we all have many privileges) as regards everything.

By contrast, there surely are no claims that a person has against everything in the universe. B is under a duty toward A to stay off A's land, so in light of

(H_1) $C_{X, Y} \, p$ is equivalent to $D_{Y, x} \, p$

we may conclude that A has a claim against B that B stay off A's land. But you are under no duty toward A that B stay off A's land, and I am also not under any such duty:

Whatever thing X you choose, $C_{A, x}$ B stays off A's land

is quite certainly false. This is a feature of privileges in respect of which they differ dramatically from claims.

And it leads us to the third and most important of the three features of privileges that I wished to draw attention to here: they are *weak*. What I have in mind in speaking of the weakness of privileges is in part (though only in part) a matter of what (H_2) tells us, namely that, as Hohfeld put it, a privilege is the mere negation of—thus the lack of—a duty. Given (H_2), it should come as no surprise that so many privileges are so extensive. No wonder a person may have a privilege as regards everything in the universe: he or she may simply not be under the relevant duty toward anything in the universe.

But I had a second thing in mind in speaking of the weakness of privileges. If a privilege is merely the lack of a duty, then it is very plausible to think that from the fact that X has a privilege as regards Y, it does not follow that X has any claims against anything, whether Y or anything else. How could lacking a duty by itself entail having a claim? No doubt everybody has some claims against somebody; what is in question here is only whether X's having a claim against somebody *follows* from the mere fact that X lacks a certain duty. It is very plausible to think that the answer is no.

We can summarize this idea about privileges compactly in the following way:

(H_3) No privilege entails any claim.

I give the thesis the name "(H_3)" since the idea is Hohfeld's.

Given (H_2), we can see that privileges are weak; given (H_3) as well, we can see how very weak they are. I have two things in mind. First, given (H_2) and (H_3), there is no such thing as according a person what a right of his or hers is a right *to*, if the right in question is a privilege. For consider D again, whom we supposed to have a right to eat C's salad. We noticed in the preceding section that the following cannot be said: C accords D what D's right is a right to if and only if D eats C's salad. It should now be noticed that there is no such thing at all as C's according D what D's right is a right to—if D's right is a privilege. For (H_2) tells us that if D's right to eat the salad is a privilege, then it is merely a lack-of-a-duty to not eat the salad. If D's lack-of-a-duty to not eat the salad entailed that he had some claims against C, then there would be things C could do to accord D what D has those claims to, and perhaps we could say that C's doing those things would thereby be C's (indirectly) according D what D's privilege is a privilege to. But (H_3) tells us that D's lack-of-a-duty does not entail that he has any claims against C.

Second, given (H_2) and (H_3), there is no such thing as infringing a person's right if the right in question is a privilege. I now have a privilege of pinching my nose, and I have that privilege as regards everything in the universe. A privilege is a right; is it possible that some person, say Bloggs, should infringe that right of mine? How is he to do that? Well, suppose Bloggs prevents me from pinching my nose. That would not constitute infringing my privilege of pinching my nose, since for me to have that privilege is nothing more than for me to lack a duty, as (H_2) tells us, and the lack of a duty entails no claims, as (H_3) tells us, and *a fortiori* entails no claim to noninterference.

It is clear, then, that given (H_2) and (H_3), X's having as regards Y a privilege of doing such and such is entirely compatible with X's having no claim against Y to X's actually doing the such and such, or to Y's assistance in doing the such and such, or even to Y's noninterference with X's doing the such and such. So Hohfeld's notion 'privilege' really is very weak.

Now I said at the end of the discussion of claims in section 2 that we needed to turn to rights of other kinds, rights that are not rights in the strictest sense and thus are not claims. Privileges being weak in the ways we have now taken note of, *can* it plausibly be thought that they are rights?

5. But first an aside. Having taken note of the ways in which privileges are weak, I think we might do well to take note that privileges are in another way strong. What I have in mind is that it is arguable that

(H_4) No claim entails any privilege

is fully as plausible as

(H_3) No privilege entails any claim.

Suppose you have a claim against me that I be in my office at 4:00. How did you acquire that claim? Perhaps I promised you I would be there then. (It is intuitively plausible to think we cause each other to have claims by making promises to each other.) It does not follow that I have the privilege as regards A, B, or C of being there then, for I might have promised them that I would not be there then. Does it follow that I have the privilege anyway as regards *you?* I think not. People are hardly ever so forgetful as to make two conflicting promises to one and the same person, but mightn't *I* have done so? I promised you I would be there at 4:00; mightn't it happen, shortly thereafter, both of us having temporarily forgotten my first promise, that I promise you I will not be there then? That seems possible. But if it does happen, then my first promise gave you a claim against me to my being there then; and my second promise gave you a claim against me to my not being there then—and if you have a claim against me to my not being there then, I am under a duty toward you to not be there then, and thus lack the privilege as regards you of being there then. (How I am to extricate myself from this moral mess is another matter.)

But this way in which Hohfeld's notion 'privilege' may be thought strong is not as interesting as the ways in which the notion is weak. Let us go back to that.

6. Given

(H_2) $P_{X, Y} p$ is equivalent to Not-$(D_{X, Y}$ Not-p)

and

(H_3) No privilege entails any claim,

privileges are weak, as we saw in section 4.

Indeed, there is an even simpler way of bring out how weak Hohfeld's notion 'privilege' is. Notice that (H₂) yields that other things besides human beings—indeed, nonhuman entities of all sorts, including your left shoe—have privileges. After all, (H₂) tells us that for any things X and Y, X has a privilege as regards Y if and only if Y lacks the relevant duty toward X. I presume that your left shoe has no duties toward anything; that being so, your left shoe has privileges as regards everything.

So how on earth could anyone think that a privilege is itself a right? On some views, animals have rights; I know of no view on which shoes have rights.

What to do? There are a number of possibilities.

One possibility is to say that Hohfeld's notion 'privilege' is really just a triviality, of no interest to the theory of rights or anything else. A man may certainly introduce technical terminology as he pleases; and no doubt, given Hohfeld's definition of the term "privilege", shoes have privileges. But they have nothing of interest in having privileges. Nothing has anything of interest in having privileges. For no privilege is itself a right.

But it would be a mistake to choose this option. We really do lose something of moral interest if we say that no privilege is itself a right.

Let us begin by taking note of the fact that Hohfeld's notion 'privilege' is not an idle invention of his own. The idea that privileges are rights—or anyway the idea that the privileges possessed by human beings are rights—has a distinguished history in political theory. There is good reason to think the idea is at work in Hobbes, for example. Hobbes says in chapter 13 of *Leviathan*[6] that the state of nature is a state of war, of all against all, and he tells us at the end of the chapter:

> To this warre of every man against every man, this also is consequent; that nothing can be Unjust. The notions of Right and Wrong, Justice and Injustice have there no place. Where there is no common Power, there is no Law: where no Law, no Injustice ... It is consequent also to the same condition, that there be no Propriety, no Dominion, no *Mine* and *Thine* distinct; but onely that to be every mans, that he can get; and for so long as he can keep it.

6. My quotations are from the edition of 1651.

How can Hobbes think those remarks compatible with the following, from near the beginning of chapter 14:

> And because the condition of Man . . . is a condition of Warre of every one against every one; in which case every one is governed by his own Reason; and there is nothing he can make use of, that may not be a help unto him, in preserving his life against his enemyes; It followeth, that in such a condition, every man has a Right to everything; even to one anothers body. And therefore, as long as this naturall Right of every man to every thing endureth etc. etc.

How can one consistently think on the one hand that people in the state of nature have natural rights (chapter 14) and, on the other, that in the state of nature there is neither Justice nor Injustice and thus no just or unjust acts (chapter 13)? There is no difficulty whatever if the natural rights one has in mind are, all of them, privileges. For if a man's rights are all privileges, then they are all lacks-of-duty [(H$_2$)], which entail no claim [(H$_3$)]. There is therefore no such thing as according him what he has a right to, thus no way of exercising justice toward him; and there is also no such thing as infringing his rights, thus no way of acting unjustly toward him. So I think it very likely that what Hobbes had in mind in these passages is this: in the state of nature, people have no claims—what they have is privileges, and their privileges are natural rights and *a fortiori* are rights.

It is not for nothing that Hobbes thinks that a privilege possessed by a human being is a right; what led him to do so will come out shortly.

7. Consider C and D and the salad again. C owns some salad, but he gave D permission to eat it. I said: it is intuitively plausible to think that C thereby gave D a right as regards C, a right to eat the salad. But I then went on to talk of "D's right" and said that Hohfeld thinks *it* is a privilege. I thereby implied that there is such a thing as *the* right that C gave D in giving D permission to eat the salad.

Is that true? Is there such a thing as *the* right C gave D in giving D permission to eat the salad? I am strongly inclined to think that in the typical case in which you give Bloggs permission to eat your salad, you give him more than merely a privilege, as regards you, of eating your salad: you surely also give him a claim against you to your noninterference with his eating of it. (If you use the words we so often use in giving permission—"You may", "Help yourself", "Feel free"—

then I think you must be supposed to give him the claim to noninterference as well as the privilege.) I do not for a moment say that in giving Bloggs permission to eat your salad, you give him a claim to his actually eating it, or even to your assistance in eating it; but a claim against you to mere noninterference seems different. If so, then there is no such thing as *the* right you give Bloggs in giving him permission to eat your salad, for you give him two: the privilege of eating it (if his privilege is a right) and a claim to noninterference with his eating it.

But the situation involving C and D was not really like the typical situation in which one person gives another permission to do a thing. Hohfeld's example was rather more complicated than I have let on. What Hohfeld wrote[7] was this:

> C being the owner of the salad, might say to D: "Eat the salad, if you can; you have my license to do so, but I don't agree not to interfere with you." In such a case the privilege exists, so that if D succeeds in eating the salad, he has violated no right of C's. But it is equally clear that if C had succeeded in holding so fast to the dish that D couldn't eat the contents, no right of D would have been violated. (p. 41)

It is not surprising that some of Hohfeld's readers have found this passage puzzling. C (for what reason?) wished to give D *only* the privilege as regards C of eating the salad and did *not* wish to give D also a claim against C to noninterference with D's eating of it. It seems to me that Hohfeld is right in thinking it possible to have only that privilege and not also a claim to noninterference, for it seems to me that privileges (mere lacks-of-duty) do not entail claims—remember

(H₃) No privilege entails any claim.

Moreover, it seems to me that Hohfeld is right in thinking it possible to *give* only a privilege and not also a claim to noninterference. (But notice how careful one has to be if one wishes to do this. C certainly was careful. "Eat the salad, *if you can*", he said. "You have my license to do so, but *I don't agree not to interfere with you*".) Indeed it seems to me that C did give D only a privilege as regards C of eating the salad, so that there really was such a thing as *the* right that C gave D in giving D permission to eat the salad. All the same, it would be

7. I have taken the liberty of eliminating three of the owners (Hohfeld imagined there were four) and altered the names of the characters to accord with my own.

no wonder if a quick reading of the passage had left one feeling puzzled. In the first place, as I said, one who gives permission typically does give a claim to noninterference as well as a privilege. Naturally enough, then, one overlooks the possibility of giving only the privilege. Second, it is not easy to imagine a background against which it can easily be understood why a man might want to give only the privilege, and thus not easy to accept that a man does want to give only the privilege. The other side of this coin is that it is not easy to imagine a background against which it can easily be understood why a man might be interested in getting the privilege, if he knows he is going to get only the privilege. What use it is to D to get the privilege of eating the salad, if C may well decide to hold "so fast to the dish that D can't eat the contents"?—and, moreover, do this without in any way wronging D?

Presumably the use to D is this: if C does not interfere with D's eating of the salad, and nothing else does either, so that D is able to, and does, eat the salad, *then C cannot complain that D wronged him.* (As Hohfeld put it: "he has violated no right of C's".) That is certainly not nothing. If you have not given me the privilege of eating your salad, and I manage to eat it anyway, then you can complain that I wronged you.

The fact that if a person X has a privilege as regards a person Y, then Y cannot complain that X wrongs Y if X exercises that privilege—this is the very consideration that led Hobbes to think of the privileges possessed by human beings as rights. If Hobbes' view of the state of nature is correct, then no one in the state of nature can complain of anyone else's behavior, and this is a morally significant feature of that state, one that it is very natural to want to redescribe in the words "They all have rights to do as they please". We make too little of the moral significance of a privilege if, in light of the weakness of privileges, we say that a privilege is not a right.

So I suggest that we say that privileges are rights.

Or anyway I suggest we say that the privileges possessed by human beings are rights, for our definition of "privilege" yields that shoes have privileges, and shoes presumably have no rights. What is important here is that we not lose sight of the moral interest there is in the fact that human beings have privileges.

To return now to C and D and the salad. Oddly enough, what I implied was true: there really is such a thing as *the* right C gave D in giving D permission to eat the salad—and it really was a privilege.

8. Privileges being weak in the ways we have been looking at, a certain idea about them is incorrect. What I have in mind is Hohfeld's idea that, as he put it,[8]

> A "liberty" considered as a moral relation (or "right" in the loose and generic sense of that term) must mean, if it have any definite content at all, precisely the same thing as *privilege*. (p. 42)

This is surely wrong.[9]

Let us begin with the phrase "at liberty". What is required for the truth of "Bloggs is at liberty to eat JJT's salad"? Two things, I think. First, Bloggs must have a privilege as regards everyone of eating my salad. If Bloggs has promised you that he will not eat my salad, then while Bloggs may well have a privilege as regards *me* of eating my salad, he is not, all simply and flatly, at liberty to eat my salad—for he is under a duty toward you to not eat it. Second, Bloggs must have claims against all others to their not interfering *in a certain range of ways* with his eating of my salad. There are, after all, interferences and interferences. I should think that Bloggs' being at liberty to eat my salad is compatible with your infringing no claim of his when you interfere with his eating of it by singing so beautifully that his attention shifts from salad to song. Similarly for your interfering by telling him (truly) that his mother-in-law is on the telephone and would like to speak to him. By contrast, Bloggs is at liberty to eat my salad only if you (or I or others) do infringe a claim of his when you (or we) interfere with his eating of it by snatching it away from him, or by holding so fast to the dish that he can't eat the salad. It is not easy to say what are the ways of interfering such that Bloggs is at liberty to eat my salad only if he has claims against everyone else that they not interfere with his eating of it in those ways. What does seem right, however, is that he is at liberty to eat the salad only if he does have claims to not be interfered with in those ways.

Or so I think, and so I will suppose. I think we do not say of a person, Bloggs for example, that he is at liberty to do a thing unless *both* he is under no duty at all to not do it (thus he has a privilege against everyone of doing it) *and* everyone else is under a duty toward

---

8. What Hohfeld actually wrote was this: "A 'liberty' considered as a *legal* relation (or 'right' in the loose and generic sense of that term)" (my emphasis).

9. It is surely wrong even as an account of legal usage. See note 11.

him to not interfere with his doing of it in some appropriately chosen set of ways. The notion 'being at liberty', I think, is a very strong one—unlike the notion 'privilege'.

If this is correct, then it would plainly be false to say that D is at liberty to eat C's salad. D has a privilege as regards C of eating it, and for all I know, D has a privilege as regards everyone of eating it. But he lacks a claim against C that C not hold so fast to the dish that D can't eat the salad, for C refused to give him that claim—C refused to give D any claim at all to noninterference by C with D's eating of the salad.

The locution "*the* liberty to do such and such" seems to be less common than the locution "at liberty to do such and such", but it does turn up from time to time.[10] I think it clear that those who use the less common locution would not ascribe it to a person unless they also thought the more common locution ascribable to that person. Thus I think it clear we would not say of Bloggs that he has *the* liberty of eating JJT's salad unless we thought he was *at* liberty to eat JJT's salad. This suggests that the liberty to do such and such contains all of those privileges, on the one hand, and claims to noninterference on the other, whose possession is necessary and sufficient for being at liberty to do the such and such.

Is the liberty to do such and such itself a right? I see no harm in our supposing that it is. There is no harm in our supposing that the liberty to eat C's salad is itself a right. D does not have this right, for he lacks a claim against C to noninterference with his eating of it, but he might have had it—indeed, he would have had it if C had been more generous and simply given D the salad outright.

Moreover, there is some reason in our usage for supposing that we do think the liberty to do such and such is itself a right. What I have in mind is this. We might say of a person that he or she has *a* right to eat C's salad and mean to be ascribing to that person only a privilege of eating it. But I think that when we say of a person that he or she has *the* right to eat C's salad, what we typically mean to be ascribing is precisely the liberty to eat it.

So I suggest we suppose that the liberty to do such and such is itself a right, thus a right that contains rights. But the fact that the liberty to do such and such is a right that itself contains rights certainly does

10. For example, Lord Lindley ascribes "the liberty to deal with other persons who were willing to deal with him" to the plaintiff in an opinion Hohfeld quotes from. See note 11.

not make it unique among rights, for the rights to life, liberty, and property also contain rights. (The right to liberty presumably contains rights such as the liberty to do this or that, which themselves contain rights.) Let us call rights that contain other rights "cluster-rights".[11]

11. Hohfeld's capacity for contempt was impressive, but his contempt was sometimes misdirected. Here, for example, is Lord Lindley, in a passage Hohfeld quotes (on p. 42) from *Quinn v. Leathem:* "The plaintiff had the ordinary *rights* of the British subject. He was *at liberty* to earn his living in his own way . . . This *liberty* involved *the liberty* to deal with other persons who were willing to deal with him. *This liberty* is *a right* . . . its *correlative* is the general *duty* of every one not to prevent the free exercise of this liberty". Hohfeld says (pp. 42–43): "A 'liberty' considered as a legal relation (or 'right' in the loose and generic sense of that term) must mean, if it have any definite content at all, precisely the same thing as *privilege* . . . It would therefore be a *non sequitur* to conclude from the mere existence of such liberties that 'third parties' are under a *duty* not to interfere, etc.". Well, of course, if "liberty" does mean "privilege", then Lord Lindley is badly confused, as Hohfeld says, for privileges do not entail claims, and in particular do not entail claims to noninterference. But *must* "liberty" mean "privilege"? It can only have been infatuation with his own taxonomy of rights that blinded Hohfeld to the fact (I take it to be an obvious fact) that Lord Lindley is here using "at liberty" in the way I said I think we do use it, and that he is taking the liberty to deal with other persons to be a cluster-right, which contains claims to noninterference as well as privileges. (Lord Lindley speaks of "its correlative"; we should presumably take him to be referring to the cluster of duties correlative with those claims to noninterference.)

It is unfortunate that Hohfeld did not accept and accommodate the fact that some, perhaps even most, of what we commonly call rights are cluster-rights—as opposed to rejecting such talk as mere confusion—and not merely because he might then have been able to see that Lord Lindley (like many of the other authors Hohfeld criticizes) meant to be referring to a cluster-right by "the liberty to do such and such". What I have in mind is that Hohfeld could have given a clearer and theoretically more satisfying account of rights *in personam* and rights *in rem* (see the second of the two articles included in the Cook edition) if the notion 'cluster-right' had been available to him. He does see the usefulness of talk of aggregates of rights, as comes out in: "Suppose, for example, that A is fee-simple owner of Blackacre. His 'legal interest' or 'property' relating to the tangible object that we call *land* consists of a complex aggregate of rights (or claims), privileges, powers, and immunities" (p. 96). But he does not make the further move of supposing that an aggregate of rights might itself be a right—and that many of the rights people attribute to themselves and others *are* aggregates of rights. This failure on Hohfeld's part may have been due to a concern that every right should be correlative with a single duty, Hohfeld having forgotten his own restriction of that idea to rights in the strictest sense. It may also have contributed to this failure that the central question in a law suit very often is, or can helpfully be seen as, whether X did have this or that simple straightforward claim against Y.

A cluster-right is of course not a right in the strictest sense, since it is not correlative with a duty. In the first place, a cluster-right may contain privileges, and they are not correlative with duties. Second, while there is nothing that stands in the way of supposing that a given cluster-right might contain only claims, and indeed claims against one and the same thing, still, if the states of affairs those claims are claims to the obtaining of are different, then each of those claims is correlative with a different duty. For example, we might suppose you to have a cluster-right that contains no privileges, but only a claim against me that I not eat your salad and a claim against me that I not squash your banana and a claim against me that I not use your toothbrush, and so on. Each of these claims of yours is correlative with a different duty in me, however, so there is not *a* duty that your cluster-right is correlative with.

Furthermore, there need not even be anything such that a cluster-right is had against that thing. A given cluster-right *might* be a cluster of claims each of which is had against the same thing, but this need not be true of a cluster-right. A given cluster-right might contain your claim against me that I not eat your salad and your claim against Bloggs that Bloggs not eat your salad, and there be nothing—neither Bloggs nor me nor anything else—such that you have both of these claims against *it,* that is, nothing such that you have against it both the claim that I not eat your salad and the claim that Bloggs not eat it.

Still, these things are no barrier to supposing that cluster-rights are rights, for not all rights are rights in the strictest sense. In particular, I said in section 2 above that it was open to us to say, if we wish, that there are rights that are not had against anything; cluster-rights are among the examples I had in mind.

To summarize, then. People have claims, and claims are rights. People also have privileges, and their privileges are rights too. People also have liberties, and liberties are not themselves privileges: the liberty to do this or that includes privileges of doing it *and* claims to noninterference with doing it. Liberties are clusters of rights, and are themselves rights. Many other familiar rights that we take ourselves to have are also cluster-rights.

9. We will be taking a closer look at some familiar cluster-rights in Part II. What we should take note of here is that a great many familiar

cluster-rights contain more than merely claims and privileges. Suppose, for example, that A owns a typewriter. It is intuitively plausible to think that for A to own that typewriter is for A to have a great many claims and privileges in respect of it. We may suppose A has a claim against B that B not use it. We may suppose A has, as regards C, the privilege of using it. And so on. The list is likely to be very long. We might then think of A's owning that typewriter as A's having a right in respect of it, a right that itself contains claims and privileges and therefore is a cluster-right. But A has more than merely a cluster of claims and privileges in owning the typewriter. He has, in addition, what Hohfeld called "powers".

Following Hohfeld, I will say that a power is an ability to cause, by an act of one's own, an alteration in a person's rights, either one's own rights or those of another person or persons, or both. For example, by virtue of owning that typewriter, A is able to make it be the case, by an act of his own, that A himself loses a claim against B that B not use it: A does this if he gives B permission to use it. If C has made an offer to rent a certain typewriter, then by virtue of owning it, A is able to make it be the case, by an act of his own, that C acquires a claim against A that A not use it: A does this if he accepts C's offer. And so on. These abilities are among the powers A has *in* owning the typewriter.

It does not take ownership of something to be able to cause oneself or others to acquire or lose a claim or a privilege. For example, whenever I release someone from a commitment, I cause myself to lose a claim and the other person to acquire a privilege. Whenever I accept an offer of something, made in exchange for my doing something, I cause myself to lose a privilege and the other person to acquire a claim.

But ownership does involve powers of special kinds. A has, and I lack, some special powers in respect of A's typewriter in virtue of its being the case that A owns the typewriter and I do not. One of them can be described, roughly, as follows. A can, by an act of his own, make it be the case (i) that A loses whole hosts of claims, and (ii) that other people acquire whole hosts of privileges and claims. Thus suppose A dumps his typewriter in a trash barrel. That under our law constitutes abandoning the typewriter, so it follows (i) that A ceases to have a claim against B that B not use the typewriter, A ceases to have a claim against C that C not smash the typewriter, and so on.

And it follows also (ii) that B acquires a privilege as regards A, C, and others of using or smashing the typewriter; and B acquires a claim against others that they not interfere (for some ways of interfering) with his use of the typewriter, with his smashing it, and so on. Certainly no comparable large-scale alteration in people's claims and privileges will take place in consequence of *my* dumping A's typewriter in a trash barrel. That is because A owns it and I do not.

I stress that it is *by an act of A's own* that A is able to cause this large-scale alterations in rights. I am also able to cause them, indirectly. I might offer money to A in exchange for A's dumping his typewriter in a trash barrel, and A might accept my offer. If he does, then I will have brought about the result by bringing about that A brings it about. But A alone can bring it about by an act of his own, such as dumping the typewriter in a trash barrel. Certainly no large-scale alteration in people's claims and privileges takes place in consequence of anything I alone do to the typewriter.

We might, for want of a better term, speak here of "large-scale powers": abilities to make large-scale alterations in people's claims and privileges. Ownership of any piece of property includes large-scale powers. (One who occupies an official status of certain kinds, as that of legislator or judge, also typically has large-scale powers.) If we think of A's owning the typewriter as a cluster-right—and I suggest we do—then there are powers in the cluster and, in particular, large-scale powers.

One who has a large-scale power is very likely also to have a further kind of power, a metapower, that is, the ability to cause oneself and others to acquire or lose powers. Thus suppose A says to B of A's typewriter, "Five dollars and it's yours". A thereby exercises a metapower, for by saying what he says, he makes B acquire a power. That is, by saying what he says, A makes B have the ability to make himself owner of the typewriter by handing A five dollars. Since having metapowers seems to be centrally involved in ownership, we should probably think of ownership cluster-rights as containing not merely small-scale powers, not merely large-scale powers, but also metapowers. (One who occupies an official status of certain kinds, as that of legislator or judge, also typically has metapowers.)

It might be worth stressing, however, that I am not saying here that ownership *is* a power. Ownership includes powers, but it includes claims and privileges as well.

Should we think of powers as themselves rights? Hohfeld said

The term 'rights' tends to be used indiscriminately to cover what in a given case may be a privilege, a power, or an immunity, rather than a right in the strictest sense. (p. 36)

Rights in the strictest sense are claims, and certainly no power is itself a claim, for no power is correlative with a duty. But there is surely no harm in that indiscriminate use of the term "rights": no harm in our allowing it to be applied to powers, so long as we remember that what is in question *is* powers. People do say such things as that a person who owns a piece of property has a right to give it away or sell it, and while they might mean to be ascribing only a privilege, I think them likely to mean to be ascribing a power. We need not be misled. If in doubt about what a speaker means, we need only ask.

10. Hohfeld says that "a power bears the same general contrast to an immunity that a right [a claim] does to a privilege" (p. 60). Thus for X to have an immunity against Y just is for Y to lack a power as regards X. You, for example, have an immunity against me if I lack the ability to make you cease to own your typewriter. (A government official might have the ability to make you cease to own your typewriter. If so, you lack the immunity against him.) And if there are inalienable rights, then we each of us have some immunities against ourselves. These are matters we will return to later.

I will suppose that, just as powers are rights, so also are immunities. It is a plausible idea that, for example, the immunity you have against me in that I have not the ability to make you cease to own your typewriter (if you have this immunity) is itself a right of yours. Indeed, it will turn out (in Chapters 11 and 14) that certain immunities are among the rights we most profoundly cherish.

11. To have a power is to have the ability to make another person have or cease to have rights of one or another kind, so we may well want an account of what it is about people in light of which they are able to do this. I have taken it for granted in this chapter that people really do cause people to have or cease to have rights, by making promises, for example, or by giving another person permission to do a thing. (Compare C's giving D permission to eat C's salad.) I have taken this for granted since it seems to me intuitively plausible, some-

thing a theory of rights should make room for. But of course we will need to see whether these ideas can be accommodated in a theory of rights. That, however, is the topic of Part II. For the time being, I will continue to suppose—without justification—that people do cause people to have or cease to have rights in the ways I have pointed to. Our concern in Part I is not which rights we have and why, but only what moral difference it would make if we had this or that right, for our concern now is only what it is to have a right.

It seems correct to think, following Hohfeld, that the moral significance of having a right is a consequence of the relations between rights and duties. So it is to the notion 'duty' that we must now turn.

Chapter 2

Duties

1. I said it seems very plausible to think that A's right against B that B stay off A's land is a claim, thus is correlative with a duty. More precisely, that A's having that right is equivalent to

(1) B is under a duty toward A, namely the duty that B discharges if and only if B stays off A's land,

or, less long-windedly, to

(1') B is under a duty toward A to stay off A's land.

But what is it, exactly, to be under a duty?

Some moral philosophers use the word "duty" very broadly: they so use it that whenever you ought to do a thing, you are under a duty to do it, and whenever you are under a duty to do a thing, you ought to do it. On their understanding of "duty" your duty is identical with what you ought to do. That seems to me an odd usage. While I ought to telephone my friend Alfred this evening, for example, I am not at all inclined to report that fact by saying that I am under a duty to do so.

Moreover, anybody who does use the word "duty" in that very broad way should have been having deep trouble understanding a good bit of what has so far been said. Consider (1'), for example. It surely cannot be thought that (1') is equivalent to

(2) B ought to stay off A's land.

For (2) omits something contained in (1'): (1') tells us that B is under the duty *toward A,* and that information is not given by (2).

The point here can be made in another, and perhaps clearer, way. Suppose A gave B permission to enter A's land, but that B promised C to stay off it. It is intuitively plausible to think that C now has a right against B that B stay off A's land, a claim in fact that is therefore correlative with a duty. More precisely, that C's having that right is equivalent to

(1″) B is under a duty toward C to stay off A's land.

There is no better reason to think (1′) equivalent to (2) than there is to think (1″) equivalent to (2); but it cannot be thought that *both* (1′) and (1″) are equivalent to (2), since (1′) and (1″) are not equivalent to each other. (1″) says that B is under the duty toward C; (1′), by contrast, says that B is under the duty toward A; and these are surely different.

Hohfeld's concept 'duty' is a concept that attaches to two people: there are in every case of its application the one who is under the duty and the one toward whom he or she is under it. We might summarize this in the words: it is a two-hat concept.[1] 'Ought' is not a two-hat concept; we might call it a one-hat concept.

But then what exactly is Hohfeld's concept 'duty'? What exactly does he mean by the word "duty"?

Not, I think, what ordinary speakers of English mean by the word "duty". I am inclined to think that ordinary speakers of English use that word only where they have in mind some job or position, such as that of night watchman ("The duties of the night watchman include making rounds every hour on the hour"), or some role, such as that of parent ("The duties of the parent include seeing to it that his or her child is vaccinated before school opens"). But nothing of that sort—no job, position, or role—need be in the offing where Hohfeld would have us speak of duties. On Hohfeld's account of the matter, given A has a claim against B that B stay off A's land, B is under a duty toward A to do so, whoever B may be, whatever job, position, or role he occupies.

Moreover, ordinary speakers of English sometimes do and sometimes do not attribute a two-hat concept in using the word "duty". When we speak of the duties of a spouse, we presumably think of them as duties toward the spouse. And perhaps we think of the duties of the night watchman as duties toward his or her employer. But do we think this of everything we think of as a duty? (Is the parent's duty to have his or her child vaccinated a duty toward the child? Or

---

1. I do not say that it is a two-place relation. For my reasons, see Chapter 1, note 5.

toward the school? Or toward the community? Does there have to be an answer to this question?) Hohfeld's word "duty", by contrast, can be used only to attribute a two-hat concept.

There are expressions that people always (almost always? typically?) use to attribute two-hat moral concepts, expressions such as "committed to", "under an obligation to", and "owes". Anyway, we very often say such things as that we are committed to, or under an obligation to, or that we owe it to, so and so to do such and such. But I do not think that any of these expressions is synonymous with Hohfeld's "duty". Take "committed to". Suppose I give you a right against me that I will do such and such by promising you that I will. That right should presumably be a claim, thus it should presumably have a duty as correlative. So

I am under a duty toward you to do the such and such

should presumably be true. I am sure—in light of the way I gave you the right—that

I am committed to you to doing the such and such

is also true. But are these two sentences synonymous? I doubt it. A has a right against B that B stay off A's land, a claim presumably. So

(1′) B is under a duty toward A to stay off A's land

is presumably true. Is

(1*) B is committed to A to staying off A's land

also true? People who have commitments typically (always?) acquire them by actually committing themselves. But we need not suppose that B committed himself to A to staying off A's land in order to suppose that A has a right that he do so: A's having the right against B is surely compatible with their being total strangers. So we seem to have to stretch the sense of the expression "committed to" if we are to think it right to say that B is committed to A to staying off A's land. If so, then it will not quite do to say that (1′) is equivalent to (1*), and thus will not do to say they are synonymous.

In sum, my impression is that there just is no familiar piece of moral terminology that is synonymous with Hohfeld's "duty". The actual English word "duty", on the one hand, and "committed to", "under an obligation to", and "owes", on the other, seem to have meanings that are markedly narrower than Hohfeld's "duty".

If I am right in thinking that there is no familiar piece of moral terminology that is an exact synonym of Hohfeld's "duty", then is there an unfamiliar one? We might try to construct an account of what Hohfeld means by "duty", but nothing springs readily to mind.

Then why did we think we knew what Hohfeld means by "duty"? Worse still, why did we think we understood Hohfeld's "claim" and "privilege" by virtue of his definitions of them in terms of "duty"? And why did I say it seems very plausible to think that A's right against B that B stay off A's land is a claim, thus is correlative with a duty? How could I have thought that seems plausible if I am not clear what a duty is?

I think we did understand Hohfeld's "duty", and thereby his "claim" and "privilege", and that we did understand it because of, and in light of, the examples he gave us. I said it is intuitively plausible to think that some people do own bits of land and that some among them have rights against some others that those others stay off the land; and I said let us suppose for the time being that A is among those owners and that B is among the others against whom A has the right. There are many things we want to know about rights, but one thing we do know about A's right is that it in *some* way constrains B's behavior. I asked "What is the moral significance of A's having that right against B?" I did not first argue *that* A's having that right against B does constrain B's behavior in some way, and *then* proceed to ask what precisely that way is; I took for granted you would agree that A's having the right against B does constrain B's behavior, and simply asked how it does. I said that a particularly interesting answer to the question is suggested in Hohfeld's article. In fact I think that no answer to the question is suggested in Hohfeld's article. We already knew that A's having the right against B constrains B's behavior; what Hohfeld does is to offer us the name "duty" to refer to the kind of behavioral constraint—whatever precisely it may be—which, as we already knew, A's having the right against B imposes on B. And we understood Hohfeld's "duty" in that we took it to be the name of that kind of behavioral constraint, whatever precisely it may be.

I suggested just above that there is no familiar piece of moral terminology that is an exact synonym of Hohfeld's "duty", and asked whether there isn't perhaps an unfamiliar one that is. Perhaps *now* the following springs readily to mind: a duty is the kind of constraint on behavior that A's having a right against B that B stay off A's land imposes on B. This, I am sure, would be correct. But, as I said, this tells us what we are to call the constraint on behavior, and not what it is.

2. I do not for a moment mean to imply that we have been wasting our time in attending to Hohfeld's article. He makes three important contributions to the theory of rights.

In the first place, although we already knew that A's right against B constrains B's behavior, Hohfeld reminds us that this is so, he draws our attention to its being so, he tells us that its being so is an important fact about A's right. Indeed, he tells us that A's having the right *is equivalent to* B's being under that constraint.

Second, he is obviously not concerned just with A and B: he has a general aim in view. What he tells us is that there is a large subclass or species of rights that are like A's in this respect: a species of rights that a person X has against a person Y such that X's having the right against Y constrains Y's behavior in the very same way as A's having his right against B constrains B's behavior. The species is, of course, the rights in the strictest sense, the claims, as he would have us call them. Thus in the case of every right in that species—every claim, that is—X's having the right is equivalent to Y's being under that behavioral constraint in respect of X.

The importance of this thesis is considerable. A student of the theory of rights is in search of an account of which rights we have; if what Hohfeld tells us is correct, then we will have found out which claims we have when we have found out who is under that behavioral constraint in respect of us. Indeed, we could as well ask who is under that behavioral constraint in respect of us as ask which claims we have.

Is what Hohfeld tells us correct? One thing is clear—that the value of having a claim arises from the fact that the behavior of the one against whom one has it is constrained in virtue of one's having it. B may wander at will on unowned land; the value to A of having a claim against B that B stay off a certain bit of land arises from the fact that, given A has that claim, B may not (other things being equal) wander at will on it.

Hohfeld of course tells us something stronger than just that the value of having claims lies in the constraints on behavior that flow from one's having them: he tells us that having claims is equivalent to there being such constraints on the behavior of others. But that is surely correct. Y's behavior is constrained in respect of X in the way we are talking of if X has a claim against Y; and X has a claim against Y if Y's behavior is constrained in respect of X in that way.

Hohfeld's third major contribution to the theory of rights is to draw our attention to the fact—it seems to me plainly a fact—that many rights outside the species of rights that are claims have immediate and simple connections with rights inside the species. Take privileges, for example, which form a second species of rights. Hohfeld defined "privilege" in terms of "duty", as follows: "a privilege is the opposite of a duty" but of a "duty having a content or tenor precisely *opposite* to that of the privilege". How were we able to understand what a privilege is, given there is no readily available expression of English synonymous with Hohfeld's "duty"? We understood that "privilege" is the name Hohfeld wishes us to use for a lack of that very kind of constraint on behavior that A's having his right against B imposes on B. Are there any rights that fall into this species? Yes, D's right as regards C to eat C's salad is intended by Hohfeld to be an example, and succeeds in being one, for D's having his right as regards C to eat C's salad surely is equivalent to D's not being under that kind of constraint to not eat C's salad.

But this being so, D's having his right as regards C to eat C's salad (a right in the second species, that is, a privilege) is equivalent to C's not having a right (a right in the first species, that is, a claim) against D to D's not eating C's salad. I offered

(H₁) $C_{X, Y}\, p$ is equivalent to $D_{Y, X}\, p$

and

(H₂) $P_{X, Y}\, p$ is equivalent to Not-$(D_{X, Y}\, \text{Not-}p)$

as displays of the use of "claim" and "privilege" that I will, following Hohfeld, abide by in what is to come. They jointly entail

(H₅) $P_{X, Y}\, p$ is equivalent to Not-$(C_{Y, X}\, \text{Not-}p)$,

from which it can be seen directly that rights in the second species have the following immediate and simple connection with rights in the first species: X's having a right of the second species as regards a person Y is equivalent to Y's lacking a right of the first species against X.

Hohfeld would prefer we reserve the term "rights" for the rights in the first species, but, as I said in the preceding chapter, there is reason to prefer a terminology by which privileges are called rights. So privileges form a (second) species of rights.

Again, we may allow ourselves to speak of powers and immunities as forming a third species of rights. Hohfeld's account of them brings out that they too have immediate and simple connections with rights in the first two species and with each other, and with rights in the fourth species, which I will mention shortly. For he tells us that powers are abilities, and immunities inabilities, to cause oneself and others to acquire and lose claims, privileges, powers, immunities, and rights in the fourth species.

The idea of a right that is itself a cluster of rights does not appear in Hohfeld's articles, but it might and indeed should have done. Cluster-rights (such as liberties) can be thought of as forming a fourth species of rights; a cluster-right is a cluster of rights each of which falls into one or other of the four species I have mentioned.

I said that it seems to me plainly a fact that *many* rights outside the species of rights that are claims have immediate and simple connections with rights inside the species. Do *all* rights have immediate and simple connections with rights inside that species? More important, do all rights fall into one or the other of the four species I have listed? Saying so is saying something very strong indeed. What it means is that if a person, say Bloggs, asserts that he has such and such a right, and we cannot find a place for his (putative) right in this list of four species, then we have reason to think he does not really have the right at all.

For my own part, I think it a very plausible idea that all rights do fall into one or the other of the four species. I have no argument to that effect, however. The plausibility of the idea is enhanced when we see (as we will in Part II) that rights we not only think we have, but think it a morally important fact about us that we do have, can be assigned places among the species; moreover, we are helped to understand what having those rights involves by going through the process of figuring out which species they fall into. I may of course have overlooked some possibilities, for I have no argument to the effect that all rights do fall into the four species. Perhaps there is a fifth species, and a sixth. But those who think there are further species of rights might themselves be helped to characterize what they have in mind if they see it as their task to contrast what they have in mind with the four species I have listed. It might pay to remember, moreover, that unlimited tolerance about what rights people have is not a virtue, for a person's really having a right, of whatever kind, must surely have consequences for the behavior of the rest of us, and the rest of us therefore have a stake in the difference between bogus right and real right.

In any case, if all rights do fall into one or other of the four species, then a considerable advance has been made. To shift metaphor, what we might think of as the realm of rights is at first glance very hard to see one's way around in. What Hohfeld has supplied us with is the means of making a map, showing the routes between the territories within it. That is no mean contribution to the theory of rights.

3. I said in Chapter 1 that Hohfeld supplied us with an answer to the question "What is the moral significance of A's having the right we supposed him to have against B?" in telling us that B is under a duty toward A. But I said in this chapter that Hohfeld does not in fact supply us with an answer to our question: what he supplies us with is only the word "duty" as a name for the moral significance of A's having the right—he does not tell us what that moral significance is. It is worth stressing that he would not in fact have supplied us with an answer to our question even if his word "duty" had been synonymous with one or another familiar piece of moral terminology of the kind I drew attention to earlier, such as "commitment", "obligation", and so on. Thus the trouble does not issue from the mere fact that (as I think) there is no familiar piece of moral terminology synonymous with Hohfeld's "duty".

What I have in mind is that the question we wanted answered in asking for the moral significance of A's right against B—or, as I should put the point, the question we *really* wanted answered—would not have been answered even if Hohfeld's "duty" had meant the same as one or another of those expressions. To see this, let us pretend that there is a familiar piece of moral terminology synonymous with Hohfeld's "duty". Let us pretend that it is "commitment", so that what Hohfeld means by

(1′) B is under a duty toward A to stay off A's land,

really is what any of us in ordinary life mean by

(1*) B is committed to A to staying off A's land.

This suggests we should say that the moral significance of A's having the right against B lies in the fact that A's having that right against

B constrains B's behavior in the following way: given A has that right against B, B is committed to A to what the right is a right *to*. But don't we now want to ask the very same question about B's commitments that we asked about A's rights?—namely, "What is the moral significance of B's being commited to A to staying off A's land?"

Let us go back. I said that our first question is this: not which rights we have, but rather what a right *is*. I went on to say: having a right is having a kind of moral status, and finding out what that status is requires finding out what the moral significance of having a right is. So finding out what a right is requires finding out what the moral significance of having a right is. So far so good. I suggest, moreover, that we will not think we have found out what the moral significance of having a right is until we have found out what is the connection between a person's having a right, on the one hand, and what if anything people ought to do about it, on the other.

That point is worth stressing. So and so has a right against us? Well, what does that come to? We have not been told until we have been told what if anything we ought to do about his having it. It is arguable that something analogous is true of every moral concept. Smith is an honorable man and Jones a deceitful one? Smith does certain kinds of things that he ought to do, and Jones does not. Such and such a state or state of affairs would be better than ours is? Other things being equal, we ought to change ours. Such and such a man's words were an outright lie? Other things being equal, he ought not have said them. Indeed, it is arguable that moral concepts generally have such content as they do have only in having such import for human behavior as they do have, and that morality itself is at heart a set of constraints on behavior. Whether that is true of morality as a whole, it is certainly true of the concept 'having a right' that making sense of it requires understanding how rights connect with what people ought to do.

It was *that* kind of information about rights that I was asking for—and am sure you understood me to be asking for—in asking "What is the moral significance of having a right?"

But if that is the kind of information we are asking for, then one who says by way of reply, "The moral significance of having a claim lies in the fact that for X to have a claim against Y is for Y's behavior to be constrained in the way in which commitments constrain behavior", has not answered our question at all unless he or she can go on in the next breath to answer the very same question about commitments. That is, unless he or she can go on in the next breath to tell us, given Y has such and such a commitment to X, what if anything follows about what Y or anyone else ought to do.

Is that an easy task to carry out? Suppose I promised you I would be in my office today at 4:00, so that I am committed to you to being there then; does it follow that I ought to be there then? What if my son suddenly falls ill and needs to be taken to hospital, and my taking him there is incompatible with my being in my office at 4:00? Ought I really, all the same, be in my office at 4:00? At a minimum, it is not obvious that I ought. The question what Y's being committed to this or that entails about what Y or anyone else ought to do is not in fact an easy question to answer.

So even if Hohfeld's "duty" meant what we in ordinary life mean by "commitment", Hohfeld's proposal to the effect that rights (in the strictest sense) are correlative with duties would not *by itself* supply any answer at all to the question we really wanted answered.

4. The time has come to ask what Hohfeld would reply to all of this. I am sure he would say: "Look, it was law I advertised myself as concerned with in that article of mine, and only law. *Not* morality". That makes a difference.

Let us have another look at

(H$_1$) $C_{X, Y}$ p is equivalent to $D_{Y, X}$ p.

Suppose we interpret this in the way Hohfeld quite certainly meant it to be interpreted, as saying

'X has a legal claim against Y that p' is equivalent to
'Y is under a legal duty toward X, namely the legal duty that Y discharges if and only if p'.

What should we make of (H$_1$) under this interpretation of it?

To begin with, what is a legal claim? Here is an example: the legal claim I have against you that you not ram your car into mine for fun. What is it for me to have that legal claim against you? The legal system under which we live attaches a penalty to a person's ramming his or her car into another person's for fun, for any pair of people governed by the legal system, and one theory about what it is for me to have that legal claim against you is this: for me to have it against you just *is* for the legal system under which we live to attach a penalty to your ramming your car into mine for fun. More generally: for X to have a legal claim against Y that Y not do such and such to X just is for the legal system under which they live to attach a penalty to Y's doing the such and such to X. I will call this theory Positivism.[2]

What would Positivists say about legal duties? I am sure they would say the same of legal duties as they say of legal claims, thus that for Y to be under a legal duty toward X that Y not do such and such to X just is for the legal system under which they live to attach a penalty to Y's doing the such and such to X. I am sure a Positivist would say that a legal duty and a legal claim are simply the same phenomenon (of penalty-attaching) looked at 'from different directions'—that is, to talk of a legal claim is to describe the penalty from the point of view of the potential victim, and to talk of a legal duty is to describe the penalty from the point of view of the potential agent. Positivists, then, would welcome (H₁), interpreted as a thesis about law: on their view it is perhaps not a very exciting truth, but all the same a truth.

It is certainly arguable that this account of legal claims is incorrect.[3] It is arguable, for example, that moral (or other) considerations enter into the content of the notion 'legal claim' in some way. A relatively simple-minded theory of this kind might say that for me to have a legal claim against you that you not ram your car into mine for fun is for it to be the case that the legal system *ought to* attach a penalty to your doing that, whether or not it actually does. For our purposes it is not necessary that we decide on the range of issues this idea points to. What is in question for us is only whether or not a friend of one of the theories offered as preferable to Positivism would take a different stand from the Positivist about (H₁). I think not. Consider the theory I just mentioned. A friend of this theory is, I think, likely to say the same of legal duties as of legal claims, so, in particular, that for you to be under a legal duty toward me to not ram your car into mine for fun is for it to be the case that the legal system *ought to* attach a penalty to your doing that, whether or not it actually does. I think that friends of this theory are likely to agree with the Positivist

2. "Positivism" is not actually the name of this theory but of a more general theory, for there are legal claims of other kinds that I do not mention above, and Positivism accounts for them as well. But our purposes do not require that we attend to them. (I should mention also that some legal theorists use the name "Positivism" for rather 'softer' theories than I point to here.)

3. See, for example, H. L. A. Hart, *The Concept of Law* (Oxford: Clarendon Press, 1961), and Ronald Dworkin, *Taking Rights Seriously* (Cambridge: Harvard University Press, 1977).

on this much anyway, that a legal duty and a legal claim are simply the same phenomenon looked at 'from different directions'—though they would disagree with Positivists as to the nature of the phenomenon. So they too would take (H_1) to be perhaps not a very exciting truth, but all the same a truth.

Hohfeld does not himself take a stand as between these theories: he does not have anything at all to say about what makes it be the case that this or that person has this or that legal claim or legal duty. What interests him is only that it should be agreed that legal claims (whatever they rest on) are correlative with legal duties. And, as I said, I think that all parties to the dispute would agree to this.

It would in fact be no wonder if they did. For what they offer as an analysis of legal claims—whether the analysis says that legal claims consist in there being penalties attached to this or that kind of conduct, or that legal claims consist in its being the case that penalties ought to be attached to those kinds of conduct, or whatever else—seems to be as plausibly viewable as an analysis of the concept 'legal duty' as of the concept 'legal claim'. None of the theories supplies material by means of which to distinguish between these two concepts. All seem best understood as taking them to apply to the same phenomenon looked at 'from different directions', as I put it.

If what Hohfeld had in mind is what I have now suggested he had in mind—and I am sure he did—then the complaints I have been making are off target. I said that it is not clear exactly what Hohfeld means by "duty". Hohfeld would justifiably reply, "You are mistaken. What I mean by 'duty' is: legal duty. And if you want to know what a legal duty is, look up those works on jurisprudence that deal with the question whether for Y to be under a legal duty toward X to not do such and such to X just *is*, or is in some more complicated way related to, the legal system's attaching a penalty to doing such and such to a person". I also said that Hohfeld supplies us with no answer at all to the question "What is the moral significance of A's having a right against Y that Y stay off X's land?" Hohfeld would justifiably reply, "I never for a moment intended to offer you an answer to that question. Given that X has, as in our society he does have, a legal claim against Y that Y not ram Y's car into X's car for fun, then Y is under a legal duty toward X to not ram Y's car into X's car for fun—as (H_1) tells us. What follows from that about what Y or anyone else ought to do? That's an interesting question, but not one I tried to answer in that article of mine which you have been so grossly misinterpreting."

If what Hohfeld had in mind is what I have now suggested he had in mind, then we cannot take him to have made an important contribution to the theory of rights. But we can take him to have made an important contribution to the theory of legal rights. In section 2 I interpreted him as offering us a map of the realm of rights; when we construe him correctly, we can take him instead to have offered us a map of the realm of legal rights.

5. It is morality, however, not law, that interests us. I said at the outset that among the rights we take ourselves to have are rights to life, liberty, and property. And I did not intend to be making an assertion about law.

Some people would say I should have said "moral rights" to life, liberty, and property—by contrast with legal rights to life, liberty, and property—in that this would have made it clearer what I had in mind. I think it worth bringing out that there is less that is helpful in this proposal than meets the eye.

I should stress at the outset that I have no objection to our saying of ourselves that we have legal rights. It is also not objectionable to think of legal rights as forming a realm, of which Hohfeld gave us a map. What is objectionable is this. Many people say, "Well, we have legal rights on the one hand and moral rights on the other", and many of those people wish to be understood as saying that what they are calling "legal rights" and what they are calling "moral rights" are two discrete territories within the realm of rights. It is *that* idea that won't do.

To shift metaphor, what won't do is the idea that legal rights and moral rights are two distinct species of the genus rights. For what exactly is supposed to be the feature by which the species are distinguished? I am sure the friends of this idea would say that the two species of rights differ according to the sources of the rights that fall into the species. I am sure they would say that the difference between the species is characterizable in some such way as this: X's right against Y that a state of affairs S obtain falls into the legal-right species just in case X has the right against Y because the legal system under which they live assigns it to X, whereas, by contrast, X's right against Y that S obtain falls into the moral-right species just in case X has the right against Y because morality assigns it to X. Let us call this idea the Two-Species Thesis.

Now I think we can already see that there is a difficulty for the Two-Species Thesis, lying in the fact that some of our rights certainly seem to have both legal and nonlegal sources. For example, I think I have a right against my neighbor that he not murder me. That right is assigned me by the legal system under which we both live, for that legal system declares murder a crime. On the other hand, I think I would have that right even if the legal system did not assign it to me. It is no doubt hard to imagine a legal system that does not assign to anyone living under it a right to not be murdered; perhaps that is an unimaginable legal system. But it is unfortunately all too easy to imagine a legal system that does not assign to (as it might be) Jews or blacks a right to not be murdered. We would surely not say of the Jews or blacks who live under such a legal system that no right of theirs is infringed if and when others murder them. If you like, no legal right of theirs is infringed; but *a* right, indeed a fundamental right, is infringed. The gravamen of the charge against such a legal system is precisely that it does not assign them a fundamental right that they do have as human beings who live under the system, the right to not be murdered.

Friends of the Two-Species Thesis could bypass this difficulty in a number of ways. Or, better, they could say a plague on the Two-Species Thesis and reject it in favor of the Three-Species Thesis— which says that legal rights are rights with only legal sources, moral rights are rights with only moral sources, and legal/moral rights form a third species, namely those rights with both legal and moral sources.

A second difficulty, however, is more serious. According to the Three-Species Thesis, legal rights are a species of rights. But which exactly are the legal rights? The Three-Species Thesis says that X's right against Y that a state of affairs S obtain falls into the legal-right species just in case X has the right against Y because and only because the legal system under which they live assigns it to X; but there are a number of ways in which we can understand what it is for a legal system to assign a right, for there are a number of ways in which we can understand what a legal right is.

Consider what I called Positivism, which says that if a legal system attaches a penalty to a kind of conduct, then potential victims have a legal claim against others that they not engage in that kind of conduct. Positivism may also be taken to say that if a legal system does not attach a penalty to a kind of conduct, then potential engagers in it have a legal privilege as regards others of engaging in it. More generally, a Positivist takes it that a legal system assigns a right wherever it does, or does not, attach a penalty. But if Positivism is correct, then the Three-Species Thesis is false. For suppose a law is passed in our community which declares that there is henceforth no penalty attached to murdering Jews, and moreover that there is henceforth a penalty attached to attempting to prevent the murder of Jews. Here is Bloggs, who hates a certain Jew, namely Smith. Does Bloggs now have a legal privilege as regards Smith of murdering Smith? Does Bloggs now have a legal claim against me that I not attempt to prevent his murdering Smith? If Positivism is correct, the answer to both questions is yes. But then at least some legal rights are not members of the genus rights. No doubt Bloggs has a *legal* privilege of murdering Smith, on this understanding of legal privileges; but he has no privilege of murdering Smith. No doubt I infringe a *legal* claim of Bloggs' if I attempt to prevent him from murdering Smith, on this understanding of legal claims; but he has no claim against me that I not do this—I infringe no claim he really has if I proceed to do it.

More generally, if Positivism is correct, so that attaching or failing to attach a penalty by itself generates a legal right, then a person's having a legal right does not by itself guarantee his or her having a right. And legal rights are therefore not a species of rights.

As I mentioned earlier, there are those who think Positivism is not correct as an account of legal claims, and thus do not think that a legal system's actually attaching a penalty to a kind of conduct by itself generates a legal claim. They would say the same of legal privileges. Many of them think that the question whether a legal system assigns a right, and indeed that the question what a particular legal system *is*, turns on moral considerations as well as on matters having to do with what penalties are or are not in fact attached to this or that kind of conduct. It is entirely open to one who adopts such an account of legal rights to suppose that legal rights are a species of rights, so that a person's having a legal right does by itself guarantee his or her having a right. But on such a view, legal rights themselves have moral sources, and there is no sharp distinction to be made between rights with only legal sources and rights with only moral sources, as the Three-Species Thesis declares there to be.

My aim here has not been to show that the Two- and Three-Species Theses are false, but only to show that the linguistic proposal I drew

attention to at the beginning of this section—that we not speak of
rights, but instead of moral rights on the one hand and legal rights
on the other—is less helpful than it might have appeared. The way
of talking it would impose on us is not itself clarifying: the work
would remain to be done of understanding what is to be meant by
those locutions, "moral rights" and "legal rights", and of understanding how what they are to be applied to connect not only with each
other but with what we think of, and prephilosophically describe as,
all simply, "rights".

It is plain enough that our rights have different sources. I have a
right against my neighbor Bloggs that he not murder me, and the
source, perhaps better, the sources of this right are not the same as
the sources of many of my other rights, such as my right against
Bloggs that he not leave his garbage on the sidewalk in front of my
house, except on Wednesdays, which under our town's regulations
are garbage-collection days. The student of the theory of rights does
better, I think, not to begin by asking whether the one is moral (or
legal/moral) and the other legal, but rather just to ask what those
sources are. Again, I acquired a right against Bloggs that he not leave
his garbage on the sidewalk in front of my house, except on Wednesdays, when our town passed its garbage-collection ordinance, but
Bloggs would not acquire a right to murder me by virtue of the legal
system's ceasing to attach a penalty to murder. The student of the
theory of rights does better, I think, just to ask why the one and not
the other. Anyone who likes can at the end try to construct an account
of what might plausibly be meant by the terms "moral rights" and
"legal rights" under which the genus rights can be seen as having
species appropriately named in those ways, but what interests us is
the genus rights itself—as I will put it throughout, what interests us
is people's *rights*.

We can, however, continue to say that there is a realm of legal
rights, of which Hohfeld gave us a map. We need merely leave open
(as Hohfeld did) what makes something be in it, and *a fortiori* leave
open what the relation is between that realm and the realm of rights.

6. But what *are* rights? I suspect that having drawn attention in this
chapter to law, I may have made it seem less clear now what a right
is than it did when I talked, as I did in the preceding chapter, simply
about rights. We know what it is for a legal system to attach penalties
to this or that kind of conduct; perhaps we also take ourselves to

know when it would be wrongful for a legal system to attach penalties to this or that kind of conduct. But what are rights, some of which may be thought to issue from legal considerations and some of which may be thought to issue from considerations that are not legal?

I said in section 4 that Hohfeld might justifiably reply to my comments on his article that he had no interest in rights generally: that it was law, and only law, legal rights and only legal rights, that interested him. Suppose, however, that we do what I did up through section 3 of this chapter, namely ignore Hohfeld's intentions and pretend that he had rights generally in mind. Then we can take him to have made the contributions to the theory of rights that I attributed to him in section 2. In particular, we can take him to have wished to say that A's having a right against B that B stay off A's land is equivalent to B's being under a certain kind of behavioral constraint in respect of A, a behavioral constraint we are to call "duty". And we can take him to have wished to say, more generally, that there is a species of rights which are rights that a thing X has against a thing Y, and which are such that X's having the right against Y is equivalent to Y's behavior's being constrained in the way in which B's behavior is constrained by virtue of A's having a right against B that B stay off A's land. We can take Hohfeld to have thought that species of rights the rights in the strictest sense, and to have invited us to call them "claims".

If these ideas are correct, and I said it seemed to me very plausible to think they are, then we can say that a right of that species—a claim that X has against Y—just is a moral fact equivalent to Y's behavior's being constrained in the way in which B's behavior is constrained by virtue of A's having a right against B that B stay off A's land.

Something stronger still could be said, namely that a claim that X has against Y is not merely a moral fact *equivalent to* Y's behavior's being constrained in that way, but more, that it *is* Y's behavior's being constrained in that way. This stronger thesis says that a claim is not merely equivalent to a constraint, but is a constraint. I see no good reason[4] for adopting the weaker thesis but refusing to go on to adopt the stronger thesis.

Again, we can take Hohfeld to have said that there is a second species of rights, the privileges, the having of which is equivalent to

----

4. I say "no good reason" advisedly. There is *a* reason, which I will later suggest is not a good reason.

a person's behavior's not being constrained in that way. We can say that having a privilege just is a moral fact equivalent to one's behavior's not being constrained in that way or, more strongly, that a privilege *is* one's behavior's not being constrained in that way.

Again, we can suppose that a third species of rights consists in abilities and inabilities to generate rights, and that a fourth consists in clusters of rights of the four species.

If these four species of rights exhaust the rights, then we have an account of what all rights *are*. Of course we should have to go on to ask the further question which of them we have, but we would at least know what those things are such that what we are asking is which of them we have.

But the adequacy of this account of what rights are rests on something that may, entirely rightly, be thought weak, namely our understanding of just what that constraint on behavior is such that B's behavior is constrained in that way by virtue of A's having a right against B that B stay off A's land. So we should now ask what it is.

Chapter 3

Ought

1. It does seem right to think that X's having a claim against Y is at least equivalent to, and perhaps just *is,* Y's behavior's being constrained in a certain way. What way? It is surely plain that

(1) A has a claim against B that B stay off A's land

is not equivalent to

(2) B ought to stay off A's land,

for (1) is equivalent to

B is under a duty toward A, namely the duty that B discharges if and only if B stays off A's land,

and that as we know is not equivalent to (2)—see the small argument at the beginning of Chapter 2.

But perhaps, although (1) is not equivalent to (2), (1) all the same *entails* (2)? Let us look, in this and the following chapter, at the idea that it does.

Quite a few people find this idea attractive. After all, very often when we ought to do a thing, we ought to do it precisely because someone has a claim against us that we do it. Doesn't it seem simplest to suppose that this is because a person's having a claim against us that we do it entails that we ought to do it? And if (1) does not entail (2), then exactly how is it related to (2)? What a task we set for ourselves if we say (1) does not entail (2)! For there surely is some relation between (1) and (2)—the truth of (1) surely gives some reason to think (2) true—and a theory of rights will have its work cut out for it if it does not accept the simple account according to which (1) entails (2). These considerations appeal to the simplification to be got by accepting the view that (1) entails (2): a simplification in our theory of rights, and thereby in our theory of morality in general. This is the major attraction of the idea that (1) entails (2).

But there are other considerations too. Many people *seem* to show by their behavior that they think the simple account true. They say "I have a right that you do such and such", plainly meaning that they have a claim against us that we do the such and such; and they *seem* to show by their behavior that they think this settles the matter—that we have, morally speaking, no other option, that it just follows that we ought to do the such and such. I say only "seem" because there are other possible explanations of their behavior. But there is no denying that we explain their behavior most simply if we attribute to them the view that their having the right does entail that we ought to do the such and such.

The fact that many people think the simple account true (supposing there is such a fact, that is, supposing we are right to attribute to them the belief that the simple account is true) does not of course show that it is true. But the fact that many people think it true surely is some reason to think it true. And isn't there independent reason to think them right? If those people really do have a claim against us that we do such and such, then aren't we at fault if we fail to do it? If we fail to do it, won't they have ground for complaint against us? And doesn't that show we ought to do it?

There is yet another consideration worth mentioning. Some philosophers have suggested that self-respect rests on one's being able to feel confident, perhaps not in one's actually being accorded what one has claims to, for a person's self-respect could hardly be thought to rest on the good behavior of others, but anyway in its being the case that others ought to accord one what one has claims to—so that if others fail to accord me what I have claims to, then that does not say *I* am unimportant; it says, rather, that they are at fault. A philosopher who holds this view may very well think not merely that the simple account is simplest, but also that we are committed to it if we think morality requires respect for people, oneself and others.

And there is a further consideration, which we will turn to in Chapter 4.

What I have been calling "the simple account" is a quite general thesis about the relation between claims and what a person ought to do. It says that (1) entails (2) *and* that sentences appropriately similar to (1) entail sentences appropriately similar to (2). We can express that thesis, compactly, in our terminology as follows:

(T$_1$) If there is an X such that $C_{X, Y}$ p, then Y ought not let it fail to be the case that p.

Another, still more compact, way of expressing the thesis is this: all claims are absolute. I should perhaps stress, since people use the word "absolute" in many different ways, that what I mean by "all claims are absolute" is nothing more or less than (T$_1$) itself. We need to take a closer look at that thesis.

2. But first an aside. If a desire to simplify is what lies behind the inclination to adopt

(T$_1$) If there is an X such that $C_{X, Y}$ p, then Y ought not let it fail to be the case that p,

then why not also adopt

(T$_2$) If Y ought not let it fail to be the case that p, then there is an X such that $C_{X, Y}$ p.

Their conjunction yields

(T$_3$) Y ought not let it fail to be the case that p, if and only if there is an X such that $C_{X, Y}$ p

and adopting that would *greatly* simplify the theory of rights, for what (T$_3$) says is that claims exactly overlap what people ought to do and call for no special attention at all.

Again, (T$_1$) tells us that "Y ought not let it fail to be the case that p" is a necessary condition for the truth of "There is an X such that $C_{X, Y}$ p"; but if it is a necessary condition, why isn't it also a sufficient condition? (That it is a sufficient condition is precisely what (T$_2$) tells us.) What might be missing? Usually where we are ready to say that P is a necessary but not sufficient condition for Q we can point to what is missing where P is true but Q is not true—the more that has to be the case, beyond the truth of P, for Q to be true as well. And what could that be thought to be here? I do not for a moment say this question has no answer, only that we ought to be struck by the question if we think (T$_1$) is true and do not also think (T$_2$) true.

It might be worth noticing that the small argument I gave at the beginning of Chapter 2 makes no trouble for one who wishes to accept (T_2) as well as (T_1), and thereby to obtain (T_3). (T_3) commits us to its being the case that

(2) B ought to stay off A's land

is equivalent to

There is an X such that $C_{X, B}$ B stays off A's land

and therefore to

There is an X such that $D_{B, X}$ B stays off A's land,

which does not say that B is under the duty toward A, or toward C, but instead leaves open who B is under the duty toward.

There certainly is no inconsistency in accepting either (T_1) or (T_2) and rejecting the other, and we should look at both. Complications should not be multiplied beyond necessity, so we should reject these theses only if it really does seem necessary to do so—thus only if accepting them means that we are unable to account satisfactorily for certain important moral facts, or if they generate their own, deeper, complications, or for some other good reason. I shall argue that there is good reason to reject both.

But if we do reject both theses, then we shall have before us the hard task of saying just how claims *are* connected with what people ought to do. Part of that task is carried out in the course of seeing what is wrong with (T_1); we start on the rest in Chapter 5.

3. Let us begin with

(T_1) If there is an X such that $C_{X, Y}$ p, then Y ought not let it fail to be the case that p,

or, as I shall for the time being express it, the thesis that all claims are absolute.

And let us first attend to what really does seem to be possible, *prima facie* at least, namely that there be a conflict of claims. I said in Chapter 1 that it is intuitively plausible to think that promises generate claims. So suppose I promise C that I will give C a banana; then I have given C a claim against me that I will give C a banana. Shortly thereafter I promise D that I will give D a banana; then I have given D a claim against me that I will give D a banana. Suppose last, however, that it turns out to my horror that I am able to locate only one banana.

Then the claims I certainly appear to have given to C and D conflict: I cannot accord both.

But if I have given C and D those claims, and if also all claims are absolute, then both of the following are true:

(3) I ought to give C a banana

and

(4) I ought to give D a banana.

Should we accept that (3) and (4) are both true?

Some philosophers have canvassed the idea in recent years that it can be the case that I ought to do alpha and ought to do beta despite the fact that I cannot do both alpha and beta.[1] Should we agree with them? It is an odd idea. I will certainly feel you have been unhelpful if when I tell you about my predicament, and ask what I ought to do, you tell me "Well, as a matter of fact, you ought to give C a banana and you ought to give D a banana." I just told you I have only one banana.

It should be stressed that what is an odd idea is that "I ought to give C a banana" and "I ought to give D a banana" are both true. There is no oddity in the idea that "I am committed to C to giving C a banana" and "I am committed to D to giving D a banana" are both true. Similarly for the ordinary English expressions "obligation" and "duty". Indeed, it is a trivial point that one can be committed, be under an obligation, or have a duty to X to do something, and also be committed, be under an obligation, or have a duty to Y to do something else, compatibly with not being able to do both. (When one does have incompatible commitments, obligations, duties, it may be very hard to figure out what one ought to do.) The idea we are

---

1. See, for example, Bernard Williams, "Ethical Consistency", reprinted in his *Problems of the Self* (Cambridge: Cambridge University Press, 1973), and Ruth Marcus, "Moral Dilemmas and Consistency", *Journal of Philosophy*, 77 (March 1980). While Williams thinks (3) and (4) can both be true even if I have only one banana, he seems to dither as to whether (3) is compatible with "I ought not give C a banana"; while Marcus thinks (3) and (4) can both be true even if I have only one banana, she seems to think (3) is not compatible with "I ought not give C a banana". I find this puzzling. If you think the physical impossibility of doing both of two things no barrier to its being the case that you ought to do the one and ought to do the other, I see no good reason for you to balk where the impossibility of doing both has its source in logic. (No one, of course, thinks (3) compatible with "It is not the case that I ought to give C a banana".)

looking at gets its interest from the fact that it says this of the ordinary English word "ought". But the very fact that it does is what makes it an odd idea.

Let us look at the reasons that have been offered for thinking we should accept this idea. The philosophers I mentioned remind us that there are situations in which morality seems to require us to do two things where we cannot do both. Here I am: I have promised to give both C and D a banana, but I have only one banana. The philosophers I have in mind say that even if I think, and rightly think, that one alternative is on balance better than the other and thus ought to be chosen, and I therefore opt for that alternative—thus even if I rightly think it on balance better to give C the banana (perhaps on the ground that my promise to him was the prior promise, perhaps on some other ground), so that

(3) I ought to give C a banana

is true, and I therefore give C the banana—it would not only not be irrational in me but may be morally required of me later that (i) I feel remorse or guilt for having failed to give D a banana, and (ii) I feel the need to make amends to D for my failure to give him a banana and compensate him for any harm or loss he suffers by virtue of not getting one. And doesn't that show that

(4) I ought to give D a banana

was also true? After all, if the truth of (3) ruled out the truth of (4), so that given (3) was true (4) was false, why would remorse and guilt be morally appropriate? Why would the making of amends and the paying of compensation be morally appropriate? In short, why would there be this twofold 'moral residue'—on the one hand in the appropriateness of remorse or guilt, on the other hand in the appropriateness of making amends—if the truth of (3) ruled out the truth of (4)?[2]

These arguments have been subjected to sharp criticism.[3] What I think is of interest in them is this: what lies behind them seems very clearly to be the idea—I will call it the Simplifying Idea—that a moral

2. Or: if the truth of (3) "eliminated" (Williams in "Ethical Consistency") or "erased" (Marcus in "Moral Dilemmas") the truth of (4)? But those are tendentious ways of putting the point, since one could not eliminate or erase what was not there in the first place.

3. See, for example, Earl Conee, "Against Moral Dilemmas", *Philosophical Review*, 91 (January 1982), and Philippa Foot, "Moral Realism and Moral Dilemma", *Journal of Philosophy*, 80 (July 1983).

consideration can have force for us only by way of *entailing* that a person ought to do such and such.[4] I made two promises and cannot now keep both. Suppose it would be better, all things considered, to keep the first of them, so that is what I ought to do; and suppose that is what I therefore do. But I later feel remorse and must make amends to the recipient of the second promise. Why should this not be explained by appeal to the fact—it remains a fact—that I broke the second promise? Why should we think we can pass from the fact of the broken promise to the fact of the later moral residue only by way of an intermediary fact to the effect that I ought to have kept the promise? You would think this true only if you thought that the broken promise could have an impact on my later thoughts and feelings only if I ought to have kept it. But why should we think that so?

I think we do think we can pass from the fact of the broken promise to the fact of the later moral residue only by way of *some* intermediary fact. "You broke a promise. So what? How does that fact yield the moral residue if it is not the case that you ought to have kept it?" One answer, which I think very plausible indeed, is this: in making a promise one gives a claim, and breaking a promise is therefore failing to accord a claim, and *that* fact explains the moral residue—for a claim is equivalent to a constraint on the claim-giver's behavior that includes such things as that the claim-giver may have to make amends later if he or she does not accord the claim.

It can be seen, however, that that answer will satisfy only if we reject the thesis that all claims are absolute. If all claims are absolute, then it is not true that a promisee has a claim against me unless I ought to accord it; so to suggest that we can pass from the fact of the broken promise to the fact of the later moral residue by way of the intermediary fact of an unaccorded claim is to offer an interme-

---

4. I think it no accident that these arguments were first taken seriously by those who interest themselves in deontic logic, which many think of as the enterprise of constructing a logic of ethics in terms of a single primitive moral notion, sometimes read in English as "it ought to be the case that", sometimes as "it is obligatory that".

Bernard Williams has more recently suggested that "It is a mistake of morality to try to make everything into obligations". See *Ethics and the Limits of Philosophy,* p. 180. Obligations, he says, are more correctly "seen as merely one kind of ethical consideration among others" (p. 182). I think he means by "morality" (sometimes he speaks of "the morality system") what I would call a certain conception of morality, a conception of it which, as is plain from my remarks above, I agree with him in thinking incorrect.

diary that itself entails that I ought to have kept the promise. Hence this answer does not explain the moral residue by means that are weaker than the supposition that I ought to have kept the promise.

It emerges here that the idea that all claims are absolute is itself a piece of the Simplifying Idea, which says that a moral consideration—whether a promise or a claim or anything else—can have force for us only by way of *entailing* that a person ought to do such and such. I said in the preceding chapter that it is arguable that morality itself is at heart a set of constraints on behavior; at a minimum, every moral concept in one or another way *connects* with what people ought to do. It would greatly simplify the task of coming to understand morality if we could suppose that every moral consideration has force for us by virtue, all simply, of entailing that some or other person ought to do such and such. If a moral consideration does not have force for us in this simple way, then how does it? How does it constrain behavior? How does it connect with what people ought to do?

But the Simplifying Idea is, as I will suggest, an oversimplifying idea. One way of bringing this out is to attend a little more closely to the notion of a moral residue, which we will turn to shortly. In any case, I think we feel considerably less sympathetic to the arguments we have been looking at when we notice that what lies behind them *is* the Simplifying Idea, for it is by no means an obvious truth.

I think myself that it was not merely odd but patently incorrect to think that

> (3) I ought to give C a banana

and

> (4) I ought to give D a banana

can both be true compatibly with my having only one banana; I think we simply do not use the English word "ought" in such a way that that is so. In any case, I will not. I will throughout so use "ought" that it cannot be the case that I ought to do alpha and ought to do beta where I cannot do both alpha and beta.

Another way to put the point is this. I will take (3) to be equivalent to "It is impermissible for me to not give C a banana" and "Morality requires me to give C a banana", and (4) to be equivalent to "It is impermissible for me to not give D a banana" and "Morality requires me to give D a banana". I hope it will be agreed all round that those cannot all be true compatibly with my having only one banana.

The word "wrong", however, is a more complex affair. Its use as an adjective or adverb seems to me to be cognate with "ought". Thus I take "It would be wrong for me to not give C a banana" and "I would be acting wrongly if I did not give C a banana" to be equivalent to (3). But the use of "wrong" as verb or noun is different: "I would wrong C if I did not give C a banana" and "I would do C a wrong if I did not give C a banana" are *not* equivalent to (3). (Notice, in particular, that "wrong" as verb or noun stands for a two-hat concept.) We will return to "wrong" as verb or noun in Chapter 4, section 9.

4. Let us go back. I said that it really does seem to be possible, *prima facie* at least, that there be a conflict of claims. Suppose we agree that promises generate claims. I promise C I will give him a banana, I promise D I will give him a banana; then I have given each of them a claim against me that I will give him a banana. If the thesis that all claims are absolute is true, then

>   (3) I ought to give C a banana

and

>   (4) I ought to give D a banana

are both true. It turns out that I have only one banana. What do friends of the thesis that all claims are absolute say in reply? One possible reply is that they use "ought" in the way discussed in the preceding section, thus a way according to which (3) and (4) *can* both be true compatibly with my having only one banana. That would, I think, be an uninteresting reply. Their thesis is interesting only if they use "ought" in the strong way in which, as I said, I would be using it, namely a way in which it is not true to say of a person that he or she ought to do a thing unless morality requires doing it—thus a way in which (3) and (4) cannot both be true compatibly with my having only one banana. So I will suppose that friends of the thesis that all claims are absolute do use "ought" in this strong way, and thus that they do not make this reply.

Three other replies are open to them. The first is to say it was simply a mistake to suppose that promises generate claims. More precisely: promises *never* generate claims. I will call this the Denial Reply. If the Denial Reply is true, then the difficulty is eliminated. I did promise to give a banana to C, I did promise to give a banana to D, but neither promise generated a claim, and thus we are not committed to the supposition that (3) and (4) are both true. We are not even committed to the supposition that either one of them is true.

But the Denial Reply is very implausible. Is there any other reason for thinking it true than that, if friends of the thesis that all claims are absolute accept it, they bypass the difficulty I have pointed to? And isn't there much reason for thinking it false? We do think ourselves born with claims—claims that others not murder or imprison us (compare the rights to life and liberty)—but we do think we cause others to have claims, and giving one's word seems to be among the paradigms of the ways in which we do this. Am I not bound by my word? And promising is giving one's word.

We can reput this objection from the point of view of the promisee. Why would a promisee pay attention to a promise if promisors do not give claims to the doing of what they promise to do? We *rely* on the promises people make to us. We make plans for the future based on the assumption that those who promise will do what they promised. That is surely because we think that, in promising, they bind themselves. If we thought that a man who promises does not bind himself, it would be weird in us to rely as we do.

The second and third replies that are open to friends of the thesis that all claims are absolute are more interesting.

The second reply allows that some promises do generate claims but insists that some do not. Which do and which do not? The short answer is: promises that it will turn out the promisor ought to keep generate claims, whereas promises that it will turn out the promisor may permissibly break do not generate claims. Consider, for example, my promises to C and D to give them bananas. I now find that I can lay hands on only one banana; it is therefore not the case both that I ought to give C a banana and that I ought to give D a banana; I may permissibly break at least one of the two promises. Perhaps I may permissibly break both of them. (For example, perhaps what I ought to do is to give each of them half a banana, in which case I do break both promises. Perhaps what I ought to do is to eat the banana myself, in which case I again break both promises.) If I may permissibly break both promises, then neither generated a claim. If I may permissibly break only one, and ought to keep the other, then whichever is the one I ought to keep is the one, and the only one, that generated a claim.

What settles whether there is one I ought to keep, and if so which?

On some views, priority in promise-making is a very weighty consideration where conflicting promises have been made: on those views, the promisor ought to keep the prior promise in the absence of some very strong ground for thinking otherwise. By hypothesis, my promise to C came first; in the absence of some very strong ground for thinking otherwise, that is the promise I ought to keep.

No one, I think, thinks priority by itself conclusive. On all views, surely, it is possible for something to outweigh priority: if D would be caused markedly more harm by my breaking my promise to him than C would be caused, then I think that on all views it is my promise to D that I ought to keep. (No doubt, however, there may be dispute as to just how weighty a consideration priority is.[5]) This is also the case if neither C nor D would be caused harm by my breaking my promise to him, but E, F, and G are in dire and desperate need of a banana. And there surely are still other considerations—considerations other than priority and harm-causing—that are relevant to the question whether I may break my promise to C or to D or to both.

In any case, the second reply says that, when Y promises X to do alpha, Y does not make

$$C_{X, Y} \text{ (Y does alpha)}$$

true. What does Y make true? There are two ways in which we can describe what the second reply says Y makes true. The short way is that what Y makes true is:

$$C_{X, Y} \text{ (Y does alpha) if and only if Y ought to do alpha.}$$

The long way is that what Y makes true is:

$$C_{X, Y} \text{ (Y does alpha) if and only if } \ldots \ldots ,$$

where the dots are filled in with a list of all of the many possible facts such that Y ought to do alpha if and only if those possible facts are actual facts—possible facts having to do with priority in promise-making, with who would or would not be caused harm by the breach, and with whatever else is relevant to whether Y ought to do alpha. For lack of the required list (who among us has it?), I will choose the

---

5. Why does priority have any weight at all? Why priority instead of posteriority? There is an interesting issue in the offing here, since priority in promise-making connects with the very attractive 'first come, first served' rule for distribution. We will come back to this in Chapter 13.

short way of expressing what the second reply says Y makes true in promising X to do alpha.

We might call this second reply the External-Condition Reply, because it says that a promisee's getting a claim is conditional on something 'external', namely whether the promisor ought to keep the promise. As is plain, adopting the External-Condition Reply would allow friends of the thesis that all claims are absolute to accommodate the kind of case we have been looking at. I did promise to give a banana to C, I did then later promise to give a banana to D, but if the External-Condition Reply is true, then at most one of the two promises generated a claim, the one (if either) that I ought to keep. And that one, of course, I ought to keep.

The third reply says that all promises generate claims but insists that they do not generate the claims you might have thought they generated. In particular, it says that we must not look just at a promisor's words to find out the content of the claim generated by the promise. I said to C "I promise you I will give you a banana". We might have thought I thereby gave him a claim to my giving him a banana, but I did not. What I gave him a claim to was only this: that I give-him-a-banana-if-and-only-if-I-ought-to-give-him-a-banana. More generally, like the second reply, the third reply says that when Y promises X to do alpha, Y does not make

$C_{X, Y}$ (Y does alpha)

true. But the third reply says Y does give a claim, for it says that Y makes

$C_{X, Y}$ (Y does alpha if and only if Y ought to do alpha)

true.[6] We might call this third reply, for obvious reasons, the Internal-Condition Reply. As is plain, adopting the Internal-Condition Reply would also allow friends of the thesis that all claims are absolute to accommodate the kind of case we have been looking at. I did promise to give a banana to C, I did then later promise to give a banana to D, but if the Internal-Condition Reply is true, then I made only

$C_{C, I}$ (I give C a banana if and only if I ought to give C a banana)

6. An obvious longer alternative is to say that what Y makes true is "$C_{X, Y}$ (Y does alpha if and only if. . . .)", where the dots are filled in with a list of all of the many possible facts such that Y ought to do alpha if and only if those possible facts are actual facts. I choose the shorter alternative here, just as I did in the case of the External-Condition Reply.

and

$C_{D, 1}$ (I give D a banana if and only if I ought to give D a banana)

true. To say that I ought to accord both claims is to say that I ought not let either of the following be false:

(i) I give C a banana if and only if I ought to give C a banana

and

(ii) I give D a banana if and only if I ought to give D a banana.

Suppose that it is not the case that I ought to give a banana to C and that it is not the case that I ought to give a banana to D (say, I ought to give my one banana to E, who is starving); then I make both (i) and (ii) true by giving the banana to neither C nor D. Suppose instead that I ought to give a banana to C but not to D. Then I make both (i) and (ii) true by giving the banana to C and not to D. Similarly if I instead ought to give a banana to D but not to C.

The Internal-Condition Reply is a first cousin of the External-Condition Reply. While the External-Condition Reply makes getting the claim conditional on whether the promisor ought to perform, the Internal-Condition Reply builds the condition of its being the case that the promisor ought to perform into the content of the claim.

And similar difficulties face both. Both certainly seem to put the cart before the horse. Surely the question what we ought to do itself turns on, and cannot be answered in advance of answering, what seems to be the prior question, namely what claims people have against us; surely the question what claims people have against us is not something that drops out as an only mildly interesting consequence once it has already been settled what people ought to do.

What I want to focus on, however, is a different set of difficulties. The same difficulties also make trouble for the Denial Reply. I will show how they make trouble for the External-Condition Reply; it will, I hope, be clear what emendations are needed so as to make them bear on the Internal-Condition Reply and on the Denial Reply. Those difficulties deserve their own section.

5. I promised to give C a banana, I promised to give D a banana, and I now discover I can locate only one banana. What to do? Oughtn't I ask one of them whether he will release me from my commitment to give him a banana, and if he tells me of his heavy

reliance on my promise, and that he will therefore be caused harm by my nonperformance, oughtn't I ask the other whether he will release me from my commitment to give him a banana? It is very hard to see why this should be so, if the External-Condition Reply is true. For if it is true, one of the two has no claim against me at all to be given a banana: I need merely figure out which of the two does have the claim, and I need no release from the other since there is nothing for him to release me from.

There isn't always time to ask for a release: perhaps there is no time at all for asking, or perhaps the promisees are out of town, or unconscious, or for some other reason unable to be asked within the available time. Again, there might be time to ask for a release but the promisees are confused, or drugged, or for some other reason incapable of responding rationally to a request for a release. If so, it is possible but pointless to ask for a release: their saying they give the release would not be their really giving it. Other things being equal, however, one ought to ask for a release.

What if there is time, and both promisees are available and competent to respond rationally, but both refuse to give a release? I stress: both might refuse to *give* a release. For one or the other might be willing to sell a release, without being willing to give it, free. And why should they give it free? They might if they are friends of mine. Whether or not they are friends of mine, they might if nothing much turns for them on my keeping my promises. But if both will suffer a heavy loss if the promises are not kept, why shouldn't they expect me to absorb at least some of that loss? (Their asking an extortionate price would be one thing; their asking a reasonable price quite another.) Why should *they* bear the full cost of my inability to keep both of the two promises?

Suppose I manufacture widgets. I contracted with C company to supply it with 100 widgets next Friday, I then contracted with D company to supply it with 100 widgets next Friday, and it turns out this morning that my regular supplier will be unable to deliver the materials I need for widget-making, so that I will be unable to produce more than 100 widgets by next Friday. Both C and D companies will suffer a loss if they fail to get the widgets I promised. Fairness requires me to notify them that I will not be able to keep both contracts so that if possible they can take steps to decrease the losses they will suffer for lack of widgets, *and* it requires me also to try to renegotiate at least one of the two contracts—to try to buy a release, in other words. Morality does not require either of them to give it free, and that is so even if I am entirely without fault for my inability to keep both contracts.

Perhaps I can buy a release from D more cheaply, since D would suffer a smaller loss from lack of widgets than C would. Then here is a fair option for me: buy the release from D, and deliver 100 widgets to C. Choosing that option is not required of me: I might have reason to prefer the more costly alternative of buying a release from C and delivering the 100 widgets to D. What is required of me is only that I try to come to some satisfactory arrangement with *both* parties. Why should that be so if, as the External-Condition Reply says, only one of them has a claim against me?

What we have just been looking at is what precedes performance of one or the other contract. But it surely connects with, and has a common source with, what follows performance—that is, with any-way part of that 'moral residue' we took note of in section 3. For suppose renegotiation is not possible in the available time. With the best will in the world, I deliver the 100 widgets to C: after all, my contract with C was the prior contract and (as let us suppose) the loss my nonperformance would cause C is greater than the loss it would cause D. I did the best I could, in the circumstances. But I cannot now simply wash my hands of the affair: I must not simply ignore D, who is after all being caused a loss by my breach of the contract I made with him. Why should *he* bear the full cost of my inability to keep both contracts? Surely I must absorb at least part of his loss. And why should that be so if, as the External-Condition Reply says, only one of them had a claim against me?

The simplest account of both phenomena—the need to renegotiate in advance if that is possible, the need to compensate later if rene-gotiation was not possible—is that both C and D did have claims against me, claims in fact to be supplied on Friday with 100 widgets, which claims I gave them when I contracted with them to do so.[7]

---

7. An alternative way of dealing with both phenomena is to make a different kind of 'conditioning' move. Thus it could be said that we accommodate both the need to seek a release in advance and the need to compensate later if no release was obtained, by saying that what Y makes true in promising X to do alpha is, not "$C_{X, Y}$ (Y does alpha)", but instead "Either $C_{X, Y}$ (Y does alpha), or Y gets a release from X, or Y compensates X for losses caused by Y's not doing alpha" (compare the External-Condition Reply) or "$C_{X, Y}$ (Either Y does alpha, or Y gets a release from X, or Y compensates X for losses caused by Y's

Business contexts obviously differ in a number of ways from those in which, in the ordinary way, one might make what turn out to be incompatible promises to two people. For one thing, business losses are normally at least roughly quantifiable: it might be quite clear that C company will lose $1000 if I fail to deliver the 100 widgets, and D company will lose only $800, both of these (perhaps) in virtue of the fact that lack of widgets will make them unable to abide by contracts they have made with still other companies. Second, a contract is normally a more formal affair than what goes on when one private person makes a promise to another: the consequences of failure to perform are often spelled out in some detail as part of what is being agreed to by contracting businesses, whereas this is rarely so in the case of private parties. Third, businesses contract with each other as part of a process aimed at making money, and that is not true of private persons in their everyday dealings with each other.

All the same, there remains a central similarity between informal promisings and formal contractings. Making a promise, like signing a contract, is positively inviting reliance. There are many things a person may say or do that cause expectations in others, and sometimes people rely on the expectations others have caused them to form. But there are ways and ways in which one can cause others to form expectations. I might unwittingly cause you to form an expectation to the effect that I will do such and such tomorrow simply by having been in the habit of doing the such and such every day in the past for some years;[8] alternatively, I might intentionally cause you to form an expectation that I will do such such and such tomorrow by telling you that I will, and that you can count on it. If I do the latter, I

not doing alpha)" (compare the Internal-Condition Reply). But these will not do. Unlike the 'conditioning' moves under consideration above, these proposals do not make nothing of the need to seek a release or to compensate; they instead make too much of the need to seek a release or to compensate. For if I have promised a man to do a thing, it is—other things being equal—*not* good enough that I merely compensate him for such losses as I cause him by not doing the thing; other things being equal, I just plain, and all simply, ought to do it.

There is of course room for the idea of combining the 'conditioning' moves pointed to here with those under consideration in the text. But wasn't the thesis that all claims are absolute supposed to simplify our theory of rights?

8. Charles Fried offers by way of example a person who rents an apartment next to mine because my friends and I regularly play chamber music in my apartment. See his *Contract as Promise* (Cambridge: Harvard University Press, 1981), p. 10.

positively invite you to repy on my doing it; not so if I do the former.

And where I invite your reliance on an expectation about my future behavior, I thereby take on myself a complex responsibility, namely to make that expectation true *or,* if I will for some reason be unable to, to take reasonable steps to see that you do not lose by virtue of having accepted my invitation to rely.

We might in fact think of promising, like contracting, as itself a 'liability-shouldering' device.

It would of course be grossly overstrong to say that anyone who makes a promise assumes liability for any and all losses the promisee will suffer in consequence of a breach of the promise. In the first place, the promisee may suffer a larger loss than any reasonable person in the promisor's circumstances could have expected him or her to suffer, perhaps because of some freakish accident, perhaps because of un-reasonable behavior on the promisee's part, perhaps for some other reason. I do not in the ordinary course of events expect my student Bloggs to stake his house and his car in reliance on my being in my office at 4:00 if I promise him that I will be there then; if he does, that is his own lookout, and I am not liable for his loss if I do not turn up.

Second, there may be no way in which one can compensate for a loss, as when the loss is the loss of a life.

Third, there might be better reason for the victim of the breach of promise to bear the costs than for the promise-breaker to bear the costs. Thus the victim might be able to absorb them very much more easily than the promise-breaker can.

Or again there might be reason to think that the victim and the promisor should share the costs. Or again the victim might, out of friendship for the promisor or for some other reason, prefer to absorb all the costs. Or again there might be an institutional arrangement (public or private insurance) that shifts costs.

Moreover, whether the promise-breaker was at fault for the breach is relevant to how the costs should be allocated, and in some cases (though certainly not in all cases) the promise-breaker's lack of fault may suggest that the victim of the breach (or perhaps someone else) should bear them.

Or of course the victim of the breach of promise may suffer no loss at all, or only a loss not worth troubling to make compensation for, perhaps because he or she did not rely on the promise, perhaps because the cost of the frustrated reliance was so small.

Compensating later, like asking for a release in advance, is an act like any other, and a great many things bear on the question whether it is required, things in addition to the fact that the promisor broke his or her promise.

But there remains this. A promisor invites reliance and therefore must take reasonable steps to see that the promisee does not suffer in consequence of relying—which includes taking action in advance of the breach where appropriate, and taking suitable action after the breach if action in advance of the breach was not appropriate. I may not simply wash my hands of the matter as no concern of mine when I learn that I will be unable to keep my promise, or after I have already broken it.

I have taken note so far of only one[9] of the two things pointed to by the philosophers we attended to in section 3 under the heading of 'moral residue'. The other was remorse and guilt. On their view, remorse and guilt are not irrational where I have made what are, as it turns out, incompatible promises to C and D, and therefore can, and then do, keep only one. That idea seems to me to be oversimple.

In the first place, while I cannot keep both promises, I may be able to buy a release in advance from one promisee and keep the other promise. Then there is nothing for me even to regret (beyond being, myself, out of pocket for the costs of my inability to keep both promises), much less to feel remorse or guilt for.

Second, while I cannot keep both promises, and perhaps also have not time for negotiations in advance, I may be able to keep one of the promises and later compensate the victim of my breach of the other for losses suffered in consequence of my breach. Here again there is nothing for me to regret (beyond being, myself, out of pocket for the costs of my inability to keep both promises), much less to feel remorse or guilt for.

And third, the victim of the broken promise may suffer no harm or loss at all from the breach, or only minimal harm or loss. The appropriate reaction here is surely plain relief that things turned out so well. Just as there is no compensation owing where no harm or loss is suffered, so no regret is called for in those circumstances.

---

9. It—the need to compensate later—is one I have been drawing attention to in a number of articles over the years. They are now reprinted in my *Rights, Restitution, and Risk*, ed. William Parent (Cambridge: Harvard University Press, 1986).

Remorse and guilt seem to me to be clearly in place for a broken promise in only three cases. They are clearly in place where breach of the promise does cause harm or loss *and* (i) the promisor's not keeping the promise was his or her fault, or (ii) the promisor could have but did not try to negotiate a release in advance, or (iii) the promisor can but does not compensate for the harm or loss. In these cases, the promisor on any view fails to do something he or she ought to do; and there is no difficulty in supposing it in place to feel remorse and guilt for that failure.

What raises a special difficulty is the kind of case in which the promisor is entirely without fault throughout but the breach causes a harm or loss that the promisor cannot compensate for. (If you cannot compensate for a loss,[10] then you certainly are not at fault for failing to do so.) Here the well-intentioned promisor may lie awake at night with a profound feeling of regret, despite knowing that he or she was without fault. Would it be irrational for such a promisor to feel not merely regret, but remorse or guilt? I should think so, for it is very plausible to think that what you feel is not properly described as "remorse" or "guilt" unless you think you were at fault. On the other hand, I should think also that it might be hard to tell about a person whether what he or she was feeling was (merely) regret or (more strongly) remorse or guilt,[11] and thus hard to mark off the rational from the irrational promisor in such a case.

To summarize. Very often when a person has a claim against us that we do a thing, we really ought to do it, and ought to do it precisely because the person has that claim against us. We take ac-

---

10. This is typically the case in the overheated examples we are given in support of the ideas we looked at in section 3. Williams offered us Agamemnon's choice at Aulis; Marcus offered us Sartre's example of the student who has to choose between joining the Free French and staying at home to care for his mother. What could count as compensation for the losses here? I think it is precisely the incompensability of the losses that fuels the idea that remorse and guilt are in place in such examples.

11. And we really ought to be suspicious of a theory that rests on our ability to make fine distinctions between kinds of feelings. I should add, moreover, that it was Bernard Williams himself who drew attention to the very interesting fact that we feel intense regret for a harm we ourselves caused—far more intense regret than we would have felt had some third party caused it—even if we are, and know we are, entirely without fault for having caused it. See his sensitive discussion of what he calls "agent-regret" in "Moral Luck", reprinted in his collection of essays *Moral Luck* (Cambridge: Cambridge University Press, 1981).

count of that fact most simply if we say that all claims are absolute. But if we do, we are unable to take account most simply of other phenomena: (i) the need to seek a release beforehand, and (ii) the need to compensate later if it was not possible to obtain a release beforehand. I said that there is a certain constraint on Y's behavior that is equivalent to X's having a claim against Y. Phenomena (i) and (ii) have excellent title to be parts of the constraint on Y's behavior—just as good a title as the one that so fascinates the friends of the thesis that all claims are absolute.

6. It is not merely in cases in which we have made two promises and cannot keep both that we may, permissibly, break a promise: sometimes it is permissible to break a promise in light of another person's need—as where I break my promise to meet Bloggs at my office at 4:00 because my child suddenly falls ill. And sometimes something similar happens where no promises are involved at all.

I said it is intuitively plausible to think that promises generate claims; I also said it is intuitively plausible to think that ownership is a cluster-right that includes claims. Which claims are included in an ownership cluster-right? One ownership cluster differs from another according to a number of different considerations, such as prevailing law, private agreements such as giving permission to others to do something that would have been impermissible without the permission, rental arrangements, and so on. Let us suppose that A owns some land and that he has not rented any part of it to B or given B permission to enter any part of it. It seems *prima facie* right to think that

    (1)   A has a claim against B that B stay off A's land

is true.

Suppose now that B's child falls seriously ill, and that by far the shortest way from B's house to the hospital lies across a corner of A's land. It seems entirely right to think that B may take his child to hospital by that shortest route, and thus that he may enter A's land—so that

    (2)   B ought to stay off A's land

is false. As we know, however, the thesis that all claims are absolute tells us that (1) entails (2). What are friends of that thesis to say about this case?

They have replies available which are analogous to those canvassed in section 4. There is first a Denial Reply, which says: owning a piece of land does not include having any claims at all. (Compare: no promises generate claims.) Or, less strongly, owning a piece of land does not include having claims against others that they stay off it. But these are very implausible ideas. After all, it is precisely in order to acquire *some* claims in respect of a thing (a typewriter, a hat, a bit of land) that one buys it in the first place; and among the claims we buy land to get are claims against others that they stay off it.

However there is, second, an External-Condition Reply, which says: owning a piece of land does include having a claim against others that they stay off it—if and only if they ought not enter it. B has a sick child whose care requires him to enter A's land, so of course B may enter it; so A lacks the claim against B that B not enter it.

And there is, third, an Internal-Condition Reply, which says: owning a piece of land does include having claims against others having to do with their staying off it, but the content of those claims is only that the others stay-off-the-land-if-and-only-if-they-ought-to-stay-off-it. B has a sick child whose care requires him to enter A's land, so of course B may enter it; so B accords A what A has a claim to—B makes

> B stays off A's land if and only if B ought not enter it

true—if he enters A's land.

But considerations of the kind we looked at in the preceding section make similar trouble for these replies. For let us now ask about the corner of A's land that B will have to cross to get his child to hospital and what B will do to it in crossing it. If the corner is part of a meadow, and B will do no harm in crossing it, then I think we suppose B may without the slightest concern just, all simply, cross it. (Though wouldn't he do well to tell A later what he had done? The land is A's, after all.) But what if B has to cross over, and thereby severely damage, some plantings that are central to A's livelihood? Then oughtn't he ask A for permission in advance if there is time for doing so? And if there isn't time for asking in advance, oughtn't he later compensate A for at least some of the damage he did in crossing the land? Oughtn't he absorb at least some of A's loss?

I stress: A's property rights pale by comparison with B's need, and it is permissible for B to cross the land—(2) is false even if the damage B will do to A's land in crossing is serious. All the same, why should the full cost of supplying B's need fall on A? (Compare: why should the full cost of my inability to keep my promises to both C and D fall on them?)

No doubt there might be good reason to think A should bear the full cost of supplying B's need. What cannot be said, however, is that B's need by itself makes it right that A should bear the full cost of supplying it. The simplest way of accommodating these facts is to suppose that—*pace* the friends of the thesis that all claims are absolute—

    (1) A has a claim against B that B stay off A's land

is true despite the fact that

    (2) B ought to stay off A's land

is not.

7. It is worth noticing that the force of the example of the preceding section issues in large part from the fact that the need is B's, for the sick child is B's own child. I think that where the need is B's, we are likely to feel that, other things being equal, B has no business making A pay any of the cost of supplying it—though of course other things may not be equal.

But I think we are likely to feel differently if the need is not B's but that of some third party. What if the sick child is C's child? Then we may well feel that A should contribute too. Not that B should pay nothing: surely it cannot be right to think a man may at will make others pay the full costs of his altruism.[12] But we may well feel that A should share.

8. It might also be worth noticing what happens when cases like that of section 6 arise in law, as they occasionally do. (But why so rarely?

12. Philippa Foot says, thinking of herself as having to break a promise to you in order to attend to the victim of an accident: "If you suffer because I cannot get to the appointment I have with you, I say that I am sorry, meaning that I regret it; but if it was not my fault I do not apologize, and I certainly do not have to 'make restitution' as some have suggested" ("Moral Realism and Moral Dilemma", pp. 388–389). This sounds remarkably cavalier to me. Can she really believe that *she* may at will make others pay the full costs of her altruism? But perhaps she is thinking of what is most common where an appointment is broken: the victim suffers only inconvenience, for which it is hard even to imagine what restitution would consist in.

That seems to me a good question, for which I have no answer.) In *Vincent v. Lake Erie Transp. Co.,*[13] a shipowner and a dockowner had agreed that the shipowner would finish unloading his ship at the dock and then cast off by 10:00. Just before 10:00 a sudden storm swept down, and if the shipowner cast off and went out to sea, there was a real risk that the ship would be lost. The dockowner was no longer there by the time the storm swept down and thus could not be asked (or bargained with) for permission to stay. But the shipowner stayed all the same. During the storm, the ship was slammed again and again against the dock and caused damage to the dock. The dockowner then sued for compensation for the damage to his dock—and won. The court said:

> Theologians hold that a starving man may, without moral guilt, take what is necessary to sustain life; but it could hardly be said that the obligation would not be upon such person to pay the value of the property so taken when he became able to do so. And so public necessity, in times of war or peace, may require the taking of private property for public purposes; but under our system of jurisprudence compensation must be made.
>
> Let us imagine in this case that for the better mooring of the vessel those in charge of her had appropriated a valuable cable lying upon the dock. No matter how justifiable such appropriation might have been, it would not be claimed that, because of the overwhelming necessity of the situation, the owner of the cable could not recover its value.
>
> [The case in hand] is one where the defendant prudently and advisedly availed itself of the plaintiffs' property for the purpose of preserving its own more valuable property, and the plaintiffs are entitled to compensation for the injury done.

On the court's view, the shipowner acted "prudently and advisedly" in remaining; yet he must compensate the dockowner for the damage he caused.

So far so good. Let us ask, however: what of the legal claims of the parties in this case? In particular, did the dockowner have a legal claim against the shipowner that the shipowner cast off? That is, was

> (5) Dockowner has a legal claim against shipowner that shipowner cast off

---

13. 109 Minn. 456, 124 N.W. 221 (1910). I have altered some details for simplification.

true? The shipowner acted "prudently and advisedly" in *not* casting off, so

(6) Shipowner ought to cast off

was false. How can (5) be true while (6) is false?

Well, why *shouldn't* it be the case that (5) is true but (6) is false? Let us go back. We have sometimes expressed

(T_1) If there is an X such that $C_{X, Y}$ p, then Y ought not let it fail to be the case that p

more compactly as the thesis that all claims are absolute; it is a thesis about morality, which many moral philosophers have thought attractive. We might call it a "bridge-thesis", in that it connects one moral notion (that of a claim) with another moral notion (that of what a person ought to do). A similar thesis has seemed plausible to many lawyers. What I have in mind is the thesis you get if you read "C" in (T_1) not simply as "claim", but as "legal claim". We might express it more compactly as the thesis that all legal claims are absolute. It too might be called a bridge-thesis: it connects a legal notion (that of a legal claim) with a moral notion (that of what a person ought to do). Now I think it plain that people who are puzzled at the idea that (5) might be true while (6) is false are puzzled precisely because they are under the influence of the thesis that all legal claims are absolute. For if that thesis is true, then (5) cannot be true unless (6) is as well.

Is it a plausible thesis? A Positivist, of course, would say it is merely silly. It is entirely open to Positivists to say that we should take account of what people ought to do in fixing on the laws that will govern us; but they would insist that no bridge-thesis from law to morality is even remotely plausible. They believe that whether people in such and such a society have such and such legal claims is a function simply and solely of the positive law in that society, and that the moral rightness or wrongness of a kind of action, while it might be evidence as to what the positive law is, is not part of the positive law in the sense of being a necessary condition for anyone's having a legal claim in respect of acts of that kind. I am sure that the affection with which lawyers regard the thesis that all legal claims are absolute is in direct proportion to the disaffection with which they regard Positivism.

In any case, friends of the thesis that all legal claims are absolute would say that (5) must be false since (6) is false. What are they to say, then, about the damage to the dockowner's dock? Some of course may say "Tough luck for the dockowner—let him pay his own bills". But this seems the wrong outcome. Why should the dockowner bear the full cost of what the shipowner had to do to save his ship?[14]

The simplest way to deal with this difficulty[15] is surely to grant that the shipowner did have a legal duty to cast off and thus that (5) was true—that having been *why* the shipowner must compensate the dockowner for the damage he caused by failing to cast off—while keeping in mind that there are breaches and breaches of legal duties, some warranting criminal penalties, which are appropriate only where there was fault, and some warranting only liability in torts,[16] which may or may not have been earned by fault. Peter Westen makes this proposal about a similar case, and I take it he would say here that the shipowner's remaining at the dock was a *noncriminal* infringement of the dockowner's "property rights against trespass and conversion".[17]

9. I suggest it is also simpler to say that

  (1) A has a claim against B that B stay off A's land

---

14. Richard Epstein points to the fact that if the shipowner had owned the dock as well as the ship, he himself would have had to absorb the cost of saving his ship, and asks the good question: why should the shipowner be able to pass on to another the cost of saving his ship merely because he does not happen to own the dock he damaged? See Richard A. Epstein, "A Theory of Strict Liability", *Journal of Legal Studies,* 2 (January 1973).

15. A more complicated way of dealing with it is to make a 'conditioning' move of the kind I drew attention to in note 7 above. Such a move is not merely available but was in fact proposed as a way of dealing with *Vincent* by Robert E. Keeton in "Conditional Fault in the Law of Torts", *Harvard Law Review,* 72 (January 1959), 401. But the proposal seems to me suspect for the same reason I gave in note 7.

16. Or liability in contracts. If I deliver the 100 widgets to C, and D suffers a loss from lack of widgets, the courts may hold me legally liable for D's loss, despite the fact that it was through no fault of my own that I was unable to deliver to D as well as to C. That is most simply understood as flowing from a legal claim D had against me for delivery of 100 widgets.

17. Peter Westen, "Comment on Montague's 'Rights and Duties of Compensation' ", *Philosophy and Public Affairs,* 14 (Fall 1985). He quotes Glanville Williams in support of this way of dealing with the matter: "a person who takes another's property to save his own life has a defense against the crime of larceny but will be held liable to the owner for the tort of conversion".

was true in the case we were imagining, *that* having been why B must compensate A for the damage he causes in crossing A's land. If we do, then, since

(2) B ought to stay off A's land

is false, so also is the thesis that all claims are absolute.

But there is yet another argument *for* the thesis that all claims are absolute. We turn to it next.

Chapter 4

Enforcing Claims

1. At the end of the preceding chapter I said there is yet another argument for the thesis that all claims are absolute. It comes out best if we approach it slowly.

We were supposing that A owns some land and that he has not given B permission to enter it. It seemed very plausible to think, then, that

(1) A has a claim against B that B stay off A's land

is true. Friends of the thesis that all claims are absolute—in our terminology,

(T_1) If there is an X such that $C_{X, Y} p$, then Y ought not let it fail to be the case that p—

take (1) to entail

B ought not let it fail to be the case that B stays off A's land

and therefore to entail

(2) B ought not enter A's land.

But we supposed also that B's child has suddenly fallen ill and needs to be taken to the hospital. The shortest route lies across a corner of A's land, and let us suppose that B would not, in crossing it, do any serious damage to A's land. Let us suppose, last, that the emergency gives B no time to ask A for permission to cross his land. It seems plain in these circumstances that B *may* cross A's land, thus that (2) is false. If all claims are absolute—that is, if (T_1) is true—so also is (1) false.

What we should take note of now is the fact that the very same features of B's situation that make (2) false also make this false:

(3) It is permissible for A to prevent B from entering A's land.

(It would in the circumstances be appalling in A to threaten to shoot B if he attempts to cross A's land.) The emergency faced by B makes it true at one and the same time *both* that B may cross the land *and* that A may not prevent him from doing so.

Let us attend to the fact that A may not prevent B from crossing A's land. It is natural to think that, if X has a claim against Y, then it is permissible for X to prevent Y from infringing it. A claim after all is a right; surely, one thinks, it is morally permissible for people to protect themselves against infringements of their rights. We might express the thesis in the offing here in the words "All claims are enforceable" or, in our terminology, as follows:

(T$_4$) If C$_{X, Y}$ p, then it is permissible for X to prevent Y from letting it fail to be the case that p.

Friends of that thesis take

(1) A has a claim against B that B stay off A's land

to entail

It is permissible for A to prevent B from letting it fail to be the case that B stays off A's land

and therefore to entail

(3) It is permissible for A to prevent B from entering A's land.

But (3) is false. If all claims are enforceable—that is, if (T$_4$) is true—so also is (1) false.

Viewed in one way, (T$_1$) and (T$_4$) are simply two theses about claims: (T$_1$) says a necessary condition for having a claim is that the person against whom it is had ought to do such and such; (T$_4$) says a necessary condition for having a claim is that the claim holder may prevent infringement of it. Viewed in this way, what we have in hand are simply two arguments to the effect that A lacks the claim ascribed to him by (1): one argument that proceeds from the fact that B may cross the land, and a second argument that proceeds from the fact that A may not prevent B from doing so.

But it is arguable that those two theses, and the arguments that relied on them, are not independent. After all, it is the very same features of B's situation—the emergency he faces—that make it be the case *both* that B may cross A's land *and* that A may not prevent him from doing so.

Suppose we could say that if it is permissible for X to prevent Y from doing a thing, then Y ought not do it. (How *could* it be the case both that X may permissibly prevent Y from doing a thing and also that Y may permissibly do it?) We could express that thesis as follows:

(T$_5$) If it is permissible for X to prevent Y from letting it fail to be the case that p, then Y ought not let it fail to be the case that p.

We now have in hand a new argument for the thesis that all claims are absolute, which proceeds as follows. If (T$_4$) is true, then

(i) $C_{X, Y}$ p

entails

(ii) It is permissible for X to prevent Y from letting it fail to be the case that p.

If (T$_5$) is true, then (ii) entails

(iii) Y ought not let it fail to be the case that p.

So if both (T$_4$) and (T$_5$) are true, (i) entails (iii). So if both (T$_4$) and (T$_5$) are true, so also is

(T$_1$) If there is an X such that $C_{X, Y}$ p, then Y ought not let it fail to be the case that p.

I think this new argument is worth paying attention to.

2. For our purposes, the interesting premise in this new argument is the thesis that all claims are enforceable, that is

(T$_4$) If $C_{X, Y}$ p, then it is permissible for X to prevent Y from letting it fail to be the case that p.

Is it a plausible thesis? Suppose I have promised you I will deliver 100 widgets to you next Friday. On my view, I thereby made this true:

(4) You have a claim against me that I deliver 100 widgets to you next Friday.

On some views, as we know, (4) is false if

(5) I ought to deliver 100 widgets to you next Friday

is false. Well, let us suppose (5) is true. Let us suppose, that is, that I have made no prior incompatible promise to deliver widgets to anybody else. I have no sick or starving child, spouse, cat, or dog who needs widgets. Nothing stands in the way of my delivering those widgets other than the fact that I simply do not feel like delivering them. (I want to go to the beach on Friday.) Then I should think that, on *any* view, it is not merely the case that I ought to deliver the widgets, but more: you have a claim against me that I deliver them. So (4) is true. (T_4) tells us we are entitled to conclude that it is permissible for you to prevent me from letting it fail to be the case that I deliver 100 widgets to you next Friday. (T_4) tells us, in short, that

(6) It is permissible for you to make me deliver 100 widgets to you next Friday

is true. Can that be right?

If all you need do to make me deliver the widgets is to phone and say, in your fiercest way, "DELIVER THOSE WIDGETS OR I'LL SUE!" then I am sure all is well: you really may make me deliver the widgets. But what if I am unmoved by threats to sue? What if in order to make me deliver the widgets you need to come round in person and shoot me in the foot? Presumably that will not do at all; if *that* is the case, then surely (6) is not true.

There is a quite general principle at work in the little argument I just gave. What I have in mind is a second cousin of a Kantian principle. Kant said that who wills the end wills the means; a second cousin of that principle says that one may will the end if and only if one may will the means. We might call this the Sole-Means Principle for Permissibility and take it to say, more precisely:

The Sole-Means Principle for Permissibility: If the only means X has of doing beta is doing alpha, then it would be permissible for X to do beta if and only if it would be permissible for X to do alpha.

It is, I think, very plausible. If it is true, then (6) really is false, since the only means you have of making me deliver the widgets is shooting me in the foot, and it is not permissible for you to shoot me in the foot.

But if (6) is false (T_4) is in trouble, for (4) is surely true. More generally, we just cannot suppose that X's being unable to prevent Y from letting a state of affairs fail to obtain except by unacceptably drastic means makes it be the case that X has no claim against Y that the state of affairs obtain.[1] I said: surely, one thinks, it is morally permissible for people to protect themselves against infringements of their rights. We have this thought only when we are forgetting that there are cases in which protecting oneself against an infringement of one's rights would require a major, itself impermissible, intervention into the life of another. *Sometimes* morality requires us to suffer the infringement and then take such rectifying action as is possible later.

It is arguable that this is true only in the 'state of society' and would not be true in the 'state of nature'. That is, the legal system of any society forbids violent self-help (except in special cases), requiring that the citizen instead use the procedures it makes available for obtaining rectification later; but what of a people without a legal system? What of self-help then? What you will feel about these ideas turns on what you think the state of nature would be like. If you think, with Hobbes, that there would be no morality at all in the state of nature ("Right and Wrong, Justice and Injustice have there no place"), then of course you think anything goes in the state of nature, including violent self-help. If you think, with Locke, that there would be morality (though no law) in the state of nature, then I think you must agree that not just any bit of violent self-help is permissible in the state of nature. No doubt more in the way of self-help would be permissible than is permissible in the state of society, in which there are legal arrangements that are intended to make violent self-help unnecessary; but it is plausible to think that not just any amount would do. It could hardly be thought permissible in Locke's state of nature to kill a man to prevent him from stealing an apple—unless,

---

1. Cases like this one could have been produced in support of the points I wished to make in section 5 of Chapter 3, for there are considerations other than priority in promise-making and how much harm would be caused *by* breaking the promise that are relevant to the question whether one may break it. Among others, there are what means one would have to use to keep the promise: they may, after all, be unacceptably drastic.

perhaps, you had good reason to think that failing to intervene would encourage him to become a serious threat to your life or your livelihood.

In any case, we do not live in the state of nature. Where legal routes to rectification are available, self-help is *a fortiori* not the only available way of protecting oneself against infringements of one's rights. And it would not be permissible for you to shoot me in the foot to get me to deliver your widgets next Friday—though you have a claim against me that I deliver them.

3. It might be a good idea to take explicit note of the fact that the objection to

> (T$_4$) If C$_{X, Y}$ p, then it is permissible for X to prevent Y from letting it fail to be the case that p

that I drew attention to in the preceding section is not bypassed if we weaken (T$_4$). What I have in mind is this. The case we looked at, in which you had a claim against me that I deliver some widgets, was a case in which your claim against me was that I *do* something—it was a claim to my *acting* in a certain way. It might be said: no wonder, then, that there was trouble. No doubt there are cases in which one can prevent a person from failing to act by taking nondrastic steps (as where one can get a person to do a thing by shouting "DO IT OR I'LL SUE!"), but typically getting people to do things they do not want to do requires more, a more that is likely to be, itself, impermissible.

But what of cases in which your claim against me is that I *not* do something? Typically you can get a person to not do something by means that are, themselves, not impermissible. You have a claim against me that I not enter your house? You need only lock your doors and windows. You have a claim against me that I not eat your salad? You need only clutch it firmly or eat it yourself. So it might strike us to think that a weakened (T$_4$), namely

> If C$_{X, Y}$ Y not do such and such, then it is permissible for X to prevent Y from doing the such and such,

has a better chance of being true.

A better chance, yes. But it isn't after all true, for there are cases in which you have a claim against me that I not do a thing and yet you may not prevent me from doing it because the means you would have to use are (as in the preceding section) unacceptably drastic. I detest the pink plastic flamingo you keep on your front lawn; one day something in me snaps, and I go for it with a sledgehammer; the only means you have of preventing me from smashing it is shooting me in the foot. You do have a claim against me that I not smash it, but you may not shoot me in the foot, and the Sole-Means Principle for Permissibility tells us that you therefore may not prevent me from smashing it. Morality, alas, requires you to suffer the flamingo smashing.

4. I fancy that some people will think that a different kind of revision in

> (T$_4$) If C$_{X, Y}$ p, then it is permissible for X to prevent Y from letting it fail to be the case that p

would eliminate the difficulties I have been pointing to, a revision that takes into consideration the means that X would have to use to prevent Y from infringing X's claim, and requires that they themselves be permissible. Thus it might strike us that

> (T$_4'$) If C$_{X, Y}$ p, then it is permissible for X to prevent Y from letting it fail to be the case that p *if* X has a means of doing this that is itself permissible

is what is wanted here. Certainly the difficulties I have been pointing to do not arise for (T$_4'$). You may not make me deliver the widgets on Friday? You may not prevent me from smashing your flamingo? This does not show that you lack the claims against me, for by hypothesis you do not have means of enforcing those claims that are themselves permissible—your only means, shooting me in the foot, not itself being permissible.

By contrast, you have a claim against me that I not enter your house? You need only lock your doors and windows, and that is on any view something it is permissible for you to do. You have a claim against me that I not eat your salad? You need only clutch it firmly or eat it yourself, and that too is on any view something it is permissible for you to do. So far so good.

The question we need to ask, however, is whether (T$_4'$) isn't a mere triviality. Consider again

> The Sole-Means Principle for Permissibility: If the only means X has of doing beta is doing alpha, then it would be permissible

for X to do beta if and only if it would be permissible for X to do alpha.

A similar principle says the following:

> The Means Principle for Permissibility: If doing alpha is *a* means by which X can do beta, then it would be permissible for X to do beta if it would be permissible for X to do alpha.

This principle too seems entirely plausible.[2] After all, the means bring about the end, so whatever considerations are relevant to the question whether the end is permissible are surely among the things relevant to the question whether the means are permissible.

But if the Means Principle for Permissibility is true, then (T_4') is trivial. (T_4') is a conditional, with

$$C_{X, Y} \, p$$

as antecedent, and

> It is permissible for X to prevent Y from letting it fail to be the case that p *if* X has a means of doing this that is itself permissible

as consequent. But the truth of the consequent follows straightforwardly from the Means Principle for Permissibility, for the principle tells us that it is permissible for X to do beta (whatever doing beta may be) if X has a means of doing beta that is itself permissible. The antecedent of (T_4') plays no role at all in making its consequent true: its consequent is true whether or not its antecedent is true, thus whether or not X has the claim against Y.

So yet another attempt to modify (T_4) is an unsuccess—on the assumption that (T_4) is to be of interest to the moral theorist.

---

2. We should keep in mind, however, that this principle does not yield that if you have *a* permissible means of doing beta, and it is therefore permissible for you to do beta, then it is permissible for you to do beta by any means you like—including impermissible means. For example, I might have two means of preventing my neighbor from smashing my headlights: back my car into my garage or shoot him. Suppose backing my car into my garage is permissible. This shows (by the Means Principle for Permissibility) that preventing my neighbor from smashing my headlights is permissible. But the fact that preventing my neighbor from smashing my headlights is therefore permissible does not show that preventing my neighbor from smashing my headlights by shooting him is permissible.

5. In section 8 of the preceding chapter, we took note of the fact that many lawyers think that the thesis you get if you read "C" in

(T_1) If there is an X such that $C_{X, Y}$ p, then Y ought not let it fail to be the case that p

as "legal claim" is very plausible. A brief aside might be in place here to take note of a similar possible reading of

(T_4) If $C_{X, Y}$ p, then it is permissible for X to prevent Y from letting it fail to be the case that p,

which has also been found attractive by many lawyers.

Under its legal reading, (T_4) is a bridge-thesis that connects a legal notion (that of a legal claim) with a moral notion (what it is morally permissible to do). Consider *Vincent* again. As we said, it just was not true that the shipowner ought to cast off from the dock: the sudden storm created an emergency, and the shipowner therefore acted "prudently and advisedly" in remaining at the dock. Suppose it had been possible for the dockowner to prevent the shipowner from remaining at the dock: suppose that if the dockowner had cut the ropes that held the ship to the dock, he would have prevented the shipowner from remaining. I am sure we would all agree that this would have been wrong: it would have been true to say of the dockowner that he ought not prevent the shipowner from remaining. Are we inclined to conclude that the dockowner had no legal claim against the shipowner that the shipowner cast off? No more than we were inclined to draw this conclusion from the fact that it would have been false to say of the shipowner that he ought to cast off. After all, it is the very same thing—the emergency created by the storm—that makes it be the case *both* that the shipowner may remain *and* that the dockowner may not prevent him from remaining; and despite that emergency, the shipowner must compensate the dockowner for the damage he caused by remaining.

6. Perhaps further tinkering with

(T_4) If $C_{X, Y}$ p, then it is permissible for X to prevent Y from letting it fail to be the case that p

would enable us to avoid the difficulties I drew attention to in sections 2, 3, and 4. But the need for tinkering in philosophy always suggests that something went wrong at the outset. Why were we in the market for a simple, nontrivial thesis connecting claims with the permissibility of enforcing them?

I said at the beginning of this chapter that it is natural to think that, if X has a claim against Y, then it is permissible for X to prevent Y from infringing it. Surely, we think, it is morally permissible for people to protect themselves against infringements of their rights.

Well, it turned out to be a mistake to think that the fact that a person would infringe a claim of mine if he did a thing makes it permissible for me to prevent him from doing it. We had the thought "Surely it is morally permissible for people to protect themselves against infringements of their rights" because we were simply not remembering that there are cases in which, though we do have the claim, it is not morally permissible to prevent the claim infringer from infringing it. You have a claim against me that I not smash your flamingo; all the same, it is not permissible for you to prevent me from doing so if the only means you have of preventing me—shooting me—are unacceptably drastic.

We should notice now that this is only one of many kinds of countercase to the idea that one may always permissibly prevent a person from infringing one's claims. It might be impermissible for you to prevent a person from infringing a claim of yours not because the only *means* you have of doing so are unacceptably drastic, but because the *consequences* of doing so are unacceptably drastic. Suppose you can easily prevent me from smashing your flamingo: you need merely shout, in your fiercest way, "DON'T OR I'LL SUE!" and I won't. So your means are fine. But suppose that if you do this, and thereby prevent me from smashing your flamingo, you will thereby cause a disaster of some sort. (Jones is balanced on the edge of a nearby cliff, and if you shout at me "DON'T OR I'LL SUE!" you will startle Jones and cause him to fall off the cliff.) If so, you ought not prevent me from smashing your flamingo—after all, you can always sue me later.

A less weird example issues from the kind of case we looked at earlier. Suppose that if A prevents B from entering A's land, then B's sick child will die. Then A ought not prevent B from entering his land: the consequences of doing so are unacceptably drastic.

Again, it might be impermissible for you to prevent a person from infringing a claim of yours, not because the only means you have of doing so are unacceptably drastic, not because the consequences of doing so are unacceptably drastic, but because you have given your word, to that person or to someone else, that you will not. As, for example, if you have promised my mother that you will not prevent me from smashing your flamingo. (Compare C and D and the salad. If C had not given D the privilege of eating C's salad, C would have had a claim against D that D not eat it. It is compatible with C's having the claim that C promised someone—perhaps even D himself—that C would not prevent D from eating the salad. We might imagine C to have said to D: "I promise I won't prevent you, I leave you on your honor to not eat it.")

What lies behind all this is the fact that *X's preventing Y from doing a thing is an act like any other* and may be made impermissible by a wide variety of different things.

And in that X's preventing Y from doing a thing is an act like any other, it may also be made permissible by a wide variety of different things—that Y would otherwise infringe a claim of X's has no special pride of place among possible reasons for thinking it permissible for X to prevent Y from acting. Paternalism, for example, is morally worrisome, but is sometimes permissible: it is sometimes permissible for X to prevent Y from doing a thing even though what makes this permissible is not that Y would otherwise infringe a claim of X's, but instead that Y would otherwise cause harm to himself or herself.

Again, there are cases like the following. You and I like to sit on the public beach in a particular place where there is room for only one. I got there first this morning and thereby prevented you from sitting in it. Was that permissible? Certainly. And my preventing you from sitting in it was not made permissible by the fact that you would have been infringing a claim of mine in sitting in it, for there is no such fact.

Again, and more important for present purposes, it is sometimes permissible for X to prevent Y from doing a thing even though what makes this permissible is not that Y would otherwise infringe a claim of X's, but instead that Y would otherwise infringe a claim of some third party, Z. Self-defense is often, though not always, permissible; but so too is other-defense often, though not always, permissible—other-defense is not permissible as in the case of self-defense, where the only available means are unacceptably drastic.

I should perhaps stress: I do not say that other-defense is permissible wherever self-defense is. It might be important for Bloggs that he learn to fight his own battles, even at the cost of losing some, and there might be cases, then, in which it would not be permissible for me to barge in to defend him. All the same, it sometimes is permissible for me to barge in to defend him.

Still, the fact that Y would otherwise infringe a claim of X's—or, as let us now include, of Z's—does have a special role in contributing to making it permissible for X to prevent Y from acting. For the fact that Y would otherwise infringe a claim has a bearing on *Y's* claims, in particular on Y's claims to noninterference. In short: other things being equal, the fact that, in acting, Y would be infringing a person's claims, makes Y *forfeit* some (though certainly not all) claims to noninterference. (We will return to this matter in Chapter 14.)

At all events, there do not appear to be any simple, nontrivial theses connecting claims with the permissibility of enforcing them. It was, I think, just a mistake to think there were.

7. The new argument for the thesis that all claims are absolute went as follows. Given

> (T_4) If $C_{X,Y}$ p, then it is permissible for X to prevent Y from letting it fail to be the case that p

and

> (T_5) If it is permissible for X to prevent Y from letting it fail to be the case that p, then Y ought not let it fail to be the case that p,

we can deduce

> (T_1) If there is an X such that $C_{X,Y}$ p, then Y ought not let it fail to be the case that p.

Our primary interest in this and the preceding chapter has been the thesis that all claims are absolute; since we are now rejecting (T_4), the new argument for that thesis fails, whatever we may thing of (T_5). So let us bypass (T_5). It is an interesting thesis, but our purposes do not require us to attend to it.

What we do need to attend to is

> (T_2) If Y ought not let it fail to be the case that p, then there is an X such that $C_{X,Y}$ p.

I said in section 2 of the preceding chapter that if we could accept both (T_1) and (T_2), we could deduce

(T₃) Y ought not let it fail to be the case that p, if and only if
       there is an X such that $C_{X, Y}\, p$,

and adopting (T₃) would *greatly* simplify the theory of rights, for
what (T₃) says is that claims exactly overlap what people ought to
do, and call for no special consideration at all. So we should not reject
either (T₁) or (T₂) without good reason for doing so. I have been
giving what I think is good reason to reject (T₁); we should now
attend to (T₂).

Fortunately we can be brief, since (T₂) is surely not true. Here are
Alfred and Bert, sitting at a lecture, taking notes. Alfred's pencil
breaks, and he has no other. Bert has plenty of pencils. Bert has no
need of all those pencils and ought to lend one to Alfred. But Alfred
has no claim against Bert that Bert lend Alfred a pencil; nor does
anyone else have a claim against Bert that Bert lend Alfred a pencil.

I am not inviting you to suppose that Alfred needs the pencil for
life itself. On some views—we will be looking at them in Chapter 6—
if you need something for life itself, then you do have a claim to be
provided with it. In my story, Alfred needs the pencil only to continue
taking notes on the lecture. That need, together with the ease with
which Bert could meet it, makes "Bert ought to lend Alfred a pencil"
true, but does not make "Alfred has a claim against Bert that Bert
lend him a pencil" true.

There are endless things we ought to do though others have no
claim against us that we do them. We ought to be generous, kind,
helpful, thoughtful; these are not merely good ways to be, but ways
we ought to be. And we certainly ought to exercise these traits when
it will cost us very little to do so. But where only small benefits will
accrue to those benefited, neither those benefited nor anyone else has
a *claim* against us that we provide the benefit.

So (T₂) has to go—and so also, therefore, does the simplifying (T₃).
The realm of rights is squarely within the morality of action, but is
not identical with it.

8. There is no inconsistency in a person who rejects (T₂) while
accepting

(T₁) If there is an X such that $C_{X, Y}\, p$, then Y ought not let it
       fail to be the case that p.

Should we accept (T₁)? I have been arguing that we should not. I drew attention in the preceding chapter to the fact that if I promise a person that I will do a thing, then this has consequences for my behavior even if it turns out to be false to say that I ought to do the thing, those consequences being most simply explained by appeal to the supposition that the person has a claim against me that I do the thing. And similarly for property ownership: that too has consequences for the behavior of others that are most simply explained by the supposition that the owner has claims against those others, for example, that the others not intrude on the owner's property.

In this chapter we looked at an argument for (T_1) that issues from the supposed permissibility of enforcing one's claims, and rejected it.

So I suggest we reject (T_1)—I suggest we reject the thesis that all claims are absolute.

Some philosophers may say, "Ah, *now* it is clear (or perhaps: for some time it has been clear) that what she means by 'rights' is what the rest of us mean by '*prima facie* rights'. If only she had made that clear at the outset! For it is as plain as day that *prima facie* rights are not absolute". But what do people who say this mean by "*prima facie* rights"? And what do they mean by "rights"?

The term "*prima facie* rights" is a piece of technical terminology, invented by philosophers to fill what seemed to them to be a gap in the language. I believe that the thinking behind the invention of the term went as follows. (i) All rights are absolute. That is, if X has a right against Y that such and such state of affairs obtain, then Y ought not let it fail to obtain. Suppose, for example, that (ii) Y promised X to do something. We cannot say that Y made it be the case that X has a right against Y that Y do the thing, for it may turn out not to be the case that Y ought to do it. All the same, (iii) Y made something, S, be the case that has two features: (a) given S is the case, it follows that, other things being equal, Y ought to do the thing,[3] and (b) given S is the case, it follows that *if* Y ought to do the thing, then X has a right against Y that Y do it. (iv) There is no compact piece of

---

3. I do not think that people who favor the use of the term "*prima facie* rights" have attended to the need to seek a release (if there is time) before infringing the *prima facie* right, or the need to compensate for loss caused by the infringement (if the *prima facie* right is infringed without release). But having now had their attention drawn to these things, perhaps they would say that given S is the case, it follows, not merely that other things being equal, Y ought to do the thing, but also that if Y is not going to do it, then other things being equal, he or she ought to seek a release in advance or make compensation later.

terminology in English by means of which we can say what S is. Let us express what S is as follows: X has a *prima facie* right against Y that Y do the thing. Thus we can now say: in making that promise to X, Y made it be the case that X has a *prima facie* right against Y that Y do the thing, which means the conjunction of (a) other things being equal,[4] Y ought to do it, and (b) if Y ought to do it, then X has a right against Y that Y do it.

I took as my example at step (ii) a promise Y made to X. We might instead have taken as our example a piece of land owned by X, which Y wishes to cross. (I am tempted to say: we might instead have taken as our example any right that X has against Y. But I am sure that would be regarded as tendentious.)

I do not know of anyone who has introduced the term "*prima facie* right" in exactly this way, but I think this captures what is intended, namely the idea that a *prima facie* right counts in support of the hypothesis that the one against whom it is had ought to do this or that, and the idea that if he or she really ought to do the relevant thing, then the holder of the *prima facie* right has a (real, full-fledged) right.

But do we really need this piece of terminology? What dominated the bit of reasoning I set out above was the thesis (i) that all rights are absolute, and if we do not accept that thesis, then the rest is a waste of our time. And there is nothing to be gained by the adoption of it, for the job would remain to be done of saying what *prima facie* rights are, which includes saying *how* they support conclusions about what people ought to do, and of saying also which of them we have.

I will continue to say that if Y makes X a promise to do a thing, then X has a right (in particular, a claim) against Y that Y do it, and that if X owns a piece of land, then X has a right (in particular, a claim) against Y that Y stay off it, and so on. (Or so, as I said, it is plausible to think.) And I do not mean by all this anything from which it follows that Y ought to do this or that. On the other hand, I certainly do mean something from which it follows that, other things being equal, Y ought to do the this or that—indeed, I have been proposing

---

4. "Other things being equal" throughout this paragraph should be supplied with the metaphysical and relatively strong reading pointed to in the Introduction, section 3. That is, a *prima facie* right is not a reason to think Y ought to do the thing of just any old kind: it is not mere evidence that Y ought to do the thing, it is an 'ought-making' fact. See Introduction, note 11.

that X's having a claim against Y is equivalent to a kind of constraint on Y's behavior, the nature of which we are in process of examining.

But of course anyone who likes is cordially invited to pencil the abbreviation "pf" (short for "*prima facie*") in front of the appropriate occurrences of "rights" (and "claims") in both what precedes and what follows.

9. When reasons have been given for a thesis, we cannot *simply* reject it, however mistaken it may seem to us to be, unless we find some way of accounting for those reasons. Why did it seem so plausible to think that all claims are absolute? I listed some reasons for thinking it plausible at the beginning of Chapter 3; so if we are to reject that thesis, we must take note of them once again.

I mentioned, first, the simplicity many people think can be got by accepting it. I hope it is now clear that accepting the thesis does not simplify the theory of rights. Too much of moral importance is explained only with difficulty if that thesis is true. There will, of course, remain the question what *is* the relation between X's having a claim against Y and what Y therefore ought to do. We have taken note of some things Y ought to do if X has a claim against Y and Y wishes for one or another reason to not accord X that claim. But there are circumstances in which Y really ought to accord the claim, and we will need to look at them.

But I mentioned other reasons for thinking the thesis that all claims are absolute attractive. I said that people anyway *seem* to show by their behavior that they think the thesis true. They say "I have a right that you do such and such!" plainly meaning that they have a claim against us that we do the such and such; and they *seem* to show by their behavior that they think that settles the matter—that we have, morally speaking, no other option, that it just *follows* that we ought to do the such and such. I quite agree that we do explain their behavior most simply if we attribute to them the view that their having the right does entail its being the case that we ought to do the such and such. But there is a less simple but I think more satisfying explanation of their behavior, namely that they think having a right has great moral weight. Not that their having a right *entails* that we ought to accord them what they have a right to, but that their having a right is strong reason to think we ought to accord them what they have a right to, and very often—though not everywhere—is sufficient for the truth of that conclusion.

A further reason for finding the thesis attractive was this: we think we must surely be at fault when we fail to accord people what they have a claim to. (Don't they have a ground for complaint against us if we fail to accord it?) Why would we be at fault when we fail to accord a claim if it were not the case that we ought to accord it? Well, we may really be at fault when we fail to accord a claim. We really are at fault when we fail to accord a claim where it was our fault that we got into a situation in which it is not possible to accord it. (Consider, for example, a man who all too casually makes incompatible promises.) Do we think we are *always* at fault when we fail to accord a claim? I doubt it—except when we fail to remember those situations where, with the best will in the world and through no fault of our own, we simply cannot do what we are bound to do, or when we remember those situations but think we would feel remorse or guilt if we were in them. But while it says something good about us that we think we would feel remorse or guilt if we were in those situations, it may be that those feelings would simply be irrational.

I think in fact that the evidence from ordinary usage on this matter is conflicting. People do say "I have a right that you do such and such", plainly meaning that they have a claim against us that we do the such and such; and they *seem* to show by their behavior that they think that settles the matter—that we have, morally speaking, no other option, that it just *follows* that we ought to do the such and such. But people also say "I know you had a right that I do such and such, but I just couldn't" and sometimes they even add that it was not their fault that they couldn't, and sometimes even, more strongly, that doing the such and such would have required failing to attend to more important and pressing concerns and thus would have been wrong.

Last, I mentioned the fact that some philosophers think self-respect itself rests on one's being able to feel confident, perhaps not of one's actually being accorded what one has claims to, but at least of its being the case that others ought to accord one what one has claims to—so that if others fail to accord me what I have claims to, then that does not say I am unimportant; it says rather that they are at fault. But self-respect is by no means threatened by the fact that it is sometimes permissible to infringe a claim, given on the one hand that claims have great weight and, on the other, that the situations that make it permissible to infringe a claim are restricted in certain special ways. We will be looking at them in the following three chapters.

In short, nothing seems to be gained by accepting the thesis that all claims are absolute, and the complexity of moral phenomena cannot be satisfactorily captured by a moral theory that contains it. So I suggest we now reject it.

Having rejected it, we can help ourselves to a piece of terminology that will from time to time be useful. Suppose X has a claim against Y that a certain state of affairs S obtain. (The state of affairs might be Y's staying off X's land.) What if Y lets that state of affairs fail to obtain? (Y enters X's land.) Then Y did not accord X what X had a claim against Y that Y accord X. Let us say that Y has therefore *infringed* X's claim against Y. Let us say that Y has *violated* X's claim against Y only if it is not merely true that Y let S fail to obtain but more, that Y ought not have let S fail to obtain. Then the thesis that all claims are absolute might have been expressed as follows: every infringing of a claim is a violating of it. We have rejected that thesis, so it will sometimes be right to say that, although Y has infringed a claim X had against Y, Y did not violate that claim. And we might, if we liked, put the question we will shortly turn to, not in the words "When is it permissible to infringe a claim?" but instead in the words "When is an infringing of a right *not* a violating of it?"

A further piece of terminology wants attention. I said in Chapter 3 that "wrong" as adjective or adverb seems to me to be cognate with "ought": thus I take "It would be wrong for Y to not do alpha" and "Y would be acting wrongly if he or she did not do alpha" to be equivalent to "Y ought to do alpha". But "wrong" as verb or noun is different. I will use "Y wronged X" and "Y did X a wrong" only where Y violated a claim of X's. So on my use of these locutions, they entail that Y acted wrongly; but they entail more than just that Y acted wrongly—they entail that Y wrongly infringed a claim of X's. I think in fact that this use of these locutions is rather stricter than our ordinary use of them. If I break your nose for no good reason, then I surely wrong you and do you a wrong; so far so good, that would be my violating a claim of yours. But what if I think you killed Cock Robin, when as things turn out you did not? I think we might in the ordinary way say I wronged you and did you a wrong, though it can hardly be thought that my merely harboring that thought was my violating a claim of yours. I suggest we bypass the question what exactly these locutions mean; what matters for our purposes is only terminological consistency.

Chapter 5

Value

1. As I said at the beginning of Chapter 3, it does seem right to think that X's having a claim against Y is at least equivalent to, and perhaps just *is,* Y's behavior's being constrained in a certain way. We have taken note of two things included in that constraint, namely the need to seek a release in advance if the claim will otherwise have to be infringed, and the need to compensate later for harms or losses caused by the infringement if a release was unobtainable.

But it is only in special circumstances that Y may permissibly fail to accord the claim; other things being equal, Y ought to accord it. What we now begin on in this chapter is the question what those special circumstances are in which it is permissible for Y to fail to accord the claim—what those other things are such that Y need not accord the claim if they are not 'equal'. It will take us three chapters to arrive at an answer to this question.

2. A certain idea—let us call it the Tradeoff Idea—seems *prima facie* plausible: it is permissible to infringe a claim if and only if sufficiently much more good would come of infringing it than would come of not infringing it. How much more good is sufficiently much more good? Let us leave this vague for the time being. We will be taking a close look at the Tradeoff Idea in the following chapter.

What is important to notice here is that the Tradeoff Idea does *not* say (i) that one ought to infringe a claim if and only if sufficiently much more good would come of infringing it than would come of not infringing it. Moreover, the Tradeoff Idea does *not* say (ii) that one ought to infringe a claim if and only if more good (even just a little more good) would come of infringing it than would come of not infringing it. (i) and (ii) are very much stronger than the Tradeoff Idea.

(ii) is a consequence of a still stronger (because more general) idea, namely (iii) that one ought to do a thing, whatever it may be, if and only if more good (even just a little more good) would come of doing it than would come of not doing it. This stronger and more general idea (iii) lies at the heart of classical utilitarianism, and I will therefore call it the Central Utilitarian Idea. Many people find it exceedingly attractive.

But it is obviously in a number of ways vague, and different theories result from different ways of making it more precise. We need to look at two of them. Much of what I will be saying by way of objection to those theories is familiar nowadays, but some, I think, is not, and in any case there is one question they raise that our purposes do require us to answer.

People very often fail to distinguish between the two theories we will be looking at, and use the names "Utilitarianism" and (the increasingly common) "Consequentialism" to stand for both of them; but the theories differ in an important way, and I will give them names that draw attention to that difference.

"One ought to do a thing if and only if more good would come of doing it than of not doing it." One way of making that idea more precise is to interpret it as saying

> CONSEQUENTIALIST ACT UTILITARIANISM: X ought to do alpha if and only if the consequences of X's doing alpha would be better than the consequences of X's doing any of the other things it is open to X to do instead.[1]

But this does not make the idea *very* precise: in particular, we need to become clear what we are to take a friend of this theory[2] to mean by that word "consequences". Suppose that X's options at a given time are these: do alpha, do beta, do gamma, and so on. It is an important fact about CONSEQUENTIALIST ACT UTILITARIANISM that it

---

1. G. E. Moore's words in *Ethics* (Oxford: Oxford University Press, 1912) suggest this thesis. But see note 5 below.

2. CONSEQUENTIALIST ACT UTILITARIANISM and NON-CONSEQUENTIALIST ACT UTILITARIANISM—which we will get to shortly—are what I called object-level moral judgments in the Introduction; thus they are not themselves moral theories, since at the heart of a moral theory is one or more explanatory moral judgment. But it is easy enough to construct explanatory moral judgments from them. Thus

tells us we are to find out whether X ought to do alpha without taking into consideration what X's doing alpha would itself consist in, and without taking into consideration what X's doing beta would consist in, and so on through X's doing gamma and all the other possibilities. The theory tells us we are to take into consideration only what would be the *consequences* of those possible events if they occurred; hence the adjective "consequentialist" in the name I gave to the theory. But the meaning of that word "consequences" is not transparent.

We may presumably suppose that a CONSEQUENTIALIST ACT UTIL-ITARIAN so uses the word "consequence" that an event E is a consequence of X's doing alpha *only if* E is discrete from the event that consists in X's doing alpha. Consider my typing of the preceding sentence. That was a complex act, containing among its 'subacts' my typing the word "We", my typing the word "may", and so on. The CONSEQUENTIALIST ACT UTILITARIAN would say that none of those 'subacts' of my typing the sentence is a consequence of my typing the sentence, since they are not discrete from (but are instead parts of) the event that consisted in my typing the sentence.

That example was simple to deal with, but others are less so. Suppose Bert killed a child. From the fact that Bert killed the child, it follows that the child died. Is the child's death a consequence of Bert's killing of the child? Well, is the child's death discrete from Bert's killing of it?

There is a theory of action according to which the child's death *is* discrete from Bert's killing of it; I will call it the Reductive Theory of Action. How did Bert kill the child? Let us suppose he shot it. How did he do that? Let us suppose he pulled the trigger of a gun that was aimed at the child. How did he pull the trigger of the gun? Let us suppose he moved his forefinger, which was curled around the trigger of the gun. The Reductive Theory of Action says that the act that consisted in Bert's killing of the child just itself *was* the act that consisted in Bert's moving his forefinger. The Reductive Theory of Action says, quite generally, that every human act is a bodily move-

---

to CONSEQUENTIALIST ACT UTILITARIANISM there corresponds the following explanatory moral judgment: if X ought to do alpha that is *because* the consequences of X's doing alpha would be better . . . , and if it is not the case that X ought to do alpha that is *because* the consequences of X's doing alpha would not be better . . . Similarly for NON-CONSEQUENTIALIST ACT UTILITARIANISM. We will not in fact need to attend to those explanatory moral judgments. See note 11 below.

ment or set of bodily movements.[3] Bert's moving his forefinger, of course, was not merely a moving of a forefinger, it was also a killing of a child; but what made it be a killing of a child is the fact that it caused a child's death. But if Bert's killing of the child caused the child's death, then the child's death is discrete from Bert's killing of it.

Is the Reductive Theory of Action true? *Should* we think that Bert's killing of the child was his moving his forefinger? Bert's moving his forefinger caused the child's death, but isn't it at best uncomfortable to suppose that his killing of the child caused the child's death? A human act is an event and typically has proper parts that are also events. My typing of the preceding sentence has the following proper parts, among others: my typing "A", my typing "human", my typing "act", and so on. Bert killed the child *by* moving his forefinger; isn't it plausible to think that his moving his forefinger was not identical with his killing of the child, but rather a part of it?—a further part being the death that Bert's moving his forefinger caused? The theory of action I point to here says that Bert's killing of the child included among its parts not merely Bert's moving his forefinger, but also all of those other events—including the child's death—such that Bert killed the child by causing them.[4] But if the child's death was part of Bert's killing of the child, then the death is not discrete from it and hence is not a consequence of it.

Anyone who likes CONSEQUENTIALIST ACT UTILITARIANISM plainly has to take a stand on the issues that arise here. If the child's death is a consequence of Bert's killing of it, then CONSEQUENTIALIST ACT UTILITARIANISM allows the badness of the child's death (I presume the death of a child is something bad) to figure in the assessment of whether Bert ought to kill it; if the child's death is not a consequence

3. This theory has many friends, among them Donald Davidson; see his *Essays on Actions and Events* (Oxford: Clarendon Press, 1980). See also Jonathan Bennett, *Events and Their Names* (Indianapolis: Hackett, 1988). What of the so-called acts of omission? Friends of the Reductive Theory of Action may wish to say that an act of omission is an event that consists in a not-making of a bodily movement or set of bodily movements. Alternatively, they may wish to say that there are no events that are acts of omission, that acts of omission have to be understood in a different way. Let us ignore the question that arises here.

4. The theory of action pointed to here is spelled out in my *Acts and Other Events* (Ithaca: Cornell University Press, 1977). Another opponent of the Reductive Theory of Action is Alvin A. Goldman, *A Theory of Human Action* (Princeton: Princeton University Press, 1970).

of Bert's killing of it, then CONSEQUENTIALIST ACT UTILITARIANISM does not allow the badness of the child's death to figure in the assessment of whether Bert ought to kill it. Since what makes it wrong to kill had better lie (at least) largely in the fact that a person who kills causes a death, I think a CONSEQUENTIALIST ACT UTILITARIAN very likely to favor the Reductive Theory of Action, according to which the death a killer causes is a consequence of the killing.

We will return to this point in the following section. Let us for the time being be satisfied with merely having taken note of the fact that what you will think a consequence of an act turns on what you think the act *is* and, in particular, on whether you think the Reductive Theory of Action true.

What we have so far is only a necessary condition for use of the word "consequence", and we need a set of conditions that are both necessary and sufficient. Let us take a CONSEQUENTIALIST ACT UTILITARIAN to have the following in mind: an event E is a consequence of X's doing alpha if and only if *both* (i) E is discrete from X's doing alpha *and* (ii) if X's doing alpha occurs then E occurs. Here is an example. Suppose that a gust of wind just blew your hat off and that it is now rolling toward a puddle. If I walk away from the situation, the hat will roll into the puddle. (No one other than me is in a position to save it.) Will the hat's rolling into the puddle be a consequence of my walking away? The hat's rolling into the puddle is on any view discrete from my walking away, so condition (i) is met. By hypothesis, if I walk away, the hat's rolling into the puddle will occur, so condition (ii) is also met. It follows that the hat's rolling into the puddle is a consequence of my walking away.

I chose that example in order to make clear that the word "consequences" in this theory is not to be understood in such a way that an event E is a consequence of X's doing alpha only if X's doing alpha *causes* E—for my walking away will not cause the hat to roll into the puddle. (It will have been the gust of wind that caused this.) An event E is a consequence of X's doing alpha if X's doing alpha causes E; if a man's shooting of a child causes the child's death, then the child's death is a consequence of his shooting of it. But E may be a consequence of X's doing alpha even if X's doing alpha does not cause E. On any plausible view of what people ought to do, the fact that if I walk away your hat will roll into a puddle should surely be relevant to the question what I here and now ought to do; the theory we are looking at makes it relevant by counting the hat's rolling into the puddle as a consequence of my walking away, and thus as among the things to be considered in figuring out what I here and now ought to do.

This interpretation of the word "consequence" yields some odd outcomes. Consider, for example, East Germany's reuniting with West Germany. It seems to me quite certain that this will occur, perhaps not sooner but anyway sooner or later, and that it will occur whatever *I* do. Then in particular, if I pinch my nose now, the reunification will occur. (Of course it is also true that if I do not pinch my nose now, the reunification will occur, since it will occur whatever I do. No matter, for the moment.) East Germany's reuniting with West Germany is on any view discrete from my pinching my nose now, so condition (i) is met. If I pinch my nose now, the reunification will occur, so condition (ii) is also met. It follows that East Germany's reuniting with West Germany is a consequence of my pinching my nose now. But that *is* an odd outcome: certainly no one uses the word "consequence" in ordinary life in a way according to which that is true.

We could have interpreted the word "consequences" in the theory more tightly: for example—this is only one of a number of possibilities—we could have taken it that an event E is a consequence of X's doing alpha if and only if the following is the case: (i) E is discrete from X's doing alpha *and* (ii) if X's doing alpha occurs then E occurs *and* (iii) if X's doing alpha does not occur then E does not occur. On that interpretation of the word, East Germany's reuniting with West Germany is not a consequence of my pinching my nose now, for it will occur whether or not I pinch my nose now.

But in the first place, this tighter way of using the word "consequences" is also out of accord with our use of it in ordinary life. Let us go back to your hat and the puddle. We were supposing that if I walk away from the situation, your hat will roll into the puddle. It might also be true that if I stand still and stare at your hat it will roll into the puddle. Then it is false that your hat will not roll into the puddle if I do not walk away from the situation. So if we are using the word "consequence" in this tighter way, then it is false that your hat's rolling into the puddle is a consequence of my walking away. (It is also false that your hat's rolling into the puddle is a consequence of my standing still and staring at the hat.) But that is not how we use the word: surely we so use it that your hat's rolling into the puddle *is* a consequence of my walking away. (As also of my standing still and staring at the hat. As also of my doing any of the things I might do that do not include saving the hat.) And, second, on any plausible view of what people ought to do, the fact that if I walk away your hat will roll into a puddle should surely be relevant to what I here and now ought to do.

It is simplest to interpret the word "consequences" in the theory in the looser way I described, thus in such a way that an event E is a consequence of X's doing alpha if and only if *both* (i) E is discrete from X's doing alpha *and* (ii) if X's doing alpha occurs then E occurs. No doubt this decision does yield odd outcomes, such as that whatever will occur no matter what I do turns out to be a consequence of everything I do. But that kind of odd outcome need not trouble the CONSEQUENTIALIST ACT UTILITARIAN. Take East Germany's reuniting with West Germany. Since that will occur if I pinch my nose now, it is among the consequences of my pinching my nose now. But since it will occur whatever I do now, it is among the consequences of all of my possible acts now. Then its goodness or badness (I leave open whether it will be good or bad) contributes equally to the goodness or badness of the consequences of all of my possible acts. But then its goodness or badness makes no difference to what I ought to do now: it cancels out.

A second way of making the Central Utilitarian Idea precise yields a theory which differs from CONSEQUENTIALIST ACT UTILITARIANISM in one and only one way. Let us say that an event is in the 'consequence-set' of X's doing alpha just in case it is among the consequences of X's doing alpha. Then we can restate our first theory as follows:

> CONSEQUENTIALIST ACT UTILITARIANISM: X ought to do alpha if and only if the consequence-set of X's doing alpha would be better than the consequence-sets of X's doing any of the other things it is open to X to do instead.

Let us say that an event is in the 'act-plus-consequence-set' of X's doing alpha just in case *either* it is among the consequences of X's doing alpha *or* it is, or is part of, X's doing alpha. Then we can state our second theory as follows:

> NON-CONSEQUENTIALIST ACT UTILITARIANISM: X ought to do alpha if and only if the act-plus-consequence-set of X's doing alpha

would be better than the act-plus-consequence-sets of X's doing
any of the other things it is open to X to do instead.[5]

As is plain, the second theory differs from the first in the following
way only: while the first theory tells us to attend only to the consequences of X's possible acts in assessing what X ought to do, the
second theory tells us to attend also to the acts themselves—to X's
doing alpha itself and to all of those events that are parts of X's doing
alpha. Hence the adjective "non-consequentialist" in the name I gave
to the theory.

More precisely, the second theory tells us that we *may* attend also
to the acts themselves—to X's doing alpha itself and its parts. For
NON-CONSEQUENTIALIST ACT UTILITARIANISM, like CONSEQUENTIAL-
IST ACT UTILITARIANISM, says nothing about what in fact is good or
bad. Both theories are compatible with any theory you like about
what is good or bad. In particular, neither theory declares itself on
whether human acts are good or bad. Of course you would be unlikely
to prefer NON-CONSEQUENTIALIST ACT UTILITARIANISM to CONSE-
QUENTIALIST ACT UTILITARIANISM if you thought human acts are neither good nor bad: there would be no point in your allowing their
goodness or badness to be relevant to whether someone ought to do
a thing if you thought they had none. Indeed, if human acts are neither
good nor bad, then the two theories yield the same conclusions about
what a person ought to do. But NON-CONSEQUENTIALIST ACT UTILI-

5. In light of the loose interpretation I gave the word "consequences", this
second theory can be seen as an approximation to a theory that says that what
matters morally is not just the consequences of an act, but the whole world that
will be actual if the act is performed.

In his "Reply to My Critics", in Paul Arthur Schilpp, ed., *The Philosophy of
G. E. Moore* (New York: Tudor, 1952), Moore says that he had not seen the
difference between the views I here call CONSEQUENTIALIST ACT UTILITARIANISM
and NON-CONSEQUENTIALIST ACT UTILITARIANISM at the time of writing his earlier
Ethics. I hazard a guess that is because philosophers of the period had not seen
the interest there is in the question what an act is, and the bearing its answer
has on moral theory. In any case, at the time of writing "Reply to My Critics",
Moore prefers the second of the two views. Very good discussion of these and
other alternatives may be found in Fred Feldman, *Doing the Best We Can*
(Dordrecht: D. Reidel, 1986).

TARIANISM does not assert that acts are good or bad: it leaves this open.

On some views about what is good or bad, then, the two theories yield the same conclusions about what a person ought to do. Suppose you think that the only things that are good or bad are feelings of pleasure or pain. If you adopted the first of the two theories I set out, we might call you a HEDONISTIC CONSEQUENTIALIST ACT UTILITARIAN; if you adopted the second, we might call you a HEDONISTIC NON-CONSEQUENTIALIST ACT UTILITARIAN. But it would not in fact matter which of those two theories you adopted. If all that is good or bad is feelings of pleasure or pain, then it makes no difference as to what X ought to do whether we consider only the consequence-sets of X's doing alpha, beta, gamma, and so on, or the act-plus-consequence-sets of X's doing those things, since X's doing alpha, beta, gamma, and so on, are not themselves feelings of pleasure or pain, though no doubt they may cause feelings of pleasure or pain.

Suppose, by contrast, you think that human acts are themselves good or bad, or that at least some are. Then it may on your view make a difference as to whether X ought to do alpha which of these two theories you adopt: for the goodness or badness of X's doing alpha, if any, is made relevant by the second theory but not by the first.

Are human acts themselves good or bad? This question may strike us as crazy, for isn't it obvious that they are? Isn't it obvious that X's throwing a child into the water is something bad, and that Y's jumping into the water to save it is something good? How could anyone think otherwise?

3. The question "Are human acts themselves good or bad?" is not as it stands a clear one. For some people might say "Yes, of course they are: they are good or bad insofar as they cause good or bad things, such as feelings of pleasure or pain."

The notion 'intrinsic value' is the one we want here, and it is unfortunately not easy to say exactly what it is. I suggest we not go into the difficulties that arise here; I suggest we say, just roughly, that a thing has positive intrinsic value in amount D just in case it is good in amount D but *not* because of what it causes or because of what causes it; and that a thing has negative intrinsic value in amount D just in case it is bad in amount D but *not* because of what it causes or because of what causes it.[6] For example, those who say that feelings of pleasure are the only good things (or perhaps: the only things 'good in themselves') mean by this that feelings of pleasure are the only things that have positive intrinsic value in this sense, that is, that although many things that are not feelings of pleasure may inherit a degree of goodness from their causing feelings of pleasure, feelings of pleasure alone are in some degree good quite apart from what they cause and from what causes them.

Let us from here on mean positive and negative intrinsic value, so characterized, by the term "value"—where unclarity would otherwise result, I will say, explicitly, "positive value" and "negative value".

Making use of an easily grasped locution, we can now rephrase the two theories as follows:

> CONSEQUENTIALIST ACT UTILITARIANISM: X ought to do alpha if and only if the consequence-set of X's doing alpha would 'maximize value',

and

> NON-CONSEQUENTIALIST ACT UTILITARIANISM: X ought to do alpha if and only if the act-plus-consequence-set of X's doing alpha would 'maximize value'.

And we can now rephrase our question as follows: do human acts have value? If human acts lack value, then the outcomes of the two theories are the same.

Is Alfred's saving a child's life at some cost to himself in a degree good quite apart from what it causes and from what causes it? It may cause many further good things, future feelings of pleasure for the child, feelings of pleasure for its parents, and so on; is it in a degree good *not* because of the causal relations in which it stands to other things? Again, was Bert's killing a child in a degree bad quite apart from what it causes and from what causes it? Many people have thought it very plausible to answer yes to these questions.

---

6. Many people have thought it plain that we need to distinguish between a thing's intrinsic value and its 'instrumental value' (the goodness or badness the thing inherits from what it causes), but nobody has seen a need to distinguish between a thing's intrinsic value and what could be called its 'product value' (the goodness or badness the thing inherits from what caused it)—presumably because it is not usually thought that anything does inherit goodness or badness from what causes it. On some views, however, there *is* reason to think this: see note 7.

Many people have held views that would make it implausible, however. I suspect that those who think human acts lack value are motivated to think this because they accept three theses.

The first thesis is our old friend the Reductive Theory of Action, which says, quite generally, that every human act is a bodily movement or set of bodily movements. (So Bert's killing of the child was his moving of his forefinger.) I said that a CONSEQUENTIALIST ACT UTILITARIAN is very likely to favor the Reductive Theory of Action for the reason that it allows the death a man who kills will cause if he kills to be relevant to whether he ought to kill. Here is a second reason: the Reductive Theory of Action is the first step in a line of argument that leads to the conclusion that acts have no value.

Some killings are unintentional, but some are intentional. The second thesis, which I will call the Causal Theory of Intention, says that what makes an act be intentional is its being caused by an intention. Suppose Bert's killing of the child was an intentional killing of the child; what made it so? The Causal Theory of Intention says that the act was an intentional killing of the child in that it was caused by an intention *to* kill the child.[7]

The third thesis is about value, and it says that bodily movements themselves lack value. I will call it the No-Value Thesis. Consider Bert's moving his forefinger. By hypothesis, it caused a child's death, and if anything has (negative) value, a child's death surely does; but this does not show that Bert's moving his forefinger itself has value—value, in our use of that term, being everywhere *intrinsic* value. Again, we may suppose that Bert moved his forefinger in order to pull the trigger of a gun and thereby kill a child. Isn't it plausible to suppose, then, that Bert's moving his forefinger did have (negative) value by virtue of the intention with which Bert moved his forefinger? Not if the Causal Theory of Intention is true. If the Causal Theory of Intention is true, then Bert's moving his forefinger was intentional only in having been caused by an intention, and it really does seem to follow that Bert's moving his forefinger itself lacks value—value, in our use of that term, being everywhere *intrinsic* value.

---

7. Anyone who thinks an intentional killing of a person worse than an unintentional killing of a person, who also thinks that intentions are involved in actions only by way of causing them, had better think that something can inherit badness not only from what it causes, but also from what causes it—thus that it can have what I called 'product value' in note 6.

It is plain that the conjunction of the three theses yields that human acts lack value. If the first two theses are true, then all human acts, whether intentional or not, are mere bodily movements; if the third is also true, then they lack value. What is of moral interest in Bert's intentional killing of the child lies wholly in what his act is causally related to.

Are the three theses true? For my part, I think all three are false. I indicated in the preceding section my reason for thinking that Bert's killing of the child includes the child's death as part; if that is correct then the Reductive Theory of Action is false. And what of the Causal Theory of Intention? Well, what is an intention that it should cause an act? My forming an intention to do such and such might well be thought to be an event, which then causes other events later, including acts of mine. But the intention itself is not an event. And even if an event that consists in my forming an intention to do such and such causes an act of mine, it does not follow that this act of mine is intentional, much less that in acting I act with that intention. I might form an intention to make some coffee, which then causes me to head downstairs to the kitchen, which then causes me to phone the plumber because the kitchen floor (as I now see) is flooded; but I do not phone the plumber to make some coffee, I phone the plumber to get the flood dealt with and perhaps have lost all desire for coffee by now. But if one rejects the Causal Theory of Intention, then the No-Value Thesis loses plausibility. If we reject the idea that a man's moving his forefinger is intentional in virtue of having been caused by an intention, we may well think it may itself have value—negative value if the intention with which he moved his forefinger was a bad one, positive value if the intention with which he moved his forefinger was a good one.

But in fact we do best to sidestep the question what we should think of the three theses, since dealing properly with the Reductive Theory of Action and the Causal Theory of Intention would require us to make too deep a foray into the theory of action. What I suggest we do is to turn to the moral issues that directly concern us, bringing out as we go how they interconnect with the issues in the theory of action that I have been pointing to.

4. If you think some version of the Central Utilitarian Idea must be right, then you have good reason to reject one or more of the three theses we looked at in the preceding section, for you have good reason

to suppose that human acts do have value, and good reason therefore to allow consideration of their value by preferring NON-CONSEQUEN- TIALIST ACT UTILITARIANISM to CONSEQUENTIALIST ACT UTILITARIAN- ISM. What I have in mind comes out as follows.

Consider a case that I will call TRANSPLANT. Here is Bloggs, who is a transplant surgeon, an extraordinarily good one—he can trans- plant anything at all sucessfully. He has five patients who need parts and will soon die if they do not get them: two need one lung each, two need one kidney each, and one needs a heart. Here is a young man in excellent health; he has the right blood type and can be cut up to supply parts for the patients who need them. (Let us bypass a possible objection by supposing that none of the patients can be cut up to supply parts for the others.) The surgeon asks the young man whether he would like to volunteer his parts, but the young man says "I deeply sympathize, but no." If the surgeon proceeds despite the young man's refusal, he saves five lives at a cost of only one. Does this mean the surgeon ought to proceed? Surely not! It is not only false that he ought to proceed, it is false even that he *may* proceed. That he ought, or even may, is so obviously false that it would be a disaster for a moral theory to yield them: a theory that yields them is a theory in dire need of revision. In short, I take their being false to be a datum.[8] If a moral theory yields anything at all about this case, it had better yield that the surgeon ought not proceed.

Suppose now that you think some version of the Central Utilitarian Idea must be right, but that you think acts lack value—perhaps be- cause you accept the three theses of the preceding section. Then it makes no difference, morally, whether you opt for CONSEQUENTIALIST ACT UTILITARIANISM or NON-CONSEQUENTIALIST ACT UTILITARIAN- ISM, since given acts lack value, the value of the consequence-set of an act is the same as the value of the act-plus-consequence-set of the act. So suppose you opt for CONSEQUENTIALIST ACT UTILITARIANISM.

Consider the following complex act: the surgeon's cutting the young man up, removing his parts, and then transplanting those parts into the five who need them. What are its consequences? On any view about the ontology of action, the consequences of that complex act include death for the one young man and life for five who would otherwise die—on balance, four more lives than if the surgeon's com-

8. As I said in the Introduction, I take certain moral judgments about what a person ought or ought not, may or may not, to be data, thus not to be argued *for* but rather to be argued *from*. This is among them.

plex act does not occur. It is very plausible to think that lives have value and therefore that the consequence-set of the complex act would maximize value. If so, then given you have opted for CONSEQUEN-TIALIST ACT UTILITARIANISM, you are committed to the conclusion that the surgeon ought to cut the young man up, remove his parts, and then transplant the parts into the five who need them: not even merely to the conclusion that he may, but to the conclusion that he positively ought to.

So if you think some version of the Central Utilitarian Idea must be right, you have good reason to suppose that human acts do have value and then to allow consideration of their value by preferring NON-CONSEQUENTIALIST ACT UTILITARIANISM to CONSEQUENTIALIST ACT UTILITARIANISM. For suppose you grant that acts do have value. You could then say in particular that the surgeon's complex act has value—negative value, of course. More strongly, you could say it has immense negative value. After all, consider the subparts of that com-plex act. One subpart is the surgeon's cutting the young man up and removing his parts. Since by hypothesis the young man did not consent to the surgeon's doing this, the surgeon's cutting the young man up and removing his parts is the surgeon's committing battery and theft. A very terrible battery and theft, since the battery is cutting up and the theft is of body parts. If any acts have negative value, this battery and theft has negative value, immense negative value.

No doubt if acts have value, then the other subpart of the surgeon's complex act—the surgeon's transplanting some by then available spare parts into five who need them—may be presumed to have pos-itive value. Still, you could say that the negative value of the battery and theft is so very great as to outweigh the positive value of the transplanting as to make the complex act itself on balance have neg-ative value, great negative value—sufficiently great negative value as to outweigh the positive value of the extra four lives in existence if the complex act occurs.

And if you then opt for NON-CONSEQUENTIALIST ACT UTILITARIAN-ISM in preference to CONSEQUENTIALIST ACT UTILITARIANISM, which allows you to count the negative value of that complex act in assessing what the surgeon ought to do, you have a way of obtaining the conclusion that the surgeon may not proceed, and even the conclusion that he positively ought not.

There is a cost to taking this line, for then you must reject one or more of the three theses we looked at in the preceding section. Perhaps, however, that will seem to you a small price to pay, or no real price to pay at all if those theses seemed unattractive to you from the outset.

More important, this is not the end of the matter, for it can certainly be asked what is supposed to make the negative value of the first subpart of the surgeon's complex act be so great as to outweigh the positive value of the second subpart of the surgeon's complex act— in fact, so great as to outweigh the sum of the positive value of the second subpart of the surgeon's complex act *and* the positive value of the four extra lives. Taking the line I indicated would require going on to deal with this further question, and it is not easy to see how it should be answered. (We will return to it in section 8 below.)

And there are further difficulties lying in wait.

5. Here is a reminder of the details of the case we have been look- ing at:

> TRANSPLANT: If the surgeon cuts the young man up, removes his parts, and transplants them into his five patients, the young man will die but the five will live. If surgeon does not do that, the young man will live but the five will die.

I did not, in telling you about this case, tell you why the surgeon's five patients need those parts. I suspect you supposed they need the parts because of ailments of one or another kind, naturally caused ailments. But that is only one possible history. Here is another: their need of the parts is due to the work of villains, one villain in the case of each patient—each of the villains will have killed one of the patients if the surgeon does not supply the needed parts. Let us call the case we get if we supply a history of natural causes for the patients' need TRANSPLANT (NATURAL CAUSES); let us call the case we get if we supply a villainous cause for each of the patients' need TRANSPLANT (5 VIL- LAIN CAUSES). I think you can see there is trouble ahead for those who think that some version of the Central Utilitarian Idea must be right.

For suppose you have taken it that acts have value, and opted for NON-CONSEQUENTIALIST ACT UTILITARIANISM. It is arguable that you can handle TRANSPLANT (NATURAL CAUSES) in the way I indicated in the preceding section. But how are you to handle TRANSPLANT (5 VILLAIN CAUSES)? The surgeon's cutting the young man up and re- moving his parts is (on your view) an act with immense negative value. But if this act does not occur, then each of the five villains will have killed someone. So if the surgeon proceeds, there is one act of immense negative value; if the surgeon does not proceed, there will have been five acts of at least as great negative value. (I say "at least as great negative value" since we may suppose that the surgeon's intention if he proceeds is to save the lives of his five patients, which is a good intention, whereas the villains' intentions, we may suppose, are villainous, whatever precisely those intentions may be.) So it looks as if NON-CONSEQUENTIALIST ACT UTILITARIANISM yields that the surgeon ought to proceed in TRANSPLANT (5 VILLAIN CAUSES).

But shouldn't the answer to the question whether the surgeon ought to proceed in TRANSPLANT (5 VILLAIN CAUSES) be exactly the same as the answer to the question whether the surgeon ought to proceed in TRANSPLANT (NATURAL CAUSES), namely no?

I hope it really is plain that the plight of the surgeon's five patients—their need of parts—no more requires the surgeon to proceed if their plight is due to villains than if their plight is due to nature. Consider two communities, both now in desperate need of food. In the case of one, the famine was due to nature; in the case of the other, the famine was due to third parties who wished to eliminate that community for villainous purposes of their own. If we cannot supply both communities with the food they need, shouldn't we share what we have between them, or flip a coin if sharing is impossible? Surely the call on us of human need is no greater on the ground that it was villainously, as opposed to naturally, caused.[9]

But then there really is trouble for those who think that some version of the Central Utilitarian Idea must be right. Allowing that acts have value and opting for NON-CONSEQUENTIALIST ACT UTILITARIANISM arguably yields the right answer to the question whether the surgeon ought to proceed in TRANSPLANT (NATURAL CAUSES), but it yields the wrong answer in TRANSPLANT (5 VILLAIN CAUSES).

9. It is of interest to notice the chilliness with which many writers treat need caused by one's own wrongful actions. That I wrongfully (say out of negligence or intention) caused my own need seems to make me less deserving of help than one whose need was not caused by his or her own wrongful acts. It is an interesting question, not easy to answer, exactly why we find ourselves thinking that true, and whether we should. But the situation in TRANSPLANT (5 VILLAIN CAUSES) is different: the needs of the five in that case are not due to their own wrongful acts.

My example of the two communities is a second cousin of one of John Taurek's in "Should the Numbers Count?", *Philosophy and Public Affairs*, 6 (Summer 1977).

It might be worth stopping for a moment over a third possible extension of TRANSPLANT: what we get if we suppose the needs of the surgeon's five patients are due not to natural causes, not to five villains, each of whom launched an attack on one of the five patients, but to villainy on the surgeon's own part. In the case I will call TRANSPLANT (SURGEON CAUSE), the surgeon ran up gambling debts last March and, knowing he is listed as heir in the wills of his five patients, gave them all a drug that causes organ failure. Now he repents and would put things right if he could. Here is a young man, in excellent health, all body parts in order. Is it permissible for the surgeon to proceed in TRANSPLANT (SURGEON CAUSE)? Surely not.

What is of interest is that there are differences: I am under very much more moral pressure to intervene to ensure that *I* will not have killed five people than I am to intervene to ensure that *you* will not have killed five people. For the moment, however, what is important is the fact that the surgeon may not proceed in TRANSPLANT (SURGEON CAUSE). And those who think some version of the Central Utilitarian Idea must be right are in as much trouble in face of this case as they are in face of TRANSPLANT (5 VILLAIN CAUSES), for in both cases there will have been five killings if the surgeon does not proceed.

6. The careful reader will have noticed the appearance of the future perfect tense in the preceding section and may already have thought of a way in which the difficulties I just pointed to can be avoided by those who think some version of the Central Utilitarian Idea must be right. What I have in mind is this. If the surgeon does not proceed in TRANSPLANT (5 VILLAIN CAUSES) and in TRANSPLANT (SURGEON CAUSE), then there *will have been* five killings; but it would be false to say that if the surgeon does not proceed in those cases, then there *will be* five killings. The killings in those two cases will not *follow* the surgeon's decision not to proceed (if that is what he decides), for they have already begun. If A has by now injected B with poison, so that B's death will soon ensue if you do not intervene by giving B the antidote, then if you do not intervene, A will have killed B; but A's killing of B is not something that will happen if you do not intervene to prevent B's death: A's poisoning of B has already occurred and thus A's killing of B has already begun.

Indeed, if the Reductive Theory of Action is true, A's killing of B has not merely already begun but has already taken place, for on that theory of action, A's killing of B is identical with the bodily movement

A made in injecting B with the poison, and that bodily movement is now wholly in the past.[10]

Even if the Reductive Theory of Action is false, however, A's killing of B is surely not wholly in the future, for A's injecting B with the poison is in the past. And similarly, whether or not the Reductive Theory of Action is true, the killings of the five patients in TRANSPLANT (5 VILLAIN CAUSES) and in TRANSPLANT (SURGEON CAUSE) are not wholly in the future relative to the time at which the surgeon has to decide whether or not to proceed.

Now those who think some version of the Central Utilitarian Idea must be right could take account of that fact. They could allow that acts have value, and opt for

> NON-CONSEQUENTIALIST ACT UTILITARIANISM: X ought to do alpha if and only if the act-plus-consequence-set of X's doing alpha would 'maximize value',

while insisting that the only acts in the act-plus-consequence-set of X's doing alpha are those wholly future to the time at which X would be starting to do alpha if that is what X chooses to do. Taking this line would make the negative values of the five killings that *will have* come about in TRANSPLANT (5 VILLAIN CAUSES) and TRANSPLANT (SURGEON CAUSE)—if the surgeon does not proceed in those cases—irrelevant to the question whether the surgeon ought to proceed in those cases, for those five killings are not wholly future to the time at which the surgeon would be starting to act. So taking this line would enable a friend of these ideas to reach the same conclusion in TRANSPLANT (5 VILLAIN CAUSES) and TRANSPLANT (SURGEON CAUSE) as they reach in TRANSPLANT (NATURAL CAUSES), namely that the surgeon ought not proceed.

So far so good. But so far is not very far. The cases we have been attending to, TRANSPLANT (NATURAL CAUSES), TRANSPLANT (5 VILLAIN CAUSES), and TRANSPLANT (SURGEON CAUSE), are extensions of TRANSPLANT, got by supplying different histories for the needs of the surgeon's five patients. Let us now turn to a variant of TRANSPLANT. In

10. But this of course itself yields an objection to the Reductive View of Action. For here is B, still alive, hoping that you will intervene to save his life; we may well think it just false to say of a man who is currently hoping you will save his life that A's killing of him has already occurred and is now wholly in the past. For further discussion, see Thomson, *Acts and Other Events*, and Bennett, *Events and Their Names*.

a case I will call MAFIA, the surgeon's five patients are recovering nicely from prior operations. (The parts they needed were supplied by the local organ bank without anyone's having had to kill anyone to get them.) The Mafia now tell the surgeon, "We will kill those five patients of yours unless you cut this young man up and remove his parts, and thereby kill him." Why do they want to surgeon to do this? Let us suppose the point is not to get the parts (the surgeon is to throw the parts away when he gets them out of the young man's body): the point is merely to get the young man killed, and in particular by a rather nasty procedure. Ought the surgeon accede to this threat? Surely not. But here the five killings that will come about if the surgeon does not proceed are wholly future to the time at which the surgeon would be starting to act. So those five killings are in the act-plus-consequence-sets of all of the surgeon's alternatives if he does not proceed. Those killings having immense disvalue, so it follows that the surgeon ought to proceed. But surely he ought not.

I hope it really is plain that the surgeon ought not proceed in MAFIA. How could you plausibly think that the surgeon may not proceed in TRANSPLANT (5 VILLAIN CAUSE) and yet that he not only may, but indeed ought to, proceed in MAFIA? You could think it impermissible for the surgeon to proceed in TRANSPLANT (5 VILLAIN CAUSE) but permissible for him to proceed in MAFIA only if you thought that the temporal difference between the cases makes a major moral difference. In MAFIA, the five villainous killings will wholly postdate the surgeon's refusal to act; in TRANSPLANT (5 VILLAIN CAUSES), the five villainous killings will not wholly postdate the surgeon's refusal to act. Can anyone plausibly suppose that this difference makes it permissible to proceed in the one case but not in the other? The idea seems crazy.

7. A summary is in order. "One ought to do a thing if and only if more good would come of doing it than of not doing it". That is the Central Utilitarian Idea. One way of making that idea precise is to take it to assert the following theory:

CONSEQUENTIALIST ACT UTILITARIANISM: X ought to do alpha if and only if the consequence-set of X's doing alpha would 'maximize value'.

But that theory is shown to be false by the fact that it yields the falsehood that the surgeon ought to proceed in TRANSPLANT (NATURAL CAUSES).

A second way of making the idea precise is to take it to assert

> NON-CONSEQUENTIALIST ACT UTILITARIANISM: X ought to do al-
> pha if and only if the act-plus-consequence-set of X's doing alpha
> would 'maximize value',

while allowing that acts (and not merely the consequences of acts) have value. But this shift does not help. NON-CONSEQUENTIALIST ACT UTILITARIANISM arguably yields the right answer (namely, no) to the question whether the surgeon ought to proceed in TRANSPLANT (NATURAL CAUSES); but it fails to yield the right answer (namely, no) to the question whether the surgeon ought to proceed in TRANSPLANT (5 VILLAIN CAUSES)—unless a proviso is attached, requiring that only the values of wholly future acts are relevant, in which case it anyway fails to yield the right answer (namely, no) to the question whether the surgeon ought to proceed in MAFIA. I know of no way of making the Central Utilitarian Idea precise that is not in trouble from these or similar cases.[11]

My arguments assumed three things. First, human need makes an equal call on us whether its causes are natural or villainous (see section 5 above), and thus that the answer to the question whether the surgeon ought to proceed in TRANSPLANT (NATURAL CAUSES) should be the same as the answer to the question whether the surgeon ought to proceed in TRANSPLANT (5 VILLAIN CAUSES). Second, the temporal difference issuing from the fact that the killings have already begun

---

11. As I said in note 2, CONSEQUENTIALIST ACT UTILITARIANISM and NON-CONSEQUENTIALIST ACT UTILITARIANISM are object-level moral judgments and hence not themselves moral theories. But if we reject them, there is no need for us to attend to the stronger explanatory moral judgments constructible from them. If CONSEQUENTIALIST ACT UTILITARIANISM is false, so certainly is the following explanatory moral judgment: if X ought to do such and such at t that is *because* the consequences of X's doing the such and such and such would be better . . . , and if it is not the case that X ought to do such and such at t that is *because* the consequences of X's doing the such and such would not be better.

It pays to take note here of the fact that even if CONSEQUENTIALIST ACT UTILITARIANISM were true—even if it were a necessary truth—there is independent reason to think the explanatory judgment constructible from it objectionable. What I have in mind is this. Many people think that CONSEQUENTIALIST ACT UTILITARIANISM can be made safe against such cases as TRANSPLANT if we keep in mind such putative facts as that secrets are always in the end found out. In particular, if the surgeon operates on the young man, then even if he does so in secret others will in the end find out what he did. And that would have dreadful

in TRANSPLANT (5 VILLAIN CAUSES), and have not already begun in
MAFIA, makes no moral difference (see section 6 above), and thus that
the answer to the question whether the surgeon ought to proceed in
TRANSPLANT (5 VILLAIN CAUSES) should be the same as the answer to
the question whether the surgeon ought to proceed in MAFIA. But
these two things seem to me plainly right. It is not *at all* plausible to
suppose that either a difference in source of need or a mere temporal
difference makes a moral difference. Suppose we are told by our
favorite, most reliable, informant that five are at risk of death and
that their deaths can be forestalled if and only if we kill one. Our
informant does not know the source of the risk, thus does not know
whether it is (i) natural causes or (ii) villainous causes that have already
begun their work or (iii) villainous causes that have not yet, but will,
begin their work if we do not kill the one. I think it implausible in
the extreme to suppose that we cannot tell whether we ought to kill
the one unless and until we are told which of (i), (ii), or (iii) is true.

   Third, my arguments assumed that the surgeon may not proceed
in any of these cases. But that I take to be a datum. Any theory that
yields that he ought to proceed—any theory that yields even that he
may proceed—is, as I said, a theory in dire need of revision.

8. I should stress, however, that I do not take myself to have shown
that human acts lack value. I said that shifting from CONSEQUEN-
TIALIST ACT UTILITARIANISM to the conjunction of NON-CONSEQUEN-
TIALIST ACT UTILITARIANISM, together with the supposition that acts

consequences! People would come to mistrust their doctors and not go in for
their checkups when they should, and then lots of people would fail to have their
cancers diagnosed early and so would die, and so on and on. Therefore (they
say) the surgeon's proceeding really would in the end have worse consequences
than his not proceeding. My view is that the idea that secrets are always in the
end found out is a piece of quite extraordinary optimism. No matter. Suppose
it were true. Then CONSEQUENTIALIST ACT UTILITARIANISM arguably would yield
the right answer to the question whether the surgeon may proceed, namely no.
But the explanatory judgment constructed from it would certainly not yield the
right answer to the question *why* the surgeon may not proceed. What makes it
impermissible for the surgeon to proceed is surely a matter of what he does to
the young man himself in doing so. It can hardly be thought that what makes it
impermissible for the surgeon to proceed is the dire consequences for others of
his proceeding.
   An analogous point can be made about NON-CONSEQUENTIALIST ACT
UTILITARIANISM.

have value, does not help the friend of the Central Utilitarian Idea; but that is not the same as saying that acts lack value. *Do* acts have value? We cannot answer that question without dealing with the Reductive Theory of Action, the Causal Theory of Intention, and the No-Value Thesis, and I have suggested that we should sidestep them.

But it might be worth taking note of the fact that some of what has come out along the way lends support to an interesting narrower idea than the idea that acts lack value. Consider the example of Bert's killing of the child. Bert moved his forefinger (which was curled round the trigger of a gun) and thereby caused a series of events—the trigger's retracting, a bullet's traveling through the air, a bullet's reaching and entering the child's body, and the child's death—such that it was by causing that series of events that Bert killed the child. If you accept the Reductive Theory of Action, you think those events were caused by, and hence were consequences of, Bert's killing of the child; if you accept the alternative theory of action I pointed to, you think they were parts of Bert's killing of the child. No matter. The narrower idea I mentioned says: whether those events were consequences of, or parts of, Bert's killing of the child, Bert's killing of the child has no *more* value than the sum of *their* values. Similarly for any killing of anybody: X's killing of Y has no more value than the sum of the values of the events X causes, by the causing of which X kills Y.

Now some of what has come out along the way lends support to this idea. For compare TRANSPLANT (5 VILLAIN CAUSES) and MAFIA, on the one hand, with TRANSPLANT (NATURAL CAUSES) on the other. Does it matter in the slightest to whether the surgeon may proceed whether the five, who will die if the surgeon does not proceed, will die at the hands of nature or at the hands of villains? Consider the two communities I mentioned, one in need of food because of nature, the other in need of food because of villains. Is there anything in morality that puts pressure on us to save those who would otherwise have been killed by villains in contrast with those who would otherwise die at the hands of nature?

If (as I think plain) the answer to these questions is no, then there is reason to think that what matters morally in deciding what to do is not that we would forestall killings, but that we would forestall deaths, there being no moral difference whether the deaths would be the outcomes of human acts or of nature.

But then if you think that differences in amounts of value to be generated by doing this or that must have an impact on what we ought to do, you really should think that a killing has no more value than the sum of the values of the events the killer causes—including the victim's death—by causing which the killer kills the victim. And in short you should think that the narrower idea really is plausible.

Accepting that narrower idea would not, of course, help friends of the Central Utilitarian Idea. Quite to the contrary. For down this road lies a generalization, to cover not merely killings but all human acts, so that—if they accepted the narrower idea and the generalization of it—they could not explain why the surgeon may not proceed in TRANS-PLANT (NATURAL CAUSES) by appeal to the immense negative value of the first subpart of the surgeon's complex act. (I pointed at the end of section 4 above to the difficulty that making this appeal generates; we here see why it will not work.) The surgeon would, on their view, have to proceed in *all* of the cases we have been looking at.

In any case, the narrower idea really is plausible. A notion we will make use of in the following chapter is intended to accommodate it.

9. Meanwhile, however, we are left with a question. *Why* ought the surgeon not proceed in the cases we have been looking at?

One answer I am sure has occurred to some readers is: because it just cannot be thought certain, by the surgeon or by anyone else, that he really will save four lives on balance by proceeding. In the extensions of TRANSPLANT the surgeon is described as capable of saving five by cutting up one and transplanting the one's parts into the five; but aren't transplants a chancy business? Don't they often fail to take? The surgeon will certainly kill the one young man if he proceeds, but there is no such certainty that he will save five by doing so. Indeed, he might kill one and then the other five die anyway, in which case there would be a net loss of one life if he proceeds. Again, in MAFIA the surgeon is described as capable of saving five by cutting up one and thereby doing what the Mafia wishes him to do; but aren't Mafia threats a chancy business? Don't threats often fail to get acted on? The surgeon will certainly kill the one young man if he proceeds, but there is no such certainty that he needs to kill the one in order that the five live. Indeed, he might refrain from killing the one and the other five live anyway, in which case there would be a net loss of one life if he proceeds.

Some people might like the idea of taking this line, but it is not open to friends of what I called the Central Utilitarian Idea. "One ought to do a thing if and only if more good would come of doing it than of not doing it". This does not say that one ought to do a thing if and only if it is probable that more good would come of doing it than of not doing it. On this view, probabilities are irrelevant to what a person ought to do. On this view, what is relevant is only what in fact is and will be the case.

There are modern variants of the Central Utilitarian Idea according to which what a person ought to do turns on 'expected utilities', thus according to which what a person ought to do is a function of what is likely to be value-maximizing.

There is good reason, and we will soon get to it, to allow probabilities to have a bearing on what a person ought to do. But even if we do allow probabilities to have a bearing on what a person ought to do, we cannot answer the question "Why ought the surgeon not operate in TRANSPLANT and MAFIA?" by appeal to them. Transplants often fail to take, and threats often fail to get acted on; but we may suppose that *this* particular operation is very likely to be successful (the surgeon we are imagining being so skillful) and that *this* particular threat is very likely to be acted on (the Mafia being so powerful in this particular part of town), and the fact would remain that the agents ought not proceed. And in any case, it can hardly be thought that the more likely it is that the transplant would succeed, and the threat be acted on, the more reasonable it is to think it permissible for the surgeon to proceed in these cases.

10. Why ought the surgeon not proceed? Here is the answer I recommend: because the surgeon would thereby infringe some claims of the young man's, and it is not the case that sufficiently much more good would come of infringing them than would come of not infringing them. (Remember the Tradeoff Idea.) We will need to see in the following chapter how that recommendation should be thought to work.

What we need to do here is to see that that recommendation so much as *can* be thought to work.

What I have in mind is this. Let us give a name to a certain fact.

> The Claim Fact: If the surgeon cuts the young man up and removes his parts, the surgeon will thereby infringe some claims of the young man's, and it is not the case that sufficiently much more good would come of infringing them than would come of not infringing them.

These things want clarification, but let us for the time being suppose this is a fact. I have been taking it as a datum that the surgeon may not proceed, so here is a second fact.

The Impermissibility Fact: The surgeon may not proceed.

My recommendation is that the Claim Fact explains the Impermissibility Fact. But it might well be replied that the Claim Fact can explain the Impermissibility Fact only by the following route: The Claim Fact makes it be the case that the surgeon's complex act would have great negative value, sufficient negative value to outweigh the positive value of the net saving of four lives that would come of it, and *that* is what explains the Impermissibility Fact—by virtue of

NON-CONSEQUENTIALIST ACT UTILITARIANISM: X ought to do alpha if and only if the act-plus-consequence-set of X's doing alpha would 'maximize value'.

But (the reply goes on) if that is how the Claim Fact explains the Impermissibility Fact, then the explanation fails—we have already seen that it fails. If you suppose the surgeon's complex act has great negative value, and accept NON-CONSEQUENTIALIST ACT UTILITARIANISM then, as we saw in section 4, perhaps (perhaps!) you can reach the right answer in TRANSPLANT (NATURAL CAUSES) but, as we saw in sections 5 and 6, you reach the wrong answer in TRANSPLANT (5 VILLAIN CAUSES), TRANSPLANT (SURGEON CAUSE), and MAFIA. So that had better not be how the Claim Fact explains the Impermissibility Fact. But how else could the Claim Fact explain the Impermissibility Fact? How else could claims constrain behavior than by way of the negative value of a claim infringement?

The idea that the Claim Fact can explain the Impermissibility Fact only by a route that passes through value issues from the quite general idea that permissibility and impermissibility in action must be a function of value. What else besides value could there be for morality to take account of? I drew attention in Chapter 3 to the idea many people have that no consideration has moral force except by way of entailing that a person ought to do a thing; what emerges here is the idea many people have that no consideration has moral force except by way of having, or generating things that have, positive or negative value.

Indeed it is this idea that makes people feel that some version of the Central Utilitarian Idea must be right. After all, if what we ought to do is a function of value, then surely what we ought to do is to produce as much of it as we can. What else besides maximizing what matters to morality could it be thought that morality requires of us? The varieties of utilitarianism do not appeal to us primarily because of the various theories of value that their friends set before us— theories to the effect that it is only pleasure or happiness or welfare or what you will that *has* value; they appeal primarily because of what they all have in common, namely the underlying idea that value is what all morality reduces to.

But it won't do. There is more to morality than value: there are also claims. And it is not because a claim infringement has negative value that we ought not infringe claims. We ought not infringe claims—when we ought not infringe them—because of what a claim *is*.

Chapter 6

Tradeoffs

1. As I said at the beginnings of Chapters 3 and 5, it seems right to think that X's having a claim against Y is equivalent to, and perhaps just *is,* Y's behavior's being constrained in a certain way. We took note (in Chapter 3) of two things included in that constraint on Y, namely the need to seek a release in advance if the claim will otherwise have to be infringed, and the need to compensate later for harms or losses caused by the infringement if a release was unobtainable. But what is central to that constraint on Y is this: other things being equal, Y ought to accord the claim. What are those other things that may or may not be equal? The Tradeoff Idea provides an answer, for it says that it is permissible to infringe a claim—that is, permissible to fail to accord the claim—if and only if sufficiently much more good would come of infringing it than would come of not infringing it. Consider the cases we looked at in the preceding chapter. If the surgeon cuts the young man up and removes his parts, he will thereby save four lives (on balance). Why may he not proceed? I recommend that we say

> The Claim Fact: If the surgeon cuts the young man up and removes his parts, the surgeon will thereby infringe some claims of the young man's, and it is not the case that sufficiently much more good would come of infringing them than would come of not infringing them

explains

> The Impermissibility Fact: The surgeon may not proceed.

But there are other cases and other claims. Suppose that A has a claim against me that I not kick him in the shin. Suppose also that I would

save four lives by kicking A in the shin. I should imagine that it would
be permissible for me to do so. It suggests itself that we should say

> If I kick A in the shin, I will thereby infringe a claim of A's, but
> it is the case that sufficiently much more good would come of
> infringing it than would come of not infringing it

explains

> It is permissible for me to proceed.

These ideas need to be looked at more closely.

2. We need in the first place to attend to the question how the notion
'good' in the Tradeoff Idea should be thought to compare with the
notion 'value' that we looked at in the preceding chapter.

Here is a reminder of the details of one of our cases:

> MAFIA: If the surgeon does not cut the young man up and remove
> his parts, the Mafia will kill five. If the surgeon does cut the
> young man up and remove his parts, the Mafia will not kill five.

On any reasonable suppositions about value, the act-plus-consequence
set of the surgeon's proceeding has more value than the act-plus-
consequence sets of his doing any of the other things open to him to
do at the time. But I suggested that we should say: it is not the case
that sufficiently much more good would come of the surgeon's infringing the claims he would infringe by proceeding than would come of
not infringing them. Are we to take that notion 'good' to be the same
as the notion 'value'? No.

What is wanted here is a notion 'good for a person'. Suppose you
are starving. Then it would be good for you to get some food now,
since you will live if you get it and die if you do not.

Moreover, it is equally good for you to get some food now, whatever
the source of your need for food, whether your need for food was
caused by villains or by negligence on someone's part or by nature.
Consider the two communities we looked at in the preceding chapter,
one in need of food because of villains, the other in need of food
because of nature. It is equally good for the members of each to get
the food they need. That the villains will have killed the members of
the one community if they do not get food, and no person (only
nature itself) will have killed the members of the other community if

they do not get food, makes no difference to how good it is for the members to get food.

Consider TRANSPLANT. It is equally good for the surgeon's five patients to get the parts they need, whether their need for parts is due to nature, as in TRANSPLANT (NATURAL CAUSES), or to villains, as in TRANSPLANT (5 VILLAIN CAUSES).

Or, as we might have put it: it is equally bad for the members of each community to not get the food they need and equally bad for the surgeon's five patients to not get the parts they need, whether the needs are due to villains or to nature or to anything else. These come to the same. That is, I will throughout use "good for a person" and "bad for a person" in such a way that if something that would have been good for a person does not happen, then something happens that is bad for that person, and if something that would have been bad for a person does not happen, then something happens that is good for that person. If a piano falls on my head, then something happens that is bad for me, a piano's falling on my head; if you very kindly intervene, so that the piano does not fall on my head, then something happens that is good for me, a piano's not falling on my head. (Compare the use by legal theorists and economists of the term "opportunity cost".)

And we are not to be looking at the acts that will have taken place if the surgeon does or does not proceed—and if we do or do not give food to those at risk because of villains—and asking what value those acts would have. That is irrelevant to us. We are to be asking only how good it is for those who would be affected by the acts if the acts do or do not take place or, alternatively, how bad it is for them if the acts do or do not take place.[1]

So we should take the Tradeoff Idea to say this: it is permissible to infringe a claim if and only if infringing it would be sufficiently much better for those for whom infringing it would be good than not infringing it would be for those for whom not infringing it would be good. Alternatively: it is permissible to infringe a claim if and only if not infringing it would be sufficiently much worse for those for whom not infringing it would be bad than infringing it would be for those for whom infringing it would be bad.

1. It will be clear, then, that the notion 'good for a person' is the same as the result of constraining the notion 'value' by what I called the narrower idea in section 8 of Chapter 5.

I will not offer an analysis of this notion 'good for a person': it is important for our purposes, and I will lean heavily on it, but I leave it to intuition. It is good for a person who is starving to get food, it is bad for a person that a piano fall on his or her head, and I hope I will not say that such and such is or would be good or bad for a person where this will strike you as implausible. Two things should be stressed, however. In the first place, I do not construe the notion in a subjective sense according to which only pleasant feelings are good for a person and only unpleasant feelings are bad for a person. I so construe it that something that happens to you can be good or bad for you even if you never find out it happened to you, and so are neither pleased nor displeased at its happening to you. Second, I do not construe the notion in a subjective sense according to which what happens to you is good or bad for you if and only if you think it is. I so construe it that something that happens to you can be good or bad for you even if you think it is not. In short, I will everywhere construe the notion 'good for a person' objectively. The Tradeoff Idea in particular is to be understood to say that what matters is not how good those affected by a claim infringement would feel, not how good they think the claim infringement would be for them, but rather how good it really would be for them.

3. Here is the idea again:

> The Tradeoff Idea: It is permissible to infringe a claim if and only if infringing it would be sufficiently much better for those for whom infringing it would be good than not infringing it would be for those for whom not infringing it would be good.

We have looked at the question how the notion 'good' in it is to be understood. Let us now take note of an important objection to it: it fails to take the claim holder seriously enough. (It fails to pay the claim holder sufficient respect, we might say.) It tells us that Y may infringe X's claim if and only if a certain balancing comes out satisfactorily, but nothing in the description of the balancing mentions X. For all it says, the claim might be anyone's, and that is surely wrong. If X is the claim holder, then the balancing must give a special place to X's own good: what is to be traded off is X's good on the one hand and the good of others on the other hand, for it is X's claim that is being traded.

We can accommodate this point by revising the idea as follows:

The Tradeoff Idea: It is permissible to infringe a claim if and only if infringing it would be sufficiently much better for those for whom infringing it would be good than not infringing it would be for the claim holder.

Very well, but how much better is sufficiently much better? We might allow ourselves to speak of an 'increment of good'; how large does that increment of good have to be?

The answer is that there is no answer. There is no one size such that for any claim you choose, the claim is permissibly infringeable if and only if infringing it would generate an increment of good of that size. One thing (of several) that I have in mind comes out as follows.

We have an intuitive notion of the strictness or, as I will say, the stringency of a claim. The claims the surgeon would be infringing if he proceeded in TRANSPLANT and MAFIA are, we think, markedly more stringent than the claim I would be infringing if I kicked A in the shin. Suppose that if I kick A in the shin, four people will live who would otherwise die; that is very good for them. So infringing A's claim would be very good for those for whom it would be good. Let us suppose that I would cause A a mild, short-lasting pain and a bruise if I kicked him in the shin; that would be in a small way bad for him; thus not infringing the claim would be in a small way good for A. The increment of good in this case seems to be sufficiently large to make it permissible for me to kick A in the shin. But an increment of good of that same size is not sufficiently large to make it permissible for the surgeon to proceed in TRANSPLANT and MAFIA: a net gain of four lives is not enough. Perhaps no increment, however large, would make it permissible for the surgeon to proceed; we will return to that possibility below. At all events, *this* increment is not sufficiently large.

In short, the size of the required increment of good seems to vary with the stringency of the claim: the more stringent the claim, the greater the required increment of good.[2]

2. Notice that according to the thesis that all claims are absolute, all claims are equally stringent—yet another count against the thesis, if another were needed.

Ronald Dworkin says that rights are "trumps", and Robert Nozick calls them "side-constraints". See Dworkin, *Taking Rights Seriously* (Cambridge: Harvard University Press, 1977), and Nozick, *Anarchy, State, and Utopia* (New York: Basic Books, 1974). You might conclude that Dworkin and Nozick think that all rights (and *a fortiori* all claims) are absolute, thus equally stringent. I doubt

Let us look more closely at stringency. I suggest that we should take the stringency of a claim itself to vary with how bad its infringement would be for the claim holder. Thus I suggest we accept

> The Aggravation Principle: If X has a claim against Y that Y do alpha, then the worse Y makes things for X if Y fails to do alpha, the more stringent X's claim against Y that Y do alpha,

and, what flows from it,

> The Comparison Principle: Suppose X_1 has a claim against Y_1 that Y_1 do alpha, and X_2 has a claim against Y_2 that Y_2 do beta. Then X_1's claim against Y_1 is more stringent than X_2's claim against Y_2 if and only if Y_1 makes things worse for X_1 if Y_1 fails to do alpha than Y_2 makes things for X_2 if Y_2 fails to do beta.

These principles[3] yield in particular that the stringency of a claim does not vary with the source of the claim. But that seems very plausible indeed. Claims generated by promises, for example, are surely no more, or less, stringent than claims generated in any other way; and similarly for any other possible sources of claims.

On the other hand, we should notice that accepting the Aggravation Principle and the Comparison Principle commits us to a conception of the stringency of a claim that might, *prima facie,* have been thought implausible.

We were supposing that A has a claim against me that I not kick him in the shin; and we were supposing that I would do nothing worse to A if I kicked him in the shin than cause him a mild, short-lasting pain and a bruise. Suppose, by contrast, that if I kick B in the shin, I will thereby kill him. (B has a new disease, the most interesting symptom of which is that a kick in the shin is fatal.) The Aggravation Principle yields that A's claim that I not kick him in the shin is not

---

that they think this. (I cannot believe they think it impermissible to kick a man in the shin to save four lives. I also cannot believe they think it no infringement of a claim to kick a man in the shin. But they are alas not very generous with detail.) In any case, since claims vary in stringency, those attractive metaphors have to go. The most we can say is that rights are more or less high cards, or that they are more or less spongy side-constraints, which I grant lack the charm of the originals.

3. They will need qualification, for reasons that will come out later. I hope the reader will take my word for it that the sources of the need to qualify are not relevant here.

very stringent whereas B's claim that I not kick him in the shin is very stringent; and the Comparison Principle yields that B's claim that I not kick him in the shin is markedly more stringent than A's claim that I not kick him in the shin. But I think we feel an inclination to deny both of these things. I think we feel an inclination to say the following: B's claim against me that I not kill him is a very stringent claim, but B's claim against me that I not kick him in the shin—like A's—is not stringent.

I think we feel an inclination to say, quite generally, that stringency attaches 'directly to the wrong itself'. For many pairs of people X and Y, X has a claim against Y that Y not kick X in the shin, and Y would be acting wrongly in kicking X in the shin. This may plausibly be taken to mean that Y's kicking X in the shin would be Y's doing X a wrong. A wrong no matter what would happen to X in consequence of the kick. Admittedly, if Y kicks X in the shin, Y may also do X some further, other, wrong; admittedly the further wrong may be so very grave as to 'swamp', that is, make seem morally uninteresting, the wrong that Y does X in kicking X on the shin. All the same, whatever else happens, Y does X a wrong in kicking X in the shin. Now it is *prima facie* very plausible to think that the degree of stringency of the claim just is the degree of gravity of that wrong: *that* wrong—not some other wrong that Y might be doing to X by kicking X in the shin. We could call the idea that lies behind these remarks the Fine-Grain Conception of Stringency.

But there really is good reason to reject the Fine-Grain Conception of Stringency. It does seem right, *prima facie,* to attach stringency 'directly to the wrong itself' in the way I indicated, but some wrongs surely are particularly grave precisely because of the wrongs we do to the victim *by* committing them. Consider, for example, cutting a person's legs off where one ought not do that. Doing it is doing the person a very grave wrong, and what makes it so is presumably the wrongs we do the person *by* cutting his or her legs off. We do not grow new legs as we grow fingernails and hair, and artificial legs are no very good substitute; so by cutting a person's legs off you permanently cripple the person. I do not say that cutting a person's legs off would be doing the person no wrong at all if we did regrow legs, or if there were happy substitutes for naturally grown legs. Trimming a person's fingernails or shaving off a man's beard, without permission, without any other justification, are wrongs, despite the fact that the person will regrow nails and beard; causing a person to have a squashed nose without justification is a wrong even though there are ways of reconstructing noses. But cutting a person's legs off has got to be counted a more grave wrong by any sane moral theory—and a sane moral theory must surely trace that to the wrong one does to the victim *by* committing it.

Similarly for the wrong the surgeon does the young man *by* cutting him up and removing his parts.

So I suggest we instead adopt a large-grain conception of stringency according to which a wrong to a person by which we commit a further wrong to that person inherits gravity from the further wrong. More precisely,

> The Large-Grain Conception of Stringency:
> *If*
> (i) X has a claim against Y that Y not do beta, and
> (ii) if Y does alpha then he or she will thereby do beta, and
> (iii) X has a claim against Y that Y not do alpha,
> *then* X's claim against Y that Y not do alpha is at least as stringent as X's claim that Y not do beta.

This conception of stringency does not attach stringency 'directly to the wrong itself'; but it does seem to capture our way of thinking about stringency better than the Fine-Grain Conception of Stringency does.

If we accept the Large-Grain Conception of Stringency—and I suggest we now do—then B's claim that I not kick him in the shin is very stringent, for it is at least as stringent as B's claim against me that I not kill him.

I suggest we should also accept something even stronger than the Large-Grain Conception of Stringency. The Large-Grain Conception of Stringency thesis tells us (roughly) that if you have a claim that a person not use a certain means, and a claim that the person not carry out the end, then your claim that the person not use the means is at least as stringent as your claim that the person not carry out the end. It is very plausible to think, more strongly, that if you have a claim that a person not carry out the end, then it follows from that by itself that you have a claim that the person not use any of the means by which the person would carry out the end, a claim that is at least as stringent as your claim that the person not carry out the end. In other words, it is very plausible to think we should accept

The Means Principle for Claims:

> *If*
> (i) X has a claim against Y that Y not do beta, and
> (ii) if Y does alpha then he or she will thereby do beta,
> *then* X has a claim against Y that Y not do alpha, that claim
> being at least as stringent as X's claim that Y not do beta.

This thesis says that more than stringency is inherited: it says that
the status of claim itself is inherited—it says that claims extend down
from ends to means.

I think it a very attractive thesis, and in two ways at that. Here is
my doorbell. So far so good. Does anybody have a claim against me
that I not press my doorbell? Nicholas, for example? What on earth
could be reason to think he does? Then we learn that if I press the
doorbell, I will thereby kill him. (He and a battery are wired to the
doorbell.) Nicholas has a claim against me that I not kill him. If he
also has a claim that I not press the doorbell, then the Large-Grain
Conception of Stringency tells us that that claim of his is at least as
stringent as his claim that I not kill him. The Means Principle for
Claims tells us that he does in fact have a claim that I not press the
doorbell. Admittedly I would be doing him no wrong if it were not
the case that by pressing the doorbell I would do him a harm. But
that *is* the case. And don't we think he therefore has a claim—a very
stringent claim—that I not press the doorbell?

A second reason for thinking the Means Principle for Claims an
attractive thesis is its link with a thesis we met in Chapter 4: the
Means Principle for Permissibility, which we can re-express in a way
similar to that in which we just expressed the Means Principle for
Claims:

> The Means Principle for Permissibility:
> *If*
> (i) if Y does alpha then he or she will thereby do beta, and
> (ii) it is permissible for Y to do alpha,
> *then* it is permissible for Y to do beta.

This thesis says that permissibility too is inherited, but in the reverse
direction—it says that permissibility extends up from means to ends.
And it would be no surprise if the two theses were jointly true. If
claims extend down from ends to means, then if there are claims
infringed in carrying out the end, there are equally stringent claims

infringed in choosing any means to it. No wonder it is permissible to carry out the end if it is permissible to choose a means to it.

So I suggest we accept not merely the Large-Grain Conception of Stringency but also the Means Principle for Claims.

Given we accept the Large-Grain Conception of Stringency, the Aggravation Principle and the Comparison Principle are safe. Consider the young man in TRANSPLANT and MAFIA. The young man has a claim against the surgeon that the surgeon not kill him. In and by killing him, the surgeon makes things very bad for him, since the young man dies. The young man also has a claim against the surgeon that the surgeon not cut him up and remove his parts. In and by doing this, the surgeon makes things equally bad for him, since the young man dies. The Aggravation Principle yields that both claims are very stringent; the Comparison Principle yields that they are equally stringent. That is surely as it should be.

Let us now go back. We were attending to

> The Tradeoff Idea: It is permissible to infringe a claim if and only if infringing it would be sufficiently much better for those for whom infringing it would be good than not infringing it would be for the claim holder.

How much better is sufficiently much better? I said that the size of the required increment of good seems to vary with the stringency of the claim: the more stringent the claim, the larger the required increment of good. In light of our account of stringency, that means: the worse the claim infringer would make things for the claim holder by infringing the claim, the larger the required increment of good.

4. The Tradeoff Idea offers us necessary and sufficient conditions for permissibly infringing a claim. But in fact it is grossly oversimple.

Consider first the possibility that the prospective claim infringer is confronted with a conflict of claims. There are Lewis and Michael. Here am I, confronted, alas, with only two alternatives: kill Lewis or kill Michael. (How so? I am driving, and my brakes have just failed. If I continue straight, I drive into and kill Lewis. My steering wheel is constricted, so my only alternative to continuing straight is turning to the right. But if I turn to the right, I drive into and kill Michael.) We may well suppose that Lewis and Michael each has a very stringent claim against me that I not kill him, and that their claims are equally stringent: I would make things bad for each in the same degree if I killed him. If we suppose also that no one other than Lewis and Michael will be affected whichever alternative I choose—and for simplicity, let us suppose this—then there is no increment of good to be got by killing Lewis and no increment of good to be got by killing Michael. Yet it is surely permissible for me to toss a coin (heads I kill Lewis, tails I kill Michael), and then kill the one who loses the coin toss. In this case, then, no increment of good is required for permissibility, though the claim I will be infringing is very stringent.

That is a very simple case of conflict of claims, because of our suppositions that the claims are equally stringent and that no one else is involved. What am I to do in a case in which only two people are involved, but one's claim is more stringent than the other's? Then I presumably ought to infringe the weaker of the claims. Again, what if many people are involved? If their claims are equally stringent, I presumably ought to choose the course of action by which I infringe fewest. What if, to pile on complications, the claims of the many are not equally stringent? Thus what if I have to choose between doing alpha, by which I would cause a number of people to suffer in a variety of different ways, and doing beta, by which I would cause a number of other people (the same number or a different number) to suffer in a variety of still other ways? Then I presumably ought to make things as little bad for those potentially affected as possible.

But I say only "presumably" throughout. For example, it might be that I can compensate Y for the harm I would cause Y by infringing Y's claim, whereas I cannot compensate X for the harm I would cause X for infringing X's; then even if Y's claim is the more stringent, it might be that what I ought to do is infringe-Y's-claim-and-later-compensate-Y-for-the-harm-I-cause-him-or-her. (Notice that if I could get a release from X or Y in advance, then I am not in fact confronted with a conflict of claims, for I have a non-claim-infringing alternative, namely get a release from X or Y in advance.) For another example, it might be that I ought to infringe Y's more stringent claim today if I (or perhaps some other person) had had to infringe X's more stringent claim yesterday. There are any number of other possibilities here too. I think that a theory of rights cannot be expected to supply a non-vague general formula by means of which it can be decided what it is permissible to do in cases of conflict of claims. At all events, this one will not so much as try to supply a decision procedure for such cases.

There are other sources of trouble for the Tradeoff Idea beyond the possibility of a conflict of claims, but there is more that comes out of consideration of conflicts of claims that is important for our purposes, and we should stop to take note of it.

5. Consider TRANSPLANT and MAFIA. The young man has a claim against the surgeon that the surgeon not kill him. But what about the surgeon's five patients in TRANSPLANT? What about the five whom the Mafia will kill if the surgeon does not proceed in MAFIA? Don't they have claims against the surgeon that the surgeon save them? If so, then these cases too are cases of conflict of claims—just as the case of Lewis and Michael is—for the surgeon cannot save the five without killing the young man.

The idea that people have a claim to be saved, or perhaps more generally to be provided with what they need, is one that many people have found attractive. There are difficulties. For example, against *whom* is the claim had? Anyone who is available and can do the saving? Everyone who is available and can do the saving? Again, suppose Y can, and Y alone can, save X but only at a considerable sacrifice; does X all the same have the claim against Y?[4]

But we can bypass those difficulties, for we are now in possession of a strong argument to the effect that there is no such claim. Of course an argument is no stronger than its premises are, and I have no doubt that some who dislike the conclusion of this argument will wish to go back and reject one or more of its premises. But if you have been coming along with me so far, you will not find that easy to do. (Indeed, this is one reason why I showed you the premises first.)

Suppose that Alfred is one of the surgeon's five patients in TRANS-PLANT: Alfred will die if he does not get a new heart. Does Alfred have a claim against the surgeon that the surgeon save his life? The surgeon can in fact save Alfred's life—for there is an available heart, the young man's, and the surgeon *can* install it in Alfred—and to bypass the difficulties I mentioned, I stress that no one else can save Alfred's life and, moreover, the surgeon can do so at no great sacrifice to himself. So let us suppose that Alfred does have a claim against the surgeon that the surgeon save his life. The young man, of course,

4. A survey and discussion of these and other difficulties may be found in Joel Feinberg, *Harm to Others*, vol. 1 of *The Moral Limits of the Criminal Law* (Oxford: Oxford University Press, 1984).

has a claim against the surgeon that the surgeon not kill him. So what confronts the surgeon is a conflict of claims.

Can it be thought that the two claims in conflict are equally stringent? Hardly. Lewis' claim against me that I not kill him is as stringent as Michael's claim against me that I not kill him; so flipping a coin was permissible—heads I kill Lewis, tails I kill Michael. But it is a datum that the surgeon must not kill the young man. Flipping a coin between Alfred and the young man is morally ruled out.

So Alfred's claim that the surgeon save him had better be less stringent than the young man's claim that the surgeon not kill him. But how can that be so? If the surgeon fails to save Alfred, that is very bad indeed for Alfred: Alfred dies. So

> The Aggravation Principle: If X has a claim against Y that Y do alpha, then the worse Y makes things for X if Y fails to do alpha, the more stringent X's claim against Y that Y do alpha

tells us that Alfred's claim against the surgeon is very stringent. Of course if the surgeon kills the young man, that is very bad indeed for him: *he* dies. Is it worse for the young man that he die than it is for Alfred that Alfred die? It's pretty terrible to die in consequence of being cut up and having one's parts distributed for use by others; so add such details as you like (as it might be, a lot of pain) to fix that Alfred's death would be equally terrible. Then we are entitled to conclude, by

> The Comparison Principle: Suppose X_1 has a claim against Y_1 that Y_1 do alpha, and X_2 has a claim against Y_2 that Y_2 do beta. Then X_1's claim against Y_1 is more stringent than X_2's claim against Y_2 if and only if Y_1 makes things worse for X_1 if Y_1 fails to do alpha than Y_2 makes things for X_2 if Y_2 fails to do beta,

that the young man's claim that the surgeon not kill him is no more stringent than Alfred's claim that the surgeon save him. So if Alfred has a claim that the surgeon save him, it is fully as stringent as the young man's claim that the surgeon not kill him. So it should be permissible for the surgeon to flip a coin. But it is not permissible for the surgeon to do that.

Consider also Bert, who is another of the surgeon's five patients but who only needs a kidney. Does Bert have a claim against the surgeon that the surgeon save him? Suppose he does. Bert will die if he does not get the kidney he needs, so the Aggravation Principle tells

us the claim is very stringent indeed. The young man has a claim
against the surgeon that the surgeon not cut him up and remove a
kidney. (That is battery and theft.) How stringent is that claim? It's
not nearly so bad to lose a kidney as to die: a healthy person can live
with only one kidney. The Comparison Principle therefore tells us
that Bert's claim against the surgeon that the surgeon save him is
more stringent than the young man's claim against the surgeon that
the surgeon not cut him up and remove a kidney. Faced with this
conflict of claims, surely it is permissible for (perhaps even morally
required of) the surgeon to cut the young man up and remove a kidney.
But that won't do at all. The fact that I need a kidney for life, and
that you can live with only one, certainly does not make it permissible
for (much less required of) a surgeon to remove one of yours against
your will.

I conclude that neither Alfred nor Bert, nor any of the surgeon's
other three patients, has a claim against the surgeon to save his life.

What this argument does is to take the (putative) claim to be saved
seriously. If there really is such a claim, then it should have the same
kind of moral weight as any other claim does (it should have some
or other degree of stringency), and then it should be assessible for
amount of moral weight (for degree of stringency) in the same way
as any other claim. But supposing it does and is has unacceptable
consequences.

Why do people want to have it that there is a claim to be saved?
The answer seems plain. (i) There are situations in which it would be
very easy for us to save and thus in which we ought to save, indeed
in which it would be monstrous in us to fail to save. Here is a child
drowning; I have a life preserver and can easily throw it to the child;
it would be monstrous in me not to do so. Moreover, (ii) there are
situations in which it would not be *very* easy to save—saving might
require a considerable effort on our part, perhaps even some sacrifice—but in which we all the same ought to save, though perhaps
"monstrous" would be too strong a word for a failure to save. There
is a child drowning; I can swim out to save it, though that would
require effort and is accompanied by some risk to me (drowning
people tend to climb up those who try to save them), but perhaps the
case is one in which I ought to expend the effort and run the risk.

But why should it be thought that those in need of saving in situations of kinds (i) and (ii) have a claim to be saved? Our old friend
(from Chapter 3)

(T_2) If Y ought not let it fail to be the case that p, then there is an X such that $C_{X, Y}p$

says that wherever one ought to do something there is someone who has a claim against us that we do it; as we saw, however, that thesis will not do.

Perhaps the thought here is that anyway those in need of saving in situations of kind (i) have a claim to be saved, in light not of the overstrong (T_2), but of the weaker

If Y not only ought not let it fail to be the case that p, but would be gravely at fault if he or she let it fail to be the case that p, then there is an X such that $C_{X, Y}p$.

But why does there have to be a claim where we would be gravely at fault if we failed to do a thing? Is positing the claim supposed to explain its being the case that we would be gravely at fault if we failed to do the thing? But why do we need *that* explanation? If someone is in dire need, and I can easily supply what is needed, then why does that not by itself yield that I would be gravely at fault if I failed to do so? Why does the explanation have to run through a claim? I have been pointing as we go to a variety of ways in which people try to simplify the phenomena of morality, and here is yet another—and it is one for which, so far as I can see, there is no need.

6. We were looking at

The Tradeoff Idea: It is permissible to infringe a claim if and only if infringing it would be sufficiently much better for those for whom infringing it would be good than not infringing it would be for the claim holder.

How much better is sufficiently much better? I had said in section 3 that the size of the required increment of good seems to vary with the stringency of the claim: the more stringent the claim, the larger the required increment of good. But I then said in section 4, that the Tradeoff Idea is all the same grossly oversimple. Cases of conflict of claims make trouble for it. Where a prospective claim infringer is confronted by a conflict of claims, it may be permissible for him or her to infringe a very stringent claim, despite not producing any increment of good at all.

In a case of conflict of claims, there are three parties: A has a claim against me that I not do alpha, but a third party B has a claim against

me that I do alpha. But third parties can make trouble for the Tradeoff
Idea in yet another way. Suppose that A has a claim against me that
I not kick A and that no one has a claim against me that I kick A;
so I am not confronted by a conflict of claims. Suppose that if I kick
A, I thereby saves four lives. Fine, we think: large increment of good,
weak claim, so it is permissible for me to proceed. But suppose that
the saving of four lives is only *net*. Villains have said they will kill
five unless I kick A; but A is standing next to B near the edge of a
cliff, and if I kick A, A will be jostled against B, and B will fall off
the cliff, so if I kick A, I will thereby kill one. Five minus one is four,
so I save four if I kick A. But surely I may not kick A. If I kick A, I
infringe only a weak claim of A's; but by kicking A I infringe a
stringent claim of B's. I may not infringe that stringent claim of B's
for a saving of four lives. It follows (by the Means Principle for
Permissibility) that I may not infringe that weak claim of A's.

In a case of conflict of claims, as I said, A has a claim against me
that I not do alpha, but a third party B has a claim against me that
I do alpha; in the case we have just looked at, A has a claim against
me that I not do alpha, and the third party B also has a claim against
me that I not do alpha. B's claim generates interference *here*, not by
conflicting with A's claim but rather by reinforcing it.

And there are other sources of trouble for the Tradeoff Idea than
cases in which the claims of third parties generate interference. Suppose that the only claims bearing on what I may do now are A's.
Suppose that I can produce a large increment of good by infringing
A's claims. So far so good. But what if I have an alternative, non-
claim-infringing, way of producing that same increment of good? (We
might notice here again that if I have a way of getting a release from
A in advance, then I do have an alternative, non-claim-infringing, way
of producing that same increment of good, though of course if I have
to buy the release from A then the distribution of the increment of
good will differ from what it would otherwise be.) However weak a
claim, a large increment of good to be got by infringing it does not
make infringing the claim permissible if one has a non-claim-infringing
way of producing that same increment of good, or even a comparably
large increment of good.

The Tradeoff Idea is obviously oversimple. It offers us necessary
and sufficient conditions for permissibly infringing a claim, but what
makes a claim infringement permissible or impermissible is an extremely complex affair, turning not only on the stringency of the claim,

and the size of the increment of good to be got by infringing it, but on other things as well. What we have noticed in particular is that it is also relevant what the potential claim infringer's *circumstances* are. Do third parties have claims bearing on whether a potential claim infringer may infringe the claim? Does the potential claim infringer have alternative ways of producing the increment of good? Its being permissible or impermissible to infringe the claim turns on these matters too. I said earlier that I think a theory of rights cannot be expected to supply a nonvague general formula by means of which it can be decided what it is permissible to do in cases of conflict of claims; *a fortiori* I think that a theory of rights cannot be expected to supply a nonvague general formula by means of which it can be decided, quite generally, when it is permissible to infringe a claim. Supplying such a formula requires having in hand an exhaustive account of all of the other things besides the fact that you would here and now be infringing a claim in doing alpha that are relevant to the question whether you may here and now permissibly do alpha, and thus seems to me to require a full-scale moral theory. Claims do of course have moral significance, they do of course bear on what one may permissibly do; but they are not the only things that do.

Still, a theory of rights must tell us what the moral significance of a claim is, and that means it must tell us *how* claims bear on what one may permissibly do. I suggested that X's having a claim against Y is equivalent to Y's behavior's being constrained in a certain way; I suggested also that central to that constraint on Y is that, other things being equal, Y ought to accord the claim. How are we to cash that "other things being equal"?

Let us go back to the Tradeoff Idea. Perhaps it is possible to emend it? Notice, after all, that what we have pointed to by way of objection to it are considerations having to do with the potential claim infringer's circumstances; thus they are considerations that, while relevant to the question whether he or she may infringe the claim, are irrelevant to the question how stringent the claim is. What if we were to stipulate them away? Suppose X has a claim against Y that Y not do alpha, but would produce an increment of good by doing alpha. May Y do alpha? Perhaps we can say: if it is or were the case that no third parties have claims against Y either that Y do alpha or that Y not do alpha, and if it also is or were the case that Y has no non-claim-infringing way of producing that increment of good, *then* it is or would be permissible for Y to do alpha if and only if the increment of good would be sufficiently large, the required size varying with the stringency of X's claim.

This is an attractive way of proceeding. What we do in this way is to zero in on X's claim itself—we stipulate away what is irrelevant to *its* moral weight and attend only to that. Doing so eliminates the blur produced in actual circumstances by Y's alternatives, the claims of third parties, and so on; it lets us see the moral significance of X's claim itself. That is exactly what we wanted to see.

But there are two further objections to the Tradeoff Idea, so that two further emendations would be called for.

7. Suppose that A has a claim against me that I not kick him. I would cause him some pain if I did but not much, so the claim is not very stringent. Suppose that no third parties have claims against me that I kick him or that I not kick him. Suppose, last, that I would produce a large increment of good by kicking him and that I have no non-claim-infringing way of producing it. Fine, we think: it is permissible for me to kick A. But what if that large increment of good would be the sum of very tiny increments of good (small satisfactions, perhaps) for a large number of people? Surely that won't do. The objection we turn to here issues not from a difficulty about the potential claim infringer's *circumstances,* but from a difficulty about the *distribution* of the increment of good.

For my own part, I think we should agree to a very strong distributive constraint on claim infringement. Let us for the remainder of this section ignore the difficulties made by the potential claim infringer's circumstances and attend only to distribution. What I suggest by way of preliminary (the need for a revision will be pointed to in the following section) is this: I may not kick A unless there is at least one person, B, for whom I would thereby provide an increment of good of a size such that, if only B gained only that amount of good, his gaining it would by itself make it permissible for me to kick A. Where the increment of good I would produce by kicking A is the sum of tiny increments of good for many, there is no such B, for there is no person whose gaining a tiny increment of good would by itself make it permissible for me to kick A. Not so if the increment of good I would produce by kicking A is or includes B's being saved from death or blindness or losing his legs, for that increment of good for B would by itself make it permissible for me to kick A. In short, where claims are concerned, the sum of goods across people does not count.

I do not mean that goods across people have no sum; I mean only that where claims are concerned, their sum across people does not matter. In still shorter form, where claims are concerned, the numbers do not count.[5] Let us call this the High-Threshold Thesis.

Though I think we should accept the High-Threshold Thesis, there is no denying that it is very strong, and in two ways at that. In the first place, I take it to be plain that one may not (other things being equal) infringe a more or less stringent claim on the mere ground that one would thereby save *one* other person from a worsening comparable in gravity to the worsening that fixes the stringency of the claim. I may not cause you pain just to save Bloggs from a comparable pain; I may not kill you just to save Bloggs from death. If we agree that the numbers do not count, then we are committed to agreeing that I may not cause you pain to save five or twenty-five or hundreds from a comparable pain, and that I may not kill you to save five or twenty-five or hundreds from death. I said that the surgeon may not proceed in TRANSPLANT in that the increment of good he would thereby produce is insufficiently large; if the High-Threshold Thesis is true, we might have said instead that the surgeon may not proceed in that the increment of good he would thereby produce does not satisfy the distributive constraint.

Where the numbers get very large, however, some people start to feel nervous. Hundreds! Billions! The whole population of Asia! I suspect that those who start to feel nervous as the numbers get larger are moved to do so by the feeling that where billions (or perhaps even just hundreds) could be saved from pain, a person ought to volunteer to suffer it, and that where the lives of billions (or perhaps even just hundreds) could be saved from death, a person ought to volunteer his or her life. Perhaps so. (But then why isn't it also the case that he or she ought to volunteer for the sake of five? Or two? Or one?) I leave open whether he or she ought to. What is in question for us is only what may be done if the claim holders refuse to volunteer. The

5. I stress that the idea here is that *where claims are concerned* the numbers do not count. The idea here is not that the numbers never count in morality. Where matters of mere distribution are concerned, the numbers arguably do count. See John Taurek, "Should the Numbers Count?", *Philosophy and Public Affairs,* 6 (Summer 1977), for an argument that they do not, and Derek Parfit, "Innumerate Ethics", *Philosophy and Public Affairs,* 7 (Summer 1978), for criticism of Taurek's argument.

mere fact (if it is a fact) that the claim holders ought to volunteer really cannot be thought to make it permissible to infringe their claims. For example, many people do not volunteer to participate in Red Cross blood drives; the mere fact that they ought to (I believe they ought to) can hardly be thought to make it permissible to extract blood from them against their will.

A second consequence of accepting the High-Threshold Thesis is that accepting it commits us to there being what we might call maximally stringent claims. Let us say that a claim is within the range of maximally stringent claims if and only if no increment of good to be got by infringing it, however large, would make it permissible to infringe it—if the potential claim infringer had a non-claim-infringing alternative to infringing it. (Why I speak of a *range* of maximally stringent claims will come out shortly.)

Suppose that if I kill you I thereby produce an increment of good for Bloggs and only Bloggs. Is there any possible increment of good I could produce for him by killing you that would be sufficiently large to justify my killing you? I should think it plain that there is not. If we accept the High-Threshold Thesis, then, the numbers do not count, and no matter how many I would save by killing you, from no matter what horrors, that does not make it permissible for me to kill you. No matter how large an increment of good I would produce, it is impermissible for me to kill you, and your claim against me that I not do so is maximally stringent. For my own part, I think it is, and thus that the fact that the High-Threshold Thesis has this consequence is no objection to it.

I said that the surgeon may not proceed in TRANSPLANT in that the increment of good he would thereby produce is insufficiently large; if the High-Threshold Thesis is true, we might have said instead that the surgeon may not proceed in that the young man's claim against him is maximally stringent.

I think that many other claims are also maximally stringent. Is there any increment of good I could produce by blinding you or cutting off your legs that would justify my blinding you or cutting off your legs? I think it plainly impermissible to do these things to you to save the life of one person; the High-Threshold Thesis yields that it therefore is impermissible to do these things to you to save the lives of any number at all. That consequence of the thesis also seems to me no objection to it.

It should be stressed, however, that the High-Threshold Thesis does not yield that just any claim is maximally stringent. The thesis does yield that I may not infringe your claim that I not cause you pain to save billions from comparable pain; the thesis is entirely consistent with its being permissible for me to infringe that claim of yours to save the lives of billions, or even to save the life of one.

Moreover, it is worth noticing that one can consistently suppose that some maximally stringent claims are more stringent than others. That is why I spoke of a *range* of maximally stringent claims. X's dying is markedly worse for X than X's going blind, or losing his or her legs, is for X, so it follows by

> The Comparison Principle: Suppose X_1 has a claim against Y_1 that Y_1 do alpha, and X_2 has a claim against Y_2 that Y_2 do beta. Then X_1's claim against Y_1 is more stringent than X_2's claim against Y_2 if and only if Y_1 makes things worse for X_1 if Y_1 fails to do alpha than Y_2 makes things for X_2 if Y_2 fails to do beta

that X's claim to not be killed is markedly more stringent than X's claim to not be blinded or maimed. One can nevertheless suppose that these are maximally stringent claims.

Perhaps even clearer is this. It is surely worse for a person to be tortured to death than just to die. The Comparison Principle tells us therefore that the claim to not be tortured to death is more stringent than the claim to not be killed. I am sure that more people could be got to agree that the claim to not be tortured to death is maximally stringent (many people believe that torture is impermissible, no matter what the circumstances) than could be got to agree that the claim to not be killed is maximally stringent. But one can consistently believe that one claim is more stringent than the other *and* that both are maximally stringent.

But, as I said, the High-Threshold Thesis is very strong. Some people would reject it. On their view, the numbers do count, or anyway very large numbers do. So while I hope you will join me in accepting the High-Threshold Thesis, I will therefore not assume it true or rest any weight on it in later argument.

On the other hand, the distributive constraint cannot just be dropped. Those who reject the High-Threshold Thesis must find some other account of that constraint, for surely it is on *no* view permissible to kill a person to save billions from a minor headache. I leave it open what move those who reject the High-Threshold Thesis should make here.

8. A quite different kind of objection to the Tradeoff Idea comes out as follows. Suppose that if I kick A, I will thereby save B's life. (B will die if I do not kick A.) Then on any view I would produce an acceptably well-distributed and sufficiently large increment of good by kicking A to make it permissible for me to proceed. (On the assumption that no other parties have claims that are relevant. Let us once again ignore the difficulties made by the potential claim infringer's circumstances.)

Suppose instead that if I kick A, I will thereby very probably save B's life. (B will certainly die if I do not kick A.) Then I would very probably produce an acceptably well-distributed and sufficiently large increment of good by kicking A to make it permissible for me to proceed. Does the fact that I would very probably produce an acceptably well-distributed and sufficiently large increment of good by kicking A to make it permissible for me to proceed itself make it permissible for me to proceed?—thus whether or not B will in fact live if I proceed?

Another way to put this question is this. Suppose that if I kick A, I will thereby very probably save B's life. So I do kick A. As things turn out, B dies anyway. *Was* it all the same permissible for me to proceed?

I think we want to say yes. If B died anyway, then I did not in fact produce any increment of good by infringing A's claim. (Quite to the contrary: B gained nothing, and A suffered some pain.) But I think we want to say it was enough to justify my kicking A that I would thereby very probably save B's life.

We do welcome getting chances of getting things it would be good for us to get; we are even glad that we did get those chances, when it later turns out that we did not get the things it would have been good for us to get. I am grateful to you for making me a gift of a ticket in the state lottery; I am still grateful to you, when it later turns out that the ticket you gave me is not the winning ticket. Let us introduce a new piece of terminology. Suppose it would be good for X to get a thing Z. Let us say that if Y makes it probable that X will get Z, Y gives X an *advantage;* and let us measure the size of the advantage in a familiar way, namely by taking it to be the product of the amount by which Y increases the probability that X will get Z and the measure of how good it would be for X to get Z. When Y makes it probable that X will get Z, it may be that Y does more than give X an advantage, for it may be that Y will produce an actual increment of good for X. But Y need not do that in order to have given X an advantage.

Then if we want to say that it was permissible for me to kick A even though B died anyway, we could say that what made it permissible for me to do this is that I thereby produced not a large enough increment of good for B, but anyway a large enough advantage for B.

Should we say that it was permissible for me to kick A? Well, what is the alternative? If it was not permissible for me to kick A, then it was the case that I ought not kick A. Is it at all plausible to say that the mere fact that B died anyway makes it be the case that it was wrong for me to kick A—despite the fact that by kicking A I was very probably going to save B's life?

There is a bad argument to the effect that it was not wrong for me to kick A, that it was not the case that I ought not, that it was not impermissible for me to do so, and we should look at it.

What I have in mind is the two-step argument that goes as follows: "Since I was very probably going to save B's life by kicking A, it follows that I was not at fault, or to blame, for kicking A; and it follows from my not having been at fault, or to blame, for kicking A that it was permissible for me to kick A." But both steps are unacceptable.

First, its having been the case that I was very probably going to save B's life by kicking A just does not entail that I was not at fault for kicking A. What relieves of fault is not probabilities, but an agent's estimates of probabilities. (These may of course differ. I might think it highly probable that a six will turn up on the next throw of a die—perhaps because no six has turned up in recent throws—and be mistaken in thinking so.) If Y kicks X out of the belief that doing so will very probably kill Z, then (other things being equal) Y is at fault for kicking X, even if *in fact* Y's kicking X will very probably save Z's life.

The second step is equally unacceptable but in some ways more interesting. The second step presupposes the general thesis that

(1) X was not at fault for doing alpha

entails

(2) It was permissible for X to do alpha.

In light of our decision on usage (Chapter 3, section 3), saying that (1) entails (2) comes to the same as saying that (1) entails

(2′) It was not the case that X ought not do alpha.

Let us call the thesis that (1) entails (2) and (2′) the Requirement-of-Fault Thesis for Ought-Not. Very often when we would not be at fault for doing a thing, it is also true that it would be permissible for us to do it, and thus that it is not the case that we ought not do it; The Requirement-of-Fault Thesis for Ought-Not says something stronger, namely that there is entailment here.

Why might a person accept the Requirement-of-Fault Thesis for Ought-Not? Here is Bloggs, trying to figure out whether or not to do alpha. His best estimate, on very careful consideration, is that it is likely to be better that he do alpha, and conscience tells him to do alpha. So he does alpha. As things turn out, his estimate was wildly off, and his doing alpha was disastrous. But isn't one's best estimate, on very careful consideration, good enough? Isn't Bloggs fault-free? It seems reasonable to think he is. How can it be right to say he ought to have acted against conscience?

But this really won't do. Suppose Bloggs' baby has a fever. Bloggs' best estimate, on very careful consideration, is that it would be best to starve the baby. (Feed a cold, starve a fever.) So he does, and the baby dies. If that really was Bloggs' best estimate, on very careful consideration—if Bloggs really was not at fault for his mistaken belief—then we do not blame Bloggs for the baby's death, we do not say he is at fault for it. Do we conclude that he did not fail to act as he ought? The doctor will later say "I quite understand, it's not your fault"; but he or she will go on to add "but you really ought not have starved the baby, you ought to have fed it aspirin dissolved in apple juice".[6] Not just that it would have been a good idea, rather that it is what Bloggs *ought* to have done.

In light of such possibilities, most people who take this line say we need to distinguish. The word "ought", they say, has two senses. It has a subjective sense according to which what a person ought to do is only what he or she would we be at fault for not doing, thus a sense for which the Requirement-of-Fault Thesis for Ought-Not is

6. Alternatively, the doctor might instead go on to add "but you really ought not have starved the baby, you ought to have called a doctor". This says that while Bloggs did what he *thought* his best in the way of careful consideration, his consideration was not careful enough. But this too sheds doubt on the Requirement-of-Fault Thesis for Ought-Not, since it might have been through no fault of Bloggs' own that he thought his consideration was careful enough.

true; and it also has an objective sense according to which what a person ought to do is not fixed by what his or her beliefs are, not fixed by those beliefs even if the person was not at fault for having them, thus a sense for which the Requirement-of-Fault Thesis for Ought-Not is not true.

For my own part, I see no such ambiguity in the word "ought". Suppose Bloggs was thinking out loud as he engaged in his very careful consideration of what to do for the baby. "Yes", he concluded, "I ought to starve it". I am inclined to think that there just is *no* sense of the word "ought" according to which he spoke truly. *No* sense of the word "ought" according to which anyone would have been speaking truly if he or she, or they, said that Bloggs ought to starve that baby.

In any case, I will throughout use "ought", and its cognates such as "permissible", in the objective sense.[7] If this practice makes you feel uncomfortable, you are invited to make emendations in the text. If you think that "ought" has two senses, a subjective as well as an objective, then you may wish to write "objective" before every occurrence of "ought". If you think that "ought" has only one sense, the subjective sense for which the Requirement-of-Fault Thesis for Ought-Not is true, then you may wish to insert clauses attributing appropriate beliefs to the agents in question.

To return now to probabilities. It was the case that if I kicked A, I would very probably save B's life. So I kicked A, but B died anyway. We were asking whether it was all the same permissible for me to kick A. What we have just done is to look at a bad argument for the conclusion that it was permissible for me to kick A, a two-step argument that proceeds via fault. But both steps are unacceptable.

I know of no good argument for the conclusion that it was permissible for me to kick A. Some people say "Well, isn't the point of

7. As is plain, I think the classical utilitarians (such as Mill and more recently Moore) were right to divorce the question whether X ought to do alpha from the question whether X would be at fault if X did not do alpha, and I follow them in that respect. On the other hand, the classical utilitarians did not allow probabilities to be relevant to what a person ought to do: on their view, what is relevant to what a person ought to do is only what in fact is and will be the case. (It is clear that Moore's way of explaining why probabilities can be ignored rests on his not having seen a difference between probabilities and an agent's estimates of probabilities; see his *Ethics*, pp. 118–120.) I am suggesting that we do well to depart from them in this respect.

saying 'ought' to guide action? And wouldn't it have been a terrible thing to say to you at the time—given the probabilities—that you ought not kick A then?" But the fact that it would have been terrible to say a thing does not mean it was false.

On the other hand, I know of no good argument for the conclusion that it was not permissible for me to kick A. And we do very naturally think it was permissible. Moreover, I will suggest in the following chapter that a certain hard problem in moral theory is best dealt with if we allow probabilities, or more precisely advantage, to have a direct bearing on what it is permissible to do.

But if we do allow this, if we do say that it was permissible for me to kick A, then much of what has preceded needs revision. We have to say that what made it permissible for me to proceed was not that I would produce an acceptably well-distributed and sufficiently large increment of good by kicking A, for I did not in fact do this, but rather that I would produce an acceptably well-distributed and sufficiently large advantage by kicking A. As is plain, any requirement on tradeoffs would have to allow for the justification of claim infringements by appeal to advantages produced. And the High-Threshold Thesis would have to be revised: presumably it should be so revised as to require that the advantage to at least one for whom infringing the claim would give advantage must be sufficiently much larger than the advantage to the claim holder if the claim is not infringed for that advantage to the one, by itself, to justify infringing the claim.

9. We were looking at

> The Tradeoff Idea: It is permissible to infringe a claim if and only if infringing it would be sufficiently much better for those for whom infringing it would be good than not infringing it would be for the claim holder.

As we saw, it is grossly oversimple. Still, tradeoffs of claims on the one hand for increments of good, or anyway increments of advantage, on the other, *are* permissible. And the thought that lies behind the Tradeoff Idea is surely right. Moreover, we can extract from the thought that lies behind it an account of what is central to that constraint on Y's behavior that X's having a claim against Y is equivalent to. Suppose X has a claim against Y that Y not do alpha. If we stipulate away matters having to do with Y's circumstances (are there third parties who have claims against Y that Y do alpha or that Y not do alpha? and so on), these being matters relevant to whether Y may infringe X's claim, but irrelevant to the stringency of X's claim, then we thereby zero in on the moral significance of X's claim itself. And we can say that the moral significance of X's claim lies in the very fact that—if matters relevant to whether Y may infringe X's claim, but irrelevant to the stringency of X's claim, are or were absent—then it is or would be permissible for Y to infringe the claim if and only if Y would thereby produce a sufficiently large and appropriately distributed increment of good, or advantage, the size of the required increment, and the appropriateness of its distribution, turning entirely on the stringency of the claim.

In light of

> The Aggravation Principle: If X has a claim against Y that Y do alpha, then the worse Y makes things for X if Y fails to do alpha, the more stringent X's claim against Y that Y do alpha,

we can rephrase the last clause as follows: the size of the required increment, and the appropriateness of its distribution, turning entirely on how bad things are for the claim holder if the claim is infringed.

That is what is central to the constraint on Y's behavior that X's having a claim against Y is equivalent to.

Some things that happened along the way might be worth mentioning just briefly again by way of summary.

I argued that we should accept the Means Principle for Claims, which says that claims, and their stringency, extend down from ends to means. And I argued also that the fact that Y can save X's life does not give X a claim against Y that Y do so.

I offered the High-Threshold Thesis as an account of the distributive constraint on increments of good, or advantage, to be produced by infringing a claim: it says that where claims are concerned, the numbers do not count. And I said that it seems to me no objection to the thesis that it yields that some claims—such as the young man's against the surgeon in TRANSPLANT—are maximally stringent. But I will not assume you join me in accepting the High-Threshold Thesis.

I also said that I would so use "ought" and its cognates that the Requirement-of-Fault Thesis for Ought-Not is not true: I throughout use them objectively, that is, in such a way that its being the case that X would not be at fault for doing a thing is compatible with its being the case that he ought not do it.

Chapter 7

The Trolley Problem

1. The surgeon may not operate on the young man in TRANSPLANT. I gave several reasons. First, the increment of good the surgeon would produce is insufficiently great. Second, the increment of good would not be acceptably well distributed. Third, the young man's claim is maximally stringent. Perhaps you do not accept the High-Threshold Thesis and therefore do not accept the second and third reasons. All the same, the surgeon may not proceed, since whatever else may be true, the surgeon would save only four lives on balance, and that is not a sufficiently large increment of good to make it permissible for him to proceed.

But then what is to be said about the following case?

> TROLLEY: An out-of-control trolley is hurtling down a track. Straight ahead of it on the track are five men who will be killed if the trolley reaches them. Bloggs is a passerby, who happens at the moment to be standing by the track next to the switch; he can throw the switch, thereby turning the trolley onto a spur of track on the right. There is one man on that spur of track on the right; that man will be killed if Bloggs turns the trolley.[1]

Most people would say it is permissible for Bloggs to turn the trolley. And wouldn't they be right to say this? If something—a trolley, an avalanche, an out-of-control satellite (does anyone remember Sky-lab?)—will kill five if nothing is done, and if also it can be deflected in such a way as to make it kill only one, surely it is permissible to

---

1. Adapted from a case of Philippa Foot's. See her "The Problem of Abortion and the Doctrine of the Double Effect", reprinted in her *Virtues and Vices* (Los Angeles: University of California Press, 1978).

deflect it. By hypothesis, the thing will do harm whatever we do (deflect it or not); how could our making it do less harm than it would otherwise do be impermissible?

On some views, it is not merely permissible for Bloggs to turn the trolley, it is morally required of Bloggs that he do so. That is not my view, and we will come back to it below. Meanwhile, however, it surely is at least permissible for him to proceed.

But if it is permissible for Bloggs to turn the trolley, then we have been overlooking something important. For how exactly is TROLLEY supposed to differ from TRANSPLANT? In both cases, the agent saves five at a cost of only one. Do the agents differ in respect of considerations of the kind we mentioned in the preceding chapter?—in respect, that is, of circumstances, distribution of the increment of good, or probabilities? There does not seem to be any reason to think they do. For example, there is no more reason to think the five on the straight track ahead have a claim against Bloggs that Bloggs save their lives in TROLLEY than there is to think the surgeon's five patients have a claim against the surgeon that he save their lives in TRANSPLANT. So why is it permissible for Bloggs to proceed in TROLLEY and impermissible for the surgeon to proceed in TRANSPLANT?

A theory of rights needs an account of the relevant difference between TROLLEY and TRANSPLANT. We cannot satisfactorily explain why the surgeon is barred from proceeding in TRANSPLANT by appeal to the considerations we have been attending to, unless we can explain why analogous considerations do not bar Bloggs' proceeding in TROLLEY.

Indeed, moral theory generally needs an account of how TROLLEY differs from TRANSPLANT. TROLLEY in fact presents a very interesting and very hard problem for moral theory generally, and not just for the theory of rights. Why is it permissible for Bloggs to proceed in TROLLEY, but not permissible for the surgeon to proceed in TRANSplant? I am sure that cases such as TROLLEY incline some people to think the Central Utilitarian idea very plausible, since in TROLLEY it seems permissible (and perhaps even required) to maximize value; cases such as TRANSPLANT make the Central Utilitarian idea unattractive, since in TRANSPLANT it is not permissible to maximize value. So how is one and the same moral theory to accommodate both cases?

I think myself that we should be far more puzzled by the fact that it is permissible for Bloggs to proceed in TROLLEY than by the fact that it is impermissible for the surgeon to proceed in TRANSPLANT, and I therefore like to call this, not the Transplant Problem, but instead the Trolley Problem. One may not in general kill one to save five; TROLLEY seems to be a representative of a narrow class of exceptions to that general rule, and what is needed is a characterization of the class of exceptions and an account of what makes them exceptions.

2. I mention two very simple candidate solutions to the Trolley Problem only to get them out of the way. It might be said first that the relevant difference between the cases is that the young man has a claim against the surgeon that the surgeon not proceed in TRANSPLANT, whereas the one on the spur of track on the right has no claim against Bloggs that Bloggs not proceed in TROLLEY, it being *that* difference that explains why the surgeon may not proceed while Bloggs may.

But why should it be thought that while the young man has the claim against the surgeon, the one lacks the claim against Bloggs? If all claims were absolute, then we could draw the conclusion that the one lacks the claim against Bloggs from the very fact that it is permissible for Bloggs to turn the trolley. But if that is how we find out that the one lacks the claim against Bloggs, then we cannot appeal to the fact that the one lacks the claim to explain its being permissible for Bloggs to turn the trolley—on pain of circularity. In any case, we have rejected the thesis that all claims are absolute.

A second candidate solution says that the relevant difference between the cases is that, while both the one in TROLLEY and the young man in TRANSPLANT have claims that would be infringed by proceeding, the one's claim in TROLLEY is less stringent than the young man's claim in TRANSPLANT, it being *that* difference that explains why the surgeon may not proceed while Bloggs may.

I do think it plausible to say that the one's claim in TROLLEY is less stringent than the young man's claim in TRANSPLANT, since death is not the only thing that matters to us. How we die also matters to us. And I think it worse to die in consequence of being cut up, one's parts then being distributed to others, than to die in consequence of being hit by a trolley. But not enough worse to be what explains why the surgeon may not proceed while Bloggs may. Consider MAFIA again. It is not permissible to cut a person up to save five from the hands of the Mafia. It is also not permissible to run a person down with a trolley to save five from the hands of the Mafia.

And it certainly cannot be said that the fact that there are five on the straight track ahead, who will be saved if Bloggs turns the trolley, makes the one's claim against Bloggs *markedly* less stringent than the young man's claim against the surgeon. It is plain enough that if there were nobody on the track ahead, so that nobody at all would be harmed if Bloggs did not turn the trolley, then Bloggs would infringe a very stringent claim of the one's if he turned the trolley. How odd an idea that the mere presence of five on the track ahead could drastically decrease the stringency of the one's claim in TROLLEY!—particularly in light of the fact that the mere presence of five who need parts does not drastically decrease the stringency of the young man's claim in TRANSPLANT.

In short, these very simple candidate solutions are no solution at all. We cannot solve this problem by a blunt appeal to claims.[2]

3. What is wanted, I think, is that we make appeal to a quite different kind of moral machinery.

---

2. Nor can we solve it by a more subtle appeal to claims, of the kind I proposed in "The Trolley Problem", reprinted in *Rights, Restitution, and Risk*. I suggested there that we should take note of the fact that if the surgeon proceeds in TRANSPLANT, then he infringes more than one claim of the young man's. If the surgeon proceeds, he infringes the young man's claim that the surgeon not cut him up and remove his heart, lungs, and kidneys *as well as* the young man's claim that the surgeon not kill him. By contrast (so we might have thought), if Bloggs proceeds in TROLLEY, he infringes *only* the one's claim that the bystander not kill him. For surely (so we might have thought), the one has no claim against Bloggs that Bloggs not turn the trolley.

But this really will not do. In the first place, if Bloggs turns the trolley, he infringes the one's claim that Bloggs not hit him with a trolley as well as the one's claim that Bloggs not kill him. After all, people do have a claim against us that we not hit them with trolleys, even if doing so does not kill them. Second, and more interesting, consider the Means Principle for Claims, which I argued for in Chapter 6. The solution I offered in "The Trolley Problem" allows that the one has a claim against Bloggs that Bloggs not kill him. Moreover, if Bloggs turns the trolley, he will thereby kill the one, for by turning the trolley he will turn the trolley onto the one and thereby kill him. The Means Principle for Claims says it follows that the one does have a claim against Bloggs that Bloggs not turn the trolley—and indeed, that this claim is at least as stringent as the one's claim against Bloggs that Bloggs not kill him. It is largely because I failed to see the good reasons there are for accepting the Means Principle for Claims that I failed to see that this way of appealing to rights does not solve the problem. I know of no other way in which it might be plausibly thought possible to explain the moral difference between TROLLEY and TRANSPLANT by appeal to the concept of a right.

Let us begin by taking note of the fact that we have not really taken a close enough look at TROLLEY. A trolley is headed for five, and if Bloggs proceeds, what he does is to turn the trolley so that it is headed instead for one. Is it really permissible for him to do this? Shouldn't we ask for some further information about those six men on the tracks? Shouldn't we ask how they came to be where they are? In telling you the story, I did not say anything at all that would supply this information. Yet when one thinks on it, that must surely make a difference.

Suppose, for example, that there is a fence protecting the straight track, and a large sign that says "DANGER! TROLLEY TRACKS!" But five thrillseekers decided "What fun!", so they climbed the fence, and they now sit on the straight track waiting for the sound of a trolley and placing bets on whether if a trolley comes the driver will be able to stop it in time. The man on the right-hand track is a gardener. Why a gardener? The right-hand track has not been used in many years, but the trolley company is in process of constructing new stations and connecting them with the old ones via that right-hand track. Meanwhile it has hired a gardener to plant geraniums along the track. The gardener was much afraid of trolleys, but the trolley company gave him its assurance that the track is not yet in use, so that the gardener will be entirely safe while at work on it. Surely all *this* being the case, Bloggs must not turn the trolley.

By contrast, if all six people on the tracks are track workmen, out doing their job on the track, and if also their assignments to positions on the tracks for the day were made by lot, then it seems to be permissible for Bloggs to turn the trolley.

In short, an account of what makes it permissible for Bloggs to turn the trolley—when it is permissible for him to do this—is going to have to be sensitive to differences in how the six came to be where they are on the tracks: it must yield that the trolley may be turned in the case of some histories and not in the case of others.

A second point that emerges here is that we cannot say that the crucial difference between TROLLEY and TRANSPLANT lies in the fact that in TROLLEY Bloggs deflects onto one something that already threatens five, whereas in TRANSPLANT the surgeon does not, for Bloggs may not deflect onto one something that already threatens five in just *any* possible instance of TROLLEY. That leaves open that the fact of deflection is relevant. But it makes clear that something else, something deeper, is at work.

4. I said that if all six people on the tracks in TROLLEY are track workmen, out doing their job on the track, and if also their assignments to positions on the tracks for the day were made by lot, then it seems to be permissible for Bloggs to turn the trolley. Why? Shouldn't it strike us that they would have said they wished Bloggs to do so if they had been asked in advance, that is, in advance of being assigned to positions on the track for the day?

Suppose the time now is (i) early morning. The company's track workmen will go out onto the tracks, that being how they make their living, but assignments to positions on the tracks for the day have not yet been made, for the lottery has not yet been held. It occurs to us that a TROLLEY-like situation just *might* arise. We do not know if it will, or who will be the six on the relevant tracks if it does, so we call a meeting of all the workmen and we ask them: "If a situation such as that described in TROLLEY arises later today, which do you prefer—Bloggs' turning the trolley or Bloggs' not turning the trolley?" Since positions will be assigned by lot, each has the same chance as every other of occupying any one of the positions on the track, and it is therefore true of each that his probability of surviving the episode is greater if Bloggs will turn the trolley than if Bloggs will not turn it.

We should stop to stress the importance here of the supposition that their positions on the tracks for the day will be made by lot. That might not have been true. There might have been a class of track workmen who are always sent out to work alone on the tracks, the others always being sent out to work in groups of five. We might suppose that those always sent out to work alone do a special kind of job called beam fitting; let us therefore call them Beam Fitters. The Beam Fitters would have good reason to object to Bloggs' turning the trolley, since while the probability of survival of the others is greater if Bloggs will turn the trolley than if Bloggs will not turn it, *their* probability of survival is smaller if Bloggs will turn the trolley than if Bloggs will not turn it.

But we are supposing that there is no such class of track workmen, for we are supposing that the workmen will all be assigned their positions on the tracks for the day by lot. Then it really is true of each that his probability of surviving the episode is greater if Bloggs will turn the trolley than if Bloggs will not turn it.

Our probability of survival is not the only thing that matters to us. Is there something that some or all of the workmen would regard as objectionable in Bloggs' turning the trolley if and when the time comes—something sufficiently objectionable to outweigh in interest to them their getting the increased probability of survival they get if he will turn the trolley? It is hard to imagine what such a something might be. Do the workmen believe that what happens when there is a runaway trolley should be left to chance? Or to Fate? Or to God? Just when there is a runaway trolley? Do they also believe that what happens when you have a toothache, or an attack of appendicitis, should be left to chance or Fate or God?

There isn't nothing here, however. To the extent to which we can understand them to hold views that would issue in their regarding Bloggs' turning the trolley later as sufficiently objectionable to outweigh in interest to them the increase in probability of survival it gives them, we have reason to believe they would not consent to Bloggs' turning the trolley later; and to that very same extent it will seem to us impermissible for Bloggs to turn the trolley when he later confronts the situation in TROLLEY. The more firmly held those views are, and the more central to their lives, the more we are going to think Bloggs really must not intervene.

But that is just mere possibility. It really can be supposed that the workmen would all consent to Bloggs' turning the trolley later, for the reason that his doing so gives them an increased probability of survival.

But why focus on (i) early morning?

Suppose the time now is (ii) noon, by which time assignments to positions have been made and the men are already at work on the tracks. If we asked them *now*, "If a situation such as that described in TROLLEY arises later today, which do you prefer: Bloggs' turning the trolley or Bloggs' not turning the trolley?" their answers would be different. It is no longer true that each has the same chance as every other of occupying any one of the positions on the track; and therefore it is no longer true of each that his probability of surviving the episode is greater if Bloggs will turn the trolley than if Bloggs will not turn it. In the case of those at work alone, the probability of surviving the episode is smaller if Bloggs will turn the trolley than if Bloggs will not turn it. (Compare the Beam Fitters I invited you to imagine.) Unless they are more than usually altruistic, those at work alone would not now consent to Bloggs' turning the trolley if and when a TROLLEY-like situation arises later in the day.

Indeed, suppose the time now is (iii) 3:00 in the afternoon and that a runaway trolley is already headed for five on the straight track. If we asked the workmen *now*, "Given TROLLEY has now arisen, which do you prefer: Bloggs' turning the trolley or Bloggs' not turning the trolley?" their answers would again be different. Perhaps those at work alone elsewhere on the system of trolley tracks would have no objection to Bloggs' turning the trolley, but unless he is *very* altruistic, the one at work on the spur of track to the right would not consent to Bloggs' turning the trolley.

Let us postpone the question "Why focus on (i) early morning?" for the following section. Let us first see how the considerations we have already noted bear on the other cases we were looking at.

Suppose we had held a meeting at (i) early morning of the city's thrillseekers and the gardener whom the trolley company has hired to go out alone to plant geraniums later in the day. The gardener would not consent to Bloggs' turning the trolley later. (Compare the Beam Fitters. Compare the track workmen already at work alone at noon.) Perhaps even the thrillseekers would not consent to Bloggs' turning the trolley in that from their point of view an increase in probability of survival is not a desideratum. Certainly anyway, the gardener would not consent.

Suppose our community's transplant surgeon Bloggs (for simplicity I assume we have only one) had called us all together before the situation in TRANSPLANT arose and asked us whether we wish him to do the following: cut one up who is healthy if and when there come to be five who are in need of parts, and there is no way of supplying the parts other than by cutting up the one. Would we have consented to his doing this? I am sure we would not. Let us take this slowly.

Some of us might have consented to Bloggs' doing this because his doing it would increase their probability of survival. If Alfred is in dire need of a new heart, then Bloggs' doing it increases Alfred's probability of survival.

But Bloggs' doing it does not increase the probability of survival of the healthy. Quite to the contrary: it decreases their probability of survival.

In the first place, as is obvious, it is the healthy who would be cut up to save the ill. (Compare the Beam Fitters. Compare the track workmen already at work alone at noon.)

Second, being or not being healthy is not a mere matter of chance: how one lives affects one's health. This means that Bloggs' proceeding might well have a further, more subtle effect: it might well itself increase the number of those who are in need of parts and thus increase the risk the healthy are subjected to. Bloggs' proceeding supplies a form of insurance against death by organ failure, and some people are likely to be more relaxed about caring for their health than they would otherwise be in light of its availability.[3] What I have in mind is the phenomenon sometimes called moral hazard: a general policy of cutting one up to save five invites shifting the risk incurred by careless conduct onto the shoulders of the careful.

Of course people who are healthy sometimes fall ill suddenly, and even those most careful of their health can find themselves in need of new organs. Everything we know, however, tells us that how one lives does affect one's health and that care does increase one's probability of being healthy. (What if it did not? I will return to that question shortly.)

So while the probability of survival of those already in need of organs would be increased by Bloggs' proceeding, the probability of survival of those who are healthy would be decreased by it.

Moreover, as I said earlier, our probability of survival is not the only thing that interests us, and there are two further reasons why the healthy might object. Those who are healthy by virtue of denying themselves the pleasures of steak, gin, and cigarettes might well feel resentment at the prospect of being cut up to save those who are ill by virtue of not denying themselves those pleasures. Second, the healthy might well be concerned with *how* they would die if Bloggs proceeds and they are the one cut up. It is not merely death that concerns us, but also how death comes on us. Dying of organ failure after a long illness, which gives time to bring one's affairs to some meaningful conclusion, is one thing; dying in consequence of being suddenly grabbed off the street, or out of a doctor's examining room, and having one's body organs removed for use to save others, is quite another, and markedly worse.

The healthy, then, would certainly not consent to Bloggs' proceeding. And there would therefore not be unanimous consent to his doing so—by contrast with the track workmen at early morning.

It would be no surprise if the following objection were now made. "You have been asking what we would say of the prospect of Bloggs' cutting one up to save five, but you imagine the healthy among us to know that they are healthy, and some of them even to know that

---

3. Similarly, acceding to the threats of villains, as in MAFIA, encourages those and other villains.

they are people who are willing to expend effort in preserving their health. But then what you have been asking about is like asking what the track workmen would say, not at (i) early morning but rather at (ii) noon, of the prospect of Bloggs' turning the trolley, where the workmen at work alone know by noon that they are at work alone and hence know that they are at greater risk if Bloggs turns the trolley than if he does not. In both cases, those who know they would be at greater risk would not consent to Bloggs' proceeding. So where is the asymmetry, where is the contrast you were going to point to?"

The fact is that there is nothing in the case of TRANSPLANT analogous to early morning in the case of TROLLEY—given we imagine that the workmen will be assigned their positions on the tracks by lot.

In the first place, there is no time at which none of the healthy among us know whether or not they are healthy. More precisely, there is no time at which none of the normal healthy adults among us know whether or not they are healthy. (Compare the Beam Fitters. Perhaps not all, but at least some of the healthy among us know about themselves the analogue of what Beam Fitters would know about themselves.) It is not of interest what children, or mental defectives, would say if asked whether they prefer Bloggs' cutting one up to save five to his not doing so.

Second, there is no time after which health or need of body parts will come on people entirely by chance—contrast the lottery for positions on the tracks. As I said, everything we know tells us that how one lives does affect one's health and that care does increase one's probability of being healthy.

In short, there is no time at which we would all consent to Bloggs' cutting one up to save five. By contrast, there is a time at which the workmen would all consent to Bloggs' turning the trolley, namely early morning.

There might have been. We can imagine a world in which there is nothing whatever to be done that can affect one's health. (Indulging or not indulging in steak, gin, and cigarettes has no effect on health in that world.) Ailments that issue in organ failure simply descend on people by chance, out of the blue, unpredictably. The probability of survival for all of the people of that world really does increase if the Bloggs of that world cuts one up to save five.

They might nevertheless object to Bloggs' proceeding for a reason I mentioned earlier. As I said, we think dying of organ failure after a long illness, which gives time to bring one's affairs to some meaningful conclusion, is one thing; dying in consequence of being suddenly grabbed off the street, or out of a doctor's examining room, and being cut up and having one's body organs removed for use to save others, is quite another, and markedly worse. It is not easy to imagine the people of that world to be recognizably human beings while being different from us in this respect, but perhaps we can. In the first place, we can imagine them to have no affairs to bring to any meaningful conclusion: they live for the day itself and have no concern for the future—except in that they wish to survive into it. (Cats have no affairs to bring to a meaningful conclusion, yet they do want to live on.) Second, we can imagine them to regard with no distaste the thought of their bodies being cut up for use to save others. (Might they have no concern for their own bodies, having a concern only for the survival of the group?[4])

With these facts added, we may well suppose that the people of that world really would consent to the Bloggs of that world's proceeding—just as the workmen would consent to the Bloggs of this world's turning the trolley if asked at early morning. I will argue in the following section that it therefore is, in both cases, permissible for Bloggs to proceed.

But the people of *our* world are not like the people of that world, and the general facts about health in this world are not like the general facts about health in that world. We would not consent to the Bloggs of this world's proceeding.

It might pay to take note of the fact that the very features we supplied for that world and the people in it make cutting one up to save five in that world possess the very features that are possessed by deflecting a threat away from five toward one in our world—the very features that issue in our sense that deflecting something (a trolley, an avalanche, a meteor) in our world is less objectionable than cutting one up to save five in our world. On the one hand, we supplied for that world the fact that organ failure is entirely a chance event, which no one can predict or affect the probability of; on the other hand, we supplied for that world the fact that the people in it have no objection to the use of their flesh to save others. From their point of view, then, cutting them up to save others from organ failure has none of the objectionable features of cutting us up to save others.

---

4. Could this be true of creatures like human beings? We will come back to the question in Chapter 8.

Doing so in that world is from their point of view no more objectionable than deflecting something (a trolley, an avalanche, a meteor) in our world, and indeed they would welcome it on the ground of the increase in probability of survival that would issue from it.

5. Let us return now to a question I left open earlier. I said that the workmen would have consented to Bloggs' turning the trolley later if they had been asked at (i) early morning; and I seemed to take that to show that it is permissible for Bloggs to turn the trolley when he finally does confront the situation in TROLLEY. It is plain, however, that the workmen would not have consented—would anyway not *all* have consented—to Bloggs' turning the trolley later if they had been asked at (ii) noon, and would not all consent to his turning the trolley at (iii) 3:00 if they were asked then. So why is it of interest that they would all have consented if they had been asked at early morning?

Indeed, why is it of interest that they would or would not have consented to this or that at whatever time you like? After all, the workmen were not in fact asked, and did not in fact consent, at any time. What was pointed to in the preceding section is mere 'hypothetical consent'. Why should we care about that? For my own part, I think we shouldn't. What I think we should care about is not that such and such people would consent if they were asked, but rather whatever it is about them in virtue of which they would consent, if they would.

Consider a case in which we are very naturally inclined to appeal to hypothetical consent to explain why a person may permissibly do a thing. Suppose a tree fell on David; his leg is crushed under the tree and he is unconscious. You are a doctor, and you can see that David will live if and only if you cut his leg off straightway. Is it permissible for you to proceed? I think we may feel inclined to say we can't tell until we hear more about David. If David is a Christian Scientist or a Jehovah's Witness, then no. A man's deeply held religious or moral beliefs cut no ice when what is in question is operating on his child; when what is in question in operating on him, they surely settle the matter. How do they settle the matter? We may well think David's being a Christian Scientist would settle the matter in that, in virtue of being a Christian Scientist, David would refuse consent to your proceeding. And we may therefore conclude that if it is permissible for you to proceed, then that is because David would consent to your proceeding.

But can this be right? It might be true of a man that he would consent to your doing a thing without its being permissible for you to do it. It might be true of a man that he would consent to your slitting his throat in that he has the mad idea that he killed Cock Robin, and deserves throat slitting for it; the fact that he would consent does not make it permissible for you to proceed. So hypothetical consent is not sufficient for permissibility. What does the moral work of making it permissible for you to proceed in the case of David, if it is permissible for you to do so, is not that David would consent to your proceeding, but rather what it is about him in virtue of which he would consent, namely the complex fact (a) that he will live if and only if you proceed, and (b) that there is nothing true of him (as there would have been if he had been a Christian Scientist) that would if true morally outweigh the fact that he will live if and only if you proceed. That complex fact is why he would consent; but it is the complex fact, and not his hypothetical consent, that makes your proceeding permissible.

More precisely, the complex fact is why he would consent *if* he would, for it might be that he would not. David is by hypothesis unconscious and cannot in fact be asked for consent. But it might be that if you *were* able to shake him awake, he would be too confused, or too distraught, or in too much pain to think clearly about your request for consent to proceed, and would refuse it. Suppose this counterfactual is true of him. We can hardly conclude from it that you may not proceed. So hypothetical consent is not only not sufficient for permissibility, it is not necessary for it either.

In short, appealing to hypothetical consent here is appealing to an epiphenomenon[5]—one that need not even be present.

5. I confess to a strong suspicion that hypothetical consent is an epiphenomenon throughout current political theory. It is argued that such and such are just rules because people would consent to live by them if asked. But would they? Perhaps some among them are confused, or full of envy, or for some other reason would not consent. What the theorist typically does in face of these possibilities is to impose constraints: we are to ask not whether people (warts and all) would actually consent if asked, but whether people would consent if they met certain conditions, such as being clear-headed, free of envy, and the like. How do we know they would consent if they met those conditions? Well, living by those rules is to their advantage—their real advantage, as opposed to what they might in the circumstances (and given their warts) think to be to their advantage. But then *that* is what does the moral work of justifying the thesis that those rules are just. The theorists argue from "It is to their real advantage" to "The rules

Let us go back to the phenomenon that underlies the epiphenomenon. I said: what does the moral work of making it permissible for
you to proceed in the case of David, if it is permissible for you to do
so, is not that David would consent to your proceeding, but rather
what it is about him in virtue of which he would consent (if he would),
namely the complex fact (a) that he will live if and only if you proceed,
and (b) that there is nothing true of him (as there would have been
if he had been a Christian Scientist) that would if true morally outweigh the fact that he will live if and only if you proceed. But exactly
how does that complex fact make it permissible for you to proceed?
One possible answer is this: given (a), we can conclude that it is in
a measure good for David if you proceed, and given (b) we can
conclude that it is not merely in a measure good for David if you
proceed, it is *on balance* good for David if you proceed.

To take this line is to suppose that if David were a Christian Scientist
then it would not be on balance good for David if you proceeded.
Why does David's being a Christian Scientist, if he is, make it impermissible for you to proceed? Let us suppose David is a deeply
committed Christian Scientist: his being one is among the facts about
him which are central to his life. Then you may not proceed, and to
take the line we are considering is to say that the reason is this: while
the fact that David will live if and only if you proceed means that it
is in a measure good for him if you proceed, the fact that David is a
deeply committed Christian Scientist means that your proceeding is
bad for him, sufficiently bad to outweigh the good of living, so that
it is not on balance good for him if you proceed. I stress: not on
balance *objectively* good for him. For we are, after all, understanding
the notion 'good for a person' objectively.

This is an attractive line to take. Operating on a deeply committed
Christian Scientist really is committing a gross invasion, a violent

---

are just" via the intermediary "They would consent to the rules"; but the intermediary is mere epiphenomenon. Or so, anyway, I strongly suspect.

What Scanlon asks is not whether people would consent to such and such rules
under constrained conditions, but whether the rules "as a basis for informed,
unforced general agreement" could "reasonably" be rejected by people under
their actual conditions; I quoted his short-hand summary of the view in the
Introduction, note 15. "Reasonably" here bears a heavy weight, and I suggest
that whatever does the moral work of making it true that no one could reasonably
reject a given set of rules is what does the moral work of justifying them. In
short, the reference to agreement can drop out. See Introduction, note 19.

assault, comparable to rape, and therefore is bad for him. If we did not think, in light of the importance to him of his being a Christian Scientist, that your proceeding would be bad for him, if we did not think that your proceeding would be on balance objectively bad for him, then why would we think you morally barred from proceeding? Contrast the situation if David is merely in midstream of a flirtation with Christian Science. Deeply held religious convictions are one thing, passing fancies quite another. Here we may well think it permissible for you to proceed, and that, plausibly enough, for the very reason that we do not think it on balance objectively bad for David if you do.[6]

This is arguably too strong a line to take, however. It could be said that what bars operating on a deeply committed Christian Scientist is not that it is bad for him to do so, but the very fact that it contravenes his deeply held moral beliefs. It could be said that operating *is* in a measure bad for him, but that what bars operating is not that the bad outweighs the good you would do by operating, but rather just (or in addition) the fact that the Christian Scientist deeply believes it wrong to operate.

I think the question that arises here is both deep and interesting. I suggest we bypass it, however. Since we need a way of characterizing the case, and since the line I mentioned seems to me very plausible, I will take it: I will say that what bars your proceeding if David is a deeply committed Christian Scientist is that it would be on balance bad for him if you proceeded. I will say, more generally, that you are barred from proceeding wherever, and only wherever, David has some feature in virtue of which, despite the fact that he will live if and only if you proceed, it is on balance bad for him that you proceed. Deeply held religious or moral beliefs are one possibility; there may be others. But I grant that closer attention to the question that arises here might bring out that explaining why David's being a Christian Scientist (or having some other comparable feature) bars proceeding requires ap-

---

6. I am indebted to Mark Johnston for drawing my attention to the following interesting difference. If David is unconscious, then his being in midstream of a mere flirtation with Christian Science (as opposed to a deep commitment to it) does not bar you from proceeding; by contrast, if David is conscious, and in full possession of his faculties, and refuses you permission to operate, then the fact that his refusal issues from a mere flirtation with Christian Science (as opposed to a deep commitment to it) does not matter—you are barred from proceeding all the same. I have no explanation for this difference.

peal to his deeply held beliefs themselves, as well as to the fact that your proceeding would be bad for him because of his holding those beliefs.

In sum, I will say that what makes it permissible for you to proceed in David's case, if proceeding is permissible, is this: it is on balance good for David that you proceed.

Let us consider another case, one that brings us closer to TROLLEY. A tree fell on Edward; his leg is crushed under the tree and he is unconscious. You are a doctor, and you can see that Edward will probably (though not certainly) live if you cut off his leg straightway, but that he will certainly die if you do not. Is it permissible for you to proceed? I think we may feel inclined to say we can't tell until we hear more about Edward. If Edward is a Christian Scientist or a Jehovah's Witness, then no.

Suppose that none of that is present in Edward. Edward is neither a Christian Scientist nor a Jehovah's Witness, Edward has no feature in light of which even a successful operation would be on balance bad for him; quite to the contrary, a successful operation would be on balance good for Edward. Then I should think you may proceed. But we cannot say here what we said in the case of David, namely that the reason why you may is that it is on balance good for Edward that you proceed, for it may very well turn out not to have been on balance good for Edward that you proceed. Suppose you do proceed, but Edward dies anyway. Then it was not on balance good for Edward that you proceeded—though it was permissible for you to proceed.

What we need here is the notion advantage that we looked at in section 8 of the preceding chapter. If you proceed, you increase the probability that Edward will survive; and by hypothesis, a successful operation would be on balance good for Edward. This means that you give him an advantage by proceeding, the size of the advantage being the product of the amount by which you increase the probability that he will survive and the measure of how good it would be for him if he does. And then we can say: what makes it permissible for you to proceed in Edward's case is this: it is to Edward's advantage that you proceed.

Let us now go back to TROLLEY. I said that the workmen would have consented to Bloggs' turning the trolley later if they had been asked at (i) early morning; and I seemed to take this to show that it is permissible for Bloggs to turn the trolley when he finally does confront the situation in TROLLEY. It was useful to ask whether the workmen would have consented to Bloggs' turning the trolley if they had been asked then: it is plain that, as of that time, their probability of survival is greater if Bloggs will later turn the trolley than if he will not later turn the trolley, but we needed to see whether there was anything true of them in light of which an increased probability of survival would not have made it permissible for Bloggs to turn the trolley later. As I said, our probability of survival is not the only thing that matters to us; do the workmen believe that what happens when there is a runaway trolley should be left to chance? Or to Fate? Or to God? And I said: the more firmly held those views are, and the more central to their lives, the more we are going to think Bloggs really must not intervene. But that was just mere possibility. We can suppose that the workmen would have consented to Bloggs' turning the trolley later on the very ground that it would give them an increased probability of survival. As we can now put the matter, by-passing talk of hypothetical consent: it is to their advantage that Bloggs will turn the trolley later. There is one workman, the one, whoever he may be, who will be on the spur of track on the right when the situation in TROLLEY actually confronts Bloggs, and for *him* Bloggs' turning the trolley later will turn out to have been bad. But as of early morning, it is to the advantage of all, including that one, that Bloggs turn the trolley later.

As of (i) early morning, that is. By (iii) 3:00, things have changed. As of 3:00 it is not to the advantage of all that Bloggs now turn the trolley: it is no longer true of each of them that his probability of survival is greater if Bloggs turns the trolley than if he does not. For it is certain death for the one on the spur of track if Bloggs turns the trolley.

That is the central knot in TROLLEY: the fact that although it was at early morning to the advantage of all that Bloggs turn the trolley later, it is no longer to the advantage of all that Bloggs turn the trolley when the time actually comes for him to turn it. Contrast the case of Edward: it is now to Edward's advantage that you cut off his leg, and now is the time for you to cut it off.

But that does not matter. What was to the advantage of all at early morning is Bloggs' turning the trolley later. Thus Bloggs' turning the trolley later even though when the time comes it will no longer be to the advantage of all that Bloggs turn the trolley.

It might be helpful to rephrase the point in terms of hypothetical consent again. The following is true:

(1) At early morning, they would all have consented to Bloggs' turning the trolley if and when the situation in TROLLEY arises.

But so also is the following:

(1) At early morning, they would all have consented to Bloggs' turning the trolley if and when the situation in TROLLEY arises, even though the one then on the spur of track on the right (whoever he may be) would not then agree to Bloggs' turning it.

The workmen do not get an increased probability of survival unless Bloggs *will* turn the trolley, whatever the then views of the one then on the spur of track on the right.

Well, it isn't hypothetical consent that matters: what matters is what there is about the workmen in virtue of which they would consent. What does the moral work here is that the following is true:

(2) At early morning, it is to the advantage of all that Bloggs turn the trolley if and when the situation in TROLLEY arises.

Moreover,

(2') At early morning, it is to the advantage of all that Bloggs turn the trolley if and when the situation in TROLLEY arises, even though it will not then be to the advantage of the one then on the spur of track on the right (whoever he may be) that Bloggs turn it

is also true, for the advantage to all is obtained only if Bloggs really will turn the trolley.

It might be asked why we shouldn't say that the fact that at early morning it is to the advantage of all that Bloggs later turn the trolley merely makes

(3) It is permissible for Bloggs to turn the trolley if and when the situation in TROLLEY arises

be *true at early morning*—while by the same token, the fact that at 3:00 it is no longer to the advantage of all that Bloggs turn the trolley makes (3) be *false at 3:00*.

Now it is certainly possible for a statement of the form "It is permissible for X to do alpha" to be true at one time and false at a later time. For example, "It is permissible for Smith to shout 'Boo' " may well be true at times when Smith is out alone in the woods and false at times when Smith is in church. But when this is the case, there is a difference between the two times that makes the moral difference—in the case of Smith, the relevant difference lies in Smith's surroundings. What could be thought to be the relevant difference in the case of Bloggs and (3)?

Well, perhaps the relevant difference is the very fact that what was to the advantage of all at early morning is no longer to the advantage of all at 3:00. That *kind* of change could have an impact on what it is permissible to do. Consider Frank. It might be to his advantage now that we operate on him on Tuesday and therefore now permissible that we operate on him on Tuesday, but no longer to his advantage on Tuesday that we operate on him on Tuesday, and therefore no longer permissible on Tuesday that we operate on him on Tuesday. Perhaps the features of his ailment have changed by Tuesday. Perhaps he has become a deeply committed Christian Scientist by Tuesday. But none of this is relevant to Bloggs and (3). The only thing that has changed between early morning and 3:00 in TROLLEY is that it is now clear who the one is who was going to lose if Bloggs turns the trolley. It is no longer to *his* advantage that Bloggs turn the trolley. But *that* change cannot by itself be thought to make a difference. For what was true at early morning was not merely

> (3) It is permissible for Bloggs to turn the trolley if and when the situation in TROLLEY arises,

but also

> (3') It is permissible for Bloggs to turn the trolley if and when the situation in TROLLEY arises even though it will not then be to the advantage of the one then on the spur of track on the right (whoever he may be) that Bloggs turn it.

That cannot be made false at 3:00 by the fact that it is no longer to the advantage of the one by then on the spur of track that Bloggs turn it. Compare

> (4) It is permissible for Smith to shout "Boo".

I said that could be true at one time and false at another, true at times when Smith is out alone in the woods and false at times when Smith is in church. But consider

(4′) It is permissible for Smith to shout "Boo" even when in church.

Smith's walking into a church might well make (4) false; Smith's walking into a church cannot possibly be thought to make (4′) false.

So I conclude that there is nothing in this idea that while it was, at early morning, permissible for Bloggs to turn the trolley, it is no longer, at 3:00, permissible for him to do so. If his turning the trolley was then permissible, it is so now too.

In sum, then, I suggest that what makes it permissible for Bloggs to turn the trolley in TROLLEY is the fact that it was, at early morning, to the advantage of all that he turn it. For similar reasons it would be permissible for the Bloggs of the world we imagined at the end of the preceding section to cut up one to save five in the that-world instance of TRANSPLANT: it is to the advantage of all that he do so. But there are no similar reasons in the case of the our-world instance of TRANSPLANT. Bloggs' cutting up one to save five in our world does not increase the probability of survival of all of us, and even if it did, we have other objections to his doing so, and his doing so is therefore not to our advantage. Advantage, it will be remembered, has to do with goods in addition to mere survival.

I said that TROLLEY seems to be representative of a narrow class of exceptions to the general rule that one may not kill one to save five. More precisely, certain instances of TROLLEY—as when all six on the tracks are workmen, assigned their positions by lot—seem to be representative of the class of exceptions. The exceptions, I suggest, are those in which the one who will be killed, and the five who will be saved, are members of a group such that it was to the advantage of all the members that the one (whoever he or she would later turn out to be) would later be killed, and the only thing that has since changed is that it is now clear who the one was going to turn out to be. The numbers five and one have no special importance, of course; what matters, I should think, is only whether more will be saved, for that is what raises their probability of survival and (other things being equal) therefore makes proceeding later be to the advantage of all.

No doubt a rich imagination can construct cases in which an agent can save many by killing a few for which it is not clear where advantage lies. But this is no objection if in those cases it is also not clear whether or not the agent may proceed. What is needed in a proposed solution to this problem is not that it everywhere deliver clear results, but that it supply an independently plausible rationale for those results clearly delivered by intuition, and it would in fact be an attractive feature of it if it faltered where intuition does.

6. The bystander Bloggs may turn the trolley. *Ought* he turn it? There is nothing in the proposal I make that issues in the conclusion that he ought to. And isn't that as it should be? For mightn't Bloggs himself think these things should be left to chance (or Fate or God)? Alternatively, mightn't Bloggs think these things should not be left to chance, but all the same feel incapable of killing a person, even to save five others? The view that morality requires Bloggs to turn the trolley seems to me to be merely a morally insensitive descendant of the Central Utilitarian Idea.

A more interesting idea is that what Bloggs ought to do is to flip a coin, heads I turn the trolley, tails I don't. If that is correct, then my proposal is not correct, for my proposal says that Bloggs may (just, all simply) turn the trolley. Why might it be thought that he ought to flip a coin? Well, doesn't he thereby give each of the workmen an equal chance at life? And doesn't fairness require him to do that?[7]

But why should we think that Bloggs ought now give them an equal chance at life? Flipping a coin is like conducting a lottery, and to say "Bloggs must now conduct a lottery" is to say "The lottery that took place this morning is morally irrelevant". Indeed, it is to say that Bloggs must proceed as if the world had just been created five minutes ago, for it tells him to ignore the past history of the people now on the tracks. But the world was not created five minutes ago, and I have been suggesting throughout that how those six people came to be on the tracks really does matter.

Moreover, Bloggs' now giving them an equal chance at life is not something they themselves would have wanted him to do if they had been asked at early morning; bypassing hypothetical consent, it was not to their advantage as of early morning that he flip a coin when the time comes. For as of early morning, their probability of survival is greater if Bloggs will (just, all simply) turn the trolley when the time comes than if he will flip a coin when the time comes. A workman

7. John Taurek suggests that fairness requires him to give an equal chance in "Should the Numbers Count?".

who will in fact be among the six at 3:00 has a five-in-six chance of surviving if Bloggs will (just, all simply) turn the trolley when the time comes; he has only a one in two chance of surviving if Bloggs will instead flip a coin.

I stress, however, that this does not mean that Bloggs must (just, all simply) turn the trolley. He may do so. But he may instead do nothing. And I should think also that—moved by the thought that he thereby gives them an equal chance at life—he may instead flip a coin.

7. There is much more of interest to be got from mulling over these cases and others like them, but I suggest we now return to where we were. We were in search of an account of what the behavioral constraint is such that X's having a claim against Y is equivalent to Y's being under the constraint. I suggested at the end of the preceding chapter that central to the constraint is this: if matters relevant to whether Y may infringe X's claim, but irrelevant to the stringency of X's claim, are or were absent, then it is or would be permissible for Y to infringe the claim if and only if Y would thereby produce a sufficiently large and appropriately distributed increment of good, or advantage, the size of the required increment and the appropriateness of its distribution turning entirely on the stringency of the claim. In light of its being the result of revising the Tradeoff Idea, we might call this the Revised Tradeoff Idea.

TROLLEY (and its ilk, for compare deflecting avalanches and out-of-control satellites) seems to make trouble for the Revised Tradeoff Idea. It is permissible for Bloggs to proceed in TROLLEY; but the claim of the one workman on the spur of track on the right is very stringent, and it just is not the case that Bloggs would produce a sufficiently large and appropriately distributed increment of good or advantage *by turning the trolley* to make it permissible for him to turn it. After all, the surgeon would produce an equally large and similarly distributed increment of good or advantage by operating in TRANSPLANT, and nevertheless may not proceed.

The cases of David and Edward that we also looked at in this chapter do not make trouble for the Revised Tradeoff Idea. It is permissible for you to proceed in those cases; how come? What makes it permissible for you to cut off David's leg is not the size of the increment of good you produce. If you proceed, you do save a life at the cost of only a leg, but it would not be permissible to cut off X's leg to save Y's life. What makes it permissible for you to cut off David's leg is, as I put it, that it is on balance good *for David* that you proceed. What justifies here is not the size of the increment of good but its distribution, that it is David who gets the good. Similarly for Edward. It would not be permissible to cut off X's leg to make it probable that Y will live. What makes it permissible for you to cut off Edward's leg is, as I put it, that it is to *Edward's* advantage that you proceed—not the size of the advantage but its distribution. Still, what the Revised Tradeoff Idea requires for permissibility is only that the increment of good or advantage to be produced be both sufficiently large and appropriately distributed. What the cases of David and Edward bring out is that an increment of good or advantage need not be large if it would be distributed to the claim holder.

But there is a question the cases of David and Edward do raise, namely how stringent the claims are that you infringe if you proceed. According to

> The Aggravation Principle: If X has a claim against Y that Y do alpha, then the worse Y makes things for X if Y fails to do alpha, the more stringent X's claim against Y that Y do alpha,

David's claim is of negative stringency, since it is on balance good for David if you proceed, and Edward's claim is more or less probably of negative stringency, according as it is more or less probable that you will save his life if you proceed. But how odd for a theory of rights to yield that some claims are, or probably are, of negative stringency!

I have been assuming that you do infringe claims of David's and Edward's if you proceed; perhaps it would be better to give up this assumption than to swallow the odd outcome that David's claim is of negative stringency and Edward's probably of negative stringency? I hope that no one finds this an attractive idea. If David were conscious, and capable of responding rationally to a request for permission to cut off his leg, then it would be morally required of you that you ask for it. Similarly for Edward. (Compare the 'informed consent' form a hospital patient is asked to sign before an operation. The surgeons are not relieved of the requirement of asking by the fact that the operation will, or probably will, be on balance good for the patient.) That is among the marks of X's having a claim against Y that Y not do alpha: among the things that the behavioral constraint on Y consists in is that, other things being equal, Y must ask X for a release before doing alpha. And it is a hard saying that we lose our rights when we become unconscious. A better saying is that David and Edward still have the claims, though since they are unconscious, other things are not equal in their cases.

A different way of avoiding the odd outcome is to revise the Aggravation Principle.

But I suggest that we should instead simply swallow the odd outcome that David's claim is of negative stringency and Edward's probably of negative stringency. In the first place, it is anyway an odd kind of case in which it is on balance good, or of advantage, for people that we infringe their claims, and it would be no wonder if *any* account of the stringency of the claim in such a case seemed odd. Second, there is positive reason to welcome this odd outcome of the Aggravation Principle. Suppose we accept that David's claim is of negative stringency. Then we have a satisfying explanation of why you need not produce any increment of good for anyone else in order, permissibly, to infringe David's claim. If a claim is of negative stringency, then it is no wonder that you may infringe it without producing any increment of good beyond that increment of good for the claim holder that fixes that the claim *is* of negative stringency. Similarly for Edward.

Again, if we accept that a man's claim is of negative stringency where it is on balance good for him that it be infringed, then we have a satisfying explanation of why the pressure on the potential claim infringer to get a release in advance is proportionately weaker. If you want to cut off X's leg to save Y's life, then you had better get X's permission or not proceed at all, and if X is unconscious, then that is that, you may not proceed. If you want to cut off X's leg to save X's life, then you had better get X's permission if you can, but if X is unconscious, then that is not that, you may proceed.

TROLLEY, however, is another matter. The fact that it was, at early morning, to the advantage of all that Bloggs later turn the trolley does not make the claim of the one workman now, at 3:00, on the spur of track on the right be any the less stringent than it would be if there were no one on the straight track. The Aggravation Principle tells us that his claim is very stringent, and that is surely as it should be. But then TROLLEY does seem to make trouble for the Revised Tradeoff Idea.

But does it really? I have suggested that the reason it is permissible for Bloggs to proceed in TROLLEY is, in short, this: all the parties are members of a group such that it was to their advantage that Bloggs later proceed. This is a feature of the parties that is relevant to whether Bloggs may now infringe the claim of the one workman on the spur of track; *but it is irrelevant to the stringency of the claim.* So if the account of TROLLEY that I have proposed is correct, no revision in the Revised Tradeoff Idea is required. That idea says that if matters relevant to whether Y may infringe X's claim, but irrelevant to the stringency of X's claim, are or were absent, then it is or would be permissible for Y to infringe the claim if and only if Y would thereby produce a sufficiently large and appropriately distributed increment of good, or advantage, the size of the required increment, and the appropriateness of its distribution turning entirely on the stringency of the claim. The feature of the parties in TROLLEY that I have pointed to is among those matters that the Revised Tradeoff Idea invites us to stipulate away. If that feature—along with the other matters relevant to permissibility but irrelevant to stringency—is or were absent in a given case, then it is or would be permissible to infringe the claim only given a suitable tradeoff between increments of good or advantage on the one hand and stringency on the other. TRANSPLANT, for example, is a case in which the feature I pointed to in TROLLEY is absent; and it is a case in which there is no such suitable tradeoff, and so is a case in which the agent may not proceed.

8. We have been asking in Part I what rights *are.* Adapting Hohfeld's account of legal rights, I have suggested that rights fall into one or another of four species: they are claims, privileges, powers or immunities, or clusters of claims, privileges, powers, and immunities. Privileges are lacks-of-claims; powers are abilities to extinguish and generate rights; immunities are lacks-of-powers. So if we have an account of what claims are, we have an account of what all rights are. Which of them we have, and why, are matters we turn to in Part II.

What is it to have a claim? X's having a claim against Y is equivalent to Y's behavior's being constrained in a certain way. What way? There emerged in Chapters 6 and 7 an account of what is *central* to the behavioral constraint on Y that X's having a claim against Y is equivalent to. But as I said earlier (in Chapter 3), there are two other things that are parts of this behavioral constraint. There is, first, that, other things being equal, Y ought not just, all simply, infringe the claim even if Y would produce great good or advantage by infringing it: other things being equal, Y ought to seek a release from X in advance before doing what would, without a release, be an infringement of X's claim. There is, second, that, other things being equal, Y ought to compensate X later for such harms or losses as Y causes X by infringing the claim if Y infringes it. Seeking a release in advance, and compensating later, are acts like any others, and more will therefore be relevant to the question whether Y ought to do these things than merely that X has the claim. The presence of the claim shows itself in the fact that there has to be good reason for *not* doing these things if it is to be permissible to not do them. We saw a number of possibilities in Chapter 3, such as that X is unavailable to be asked for a release (compare David and Edward, who are unconscious). Another possibility is that seeking a release in advance might make it impossible for Y to do for X what infringing X's claim straightway would do for X. (Consider a man whose life can most probably be saved if we operate straightway, the probabilities declining rapidly if we wait until he becomes conscious or if we bring him to consciousness by shaking him awake or giving him a drug.) Yet another possibility is that X would refuse to give a release out of confusion or pain. Still another possibility is what is at work in TROLLEY: what makes it permissible for Bloggs to turn the trolley at 3:00 also makes it unecessary for Bloggs to get a release in advance from the one workman then on the spur of track on the right. Similarly for compensating later: there are a great many things that might make compensating later be unnecessary.

Is a claim merely *equivalent to* that constraint on behavior? Or can we say, more strongly, that a claim *is* that constraint on behavior? I think it does not really matter which we say. There is reason to prefer the weaker thesis, lying in the fact that we may say to Y, "Your behavior is constrained in the following way: . . .", listing what we have surveyed as the features of the constraint on behavior that a claim is equivalent to, and we may well think of ourselves as having given a reason for saying it, an explanation of its being the case, when we add "Because X has a claim against you." It could be argued that if X's having the claim just is Y's behavior's being constrained in those ways, then X's having the claim does not *explain* why Y's behavior is so constrained.

But there is also reason to prefer the stronger thesis, since if we say a claim is not itself a constraint on behavior but is rather 'a something else' that explains a person's being under that constraint, then we may well find ourselves thinking claims more puzzling than they are.

Moreover, we should remember that a fact can be explained by appeal to the same fact, so long as the description of it given in the explanans is a deeper one than the description of it given in the explanandum.

My own view is that we can plausibly say that a claim just is a constraint on behavior, in that the moral interest in the fact that X has a claim against Y issues entirely from the constraint on Y that X's having the claim against Y is at least equivalent to. In short, we lose nothing of moral interest if we choose to adopt the stronger rather than the weaker thesis. But nothing to come will turn on that choice, and anyone who likes is free to reject the stronger thesis in favor of the weaker.

PART II

Rights: Which They Are

Chapter 8

Trespass and First Property

1. I am sitting in the library feeling bored. Across from me a young man is taking notes busily. Such a lovely young man! So I go round the table and kiss him on the back of the neck. This is an infringement of a claim and an instance of a subclass of claim infringements I will call "trespass".

A traditional metaphor for a person's claims is a boundary: all around a person is a boundary (a fence or film or membrane) such that to cross it is to infringe one of his or her claims. In light of that metaphor the name "trespass" would have been a good metaphorical name for all claim infringements,[1] for if I cross your (literal) boundary, I (literally) commit trespass. But I want to reserve the name "trespass" for an important subclass of claim infringements.

Trespass is claim-infringing bodily intrusion or invasion. Consider A's claim against B that B not pinch A's nose. That is a very weak claim, but it is a claim all the same, and if B infringes it he commits trespass. But trespass is not restricted to infringements of weak claims. Rape and cutting off a person's leg are infringements of stringent claims, and these too are instances of trespass.

"Trespass" strikes me as a good name for this subclass of claim infringements in light of what it stood for in early English law. Prosser[2] tells us that there were two headings under which one person could

---

1. Compare: "Forgive us our trespasses as we forgive those who trespass against us".

2. William L. Prosser, *Law of Torts,* 4th ed. (St. Paul: West Publishing Co., 1971). Page numbers in parentheses are to this edition. (I throughout omit Prosser's footnotes.)

bring suit against another in torts: trespass, which emerged in the thirteenth century, and the later trespass on the case.

> Trespass was the remedy for all forcible, direct and immediate injuries, whether to person or to property—or in other words, for the kind of conduct likely to lead to a breach of the peace by provoking immediate retaliation. Trespass on the case, or the action on the case, as it came to be called, developed somewhat later, as a supplement to the parent action of trespass, designed to afford a rememdy for obviously wrongful conduct resulting in injuries which were not forcible or not direct. The distinction between the two lay in the immediate application of force to the person or property of the plaintiff, as distinguished from injury through some obvious and visible secondary cause. (pp. 28–29)

We need examples of trespass and the action on the case—"case" for short—if we are to see what these generalizations come to.

> The classic illustration of the difference between trespass and case is that of a log thrown into the highway. A person struck by the log as it fell could maintain trespass against the thrower, since the injury was direct; but one who was hurt by stumbling over it as it lay in the road could maintain, not trespass, but an action on the case. (p. 29)

I think we have an intuitive feel for the difference between what is done in the two kinds of acts pointed to here. If B threw a log in A's direction and it hit A, we can truly say that B caused the log to come into contact with A, but we can also truly say that B hit A with a log. By contrast, if D threw a log into the highway and C later came along and stumbled over it, we can truly say that D caused the log to come into contact with C, but we cannot also truly say that D hit C with a log. Those adjectives "forcible", "direct", and "immediate" come very naturally to us in trying to describe the difference between the examples of A and B on the one hand and C and D on the other: B caused the contact between log and victim forcibly, directly, and immediately, whereas D did not.

There is a quite general distinction lurking here, and we are all familiar with it. If I throw or leave a log in your path and you stumble over it, I cause the log to be in contact with you; I do more if I hit you with the log. Similarly, if I coerce a man into buttering my bread ("BUTTER THAT BREAD OR I'LL KILL YOU!" I say, in my most menacing way) I cause the bread's being covered with butter, but I do not (myself) butter it. Again, if I pay a man to break my mother-in-law's head I cause her head to be broken, but I do not (myself) break it. There is a large and important class of verbs—they are often called causal verbs—which includes "hit", "butter", "break", as also "kill", "melt", and "drown", which we use to say of an an agent that he or she caused a certain outcome, *and* moreover that he or she caused the outcome in one or other of a restricted range of ways. We all know what is well inside the range and what is plainly outside the range: we all know that if I punched a man in the nose then I hit him with my fist, whereas by contrast if I paid someone to hit someone else with my fist, or if I left my arm (fist clenched) extended outside my window and someone walked into it, then, while I caused my fist to come into contact with the victim, I did not hit the victim with my fist. This difference is one we learn when we learn the rudiments of our langugage.

It is therefore surprising that it should be so hard to say what the difference consists in.[3] We find ourselves saying, quite generally, that in the example to which the causal verb applies, the outcome was caused forcibly, directly, and immediately.[4] But if asked what this forcibleness, directness, and immediacy come to, we find it very hard to explain.

Still, the difference is one we are familiar with, and that is enough for our purposes. Trespass in early English law was the writ under which A could sue B for hitting A or A's property with a log; case was the writ under which C could sue D for causing a log to come into contact with C and thereby causing C a harm. Trespass in our use of the term is a kind of claim infringement in which the agent causes a bodily occurrence (an intrusion or invasion) in the way in which B caused a log to be in contact with A, and not in the way in which D caused a log to be in contact with C.

Trespass in early English law was the writ under which A could sue B for hitting A *or A's property* with a log, and I should stress that in our use of the term, causing something to come into contact with a person's property is *not* trespass: the contact must be with the person himself or herself. Though let us allow the victim to be clothed. If Bloggs fondles my shoes as he passes down the hotel corridor where I have left them to be polished, he may perhaps be thought to infringe

---

3. Some discussion appears in my "Verbs of Action", *Synthese*, 62 (1988).
4. Compare the legal locution: did the force "come to rest"?

a property right of mine, but he does not commit trespass in our use of the term. If Bloggs fondles my shoes when they are on my feet he infringes a property right of mine, but the interesting fact about what he does for present purposes is that he also commits trespass in our use of the term. Who strokes the sleeve of my coat while it is on the hanger strokes only my coat; who strokes the sleeve of my coat while my arm is in it strokes *me*.

And I should perhaps stress that to single trespass out from other claim infringements is not to say that the claims infringed in trespass are more stringent than other claims. Or that they are less stringent. We do well to start with them, however.

2. What is the source of the claims infringed in trespass? Well, what at the outset shows that we do have such claims? In Part I, we were merely supposing tentatively that we have this or that claim, with a view to finding out what a claim *is*—more precisely, what it would mean to have this or that claim, if we had it. I chose what I thought were plausible examples: I took it that you would agree that a theory of rights should yield that we do have the claims I invited you to suppose we have. But I have nowhere yet argued that we do have them. So far as the putative claims infringed in trespass are concerned, however, the argument is now an easy one. For X to have a claim against Y that Y not do alpha is for Y to be under the behavioral constraint described in Part I, and we are under that behavioral constraint in respect of bodily intrusions or invasions committed on others. Other things being equal, I may not kiss you on the back of the neck, or cut off your leg, without your consent.[5] So we can speak not merely of the putative claims infringed in trespass, but, all simply, of the claims infringed in trespass.

Sometimes, of course, people consent to bodily intrusions or invasions—I will henceforth say merely bodily intrusions, for short. Should we say that *what* we have a claim against is not bodily intrusion but unconsented-to bodily intrusion? No. If X consents to Y's doing alpha, then X no longer has a claim against Y that Y not do alpha, but the claim X had prior to giving consent was (all simply)

---

5. It should be remembered—see Introduction, sections 2 and 10—that we are not setting ourselves to construct all of morality out of elementary particles. I take certain judgments about what we ought or ought not do, may or may not do, as data.

that Y not do alpha. Similarly for forfeiture of claims: what X had before forfeiting his or claim against Y that Y not do alpha was, not that Y not do-alpha-unless-X-forfeits-the-claim-that-Y-not-do-alpha, but (all simply) that Y not do alpha.

So what we have is (all simply) claims that others not commit bodily intrusion on us, and let us ask: what is the source of those claims?

Trespass may cause harm, and don't we have a claim to not be caused harm? If a man hits you with a log, his doing so may cause you a broken bone. But that is not unique to trespass. If a man throws a log into the highway, his having done this may also cause you a broken bone: you may later come along, fail to see the log, stumble over it, and have a bad fall. Moreover, a given instance of trespass may cause no harm at all.[6] If I go round the table and kiss the lovely young man on the back of the neck, I am not going to cause him any harm, but I infringe a claim of his all the same.

Trespass may cause fear. That lovely young man is very likely to feel a stab of fear. Is she crazy?! And if she's crazy, who can tell what she'll do next? But so also may many claim infringements that are not instances of trespass cause fear; and so also may many acts that are not claim infringements at all.

More interesting is the fact that trespass insults, affronts, offends. At a minimum it does these things, for it may do more: we should remember that rape and cutting off a person's leg are also trespass.

But trespass need not insult. In the first place, trespass may be committed on a person and the person never find out. Trespass can be committed on a person who is asleep, for example, or in a coma. Second, trespass can be welcomed after the fact. Compare David, of the preceding chapter, who will later be pleased that you cut his leg off to save his life. Trespass can even be welcomed before the fact, as where one person hopes that another will make a sexual advance but is afraid to make clear that the advance would be welcomed.

---

6. Prosser tells us about trespass in early English law: "Trespass, perhaps because of its criminal origin, required no proof of any actual damage, since the invasion of the plaintiff's rights was regarded as a tort in itself; while in the action on the case, which developed purely as a tort remedy, there could ordinarily be no liability unless actual damage was proved" (p. 29). If damage need not have been proved, then damage need not have been present. The gravamen of the charge in trespass was that a kind of right was infringed, whether or not harm was caused.

Moreover, insult is not unique to trespass. If a man who owns a shop cheats me, and I then find out I have been cheated, I am insulted, for he shows lack of respect for my claims; yet he does not commit trespass. Indeed, every violation of a claim (that the victim learns of) insults in just this way. It is arguable that trespass is the greater insult. The shopowner who cheats me insults me, but he probably insults me more profoundly if he instead leans across the counter and pinches my nose. It is arguable, more strongly, that trespass that takes the form of sexual use of a person is the profoundest insult. I am offended if a man suddenly leans forward and taps me gently on the forehead with a ruler he carries around with him; I am the more offended if I see his act as an odd way of obtaining sexual gratification. But I say only that these things are arguable. Much trespass that is not aimed at sexual gratification is profoundly insulting, as where it involves ignoring one's presence altogether; and many claim infringements that are not trespass are arguably equally offensive—compare a case in which someone tells you an obvious lie, a lie any fool could see through.

More important, while lack of respect for one's claims can insult, it cannot be the insult itself that makes an act be an infringement of a claim. If I have told my neighbor how much I dislike plastic garden ornaments, then he insults me if he pays no attention and lines his path with pink plastic flamingoes. If Bloggs says to me after the department meeting "That was a dumb idea you wasted our time on!" then he insults me. But neither my neighbor nor Bloggs infringes any claim of mine. It could, I think, be said that trespass *bothers* us because (perhaps among other things) it insults—so long as we allow that other acts can insult us too—but it cannot be said that an act is a claim infringement because it insults, and *a fortiori* it cannot be said that the source of the claims infringed in trespass lies in the fact that trespass is insulting.

There is a general point in the offing here. It is often said that our rights (and on some views morality as a whole) have their source in the respect that a person owes to other people. But the nature of that respect wants careful spelling out. I certainly do not have a general right that other people respect me. (Perhaps my idea really was dumb.) And I certainly do not have a general right that other people respect my wishes. (Perhaps my neighbor thinks it merely freakish in me to dislike plastic garden ornaments.) It certainly can be said that we must respect the rights of others; but if respect for persons just is respect for their rights—that is, if respect for persons just is (other things being equal) according them what they have a right to—then their having those rights is presupposed by, and does not issue from, the respect we owe them. Perhaps respect for persons is something other than respect for their rights. Then the work would remain to be done of saying what it is, and how this or that in morality issues from it.

3. I said that to single trespass out from other claim infringements is not to say that the claims infringed in trespass are more—or that they are less—stringent than other claims. They are nevertheless fundamental.

We can suppose that A lacks claims against X, Y, and Z that they not commit bodily intrusion on him compatibly with supposing that A has other claims against X, Y, and Z. He might, for example, own a piece of property, such as a pair of shoes; ownership being a cluster of claims, privileges, and powers in respect of a thing, A therefore has claims against X, Y, and Z in respect of his shoes, perhaps among others, that they not wear the shoes.

It is arguable that people have a claim to not be caused harm. Is having that claim (supposing people have it) compatible with lacking the claims infringed in trespass? Interestingly enough, no. One who causes harm very often causes it by committing bodily intrusion (hitting the victim with a log, shooting the victim in the foot). Now if A has a claim against others that they not cause him harm, then the Means Principle for Claims tells us that he has a claim against others that they not commit such bodily intrusions or invasions on him as would thereby cause him harm. So if A lacks the claims infringed in trespass, then he lacks the quite general claim to not be caused harm. The most he could be thought to have in respect of harm, compatibly with lacking the claims infringed in trespass, is a claim to not be caused harm by means that do not involve bodily intrusion.

Similarly for the claim to not be caused pain (supposing people have such a claim). The most A could be thought to have in respect of pain, compatibly with lacking the claims infringed in trespass, is a claim to not be caused pain by means that do not involve bodily intrusion.

Of course A could be supposed to have privileges compatibly with lacking the claims infringed in trespass, privileges of doing this or that. But A's moral status is very thin if he lacks claims against bodily intrusion. In particular, you not only infringe no claim of his if you

commit harmless, nonpainful bodily intrusion on him, you infringe
no claim of his if you cause him harm or pain *by* committing bodily
intrusion on him.

Moreover, the claims A does have would not be worth much to
him. Consider A's property claims over his shoes. Suppose I want
those shoes. I must not just walk off with them, for that would be
theft, an infringement of a property claim of his. The thing for me to
do is to wring his neck to get him to give them to me, for doing that
is no infringement of any claim of his. Even his privileges of action
(if he has privileges of action) would be of little value to him, for
given he lacks claims against bodily intrusion, no claim of his stands
in the way of anyone's preventing him from acting, by whatever
ghastly laying on of hands we might choose to imagine.

So the claims infringed in trespass are fundamental. We might put
this point in terms of our metaphor as follows: the claims infringed
in trespass are at the center of the realm of rights.

What is their source? It is possible to give claims. We will be looking
later (in Chapter 12) at the giving of claims that goes on when we
make promises, and (in Chapters 13 and 14) at the giving of claims
that goes on when we make law, and it is arguable that one source
of at least some of the claims infringed in trespass is that we were
given them in one or another of those ways. Our law, for example,
does assign us claims against others that they not cut off our legs.
But I say only "one source", for we would have had that claim even
if law had not assigned it to us. More generally, we would have had
all of the claims infringed in trespass even if private commitments or
law had not given us any of them. Neither private commitments nor
law are necessary for the having of claims against bodily intrusion.
So what is the other source? What contributes to our having them
and would have made us have them even in the absence of private
commitments and law? Presumably this other source has to consist
in some feature of *us,* and we need to know what it is.

Well, what would have had to be different about us for it to have
been the case that we lacked the claims infringed in trespass—or
anyway, if we had them, to have had them only because of private
commitments or law? Since the claims infringed in trespass are fundamental in the ways I mentioned, let us for simplicity ask instead:
what would have had to be different about us for it to have been the
case that we had no claims at all—or anyway, if we had any claims,
to have had such claims as we had only because of private commit-

ments or law? In what ways would the inhabitants of a possible world have to be different from us in order for this to be true of them?

It would be no surprise if we found ourselves thinking here of Hobbes' description of the state of nature. Let us think of that as a description of a possible world, which I will call Hobbes' State of Nature. Hobbes said (in passages I quoted in Chapter 1) that in the state of nature there is

> no Propriety, no Dominion, no *Mine* and *Thine* distinct; but onely that to be every mans, that he can get; and for so long as he can keep it

and therefore that "every man has a Right to everything; even to one anothers body". So Hobbes' State of Nature is a world in which everybody has a privilege of doing as he or she pleases, thus a world in which nobody has any claims. Of course Hobbes thought that the inhabitants of the state of nature would come to realize that they would live better lives if they gave each other claims, and would therefore proceed to do so. How? By committing themselves to each other to obey a jointly chosen authority whose role is to make and enforce law. But even if the inhabitants of Hobbes' State of Nature did give each other claims, such claims as they would thereby come to have are all of them claims they would then have only because of private commitments and law.

In what ways are the inhabitants of Hobbes' State of Nature different from us? Hobbes described them as indifferent to each other. We by contrast do feel a considerable amount of fellow feeling toward others—at least toward some others—and it must surely be a deep fact about us that we do. As Aristotle said, we are by nature social animals. So in this respect the inhabitants of Hobbes' State of Nature are not merely different from us but radically different from us.

Hobbes also described them as roughly equal in their capacity to do each other harm, and we certainly do not seem to be. Does that mark them as radically different from us? I should think not. In any case, Hobbes did not have in mind that they are all equal in strength.[7]

7. "NATURE hath made men so equall, in the faculties of body, and mind; as that though there bee found one man sometimes manifestly stronger in body, or of quicker mind then another; yet when all is reckoned together, the difference between man, and man, is not so considerable, as that one man can thereupon claim to himselfe any benefit, to which another may not pretend, as well as he. For as to the strength of body, the weakest has strength enough to kill the strongest, either by secret machination, or by confederacy with others, that are in the same danger with himselfe." Hobbes, *Leviathan*, part 1, ch. 13.

The role of the 'rough equality' provision in Hobbes' discussion of the state of nature was merely to contribute—along with the provision of material scarcity—to explaining why the inhabitants would realize it would improve their lives to give each other claims.

So the inhabitants of Hobbes' State of Nature are radically different from us in their being indifferent to each other. Hobbes tells us they lack claims until such time as they give each other claims. We might therefore conclude that it is our fellow feeling that is the source of the fact that we would have claims even in the absence of private commitments or law.

But is this correct? For let us ask: what is supposed to make it *true* that the inhabitants of Hobbes' State of Nature have no claims, or only such claims as they have because of private commitments or law? Consider a time in the history of that world before the inhabitants started giving each other claims; what is supposed to make it *true* that the inhabitants do not have any claims at that time? Hobbes has an argument to this effect: there is not yet any law in that world. Hobbes said "Where there is no common Power, there is no Law: where no Law, no Injustice". It is, he said, consequent to there being at that time no law that there is at that time "no Propriety, no Do-minion, no *Mine* and *Thine* distinct; but onely that to be every mans, that he can get; and for so long as he can keep it", and thus "every man has a Right to everything; even to one anothers body". On Hobbes' view, in short, there being law is a necessary condition for having claims. So on his view there not yet being law in Hobbes' State of Nature means that no inhabitant as yet has any claims.

But law is not a necessary condition for having claims. There are claims that we in our world are assigned by law but that we would have even if there had been no law to assign them to us. So the mere fact that there is not yet law in Hobbes' State of Nature does not mean that no inhabitant has any claims. Why shouldn't we suppose that the inhabitants do have claims against each other, but infringe them from time to time, indeed, violate them from time to time?

A claim is a behavioral constraint: X's having a claim against Y that such and such be the case consists, centrally, in its being the case that other things being equal Y ought not let the such and such fail to be the case. So one way in which it could be fixed that no inhabitant of Hobbes' State of Nature yet has any claims is by supposing that the inhabitants are not—or anyway are not yet—subject to moral law at all. If moral law issues no directives to them at all, then *a fortiori* it does not issue the directive to not (other things being equal) let such and such fail to be the case.

But supposing that there is a time in the history of that world at which the inhabitants are not subject to moral law requires supposing that they are at that time in yet another way radically different from us, so different as perhaps not even to be thought of as human beings. What I have in mind is a Kantian idea, and surely a very plausible one, that the capacity to conform your conduct to moral law is a necessary and sufficient condition for the moral law to apply to you. Typewriters and animals lack the capacity to conform their conduct to moral law—there is no such thing as a typewriter's or a cat's doing a thing because it ought to—and therefore it is never true to say of a typewriter or cat that it ought to do such and such. Human beings, by contrast, do possess the capacity to conform their conduct to moral law—there is such a possibility as a human being's doing a thing because he or she ought to—and therefore it is sometimes true to say of a human being that he or she ought to do such and such. So to suppose that the inhabitants of Hobbes' State of Nature are at a time not subject to moral law requires supposing that they are not then capable of conforming their conduct to moral law. How so? Are they animal-like in the ways that mark an animal as incapable of conforming its conduct to moral law?

An alternative hypothesis is, not that they are not subject to moral law at all, but rather that they are subject to a different moral law from the one we are subject to. A claim is a behavioral constraint of a quite special kind. Perhaps the moral law true of their world does not prescribe action in accordance with that kind of behavioral constraint?

It is of interest that Hobbes himself thought this of them and their world: he thought that the inhabitants of Hobbes' State of Nature *are* subject to moral law, even prior to their establishing a legal system, but that the moral law they are subject to during that time does not require action in accordance with the kind of behavioral constraint that a claim is to be identified with. Hobbes is sometimes said to have thought that morality requires nothing at all of the inhabitants of Hobbes' State of Nature until after they have come together to establish law, morality itself only coming into existence along with law. But this is not true: he thought that morality does require something of the inhabitants of Hobbes' State of Nature right from the outset. He thought it plainly in the interest of each that they give and acquire claims, and *therefore* concluded that each ought to try to bring about what (as he thought) was necessary for doing so, namely the establishment of law. More precisely, he thought that each ought to try to bring this about where, and only where, it is not too dangerous to make the effort, thus only where it is in his or her own long-range interest to make the effort. (Hobbes thought moral law does not require approaching your neighbor with the suggestion that your neighbor join the social compact if your neighbor would kill you for the apples in your pocket by way of reply.) So it is a very plausible idea that Hobbes thought that what the inhabitants ought to do— prior to the establishment of a legal system—is to follow the dictates of ETHICAL EGOISM, which says that a person ought to do that which, and only that which, it is in his or her interest to do. But if ETHICAL EGOISM is true of them, then—given their interests—they lack claims. For the inhabitants of Hobbes' State of Nature are, by hypothesis, indifferent to each other, and it is therefore entirely possible to imagine an occasion on which it is in A's interest to shoot B to forestall B's eating some apples A would like to eat. (A is indifferent to B, and B's plight is a matter of indifference to C, D, and the rest, so A need not fear that anyone will take revenge on him for the loss of poor B.) Suppose that is the case. Then ETHICAL EGOISM says A ought to shoot B, where a moral law incorporating claims would say he ought not.

But is Hobbes right about Hobbes' State of Nature? That is, is it true that the inhabitants of Hobbes' State of Nature—prior to their establishing a legal system—really are subject to the dictates of ETHICAL EGOISM? Why should we believe this true? If B were about to cause A a serious harm, and A could forestall that harm only by shooting B, then it would not only be in A's interest to shoot B, we might well think that, other things being equal, moral law permits A's shooting B. Moral law surely permits A's cherishing his own life and bodily integrity. But it equally surely does not require A's shooting B. Moreover, it does not require, or even permit, A's shooting B just on the ground that shooting B would be in A's interest, however minor the interest and however slight the advancement of the interest. That A happens to be indifferent to B can hardly be thought to matter.

Indeed, the fact that the inhabitants of Hobbes' State of Nature are indifferent to each other does not make it the case that they lack claims; it yields at most that they will not accord any claims unless it suits them to do so. So it is not our fellow feeling that makes *us* have claims.

As I said, moral law surely permits A's cherishing his own life and bodily integrity, and so also for everyone else. This means that the inhabitants of Hobbes' State of Nature—prior to their establishing a legal system—are also not subject to the dictates of one or other of the versions of ACT UTILITARIANISM we looked at in Chapter 5. ACT UTILITARIANISM would require of the inhabitants that they submit to an attack, indeed, that they positively offer themselves for attack, wherever doing so would be value-maximizing. That is certainly not correct. (Hobbes himself would have thought it a quite wild idea.)

I should perhaps stress that I am not saying that self-defense is always permissible. It is arguable that criminals may not defend themselves against assaults on them by a lawful authority pursuant to the carrying out of their sentences. (It is worth reminding ourselves that this view is not universally held. Hobbes, we may remember, insisted that all bets are off when they come at you with chains and whips, and that anything goes in defense of your life.) Again, it is arguable that a man might sell himself into a form of slavery that includes forgoing self-defense.

Again, as we saw in Chapter 4, morality does require people to submit to some attacks even where they are not criminals and have not sold themselves into slavery. For example, my neighbor must submit to my attack on his pink plastic garden ornaments if the only way in which he can defend against it is by shooting me in the foot. But that is because what I threaten is infringement of a minor property right, and what he must do to defend his property is to cause me a serious harm. If my attack is not on his garden ornament but on his person—if I am threatening to kill him—and if also it is true that the only way he can defend against my attack is by shooting me in the foot, then it is entirely permissible for him to shoot me in the foot. (Indeed, if defending himself requires shooting me in the head, and thereby killing me, then he may do that too.)

Moreover, I am not saying that self-defense on the part of a human being is (sometimes) permissible on the ground that the human being *is* a human being. Morality permits animals to defend themselves against threats to their lives, for morality requires nothing at all of animals.

In any case, morality permits a measure of cherishing of one's own life and bodily integrity: it permits self-defense where ACT TILITAR-

IANISM would require submission. So it cannot be said that the inhabitants of Hobbes' State of Nature are subject to the dictates of ACT UTILITARIANISM.

Perhaps looking at Hobbes' State of Nature is looking in the wrong direction. We were asking: what would have had to be different about us for it to have been the case that we had no claims at all—or anyway, if we had any claims, to have had such claims as we had only because of private commitments or law. And we straightway turned to Hobbes' State of Nature, and found that it is not at all clear what is supposed to make it be the case that the inhabitants of that world have no claims prior to the generating of claims by private commitments of law. But perhaps that is not the only candidate possible world in which people have no claims against each other? Perhaps we should begin with ETHICAL EGOSIM or ACT UTILITARIANISM and try to imagine a possible world in which one or other of them is true.

Consider ACT UTILITARIANISM. As I said in Chapter 5, it is claims that block value-maximizing, so if ACT UTILITARIANISM is true in a world, then *a fortiori* the inhabitants of that world lack claims. What we need, however, is to get a characterization of the inhabitants of such a world that makes clear that ACT UTILITARIANISM *is* true in their world.

We might begin by imagining a world whose inhabitants all believe that ACT UTILITARIANISM is true. So what happens when Y attacks X, threatening to do X a serious harm, but it would be value-maximizing for X to submit? If all the inhabitants believe that ACT UTILITARIANISM is true, then in particular X does, so perhaps X submits to the attack, and does so precisely because of thinking he or she ought to. (I say only "perhaps", because we do not always do what we think we ought to do.) Does that mean that X really was morally required to submit? Hardly. Consider TRANSPLANT, for example. The surgeon and the young man might both believe that the young man ought to submit to the aggression. Indeed, they might both believe that the young man ought to volunteer his parts, so that no aggression is necessary. It certainly does not follow that moral law requires either of these things of the young man.

We need to dig deeper into the inhabitants than the level of belief if we are to get it fixed that ACT UTILITARIANISM is true in a world: we need to supply information about the inhabitants' interests.

Let us try this. In the world we are to be imagining, it is in each inhabitant's interest to act in accordance with ACT UTILITARIANISM.

How could that be—given that ACT UTILITARIANISM requires sacrifice of life or bodily integrity where making the sacrifice would be value-maximizing. Let us suppose that sacrificing life or bodily integrity, where making the sacrifice would be value-maximizing, is itself in each inhabitant's interest. Now we have that it is in the young man's interest to volunteer to be a donor for the surgeon's patients in the that-world instance of TRANSPLANT: but for ignorance or confusion about his own interests, the young man would positively want to volunteer. More generally, we will suppose it true of each inhabitant that it is in his or her interest to do whatever ACT UTILITARIANISM requires.

Among the things that ACT UTILITARIANISM requires is putting up with, indeed getting oneself to positively welcome, that others also do what ACT UTILITARIANISM requires—lest anger lead to resentment, and resentment to wrongful action, and wrongful action to a decrease in value. So let us add that it is in each inhabitant's interest that others do what ACT UTILITARIANISM requires. If the young man does not know of the needs of the surgeon's five patients, then ACT UTILITAR-IANISM may or may not require the surgeon to tell the young man about them and ask him to volunteer to be a donor: whether the surgeon is required to do this turns on whether it would be value-maximizing for him to do so. No matter: we are supposing that if it would be value-maximizing for the surgeon to proceed without asking the young man to volunteer, then that too is in the young man's interest.

More generally, we are supposing that it is in each inhabitant's interest that he or she do what ACT UTILITARIANISM requires, and in each inhabitant's interest that each of the others do what ACT UTIL-ITARIANISM requires.

Let us ask: what would these people have to be like if they are to have a structure of interests of which this is true?

They have to be like bees or ants. Perhaps even more bee- or ant-like than common or garden bees or ants. Many bits of bee behavior contribute to the good of the hive, and we may suppose that it is in general in an individual bee's interest both that it, and all the other bees in the hive, act in such a way as to contribute to the good of the hive; but I cannot quite bring myself to believe that it is *really* in the queen bee's interest that the worker bees kill her when the hive needs a more productive queen.

In any case, it is in the interest of an inhabitant of this world to get or have or do a thing only if it is in the interest of the group as a whole that he or she get or have or do the thing. As we might put it: they have no inherently individual interests—there is nothing that would be good for the individual which would not also be good for the group as a whole. Metaphorically, each is no more than a cog in the machinery.

Now have we a world of which ACT UTILITARIANISM is true? Well, are the inhabitants of this world subject to moral law at all? Bees and ants are not, but I suppose it just barely possible to think that the inhabitants of this world are, for I think we can suppose they are sufficiently like us to be capable of conforming their conduct to moral law. And what does moral law tell them to do? Given their interests, it is surely right to think that no claim of the young man's is infringed in a that-world instance of TRANSPLANT. More generally, it is surely right to think that no value-maximizing act in that world infringes any claim. And I should think that if they are subject to moral law at all, then—given their interests—what moral law tells them to do is to maximize value, value-maximizing being precisely what suits them all. Thus whatever ACT UTILITARIANISM says they ought to do is exactly what they ought to do, and no one has any claims.

It is striking, however, that—given their interests—the prescriptions for action that are issued to them by ACT UTILITARIANISM are exactly the same as the prescriptions for action that would be issued to them by ETHICAL EGOISM. For that world, the dictates of ACT UTILITARIANISM and ETHICAL EGOISM converge.[8]

We have been trying to imagine a world in which ACT UTILARIANISM is true, and found a world in which the dictates of both it and ETHICAL EGOISM are true. What if we had instead tried to imagine a world in which ETHICAL EGOISM is true? One possible outcome is that we would have arrived at the same place. Making it seem plausible that ETHICAL EGOISM is true of a world requires supplying the inhabitants with interests of a kind which make action in accord with interest not be patently wrongful, and it is clear that one way to secure that is to do exactly what we did above, namely include in our description of the world that its inhabitants have no inherently individual interests.

---

8. The explanatory moral judgments of these two theories diverge, however. (See Introduction, section 8.) What converge are the object-level judgments of the two theories.

Is there another possible world we can get to if we try to imagine a world in which ETHICAL EGOISM is true? I fancy it is possible to imagine a world whose inhabitants do have claims, but in which it is in the interest of each to accord them wherever he or she ought to. (In a that-world instance of TRANSPLANT, it is in the surgeon's interest to refrain from operating on the young man. It is also in his five patients' interests to not lay hands on the young man to force him to volunteer. How so, given they will live if and only if they get his parts? Well, that is just a fact about what their interests are like.) I should think that if we allow ourselves sufficiently free play in characterizing the interests of the inhabitants of a world, we can make the dictates of ETHICAL EGOISM for the world converge with those of any moral theory you like, including a moral theory that incorporates the special kind of constraint on behavior that having claims consists in. The central dictates of ETHICAL EGOISM are interesting only when conjoined with one or other particular assumption about the interests of those its dictates are issued to; otherwise they are empty.

But I think it emerges that in order to get it clearly fixed about a world that its inhabitants *lack* claims by way of imagining that either ACT UTILITARIANISM or ETHICAL EGOISM is true of them, we have to imagine a hive-like world whose bee-like inhabitants are radically different from us. For we do have inherently individual interests, and that is a deep fact about us. I will come back to it shortly.

Aren't there any other candidates? Is there some other moral theory that might be true of a world, from which it would follow that no inhabitant Y has the special kind of behavioral constraint in respect of X that X's having a claim against Y consists in? One can invent any number of possible moral theories of a Sunday afternoon; the hard part is to invent a moral theory that can plausibly be supposed true of a world inhabited by creatures sufficiently like us to be subject to moral law, *and* that is incompatible with the supposition that its inhabitants have claims against each other. It is just barely possible to do this in the case of ACT UTILITARIANISM and ETHICAL EGOISM, for I think we can think of the bee-like creatures of a hive-like world as subject to moral law; and they do not have claims against each other. But I know of no other candidates.

Let us go back. We were in search of the source of the claims infringed in trespass. I said that what makes us have those claims must be some feature of us. In order to find out what that feature is, we should therefore ask what would have had to be different about

us for us to have lacked them. Since the claims infringed in trespass
are fundamental, I said we should ask what would have had to be
different about us for us to have had no claims at all—or anyway,
no claims not generated by private commitments or law. We have
surveyed two possibilities. (i) We would have had no claims if we had
not been subject to moral law, for if we were not subject to moral
law, then *a fortiori* morality would not require of us that we accord
any claims. But for that to have been true of us, we would have had
to be radically different: we would have had to be incapable of conforming our conduct to moral law. (ii) We would have had no claims
if we had been subject to moral law, but to a moral law that requires
what is incompatible with Y's being, in respect of X, under the behavioral constraint that X's having a claim against Y consists in. What
moral law? The dictates of ACT UTILITARIANISM would hold of us if
and only if we were radically different from what we are: we would
have had to have no inherently individual interests—it would have
had to be true of us that there is nothing that would be good for an
individual which would not also be good for the group as a whole.
We should conclude, then, that it is those two features of us that are,
together, the source of our having claims: on the one hand that we
are subject to moral law, on the other hand that we have inherently
individual interests.

Let us focus on the second of these two features. We certainly do
not have only inherently individual interests: there are lots of instances
of convergence of interest between individuals, instances of things
good for one that are also good for another. For example, much of
what is in the interest of the child is in the interest of the parent, and
vice versa. We plainly differ from the inhabitants of Hobbes' State of
Nature in this respect, for the inhabitants of Hobbes' State of Nature
are indifferent to each other. Moreover, there are lots of instances of
convergence of interest between individuals on the one hand and the
group as a whole on the other. Much of what is in the interest of the
community as a whole really is in the interest of each. But not all.
The surgeon would maximize value if he proceeded in a this-world
instance of TRANSPLANT, but it is not in the interest of the this-world
young man that he do so. It is *because* the young man has interests—
interests, in particular, in life and bodily integrity—that are not identical with the interest of the group as a whole that the young man
has a claim against the surgeon that the surgeon not operate, and
therefore that the surgeon must not operate. Creatures who lack that

divergence of interest, such as the bee-like inhabitants of the hive-like world, are on any view radically different from us; and it is because they are different from us in this respect that they lack claims.

This second feature must surely connect with the first. Bees and ants are of course not subject to moral law; are the bee-like creatures of the hive-like world subject to moral law? I said I think we can suppose they are sufficiently like us to be capable of conforming their conduct to moral law. But can we really get a grip on this idea? If the members of a group of creatures cannot distinguish between their own interests and the interests of the group as a whole, for the reason that there is no such distinction to be made, then it is hard to get a grip on the idea of a member's doing a thing because he or she ought to—certainly there is no such thing as a member's so much as thinking he or she ought to forgo what is in his or her interest for the sake of the interest of the group as a whole.

In any case, it is not our fellow feeling that makes us have claims; it is not what makes us different from the inhabitants of Hobbes' State of Nature that makes us have claims. What makes us have claims is precisely what sets limits to our fellow feeling—it is that about us in respect of which we resemble the inhabitants of Hobbes' State of Nature more than we resemble bees in a hive.

Given the evil that human beings do to each other, it is no wonder that so many people feel it to be a bad thing in us that we have inherently individual interests. How much kinder bees are to each other! How much more satisfying the life in an 'organic community' than the life of alienation in a modern state! The ideal of the hive is seductive and fuels all communitarian ideologies. But the bee-like creatures of our hive-like world are not in fact kind to each other; each is indifferent to the others except insofar as the others are parts of the whole. (It is arguable, in fact, that without inherently individual interests, we would have no personal attachments to individual others, for the possibility of X's forming a personal attachment to Y rests on the possibility that at least some of Y's interests will come to be more in X's own interest than is the interest of the group as a whole—X has to be capable of preferring Y to the group.) And given the creatures we are, the ideal of the state as hive cannot be made real: it is amazing that communitarians have expected otherwise.

No doubt we do not have a claim to everything it is in our inherently individual interests to have. There are limits, and we will be looking at them later.

4. Some of these considerations bear on an actual as opposed to merely imaginary state of affairs. I have slavery in mind, and a brief aside on it might not be out of order here. The South's antebellum slaveowners declared (i) that their slaves had no claims other than those given by their owners,[9] and yet (ii) that their slaves were subject to moral law, and not only subject to moral law but subject to a moral law under which their owners have claims against them, and they therefore have duties toward their owners. (Consider eating one of the owner's pigs without permission. Consider running away. Aren't these theft of the owner's property?[10]) How on earth could anyone have kept both of these views in mind at once? For (i) to have been true of the slaves requires that the slaves have been markedly less than fully human; but then what moral law could they have been thought subject to? ACT UTILITARIANISM? ETHICAL EGOISM? No, for given (ii), the moral law they are subject to has to make room for the special kind of behavioral constraint that a claim consists in. It was of course profitable for the slaveowners that it be thought their slaves had no claims other than those given by their owners: that made ownership of them possible. But it was also profitable for the slave-owners that they were able to get as many as possible of their slaves

9. The classic statement is Justice Ruffin's opinion in *State v. Mann*, 13 N. Car. (2 Devereux) 263 (1829): "The end [of slavery] is the profit of the master, his security and the public safety; the subject, one doomed in his own person and his posterity, to live without knowledge and without the capacity to make anything his own, and to toil that another may reap the fruits . . . Such obedience is the consequence only of uncontrolled authority over the body . . . The power of the master must be absolute to render the submission of the slave perfect . . . This discipline belongs to the state of slavery. They cannot be disunited without abrogating at once the rights of the master and absolving the slave from his subjection". The slaves themselves, not surprisingly, made efforts to get their owners to regard the relation, not as one of ownership, but rather as contractual. See Eugene Genovese, *Roll, Jordan, Roll* (New York: Vintage Books, 1976).

10. Here is one planter: "To keep a diary of their conduct would be a record nothing short of a series of violations of the laws of God and man. To moralize and induce the slave to assimilate with the master and his interest has been and is the great desideratum aimed at" (quoted in Genovese, *Roll, Jordan, Roll,* p. 602). On the other hand, Genovese says, the slaves themselves saw nothing wrong in 'stealing' from the master: "Their logic was impeccable. If they belonged to their masters—if they were in fact his chattels—how could they steal from him? Suppose they ate one of his chickens or hogs or some of his corn? They had only transformed his property from one form into another, much as they did when they fed the master's corn to the master's chickens" (p. 602).

(and as many as possible of those who were not slaves) to think of the slaves as having duties toward their owners. So no wonder the slaveowners held this stew of views concurrently—what made it possible was the phenomenon I called failing to connect (Introduction, section 5).[11]

5. We have been looking at the claims infringed in trespass, that is, claims against bodily intrusion.

Let us step back from the body for a moment. You own a great many things: a house, a typewriter, several pairs of shoes. Ownership is a cluster of claims, privileges, and powers in respect of the thing owned; so anyone who makes use of your house, typewriter, or shoes, without your consent—for example, anyone who hits any of those things with a log without your consent—infringes a property claim of yours.

We have similar rights in respect of our bodies. Anyone who makes use of your body without your consent—for example, anyone who hits it with a log without your consent—infringes a claim of yours. Is there any good reason to object to saying that this claim is a property claim? Is there any good reason to object to saying that you own your body?

No doubt it sounds odd to say that people own their bodies. How could a person X be thought to *own* something that has as intimate a relation to X as X's body has to X? But ownership really is no more than a cluster of claims, privileges, and powers; and if the cluster of rights that a person X has in respect of his or her body is sufficiently like the clusters of rights people have in respect of their houses, typewriters, and shoes, then there is no objection in theory to saying that X does own his or her body—however odd it may sound to say so, however unaccustomed we may be to saying so.

And isn't the cluster of rights that a person X has in respect of his or her body sufficiently like the clusters of rights people have in respect of their houses, typewriters, and shoes?

There are differences as well as similarities between ownership of the likes of a typewriter on the one hand and ownership of one's body

11. Not merely failing to connect but positive walling off was rife among slaveowners, among the highest as well as the lowest. James Oakes reports: "With respect to slavery, George Washington admitted, 'I shall frankly declare to you that I do not like even to think, much less talk, of it'". *The Ruling Race*, (New York: Vintage Books, 1983), p. 120.

on the other. There is a lot of me left to myself if I sell my typewriter: all of me is left. What is there left to me if I sell my body? My soul? Anything at all? On some views, I just am my body, so to sell my body is to sell myself. On *any* view, I am more intimately related to my body than I am to my typewriter.

To mark the similarities, I will say that people own their bodies. To mark the differences, I will say that people's bodies are their First Property, whereas everything else that they own—their houses, typewriters, and shoes—is their Second Property. We will be looking at the source of Second Property in Chapter 13.

Meanwhile, however, there is more to First Property than merely having the claims infringed in trespass. There are also claims to not be caused harm, some of which are very like claims we have over our typewriters that *they* not be caused harm, and should therefore be thought of as also among the rights we have in owning First Property. So let us turn to causing harm.

Chapter 9

Harm

1. We have claims against others that they not commit bodily intrusion on us; those are the claims infringed in trespass. That a person X has such claims against a person Y is shown by the fact that Y is, in respect of X, under the behavioral constraint governing bodily intrusion that X's having those claims against Y consists in.

Don't we also have claims against others that they not cause us harm? Isn't it true of Y that—other things being equal—he or she ought not cause X harm?

It might pay first, however, to bring out explicitly that it does not *follow* from the fact that we have claims against trespass that we also have claims against being caused harm. What I have in mind is this. We do often cause each other harm by committing trespass. Suppose it is the case that if you hit me with a log, you will thereby cause me harm. I have a claim against you that you not hit me with a log: your doing that would be trespass. If we could accept the following principle,

> The Ends Principle for Claims:
> *If*
> (i) X has a claim against Y that Y not do alpha, and
> (ii) If Y does alpha then he or she will thereby do beta,
> *then* X has a claim against Y that Y not do beta, that claim being at least as stringent as X's claim that Y not do alpha,

then we could conclude that I have a claim against you that you not cause me harm, for it tells us that the conjunction of (i) I have a claim against you that you not hit me with a log, and (ii) If you hit me with a log you will thereby cause me harm, entails that I have a claim against you that you not cause me harm. More generally, if it ever is the case that Y would cause X harm by committing a trespass on X, the Ends Principle for Claims yields that X has a claim against Y that Y not cause X harm.

But that principle won't do. I have a claim against you that you not hit me with a log: your doing that would be trespass. Suppose that if you hit me with a log you would thereby cause the bells to ring in the local Baptist church. (I am standing next to the lever that controls the bells, and if you hit me with a log you will thereby cause me to fall against it.) Does it follow that I have a claim against you that you not cause the bells to ring in the local Baptist church? Certainly not. Doing that is something you might perfectly well do without wrong to me—as, for example, if you don't do this by hitting me with a log but instead by walking over to the lever and depressing it. My having a claim against you that you not cause the bells to ring does not follow from the conjunction of (i) I have a claim against you that you not hit me with a log and (ii) If you hit me with a log you will thereby cause the bells to ring; and we must reject the Ends Principle for Claims.

We should be clear that the Ends Principle for Claims differs radically from

> The Means Principle for Claims:
>   *If*
>   (i) X has a claim against Y that Y not do beta, and
>   (ii) If Y does alpha then he or she will thereby do beta,
>   *then* X has a claim against Y that Y not do alpha, that claim being at least as stringent as X's claim that Y not do beta.

This says that the status of claim extends down from ends to means, and it is very plausible; The Ends Principle for Claims, by contrast, says that the status of claim extends up from means to ends, and it is unacceptable.

We cannot, then, draw the conclusion that we have claims to not be caused harm from the fact that we have claims against bodily intrusion together with the fact that people do often cause harm by causing bodily intrusion. Harm calls for separate attention, beyond that which we paid to trespass.

I suggest that we should adopt the following thesis:

> The Harm Thesis: We have claims against others that they not cause us harm.

There is something that might incline one to reject it, however.

2. Consider

> DAY'S END: B always comes home at 9:00 P.M. and the first thing
> he does is to flip the light switch in his hallway. He did so this
> evening. B's flipping the switch caused a circuit to close. By virtue
> of an extraordinary series of coincidences, unpredictable in ad-
> vance by anybody, the circuit's closing caused a release of elec-
> tricity (a small lightning flash) in A's house next door. Unluckily,
> A was in its path and was therefore badly burned.

B caused A to be harmed in DAY'S END. The Harm Thesis therefore
tells us that B infringed a claim of A's in DAY'S END. But did he? B
was certainly not at fault for causing A harm. If you think that being
at fault for doing a thing is a necessary condition for infringing a
claim in doing it, then you will of course conclude that the Harm
Thesis has to go: you will conclude that while some harm-causings
may well be infringements of claims, others are not, namely those
others the agent is not at fault for. And I think we do feel at least
some inclination to accept

> The Requirement-of-Fault Thesis for Claim Infringement: Y infr-
> inges a claim of X's in doing alpha only if Y is at fault for doing
> alpha.

Accepting that thesis would have consequences elsewhere too. I
have been saying that we have claims against bodily intrusion, but
aren't some bodily intrusions committed without fault? Mightn't I
blunder into you through no fault of my own? If the Requirement-
of-Fault Thesis for Claim Infringement is true, then not just any bodily
intrusion is an infringing of a claim: perhaps those the agent is at
fault for are, but those the agent is not at fault for are not. So not
merely does the Harm Thesis have to go, but so does the very broad
thesis that we have claims against any and all bodily intrusions.

I postponed discussion of the Requirement-of-Fault Thesis for
Claim Infringement since it may be much more striking that we can
cause harm without fault than that we can commit bodily intrusion
without fault. We can of course commit bodily intrusion without
fault, as we remember the moment we think about fault in connection
with bodily intrusion. But the causal connection between Y's act and
the bodily event Y causes in X in committing bodily intrusion on X

is severely constrained. If Y swings a log in X's direction, and thereby causes X to be in contact with the log, the causal connection between Y's swing and X's being in contact with the log is of the constrained kind we were pointing to: Y has hit X with the log, and that was our paradigm instance of trespass. But you can cause a person to be in contact with a log in any number of ways in which the causal connection is not of the constrained kind. If Y throws a log into the highway, and X comes along later and stumbles over the log, Y has caused X to be in contact with a log, but Y has not committed bodily intrusion on X: this was our paradigm instance of trespass on the case. Causal connections can in fact be quite as freakish as you like. If Y peels a banana, his doing that might cause X to be in contact with a log through some thoroughly weird series of coincidences, and that would certainly not constitute bodily intrusion in our sense of that term. But the more freakish the causal route from Y's act to X's harm—that is, the more we are inclined to think that nobody, with the best will in the world, could have foreseen the outcome—the more obvious it is that Y is not at fault for X's harm.

Freakishness in a causal route is not the only thing that negates fault. If Smith had caused Jones to be wired to your light switch, so that your flipping it caused Jones to be burned, then it may be that there was nothing freakish in the causal connection between your flipping the switch and Jones' being burned. (No doubt from your point of view it was a nasty coincidence that Jones was wired into the circuit, but once Jones had been wired in, all was not only predictable but was predicted by Smith.) Where a first party has so arranged things that an innocuous-seeming and thoroughly ordinary act of a second party causes a third party harm, the second party is not at fault.

Indeed, a causal route can pass right through a voluntary act.[1] If my neighbor says to me on a blisteringly hot day "Hot enough for you?" he may cause me to feel a surge of rage, out of which I shoot the mailman in the foot. Then my neighbor caused me to feel rage, and my rage caused me to fire my gun at the mailman, and that caused the mailman harm. Causality being transitive, my neighbor caused the mailman harm. But he was certainly not at fault for doing so.

---

1. I here part company with H. L. A. Hart and A. M. Honore, *Causation in the Law* (Oxford: Clarendon Press, 1959). More will be said about causality in sections 3 and 4 below.

But however obvious it is that we can cause harm without fault, it is also true that we can commit bodily intrusion without fault. So what should we think of

> The Requirement-of-Fault Thesis for Claim Infringement: Y infringes a claim of X's in doing alpha only if Y is at fault for doing alpha.

If we accept it, we must not only reject

> The Harm Thesis: We have claims against others that they not cause us harm,

we must also grant that a fault-free instance of bodily intrusion is not a claim infringement, and, since trespass is by definition a claim infringement, we must also grant that some bodily intrusions are not trespass.

But we really must reject the Requirement-of-Fault Thesis for Claim Infringement.

In the first place, there are cases that we looked at in Chapter 3 in which—as I hope you agreed—the agent does infringe a claim, but entirely without fault. Consider the manufacturer who contracted to supply each of C company and D company with 100 widgets but who, entirely without fault, now finds it impossible to produce more than 100 widgets in the available time. Similarly for some cases that we looked at in Chapters 6 and 7. If I am so situated as to have to kill Lewis or to kill Michael, then I do have to infringe a claim, but I may be entirely without fault throughout the episode. If I am so situated as to be able to turn a trolley onto one track workman to save five, I may choose to turn the trolley, thereby infringing a claim, but am without fault in doing so. When we remember those cases I hope the Requirement-of-Fault Thesis for Claim Infringement will now strike us as less plausible.

Moreover, there is something I said *I* would do, and hoped you would accompany me in doing, namely use "ought" and its cognates objectively. But if we do use "ought" objectively, then in light of the link between claims and permissibility set out in Chapter 6, we *must* reject the Requirement-of-Fault Thesis for Claim Infringement. What I have in mind comes out as follows.

The Requirement-of-Fault Thesis for Ought-Not (we met it in Chapter 6, section 8) may be rephrased as follows: one ought to do alpha only if one would be at fault for not doing alpha. I said we should reject that thesis; I said that it can be true that Bloggs ought to feed the baby aspirin even if he would not be at fault if he did not feed the baby aspirin. And I said that I would, in any case, so use "ought" that the Requirement-of-Fault Thesis for Ought-Not is false. Suppose you accompany me in that usage.

Let us now turn to claims. X's having a claim against Y that Y do alpha consists in Y's being under a certain behavioral constraint in respect of X. Central to the behavioral constraint is that, other things being equal, Y ought to do alpha. But if it can be the case that Y ought to do alpha even if Y would not be at fault for not doing it, then Y can be under the behavioral constraint in respect of X without its being the case that Y would be at fault for not doing alpha; thus it can be that X has the claim against Y even if Y would not be at fault if he or she failed to accord it. Put another way, it can be that Y infringes X's claim even though Y is not at fault for doing so. That means that the Requirement-of-Fault Thesis for Claim Infringement is false.

All of that was abstract, so let us take a particular case; DAY'S END will itself serve the purpose. B did not know that if he flipped his light switch he would cause A to be burned. Nevertheless it would have been true to say, just before he flipped the switch, using "ought" objectively, that he ought not flip it. Why? Because he was as a matter of fact going to cause A to be burned by doing so if he did so. If it had been the case that B would save five lives by flipping the switch, and the burn he would thereby cause A very minor, then that would be another matter: it would be permissible for B to flip the switch, and indeed permissible because of the large increment of good he would produce by doing so. On the other hand, five lives saved would not be enough if A's burn would be very grave, if the burn would seriously and permanently disable A. In DAY'S END, however, A's burn will be a bad one, and (let us suppose) B will save no lives by flipping the switch. It emerges that what is central to the behavioral constraint that a claim consists in is present in DAY's end—given we are using "ought" objectively.

Another part of the behavioral constraint is present here too, given we are using "ought" objectively. Suppose B would save five lives by flipping the switch but would also cause A a burn, and suppose there in fact is time for B to ask A for a release in advance. It may be that none of this is known to B, so he is not at fault if he does not ask A for a release in advance. But speaking objectively, he ought to.

The need to compensate later is of course absent. But the need to compensate later is, as I said, a complex affair, and one thing that is relevant (though not conclusive) is whether the agent was at fault in acting.

Consider again a time just before B flips the switch. It would be true to say then, using "ought" objectively, that he ought not flip it. Wouldn't it be weird in us, knowing what will happen if B flips the switch, to say "Look B, we know something that you don't know. If we tell you, then it will be true to say that you ought not flip the switch, but not if we don't tell you". The weirdness of that performance is a sign that "ought" is at least typically used objectively. Something similar is at work in our use of "has a right." We would look equally weird if we were to say "Look B, we know something that you don't know. If we tell you, then you will violate a right of A's if you flip the switch, but not if we don't."

Indeed, I think we should not even in the first place have been attracted by the idea that B infringes no claim of A's in DAY'S END. If B knew that he would be causing A harm by flipping the switch, he would be infringing a claim of A's if he nevertheless proceeded to flip it. But how could X have a claim against Y that Y not do-alpha-being-at-fault-in-doing-it if X does not have a claim against Y that Y (all simply) not do alpha?

Similarly for all of the other cases in which Y causes X a harm without fault. Freakishness in the causal route, the causal route's passing through some voluntary act of another agent, none of this matters to the question whether the agent ought to have done what he or she did, or whether in so acting he or she was infringing a claim of the victim's. If I will in fact cause a person harm by peeling a banana, then—other things being equal—I ought not peel it, and will infringe a claim if I proceed. If my neighbor will in fact cause the mailman a harm by saying "Hot enough for you?" then—other things being equal—he ought not say that, and will infringe a claim if he proceeds. *Of course* the agents are not at fault in these cases if they do proceed. But they will infringe a claim if they know they will cause these outcomes to come about, and nevertheless proceed anyway. And how could their victims have a claim against them that they not proceed-being-at-fault-in-doing-so, if they do not have a claim that they (all simply) not proceed?

In any case, I am throughout using "ought" objectively, and if you join me in that usage, you will have also to join me in using "claim" objectively, in light of the link between the two notions. Thus you have to join me in rejecting

> The Requirement-of-Fault Thesis for Claim Infringement: Y infringes a claim of X's in doing alpha only if Y is at fault for doing alpha.

The possibility of causing harm without fault therefore does not constitute an objection to

> The Harm Thesis: We have claims against others that they not cause us harm.

A person might, of course, consent to being caused harm, or forfeit a claim to not be caused harm, just as a person might consent to bodily intrusion, or forfeit a claim against bodily intrusion. So the fussy reader may wish to say, not that we have claims against others that they not cause us harm and that they not commit bodily intrusion on us, but rather that we have these claims unless we have consented to the actions, thereby divesting ourselves of the claims, or forfeited the claims. But I will make these provisions explicit only where confusion would otherwise result.

3. I made an assumption in the course of discussing DAY'S END that we should now take a closer look at. I said: B caused A to be harmed in DAY'S END. I therefore concluded that the Harm Thesis tells us B infringed a claim of A's in that case. But *did* B cause A the harm in DAY'S END? I know of no plausible analysis of causality and am not going to offer one. Still I do make certain general assumptions about causality, and these should be made explicit now.

The first general assumption I make comes out as follows. What is it for a person X to cause an outcome O? I assume

> (1) For a person X to have caused an outcome O is for some event E that is in the appropriate sense 'a doing of something by X' to have caused O.

What exactly that appropriate sense of "a doing of something by X" is I will leave aside. I could instead have said that E must be in the appropriate sense 'an act of X's'. These phrases "a doing" and "an act" are certainly by no means transparent, but I do not mean to be offering an analysis of anything here. What I wish to point to here is only our intuitive sense that for a *person* to cause an outcome is for an *event* he or she is appropriately involved in to cause it. What is it in virtue of which *I* caused your teacup to break? Well, there was an event, my moving of my arm, which on any analysis of the phrase appropriate to (1) was a doing of something by me, and *it* caused your teacup to break.

We will take note in the following section of a reason to think that assumption (1) should be weakened. Meanwhile I think it seems at any rate *prima facie* plausible.

I also assume

(2) Causality is transitive

and

(3) The fact that a person X is not at fault for, or to blame for, an outcome O is compatible with its being the case that X did cause O.

These, I should think, are obvious enough. B flipped a switch in DAY'S END, and the event that consisted in his doing so was on any analysis of the phrase appropriate to assumption (1), a doing of something by B. B's flipping the switch caused a circuit to close, thereby—by virtue of an extraordinary series of coincidences—causing A to be burned, thereby causing A to be harmed. By transitivity, B's flipping the switch caused A to be harmed. It follows from assumption (1) that B caused A to be harmed. No doubt B did not intend harm to A, no doubt B was not at fault for A's harm, but that is surely irrelevant to the question whether B in fact caused A to be harmed. We often make use of causal notions in moral theory, but it cannot at all plausibly be thought that causality is itself a moral notion. What fixes what events cause what other events is not morality but rather the properties of switches and circuits and flesh.

In the preceding section, I mentioned cases in which a first party has so arranged things that an innocuous-seeming and thoroughly ordinary act of a second party causes a third party harm, and the second party is not at fault. But the second party does cause the harm. Doesn't the first party also cause the harm? A fourth assumption I make is this:

(4) Its being the case that an entity X caused an outcome O is compatible with its being the case that another entity Y also caused that same outcome O.

Its being the case that Booth caused Lincoln's death is compatible with its being the case that a certain bullet caused Lincoln's death, and with its also being the case that a certain wound caused Lincoln's death. So also where many people are causally involved: its being the case that X caused Z harm is compatible with its being the case that Y also caused Z the harm. Perhaps we feel the need to choose one of the parties, and say of that one that he or she was *the* cause of the third party's being harmed, out of a desire to fix blame. (Though why should we suppose at most one is to blame?) But as assumption (3) says, the question who is to blame for an outcome simply is not the same as the question who caused it.

Sometimes where more than one person (and even where more than one thing) is 'involved in' the causing of an outcome, we do not say of *each* that he or she caused the outcome; we say only that they jointly caused it. Suppose that you and I each poured a bit of poison in a lake, neither of us pouring in enough for the amount each poured in to poison the fish, though the total amount was fatal. Here I think that if we did our pourings concurrently, it would be wrong to say of you that you caused the death of the fish, and wrong to say of me that I caused the death of the fish, though of course right to say that we jointly did. By contrast, if you did your pouring yesterday and I did mine today, then I think it would be right to say not merely that we jointly caused the death of the fish, but also that you did and that I did. This is because if you did your pouring yesterday, then your pouring is, as it were, stage setting: you brought the lake into a condition such that my pouring would cause the death of the fish. Perhaps we will sometimes feel inclined to say that the individual poison pourings were stage settings for each other when they took place concurrently, but I think this is relatively rare.

A fifth assumption I make is this:

> (5) The causal route from an event E to an outcome O can have been freakish and full of coincidences.

The causal route from B's flipping the switch to A's being harmed in DAY'S END was full of coincidence, yet B caused A harm in that case.

There is even room for randomness in a causal route. I have a device such that if I press a button, a roulette wheel spins, and if the ball lands on 23, a bullet is ejected from the far end. I held the device to Smith's head and pressed the button, and the ball did land on 23, so a bullet was ejected, causing Smith's death. It was a matter of chance whether the bullet would land on 23; but my pressing the button did all the same cause Smith's death, and so did I.

The possibility of a freakish causal route from cause to effect makes it clear that one can cause an outcome, such as a harm, without fault and therefore may have contributed to the sense that

> The Harm Thesis: We have claims against others that they not cause us harm

is unacceptable. But the considerations of the preceding section remain. It was true of B before he flipped the switch that he would cause A harm by flipping it. Nobody could have foreseen that he would cause A harm, and he was not going to be at fault for the harm. Still, given what B was going to cause by flipping the switch if he flipped it, it was true of him that he ought not flip it, and so it was also true that he would infringe a claim of A's if he did.

4. Let us have a second look at

> (1) For a person X to have caused an outcome O is for some event E that is in the appropriate sense 'a doing of something by X' to have caused O.

Can this be right? Consider a train switchman, whose job requires him to throw the switch at 4:00 so that the four-fifteen goes to the right rather than the left. And suppose he just forgot to do this. In consequence, the four-fifteen went to the left rather than the right and crashed into an oncoming train—much loss of life, and so on. I am sure we will want to say that the switchman caused those deaths. If (1) is true, then for the switchman to have caused those deaths is for some event E that is in the appropriate sense a doing of something by him to have caused them. But what event could that be? What did the switchman *do?* The gravamen of the charge against him is precisely that he *didn't* do something he was under a duty to do.

Finding assumption (1) attractive, many people are therefore inclined to say that there really was an event E that was a doing of something by the switchman, which then caused the deaths. That event E was the switchman's failing to throw the switch, that having been not an act of commission but an act of omission.

But this is a very problematic move. The switchman did not throw the switch, but so also did you not throw the switch. There is supposed to have been an event (an act of omission) that consisted in the switchman's failing to throw the switch. Should we say that there was also an event that consisted in your failing to throw the switch? And then did you too cause the deaths that ensued?

Most people, I am sure, would say no: they would say that though the switchman caused the deaths, you did not. How so? One possible answer is this. The switchman was under a duty to throw the switch, so there was an event (an act of omission) that was his not throwing the switch; indeed, that event was not merely a not-throwing of the switch but a failing to throw the switch. By contrast, you were not under a duty to throw the switch, so although you did not throw the switch, there was no event (no act of omission) that was your not throwing the switch; *a fortiori,* there was no event that was your failing to throw the switch. No wonder, then, that though the switchman caused the deaths, you did not. But it is very hard to see how a person's being or not being under a duty to do a thing could be thought to fix what events there *are*—how it could be thought that the switchman's having been under a duty to throw the switch and your not having been under a duty to throw the switch makes it the case that there was an event that consisted in his not throwing it but no event that consisted in your not throwing it.

Alternatively, I suppose, it could be said that there was an event that consisted in your not throwing the switch just as there was an event that consisted in the switchman's not throwing the switch, though the latter (but not the former) was not merely a not-throwing of the switch, it was also a failing to throw the switch, since the switchman was (but you were not) under a duty to throw the switch. And then it could be said: since the switchman's not-throwing the switch was a failing to throw the switch (whereas yours was not), the switchman's not-throwing the switch caused the deaths (whereas yours did not). No wonder, then, that though the switchman caused the deaths, you did not. But it is very hard to see how a person's being or not being under a duty to do a thing could be thought to make one event cause another. As I said in the preceding section, it cannot at all plausibly be thought that causality is itself a moral notion. What fixes what events cause what other events is not morality but rather the properties of switches and trains and flesh.

I think, myself, that there is a real difficulty here, which has not been adequately appreciated. We do want to say that a person might have caused an unwanted outcome O by virtue of having failed to do a thing he or she was under a duty to do;[2] on the other hand, we are in trouble in such cases when we try to locate an event E such that the person caused O in that that E caused O.[3]

Yet we cannot just give up assumption (1). There has, after all, to be *something* that constrains the range of things a person causes.

I suggest we bypass this difficulty. I have been concerned primarily to provide a reminder that harms can be caused by failing to act as well as by acting, however we are to understand what is at work when they are. This means that—as the Harm Thesis tells us—you can infringe a claim by a failing to act as well as by an acting. But that is certainly as it should be. So let us replace (1) with the following: For a person X to have caused an outcome O is for one or the other of

> An event E that is in the appropriate sense 'a doing of something by X' caused O

or

> X's failing to do such and such caused O,

to be true. And let us leave aside the question whether when the latter is true, so also is the former.

5. We have been looking at

> The Harm Thesis: We have claims against others that they not cause us harm.

I said earlier that the fact that one can cause harm without fault is no barrier to accepting it. And we took note in the preceding section of the fact that one can cause harm by failing to do something as well as by doing something. Nondoings are relevant to a point we should now turn to.

2. Presumably the difficulty is not restricted to human agents: can't we say that the cat caused the explosion in the mouse population by virtue of failing to catch the mice? Or to in-animate agents: can't we say that the computer caused the fire by virtue of failing to shut off when I flipped the switch? In passing, these possibilities bring out that what makes us speak of failing to do a thing (as opposed to merely not doing it) is not any moral flaw in the nondoer, but rather issues from what is expected of the nondoer.

3. Further objections to 'acts of omissions' appear in my *Acts and Other Events,* ch. 15.

What I have in mind is that there is room for an argument for the Harm Thesis that I have not offered. The argument issues from a very interesting phenomenon drawn attention to by Bernard Williams.[4] We feel acute regret for bad outcomes we caused when we were at fault for them; that is and always was familiar enough. What Williams noticed was that we also feel acute regret for bad outcomes we caused when we were not at fault for them. Consider DAY'S END, and suppose that the burn B caused A was a bad one. When others read in the newspapers about what happened, they will feel at most mild regret: "Someone was badly burned, how sad". B, however, caused the someone to be badly burned, and he will not feel at most mild regret, he will not think merely "Someone was badly burned, how sad" when he learns of what happened. B will feel terrible; B will lie awake at night; in after years, B will shudder when he thinks of the episode. And this despite the fact that B was in no way at fault for what happened. Williams suggests we call the acute regret felt by a person who caused a bad outcome *agent regret;* what Williams noticed is that agent regret is felt even by one who knows he or she was not at fault for the bad outcome—a phenomenon we might call *agent regret without fault.*

Williams adds—rightly, I am sure—that it is not mere irrationality to feel agent regret without fault. The point is not that B's shudder is intelligible, for we stand in need of an explanation of why B shudders, given he was not at fault for what happened. The point is rather that B's shudder seems fitting and right, and not a piece of craziness. Indeed, Williams seems to be right in going on to add that morality calls for a measure of agent regret, even where we were not at fault. We would regard it as discreditable in B if his only response to the episode were "Someone was badly burned, how sad."

Now the following might be offered as an explanation of why B shudders: though without fault, B infringed a claim of A's. And then we could offer the fact of B's shudder as reason to think that B did infringe a claim of A's, in that B's infringing the claim is the best explanation of B's shudder. More generally, we could argue for the Harm Thesis as follows: people do feel agent regret when they have caused harm, whether or not they were at fault, and the best explanation of their feeling it is the truth of the Harm Thesis.

---

4. In "Moral Luck," reprinted in his collection of essays *Moral Luck.* So far as I know, he was the first to draw attention to it.

This is a very attractive idea. What gets in its way is fault-free nondoings. Suppose a woman left her baby on my doorstep last night, hoping I would find it and do something for it. I did not have the slightest idea she had done this and, since I go to bed early, I did not find the baby until morning. But the night had been more than usually cold, so by morning the baby was dead. If only I had known it was there! I could easily have saved it. I was not at fault for anything that happened, but all the same, I did not save the baby and it died on my doorstep. So I feel terrible; I will lie awake at night; in after years, I will shudder when I think of the episode. Moreover, my shudder seems fitting and right, and not a piece of craziness. Indeed, you would regard it as discreditable in me if my only response to the episode were the newspaper reader's response "A baby died, how sad". But I infringed no claim of the baby's, or indeed of anyone else's. *A fortiori,* my shudder cannot be explained by appeal to my having infringed a claim.

It should be stressed that I infringed no claim of the baby's. Admittedly I did not save it, but as we saw in Chapter 6, nobody has a claim to be saved.

In light of the existence of cases of this kind, we might think to rename the phenomenon Williams drew attention to: we might think to call what Williams drew attention to *doer's regret without fault.* Then we could call the analogous phenomenon I just drew attention to: *nondoer's regret without fault.* I apologize for the inelegance of these names. (I avoid the pair of terms "commission" and "omission", since the latter term, as I indicated in the preceding section, is so often thought by philosophers to require fault for its correct application, whereas the pair of phenomena we are looking at here do not involve fault.) But whatever we think best to call them, these phenomena need explanation. And we cannot explain them by appeal to the hypothesis that the regret is a sign of an infringed claim, for though the doer did infringe a claim (in DAY'S END), the nondoer did not (in the case of the baby and me).

I strongly suspect that what lies behind them is our commitment to the objective sense of "ought", that is, that what they show is that we really do think there are things we ought to do even though we do not know of them and are not at fault when we do not do them.

(i) B ought not flip the light switch (objective "ought")

was true of B in DAY'S END before he flipped the switch; and I suggest that it is B's recognition that (i) was true of him that explains his later shudder, and that it is our recognition that (i) was true of him that explains our thinking it would be discreditable in him if he did not shudder. Wasn't

(ii) I ought to do something to save the baby (objective "ought")

true of me last night? Not necessarily adopt it for life, but anyway take it in from the cold and call the police? I suggest that it is my recognition that (ii) was true of me that explains my later shudder, and that it is your recognition that (ii) was true of me that explains your thinking it would be discreditable in me if I did not shudder.

Not just anyone who did not save the baby will feel nondoer's regret without fault for the baby's death. Bloggs lives across the river in another city. He *could* have saved the baby and did not. But the baby was not on his doorstep, and morality did not call on him to save it.

(iii) Bloggs ought to do something to save the baby (objective "ought")

was not true of Bloggs last night, and I suggest that that is why he does not feel nondoer's regret without fault—why his reaction is the mere "A baby died, how sad", and why we expect no more of him. Compare your not throwing the switch in the example of the train in the preceding section. If you could easily have done so, if it seems right to think it was true that you ought (objective "ought") to do so, you will feel nondoer's regret without fault; otherwise you will not.

At all events, this way of explaining B's shudder in DAY'S END does not appeal to B's having infringed a claim, and to the extent to which it is plausible to explain doer's regret without fault (like nondoer's regret without fault) in this way, it is implausible to say that the best explanation of doer's regret without fault is that the doer infringed a claim. It is for this reason that I did not offer doer's regret without fault as an argument for the Harm Thesis.

6. I have suggested that we should accept

The Harm Thesis: We have claims against others that they not cause us harm.

Accepting it commits us to supposing that B infringes a claim of A's in DAY'S END, but I have suggested that we should agree that he does.

Again, if you throw a log toward a man and it hits him, then you have hit him with the log and therefore have committed trespass on him; if in addition, you thereby cause him harm, then you do not merely infringe a claim of his in committing the trespass on him, you infringe a further claim of his, namely the claim he had against you that you not cause him harm.

Again, if you throw a log into the highway and a man comes along later, trips over the log, and breaks an arm, then while you do not commit trespass on him, you do infringe a claim of his, namely the claim he had against you that you not cause him harm.

A particularly interesting variant of this story is the following:

> LOG (NO HARM): D was clearing his land, which abuts the high-way. He did not care where he threw the logs he wished to clear off and in fact threw one of them into the highway. C came along later, but luckily saw the log in time and did not trip over it.

Did D infringe a claim of C's in LOG (NO HARM)?

The Harm Thesis tells us that we have claims against others that they not cause us harm, but it does not tell us anything about imposing risk of harm. Did D impose a risk of harm on C in LOG (NO HARM)? If he did, and if also we can accept

> The Risk Thesis: We have claims against others that they not impose risks of harm on us,

then D did infringe a claim of C's in this case.

We need to attend to the Risk Thesis since a theory of rights should take a stand on it. And moral theory generally should take a stand on it. Indeed, it would be a boon to the moral theorist if it were true. What I have in mind is this. We are surely inclined to think that D acted wrongly in LOG (NO HARM). But what makes that so? We would have a simple answer to the question what makes it the case that D acted wrongly in LOG (NO HARM) if D imposed a risk of harm on C and the Risk Thesis is true: if those things are so, we can say that D infringed a claim of C's and the conditions in which he did so were not among those that make a claim infringement permissible. How are we to answer the question what makes it the case that D acted wrongly in LOG (NO HARM) if we cannot accept the Risk Thesis?

There is even room for an argument for the Risk Thesis. We adopted the following piece of terminology in Chapter 6, section 8: if it would be good for X to get a thing Z, and if Y makes it probable that X will get Z, then Y gives X an *advantage*. We can also say: if it would be bad for X to get a thing Z, and if Y makes it probable that X will get Z, then Y causes X to be at a *disadvantage*. Now just as we welcome getting an advantage, so also are we dismayed when placed at a disadvantage. More strongly, if Bloggs were asked to rank possible outcomes for himself, he might well prefer the certainty of a minor harm, such as a bruise, to a small probability of a major harm, such as death. Certainly people do quite generally prefer minor harms to risks of major harms. Suppose we could say that causing a person to be at a disadvantage is itself causing the person a harm. Then it would follow (by the Harm Thesis) that causing a person to be at a disadvantage is infringing a claim. Since imposing a risk of harm on a person is causing that person to be at a disadvantage, imposing a risk of harm on a person is infringing a claim, and it follows that the Risk Thesis is true.

But this is a bad argument, for we cannot really say that causing a person to be at a disadvantage is itself causing the person a harm. Suppose we grant that D imposed a risk of harm on C in LOG (NO HARM), and thus caused C to be at a disadvantage. Peer though we may, it is hard to see any reason to think that D caused C harm. Suppose I played Russian roulette on Smith, but there was no bullet under the firing pin when the gun went off. Let us suppose that Smith did not know at the time, and never finds out later, that I imposed this risk of harm on him. What reason could there be to think I caused him a harm? That people prefer a minor harm to a risk of a major harm does not make the risk of the major harm itself be a harm.

Still the Risk Thesis might be true even though that argument for it is a bad argument. Is it true?

We might well ask: are we to think that imposing just any risk of harm on a person is an infringement of a claim?—however small the risk? D threw a log into the highway. Did D impose a risk of harm on C? If he did, the risk cannot have been very large, even though (let us suppose) C walks along that highway to work every morning.

On whom else did D impose a risk of harm? E and F? Perhaps they do not walk along that highway to work every morning, but they sometimes do. And what about G? G wasn't even in town that day (he was in Hong Kong) and therefore wasn't at all likely to come along later and trip over the log. Still G might just have had a change in plan, flown in, walked along the highway, and tripped over the log. So is it the case that for every person in the universe who could have got to the highway and tripped over that log, D infringed a claim of his and hers? We might well prefer that our theory of rights avoid saying this.

One possibility is to give up the Risk Thesis in favor of something weaker. Consider

> The High-Risk Thesis: We have claims against others that they not impose *high* risks of harm on us.

But how high is high? Are we to suppose that D imposed a high risk of harm on C (since C walks along the highway every morning), but did not impose a high risk of harm on E, F, and G?

Moreover, the gravity of the harm risked ought to figure along with the probability of the harm in assessing how high a risk of harm a person imposes in acting. (Compare our earlier account of the size of the advantage one person may give another.) A one-in-ten chance of a bruise is one thing, a one-in-ten chance of death is quite another. The case of Smith is perhaps clear enough: if I played Russian roulette on him, I imposed an n in m chance (where n is the number of bullets and m the number of chambers in the gun I used) of a quite particular harm on him, namely death. But what is *the* harm the risk of which D imposed on C in throwing that log into the highway? If C had tripped over that log, he might have fallen and been bruised. He might instead have fallen and broken an arm. He might instead have fallen and broken his neck and died. There just is no such thing as *the* harm the risk of which D imposed on C. *A fortiori,* there is no such thing as *the* size of the risk of harm that D imposed on C.

But if we cannot appeal to either the Risk Thesis or the High-Risk Thesis to warrant saying that D infringed a claim of C's in LOG (NO HARM), why was it wrong for D to throw that log into the highway?

Indeed, why was it wrong for me to play Russian roulette on Smith? The simplest answer seems to be this: it was wrong for me to play Russian roulette on Smith because I imposed a high risk of harm on him, and (I am assuming) nothing in the circumstances made it permissible to do that. We allowed that it may be permissible, other things being equal, to do a thing on the ground that doing so gives an advantage, even though no good in fact ensues—permissible to do this even where doing so requires infringing a claim. (Remember the

246 Rights: Which They Are

case of Edward in Chapter 7.) There is no reason to refuse to allow that it may be impermissible, other things being equal, to do a thing on the ground that doing so causes a person to be under a disadvantage. Other things may not be equal, of course: there may be good reason for imposing a risk of harm on a person, even a high risk of harm. On the other hand, other things may be equal. What is important is that we can explain why my act was wrongful without appeal to a claim of Smith's.

If we take this line on the case of Smith, what are we to say of F in the following variant on DAY'S END?

> DAY'S END (NO HARM): F always comes home at 9:00 P.M. and the first thing he does is to flip the light switch in his hallway. He did so this evening. F's flipping the switch caused a circuit to close. By virtue of an extraordinary series of coincidences, unpredictable in advance by anybody, the circuit's closing caused a release of electricity (a small lightning flash) in E's house next door. Luckily, E was not in its path.

Did F impose a high risk of harm on E in this story? If we think of the coincidences as having taken place before F acted (so that they were part of the stage setting for F's act), then we will think F did impose a high risk of harm on E.[5] Moreover, there was nothing in the circumstances that made it permissible for F to impose that high risk of harm on E. But did F act wrongly? We are inclined to think not. But I suggest that this is only because of a residual desire in us to hold fast to the Requirement-of-Fault Thesis for Ought-Not: it is

---

5. It might be worth drawing attention to the likelihood of 'regret without fault' in such cases as this. (Compare the two kinds of regret without fault discussed in the preceding section.) For F too will feel terrible; F too will lie awake at night; in after years F too will shudder when he thinks of the episode. "I nearly caused E harm!" Should we call this phenomenon *risk imposer's regret without fault*? I have no better name for it.

F nearly caused a harm, so his shudder is not crazy. Contrast the profound neurotic, to whom it occurs while on the way to work that there just might have been, there *could* have been, it was logically possible for there to have been, a (very very thin) baby under the doormat he trod on in walking out his front door. The shudder whose content is "I nearly caused a harm!" is rational; the shudder whose content is "It was logically possible that I would cause a harm!" is not.

The kind of explanation I offered for doer's and nondoer's regret without fault is available here too.

only because we are inclined to feel that fault is a necessary condition for the applicability of "ought not" and its cognates (such as "acted wrongly") that we think it will not do to say F acted wrongly in this case. On any view, F would certainly have acted wrongly if he had known of the coincidences, and of the high risk he would therefore impose on E by flipping his light switch, and proceeded to flip the switch anyway, not caring about E.

Unlike F in DAY'S END (NO HARM), and like me in the case of Smith, D was at fault in LOG (NO HARM): he was negligent. No matter, for fault is not a requirement for the applicability of "ought not" and its cognates. But LOG (NO HARM) is, all the same, a more complex case. In the first place, the probability that C would come to grief of any kind (bruise? broken arm? death?) in consequence of D's throwing a log into the highway cannot have been very great, even if it is true that C walks along the highway to work every morning. So it really is not plausible to explain the wrongness of D's act by appeal to D's having imposed a risk of harm on C. (A fortiori, it would not be plausible to explain the wrongness of D's act by appeal to D's having imposed a risk of harm on E, F, G and the rest of us.)

Not that risk is irrelevant. For, second, what must be crucial to LOG (NO HARM) is the mundane fact that throwing the logs one clears off one's land into the public highway is illegal, and its having been made illegal is presumably in part a consequence of the recognition, not that each and every instance of log throwing creates a risk of harm (that must surely be false), but rather that the risk to the rest of us increases dramatically if people generally are legally permitted to dump their debris in the highway. This is of course not the only reason for making log throwing illegal: there is also disruption of traffic, nuisance, and aesthetic considerations. (Compare the law that prohibits my neighbor from putting his garbage on the sidewalk in front of my house, except on Wednesdays, which are our town's garbage-collection days. No doubt a concern about health is in part, perhaps even largely, responsible for the adoption of such a law, but the sheer look of the neighborhood concerns us too.) Whatever the source of the law, however, what must be crucial to this case is, as I said, that there is one. For if there had been no such legal constraint, if D's town had marked off a (one would hope, only rarely used) stretch of highway, and given residents the legal privilege of dumping debris in it, there would have been nothing wrong in D's throwing a log into it, despite the fact that C chooses to walk there every day.

7. I have suggested that we should accept

> The Harm Thesis: We have claims against others that they not
> cause us harm.

We need to connect the notion 'harm' with the ideas that came out
in the preceding chapter. We do well first, however, to look beyond
harm to other unwelcome outcomes one might cause in acting. We
have looked at one, namely risk of harm, and disadvantage generally,
but there are others.

Chapter 10

Distress and Harm

1. If a person Y hits a person X with a log, Y infringes a claim of X's. If Y causes X harm by hitting X with a log, then Y infringes a further claim of X's. What if Y causes X pain by hitting X with a log? Does Y infringe yet another claim of X's? Is causing pain an infringement of a claim?

Pain is a particularly salient member of a class of feelings—sensations, sense experiences, experiences generally—that people on the whole dislike having. Let us say that if a person has a feeling at a time that he or she dislikes having at that time, then he or she suffers *distress* at that time.

I should think that everyone always dislikes having feelings of intense pain. Similarly, I should think, for feelings of nausea or dizziness. But there are some feelings of relatively minor pain that some people do not dislike having whereas others do. I do not merely have masochists in mind. Some people positively like the feeling of mild pain they have when they drink very hot coffee, or when they pick off a scab, or when they poke the tip of their tongue in a cavity in a tooth; others do not. I am so using "distress" that if a person does not dislike having any of the feelings he or she has at a certain time, then he or she is not suffering distress at that time, even if others would have disliked having some of those very feelings.

But it will sometimes be useful, for brevity, to speak of a certain feeling as itself an instance of distress. I will only do this, however, where the feeling is itself one that everyone always dislikes having, or where the context makes clear that the person under consideration does dislike having the feeling at the time of having it (so that the person who has it is—though perhaps not everyone else would be—suffering distress at that time).

249

I suggested in the preceding chapter that we should accept

> The Harm Thesis: We have claims against others that they not cause us harm.

I suggest that we should also accept

> The Distress Thesis: We have claims against others that they not cause us 'non-belief-mediated' distress.

2. It is, I think, a familiar practice to divide feelings into two kinds. First, there are those we 'just have'; second, there are those we have because we have a certain belief.

Some examples of the first kind that people typically dislike having are feelings of pain, nausea, and dizziness, and such sense experiences as smelling rotten fish and hearing the screech of chalk on a blackboard. When the dentist starts to drill before the novocaine has taken effect, I have a feeling of pain, and there is no belief I have such that I have the feeling because I have that belief. I will call these feelings non-belief-mediated.

Some examples of the second kind that people typically dislike having are feelings of fear, disappointment, insult, frustration, embarrassment, envy, humiliation, guilt, shame, sadness, and grief. I feel fear because I believe that a bull is rushing toward me, and I would not feel the fear if I did not have that belief. I will call these feelings belief-mediated.

There are feeling-kinds about which we may be inclined to say that some instances belong on one of these lists and some on the other. Consider anxiety, for example. People typically dislike feeling anxiety. But which list should it be placed on? Well, you might feel anxiety because you believe you are about to undergo a final exam in chemistry, and you would not have the feeling if you did not have that belief. That feeling of anxiety is belief-mediated. On the other hand, you might just, all simply, feel anxious—free-floating anxiety, as the feeling is sometimes called. That feeling of anxiety is non-belief-mediated. (Or should we instead say that anxiety is not *a* kind of feeling, that there are two kinds of anxiety, one belief-mediated, the other not? We have not the least need to settle the matter.)

More important, I have omitted two kinds of feeling from the list of belief-mediated feelings which might well be thought of particular interest to the moral theorist: feelings of anger and of moral indignation. My impression is that women mostly dislike feeling angry, whereas many men rather enjoy it; perhaps people generally enjoy anger when they take themselves to be capable of putting a stop to what angers them, or at least think they will be safe if they express their anger, this being something women are not brought up to do. If this is right, then feelings of anger are not *typically* disliked by those who have them. Moral indignation is another matter entirely, for I am inclined to think we all quite enjoy it. Obviously we dislike the activity that generates indignation in us, and we want it stopped. But I fancy we like having the feeling of indignation itself; we often wallow in it. Perhaps I am mistaken about both anger and moral indignation. Anyone who thinks I am is cordially invited to insert them into the list I gave above—among the belief-mediated feelings of course, since these are feelings we have because of beliefs we have. And whether or not it belongs on the list, moral indignation is a feeling we will want to come back to.

There are of course non-belief-mediated and belief-mediated feelings that are typically liked by those who have them. The cozy feelings one has on getting into a warm bath are non-belief-mediated; the feelings of satisfaction at a job well done are belief-mediated; both kinds of feeling are typically liked by those who have them. But what interests us here is only the disliked feelings, for our concern is distress.

Now I have suggested that we should accept

> The Distress Thesis: We have claims against others that they not cause us 'non-belief-mediated' distress,

and thus that we have claims against others that they not cause us pain, nausea, dizziness, and the like, supposing that we would dislike having those feelings. Why should it be thought that we have such claims?

One possible reason is this. Suppose B hit A with a log and thereby caused A pain. Isn't what B did worse than it would have been had the hitting not caused A pain? And doesn't *that* show that A had a claim against B that B not cause A pain? Similarly for all the other instances of non-belief-mediated distress.

But this is a dubious reason for attributing to A a claim to not be caused pain. Consider again a thesis we first met in Chapter 6:

> The Aggravation Principle: If X has a claim against Y that Y do alpha, then the worse Y makes things for X if Y fails to do alpha, the more stringent X's claim against Y that Y do alpha.

Given that principle, there is no need to appeal to a claim in A to not be caused pain in order to explain why what B did was worse than it would have been had the hitting not caused A pain. For given B caused A pain by hitting him with the log, B made things worse for A than he would have done had the hitting not caused A pain, and the Aggravation Principle therefore tells us that A's claim to not be hit with a log was more stringent than it would have been had the hitting not caused him pain. It is common enough, after all, that the infringing of a more stringent claim is worse than the infringing of a less stringent claim.

But there are other reasons for accepting the Distress Thesis. In the case we just looked at, B caused A pain by hitting A with a log, thus by doing what was trespass. Yet there are cases in which one causes a person non-belief-mediated distress without infringing any other claim of that person's. I might stand under your bedroom window, making that horrible screeching noise with chalk on a slate. You would then suffer non-belief-mediated distress. But it might be that I infringe no other claim of yours: commit no trespass, cause you no harm, infringe no property right of yours, and so on. More generally, if we want certain kinds of nuisances to turn out to involve infringements of claims, we had better allow that causing non-belief-mediated distress is itself an infringement of a claim.

What settles the matter, however, is that we surely are in respect of non-belief-mediated distress under the special kind of behavioral constraint that others' having claims against us consists in. Would it be permissible to cause one person pain on the ground that, if one does not do so, five others will suffer a comparable pain? (Compare TRANSPLANT.) Hardly.

Nausea and dizziness are presumably of much less moral moment than pain. Or they are of much less moral moment if what we contrast is mild, relatively short-lasting nausea or dizziness with intense, relatively long-lasting pain. Similarly for the experience of smelling rotten fish. But the same test yields the same result about them. Would it be permissible to save B's life at the cost of causing A ten years of nausea or the smell of rotten fish? I should think not.

I conclude that the Distress Thesis is very plausible. No doubt one can cause non-belief-mediated distress unwittingly, and entirely without fault; that is no more reason to object to the Distress Thesis than the possibility of causing harm unwittingly, and entirely without fault, is reason to object to the Harm Thesis. Again, X might consent to being caused non-belief-mediated distress by Y, or X might forfeit his or her claim to not be caused it; but we can say that where there has been consent or forfeit, a claim that had been had is no longer had.

3. But what of belief-mediated distress?

> The Distress Thesis: We have claims against others that they not cause us 'non-belief-mediated' distress

says not a word about belief-mediated distress, and it might well be asked why these two kinds of distress should be thought different in the respects that interest us here. After all, some belief-mediated distresses are vastly worse than some non-belief-mediated distresses: I should think we all dislike feelings of embarrassment, humiliation, shame, and grief, and that we dislike them far more than we dislike minor pains and the smell of rotten fish. Would it be permissible to cause one person embarrassment on the ground that, if one does not do so, five others would suffer a comparable degree of embarrassment? So why should causing non-belief-mediated distress be a claim infringement where causing belief-mediated distress is not? I think it very much worth emphasis that these distresses really are different in the respects that interest us here.

The first fact we should take note of about belief-mediated feelings is that people can have them rationally or irrationally, and bear some responsibility themselves for how long they have them and how intense they are, even for whether they have them at all. You sneeze, and I feel a mix of horror, fear, and rage. How so? I think you are sneezing *at* me, I think you have cancer and are trying to spread your cancer germs to me. By contrast, if my dentist starts drilling before the novocaine has fully taken effect, there is no question whether it is rational or irrational in me to feel pain, or to feel an intense pain, or to feel pain for such and such a time. It might well be irrational in me to make a great scene about the pain he causes me. It might well be irrational in me to dwell on the pain in memory later, bringing it back to mind so vividly as to be almost feeling it all over again. It might well be irrational in me to have taken so little care of my teeth in the past as now to need all that drilling. But whether I feel the pain at the time, and for how long, and how intense it is, that is not up to me—it is up to the condition of the dentist's drill and my tooth.

In some instances of irrational belief-mediated feeling, the irrationality issues from the irrationality of the belief itself; that is true in the example I just gave, for while fear of cancer is rational, my belief that when you sneeze you are trying to share your cancer germs with me is not rational. In other cases, the belief is not irrational, but the underlying attitude (because of which the onset of the belief triggers the feeling) is itself irrational. You draw my attention to the fact that there are three bits of lint on my carpet, and I therefore feel profound grief. How so? I cannot bear that the condition of my carpet be anything less than perfection. There is nothing irrational in my belief that there are three bits of lint on it; there is everything irrational in the underlying attitude because of which my coming to have that belief triggers grief. And it is of course possible that there are cases in which both the belief and the underlying attitude are irrational.

The fact that belief-mediated feelings can be irrational has a direct bearing on the question that interests us. You say to me "There are three bits of lint on your carpet," thereby causing me to feel profound grief. You sneeze, thereby causing me to feel a mix of horror, fear, and rage. Did you infringe a claim of mine in either case? I should think the better answer is no.

We could say no while nevertheless saying that one who causes belief-mediated distress does infringe a claim if we say that one whose belief-mediated distress is irrational has forfeited his or her claim to not be caused that distress, by virtue of the irrationality. But should we say this? Is causing *rational* belief-mediated distress an infringement of a claim?

Suppose I am a judge, and Alfred is plaintiff's lawyer in a case now before me. I called Alfred and defendant's lawyer to the bench for a conference. I think Alfred a lovely young man—so I pinched his nose. That was trespass, hence an infringement of a claim of his. Alfred felt insulted, and not at all irrationally. Was my causing him to feel insulted an infringement of a further claim of his? If we say so, we are committed to something implausible. For suppose that causing belief-mediated distress is a claim infringement. And suppose that you have to choose between a trespass against A, thereby causing A belief-mediated distress, and a comparably grave, or even slightly more grave, trespass against B, who has steeled himself against distress in consequence of such trespasses and hence would not be caused belief-mediated distress by the trespass. Then it would be morally preferable for you to commit the trespass on B, since in committing the trespass on A you would be infringing a further claim that you would not be infringing if you committed the trespass on B. That can hardly be right.

Indeed, this consideration suggests, not merely that causing belief-mediated distress is not itself an infringement of a claim, but also that the fact that one would cause belief-mediated distress by an infringement of a claim does not make the claim be more stringent. Consider Alfred again. I committed trespass on him: I infringed a claim of his. That was a stringent claim, in light of the circumstances in which the trespass was committed. Was Alfred's claim against the bodily intrusion more stringent because he felt insulted by it? Would the claim have been less stringent if—having come to regard me with contempt, in light of his own and other lawyers' past experiences with me—he had steeled himself against insult from me? The answer seems plainly to be no.

Again, if all but one of the teacups I inherited from my grandmother have been broken, I might have steeled myself against grief at the loss of the remaining one. Your smashing or stealing the remaining one can hardly be thought an infringement of a less stringent claim than it would have been had I not so steeled myself.

The possibility of steeling oneself against belief-mediated distress obviously has a common source with the possibility of feeling belief-mediated distress irrationally.

What these examples show is that

> The Aggravation Principle: If X has a claim against Y that Y do alpha, then the worse Y makes things for X if Y fails to do alpha, the more stringent X's claim against Y that Y do alpha

needs qualification. You do make things worse for a person by infringing a claim if you do not merely infringe the claim, but also cause your victim belief-mediated distress by doing so, and this whether or not the distress you cause your victim is irrational. But the claim you infringe is no more stringent by virtue of your causing the distress than it would have been had you not caused it. Trespass, for example, can have been committed even if the victim never comes to learn it has been, thus *a fortiori* even if the victim is not insulted by it. Similarly for the claims infringed in destruction or theft of property. And if the victim of a trespass or property-claim infringement does not feel distress by virtue of having so arranged his or her emotional life as to not feel the distress, then that does not make the claim less stringent than it would otherwise have been. So let us from here on in take the Aggravation Principle to read as follows:

> The Aggravation Principle: If X has a claim against Y that Y do alpha, then the worse Y makes things for X if Y fails to do alpha, the more stringent X's claim against Y that Y do alpha—but for 'worsenings' that consist in X's being caused belief-mediated distress.

That emendation[1] allows us to say what seems to be entirely plausible in the case of Alfred: the claim of his that I infringed was very stringent in light of my position, his position, and the surroundings in which the claim was infringed, and would have been no less stringent had he not felt the insult. Similarly in the case of my last teacup: the claim you infringed in smashing it was very stringent, in light of what it meant to me (it was the last of the set I inherited from my grandmother), and the claim was no more or less stringent according as I did or did not feel grief at its loss.

In short, then, causing belief-mediated distress is not itself an infringement of a claim, even if the distress is not irrational, and the fact that one is caused belief-mediated distress by a claim infringement does not mean that the claim infringed was more stringent than it would otherwise have been.

It was because of the first of those two facts that the thesis I suggested we should accept—

> The Distress Thesis: We have claims against others that they not cause us 'non-belief-mediated' distress—

is restricted to non-belief-mediated distress. One may cause belief-mediated distress by an act that is itself a claim infringement; that one thereby causes belief-mediated distress does not mean one has infringed a further claim of the victim's, even if the distress is not irrational.

Saying that, however, is entirely compatible with saying that one can have a claim to not be caused belief-mediated distress in consequence of private commitments or law. And one can have a claim to

---

1. The need for yet another emendation in the Aggravation Principle will emerge when we look more closely at the forfeiture of claims in Chapter 14.

not be caused belief-mediated distress in consequence of having some other claim. There is A, standing on a ladder. If B shouts "I'M COMING TO GET YOU!" at A, he will thereby cause A fear, thereby cause A to topple off the ladder, and thereby cause A harm. A has a claim against B that B not cause A harm. It follows by the Means Principle for Claims that A has a claim against B that B not cause A fear, as of course also that B not shout those words at A.

4. One reason why it was worth emphasis that belief-mediated distress differs from non-belief-mediated distress in the respects that interest us here is that a number of people have rested moral weight on feelings of moral indignation, a weight they will not carry. The people I have in mind are lawyers. Let us, for example, accept Robert Bork's invitation to consider

> Griswold v. Connecticut, in many ways a typical decision of the Warren Court. Griswold struck down Connecticut's statute making it a crime, even for married couples, to use contraceptive devices. If we take the principle of the decision to be a statement that Government may not interfere with any acts done in private, we need not even ask about the principle's dubious origin for we know at once that the Court will not apply it neutrally. The Court, we may confidently predict, is not going to throw constitutional protection around heroin use or sexual acts with a consenting minor.
>
> Griswold, then, is an unprincipled decision . . . The truth is that the Court could not reach its result in Griswold through principle. The reason is obvious. Every clash between a minority claiming power to regulate involves a choice between gratifications of the two groups. When the Constitution has not spoken, the Court will be able to find no scale, other than its own value preferences, upon which to weigh the respective claims to pleasure. Compare the facts in Griswold with a hypothetical suit by an electric utility company and one of its customers to void a smoke pollution ordinance as unconstitutional. The cases are identical.
>
> In Griswold a husband and wife assert that they wish to have sexual relations without fear of unwanted children. The law impairs their sexual gratifications . . . The majority finds use of contraceptives immoral. Knowledge that it takes place and that the State makes no effort to inhibit it causes the majority anguish, impairs their gratifications.
>
> Neither case is covered specifically or by obvious implication in the Constitution . . . Why is sexual gratification more worthy than moral gratification? Why is sexual gratification nobler than economic gratification? . . . Courts must accept any value choice the legislature makes unless it clearly runs contrary to a choice made in the framing of the Constitution.

It follows, of course, that broad areas of constitutional law ought to be reformulated.[2]

I have nothing to say about this passage as a criticism of the Warren Court or as a hint at a way in which the Constitution ought to be interpreted. I have nothing to say about the propositions of law argued for or hinted at here. But there are propositions of moral theory argued for and hinted at here, and among them is a serious mistake.

The majority in Connecticut made use of contraceptives illegal. Let us suppose they did so—as Bork implies—because they thought it immoral. A good question arises here: is the immorality of a practice sufficient ground for the majority to make it illegal? Making a practice illegal is constraining liberty; and it can hardly be thought right in general that the majority may constrain the liberty of the minority *just* on the ground that the practice which the illegalizing will constrain is immoral. Something would need to be added to get from immorality to permissible illegalizing.

Bork suggests a possible addition. What if the practice is not merely immoral but causes feelings of moral indignation? The majority of the residents of Connecticut were caused to feel moral indignation by the knowledge that contraceptives were being used. Moreover, their indignation would have been more intense if their elected officials had made no effort to put a stop to the practice. "Knowledge that it takes place and that the State makes no effort to inhibit it causes the majority anguish." Anguish! This is pretty serious. Doesn't adding to the fact that the practice is immoral the further fact that its being freely engaged in causes anguish give good enough reason for illegalizing it?

Now I suggested earlier that moral indignation is a feeling we rather enjoy. Hence the use of the term "anguish" for what would be felt by the majority of Connecticut residents if the state made no effort to inhibit the use of contraceptives is, I think, disingenuous at best. But suppose I am mistaken: suppose moral indignation is a feeling we dislike having, and thus is an instance of distress. Then what?

Why should we think that the fact that practice P causes distress in the form of moral indignation is a less weighty ground for illegalizing P than the fact that practice Q causes distress in the form of nausea or dizziness is for illegalizing Q? Indeed, Bork invites us to

2. Robert Bork, "Neutral Principles and Some First Amendment Problems", *Indiana Law Journal*, 1 (1971).

compare a suit to have the Connecticut law overturned as unconstitutional with a suit to have a smoke-pollution ordinance overturned as unconstitutional. Declaring the Connecticut law unconstitutional would cause the majority distress in the form of moral indignation; declaring the smoke-pollution ordinance unconstitutional would cause the majority distress in the form of nausea and dizziness.[3] Why should we think the one consideration weightier than the other? Bork has no objection to a legislature's making such value choices as would lead to assigning different weights to the two kinds of distress—moral indignation on the one hand, nausea and dizziness on the other—but he thinks there is nothing in the nature of the distresses which could make it incorrect for a legislature to decide in the one way rather than the other.

But there is an important difference between the two kinds of distress. Causing nausea and dizziness is causing non-belief-mediated distress and hence is a claim infringement; causing moral indignation is causing belief-mediated distress (if it is causing distress at all) and is not infringing a claim, however intense the moral indignation may be ("anguish"). So the fact that practice P causes moral indignation *is* a less weighty ground for illegalizing P than the fact that practice Q causes nausea or dizziness is for illegalizing Q.

I do not for a moment say that the fact that a practice is claim-infringing is conclusive ground for illegalizing it. The claims infringed by the practice might be relatively weak, infringeable given a sufficient increment of good to be got by permitting the practice. But the burden of proof is on the other side, to show that the increment of good *is* sufficiently great.

Moreover, the fact that a practice is not claim-infringing is not conclusive ground against illegalizing it. In particular, there might well be reasons for illegalizing an immoral practice other than the fact that it causes moral indignation.

I have wished to bring out only that there is distress and distress, and that we have good reason to resist legal—or any other—arguments that rest on the supposition that all distress is the same.

5. The Harm Thesis of the preceding chapter tells us that we have claims against others that they not cause us harm; the Distress Thesis

---

3. And perhaps pain and harm. Arguments for smoke-pollution ordinances typically appeal to more than mild unpleasantness caused by the smoke.

of this chapter tells us that we have claims against others that they not cause us non-belief-mediated distress, and we have seen reason to say that we have no claim against others that they not cause us belief-mediated distress. But why did we need to attend to distress at all? Isn't causing distress causing harm?

In the preceding chapters, I left the notion 'harm' unanalyzed. I assumed it to be clear that you cause people harm when you cut their legs off or when you break their arms, and quite clear, moreover, that you might commit trespass or cause distress without causing harm. I also assumed it to be clear that causing a risk of harm is not, itself, causing a harm. But suppose someone asks, "What exactly is harm?"

We could reply: harm is damage. So causing a person harm is causing the person to be damaged. This certainly captures the examples I gave. Cutting a person's legs off or breaking a person's arm is causing that person to be damaged—permanently in the case of cutting off legs, not permanently in the case of breaking an arm. Killing a person is also causing the person to be damaged, damaged in a way that is both as serious as damage gets to be and permanent.[4] But what if we are next asked, "What exactly is damage?"

There seem to be two connected sources of the pressure many philosophers have felt under to produce analyses of harm. In the first place, the word slithers. Some harms—such as the loss of one's legs, the breaking of an arm, and death—are central, paradigm cases of harm; these cases are the heart of harm. But many people use the word for cases that are well outside the range of central cases of harm. If someone kills my cat, and I therefore grieve at its death, has he or she caused me a harm? If my neighbors refuse to mow their lawns, so that the street begins to look run down and the value of my house decreases, have they caused me a harm? Some would say yes. (Others would say no.) Where does harm end? Have I suffered a harm when just anything at all happens that I would have preferred not to have happened? Presumably not. But (as people say) where do you draw the line?

The second source of the pressure to analyze harm issues from what makes people want to use "harm" for cases outside the range of central

---

4. On some accounts of what harm is, it is unclear how killing a person could be causing him or her a harm. (See, for example, Joel Feinberg's account of harm as a 'setback' to an interest in *Harm to Others*.) But I should think that that would be a worrisome fact about those accounts of harm.

cases of harm. On any view, it is a morally significant fact that you would cause a person harm by doing a thing: other things being equal, you had better not do it. So if I want to get you to stop doing a thing, it will pay me to make out that you would cause me harm if you did it.[5] But then we might well wonder what exactly it is about causing harm that gives it this moral significance. And of course the pressure is the greater if we wish to accept—as I suggested we should accept—the Harm Thesis, which tells us that causing harm is an infringement of a claim.

So we really do need to look into the question what harm is.

As I said, harm is damage. But what is damage? The notion 'harm', or 'damage', is evaluative, and *causing harm* may be thought *prima facie* to be analyzable as follows:

> The *Prima Facie* Plausible Analysis of Harm-Causing: Y causes X harm if and only if an event E that is an act of Y's causes X's condition to be worse ·han it would have been had E not occurred.[6]

That is an analysis of causing harm. What is harm itself? We will come back to that shortly.

But analyses of causing harm that make use of counterfactuals—as this one does—really won't do. Suppose B fired a gun at A, thereby causing a bullet to lodge in A's head and thereby killing A. According to this short story, there was an act of B's, namely B's firing a gun at A, that made A's condition very bad indeed. Now let us slightly lengthen the short story, by adding to it that if B had lost his nerve and failed to shoot, C would have stabbed A and thereby killed A. Then it is not true that B's firing a gun at A caused A's condition to be worse than it would have been had B's firing a gun at A not occurred: A's condition would have been equally bad if that event had not occurred. So the *Prima Facie* Plausible Analysis of Harm-Causing requires us to conclude that B did not cause A harm in the slightly lengthened short story. That is certainly incorrect. The fact

5. Some years ago a Cambridge resident sued his neighbor for not having mowed his lawn in fourteen years. The suit of course argued that the neighbor's failure to mow his lawn caused the plaintiff harm. (In passing, the plaintiff lost his case.)

6. I abbreviate here. In particular, I here omit the complication required to deal with causings by 'acts of omission'; see the considerations pointed to in Chapter 9, section 4.

that someone else would have caused an equally grave harm if you had not caused a harm does not in the least count against the supposition that you did cause a harm.

This is a familiar kind of difficulty for analyses of causation that appeal to counterfactuals, and we must therefore avoid counterfactuals here. So let us instead try:

> The Non-Counterfactual Necessary and Sufficient Condition for Harm-Causing: Y causes X harm if and only if an event E that is an act of Y's causes X's condition to be worse than it was before E occurred.[7]

But that still won't do: it allows too much in under the heading of harm, for surely an act of Y's might make X's condition worse than it was without its being the case that Y causes X harm. Or at least so I suppose. For example, you ran faster than I did in the race we ran last Friday: you came in first and I came in second. Your winning was an act of yours, and it made my condition worse than it was, for here I am, positively miserable at losing. But I take it that we cannot conclude from this, by itself, that you caused me *harm*.

But I should think it clear that we can say, more weakly,

> The Non-Counterfactual Necessary Condition for Harm-Causing: Y causes X harm only if an event E that is an act of Y's causes X's condition to be worse than it was before E occurred.

That leaves us with the task of working out which the worsenings of X's condition are such that *if* an act of Y's causes one or other of them, then Y has caused X harm. Let us turn to it.

6. There are *bodily events*—such as losing one's legs, one's arm breaking, and death—such that *typically* when an act of Y's causes such

---

7. What of cases such as those discussed by Derek Parfit, in which a woman takes a drug that causes the child she then conceives to be defective? See his *Reasons and Persons* (New York: Oxford University Press, 1984). If we want to have it that the woman in such a case causes her child to be harmed, and I think we do, then a revision is called for. A number of possibilities present themselves. One is to add a clause to the effect that if X did not exist before E occurred, then E need not make X's condition be worse than it was before E occurred—it need only make X's condition be bad.

an event in X, Y thereby causes X's condition to be worse than it was before Y acted, and Y has on any view caused X harm. These are, as I said, among the central cases of harm.

I said only typically, however. Sometimes when an act of Y's causes X to lose his legs, Y has not caused X's condition to be worse than it was before Y acted. What I have in mind are cases such as that of David, which we looked at in Chapter 7. By hypothesis, David's leg is crushed under a fallen tree, and he is dying; if you do what will cause him to lose that leg, you will thereby cause his condition to be not worse but better. This is a case in which an act of yours does cause a bodily event of the kind I mentioned, but no act of yours causes David's condition to be worse than it was, and the Non-Counterfactual Necessary Condition for Harm-Causing therefore tells us that you do not cause him harm if you proceed. But that is exactly the outcome our theory should yield, for you surely do not cause David harm if you proceed.

Similar possibilities are available in the case of arm breakings. What of death? It is arguable that an act of Y's that causes X's death might make X's condition not worse but better: I have in mind cases in which X's condition is already so bad—perhaps so full of pain—that death would arguably improve X's condition. Let us bypass the question whether this can really be so. What matters for our purposes is that in cases where it is so, Y would not cause X harm in acting in such a way as to cause X's death.

Still, *typically* when an act of Y's causes a bodily event of the kind we are looking at—such as losing one's legs, one's arm breaking, and death—Y thereby causes X's condition to be worse than it was before Y acted, and Y has on any view caused X harm.

But what is 'the kind' of bodily event in question here? They are bodily events that *impair* for a longer or shorter period of time. Losing one's legs makes one unable to walk easily or at all. (Artificial legs may enable one to walk, but not easily.) One's arm breaking makes one unable, until the break heals, to do the things it takes two arms to do. Death makes one unable to do anything at all, ever.

I think we can say not only that if Y's act causes such an event in X then typically Y causes X harm, but also that where Y does cause X harm by causing such an event, the event itself is the harm. Causing the loss of legs is typically causing a harm, suffering the loss of legs is typically suffering a harm, and the event that is the losing of legs is typically itself a harm.

It is very plausible to think that the gravity of the kind of harm mentioned here turns on the gravity of the impairment it causes, and that this turns on the 'reach' of the impairment, by which I mean to include how large a role in the life of the victim the impaired abilities played as well as the duration of the impairment. Being able to walk is very important to all of us; so losing a leg is typically a very grave harm. Being able to walk is very important to all of us; but a leg's breaking is typically a less grave harm than losing a leg since the disabilities do not last as long. Death, of course, is complete and permanent disability.

Some abilities are very important to some people and markedly less important to others. In the case of each of us it is in *a* measure important to be able to waggle our fingers; the ability to do so is far more important to a violinist than to a mathematician, so the gravity of the harm suffered by a violinist whose finger breaks is greater than the gravity of the harm suffered by a mathematician whose finger breaks.

On the other hand, the fact that the victim is caused distress by the bodily event, or by the impairment that the bodily event causes, is not relevant to the gravity of the harm. More precisely, distress suffered in consequence of a bodily event that is harm does not make the harm more grave unless it does so by making the impairment more grave. Consider pain, which is non-belief-mediated distress. That my finger's breaking causes me pain does not make the finger's breaking a more grave harm than it would have been had it not caused me pain—unless the pain will recur whenever I try to move my finger in future (after it has set) in such a way as to make the impairment more severe or more long-lasting.

Similarly for belief-mediated distress. Anybody whose finger breaks (mathematician *or* violinist) will feel dismay, but that does not make the finger breaking a more grave harm than it would have been had the finger breaking not caused dismay. If a violinist's finger breaks, he or she may feel not merely dismay but also frustration, disappointment, perhaps even grief, but that too does not make the finger breaking a more grave harm than it would have been had the finger breaking not caused these feelings. What fixes the gravity of the harm is what fixes the importance to a person of the ability impaired (together with its duration); and what fixes *that* is not the feelings the victim will have but rather the role the ability actually plays in the victim's life.

More generally, distress in the case of harms of the kinds we are now considering is an epiphenomenon: its presence or absence does not make the harm more grave.

7. Harms of the kind we just looked at—bodily events that impair— are the central cases of harm. Two other kinds of harm are very near the center.

What I have in mind first are what might be called psychological harms. A parent might for one or another reason so abuse a child as to cause it to be psychologically crippled: unable to interact with others in normal ways. For all I know, there is a drug one can inject a person with and thereby cause schizophrenia; injecting such a drug would also cause a person to be psychologically crippled. This is certainly damage, it is certainly harm: the metaphor of the crippled or lamed is clearly in place. No doubt there is always an array of bodily events that cause the impairment in such cases, but the bodily event (such as being beaten or injected) is not the harm; the harm is rather the impairment that such a bodily event causes. Contrast break- ing a person's arm. In that case the bodily event—the arm breaking— is the harm, more or less grave according as the impairment it causes is more or less grave.

Psychological impairment might be caused by distress, as where pain or grief incapacitates. Then although distress is not itself harm, it may cause harm.

What harms of this kind have in common with harms of the kind we looked at in the preceding section is that both kinds involve im- pairment, the gravity of the harm turning on the gravity of the im- pairment. A third kind of harm has something different in common with harms of the kind we looked at: harms of this third kind are themselves bodily events. But they are unlike harms of the two kinds we have now looked at, for they do not involve impairment. What I have in mind are disfigurements. You lop off the tip of my nose. Do I suffer an impairment? No. (I can still breathe as easily as I did before.) But the loss of the tip of my nose is certainly damage, it is certainly harm. The gravity of this kind of harm is a function of the gravity of the disfigurement and its duration.

Of course some bodily events by which the victim is impaired are also bodily events that are disfigurements. But some harms are pure disfigurements.

The gravity of a disfigurement is itself in part a function of social practice. Since we mostly cover the knee and not the face, a scar on one's knee is a less grave disfigurement than a scar on one's face. But the gravity of a disfigurement is presumably not a function only of social practice, for it is presumably not merely a matter of social practice (not merely a matter of a social practice which could as easily have been otherwise) that the look of a person's face is more important both to that person and to the rest of us than is the look of the person's knee.

Moreover, just as the impairment you cause if you break a violinist's finger is more grave than the impairment you cause if you break a mathematician's finger, so the disfigurement you cause if you lop off the tip of an actor's nose is more grave than the disfigurement you cause if you lop off the tip of my nose. An actor's appearance is more important to him than mine is to me—among other things, his live-lihood depends on it and mine does not. The role of an ability in a person's life fixes the gravity of its impairment; the role of a person's appearance in his or her life fixes the gravity of a disfigurement.

It is these three kinds of harm only that I had in mind in the preceding chapter, and thus these only that the Harm Thesis should be understood to tell us we have claims against.

8. Let us turn now to what I called the slithering of the word "harm"—its tendency to spread to what is (as I think) not strictly called "harm" and what I at any rate will not call "harm". Four kinds of example seem to be of particular interest.

In the first place (i) there is the worsening of a person's condition that consists in a worsening of *status*. If you cause me to lose my job, my chairmanship of a committee, my position as champion runner, my position of respect in the community, then you cause my condition to be bad, and I think some people would be inclined to say you have caused me a (more or less grave) harm. Have you?

If we want to accept the Harm Thesis, then it would be a good idea for us to say that these outcomes of your acts are not harms, since causing a person to lose a job or position or good name is not itself an infringement of any claim of his or hers. It is of course possible to cause such outcomes by acts that are themselves infringements of claims. You might cause me to lose my job or good name by lying about me, you might cause me to lose my position as champion runner by breaking my leg. But if you caused me one or another of these outcomes and did so by no infringement of any claim of mine, then it is hard to see how anyone could think you infringed any claim of mine at all. Surely you do not infringe any claim of mine if you cause me to lose my job by doing the work attached to the job better than I do it. Surely you do not infringe any claim of mine if you cause me to lose my position as champion runner by making the effort required for running faster than me.

The gravamen of the charge against one who causes a status worsening lies in the means used. If those means are no infringement of a claim, then causing the status worsening is no infringement of a claim. I therefore suggest we say that status worsenings are not themselves harms.

Saying this is of course compatible with saying that some status worsenings are worse than some harms. I would sooner suffer a broken finger than loss of my job. But so also would I sooner suffer a broken finger than profound and long-lasting grief, and yet grief is not itself (though it may cause) harm.

Moreover, saying that status worsenings are not themselves harms is also compatible with saying that the fact that a claim infringement will cause status worsening means that the claim infringed is more stringent than it would otherwise be. If your breaking your promise to me will cause me to lose my job, then the claim you would be infringing in breaking your promise is more stringent than it would otherwise be. A status worsening *is* a worsening, and we can make moral room for that fact well enough—without supposing that causing a status worsening is itself a claim infringement—by appeal to

> The Aggravation Principle: If X has a claim against Y that Y do alpha, then the worse Y makes things for X if Y fails to do alpha, the more stringent X's claim against Y that Y do alpha—but for 'worsenings' that consist in X's being caused belief-mediated distress.

A second kind of example is (ii) the worsening of a person's condition that consists in *financial loss*. If you smash my computer or burn down my house, you cause me a financial loss, and I think some people would be inclined to say you have caused me a more or less grave harm according as the loss is larger or smaller. Have you?

I think that the right reply to make here is the same as the reply in the case of status worsening. You may cause me a financial loss by means that are themselves infringements of claims, as when you smash my computer or burn down my house; but then the gravamen of the charge against you is precisely that you infringed those claims. But you may cause me a financial loss by means that do not involve claim infringements, as when you just happen to manufacture better widgets than I do and thus cause me to go bankrupt. If that is how you cause me a financial loss, then you surely infringe no claim of mine at all in doing so. But (as in the case of status worsening) the Aggravation Principle applies so that, other things being equal, a claim the infringing of which will cause a large financial loss is more stringent than it would otherwise be.

A third kind of example is (iii) the worsening of a person's condition that consists in *his or her property's being damaged*. Property damage often causes financial loss, but need not. If you smash the teacups my grandmother left me, you cause me no financial loss at all: they were worth nothing on the market even before being damaged, and there is no such thing as replacing them, at any cost. But if you do do this, you cause my condition to be worse; and I think some people would be inclined to say you have caused me a more or less grave harm according as the teacups were more or less valuable to me. Have you?

This seems to me an even less interesting idea than the idea that status worsening and financial loss are harms. Causing property damage *is* itself an infringement of a claim, a property claim; there is no need to have it turn out to be the causing of harm in order for it to be a claim infringement. And if what the property damage causes is merely belief-mediated distress, then in light of the qualification we made in the Aggravation Principle, the property claim is not made more stringent by virtue of causing the distress than it would be if it did not cause the distress.

One final kind of example is much more interesting: (iv) the worsening of a person's condition that consists in his or her becoming a *morally bad person*. It does seem possible to cause a person to be morally bad, and if Y does this to X, then Y has surely acted very badly indeed. Shall we say that that is because Y's making X be morally bad was Y's causing X a harm, and thus an infringement of a claim of X's?

I think we all recognize that there is a difficulty here, a kind of knot. How does one make a person be a morally bad person? Perhaps we think of corruption, say bribery. But an attempt at bribery will not succeed unless the person to be bribed is already so far corrupt as to be prepared to accept the bribe.[8] Of course Bloggs might never have accepted a bribe before—yours being the first. Was that due merely to the fact that he had no prior offers? Then he always had his price, but no one offered anything. Or to the fact that prior offers were too small? Then he always had his price, but you were the first to meet it. Or because he thought he could not get away with accepting the prior offers? It is hard to see how a bribe could operate on a man like a sudden rainstorm, to make him a bad person though he was not before.

But there no doubt are causes in a bad person's background for his or her having become a bad person, perhaps parental abuse, perhaps abuse of other kinds. I think we can suppose that this is having caused harm, for we can see this as having caused what I earlier called psychological harm, a kind of psychological crippling in light of which the victim is unable to interact with others in normal ways. There is no reason to deny that interacting with others in normal ways requires a capacity for both trusting others and acting so as to be trusted by others. If we do suppose that moral worsening is harm, however, then we are committed by the Harm Thesis to supposing that causing moral worsening is infringing a claim, and that seems an intuitively dubious idea. But perhaps its seeming dubious is a product on the one hand of our not feeling entirely clear about what it is to cause a person to be morally bad (see the knot of the preceding paragraph) and, on the other hand, of our not feeling convinced that being morally bad really is being psychologically crippled. I leave this question open.

9. A summary is in order. Some of our claims we only have by virtue of private commitments or law; some of our claims we have both by nature and by virtue of private commitments or law; some of our claims we only have by nature. I suggested in Chapter 8 that the claims we have by nature have their source in two features that we possess: on the one hand we are subject to moral law, on the other we have inherently individual interests. It is because we have those features that we are subject to the special kind of behavioral constraint that others' having claims against us consists in, even where that

---

8. An interesting article on the cluster of issues that arise here is W. G. Ma-clagan's "How Important Is Moral Goodness?", *Mind*, 64 (1965), reprinted in Judith J. Thomson and Gerald Dworkin, eds., *Ethics* (New York: Harper and Row, 1968).

behavioral constraint was not generated by private commitments or law.

Among the claims we have by nature are the claims infringed in trespass. That we have them is shown by the fact that we are subject to the special behavioral constraint in the particular case of bodily intrusion. These claims are fundamental in that, if we lacked them, we would have at most very few other claims, and those we had would be worth little to us. If no bodily intrusion by another infringes a claim of yours, then you have no general claim to not be caused harm, no general claim to not be caused pain, no general claim to not be caused any of the untoward outcomes that can be caused by bodily intrusion, for as the Means Principle for Claims tells us, if you had those other claims, you would have claims against at least the bodily intrudings by which those other claims would be infringed. You might have other claims (property claims, for example) but they would be worth little to you, for no claim of yours would stand in the way of a bodily intrusion designed to force you to waive them.

In Chapters 9 and 10, we looked at claims to not be caused harm, more precisely at claims to not be caused what I suggest is central to harm, namely impairment and disfigurement. That we have such claims is shown by the fact—I take it to be plainly a fact—that we are subject to the special behavioral constraint in the particular case of impairments and disfigurements. The claims infringed in trespass are fundamental in the way I pointed to just above, but these claims are in another way fundamental, for they issue directly from the source of claims. Impairment by definition curtails the ability to secure what is in one's interest, whether the interest is inherently individual or not, and *a fortiori* curtails the ability to secure what is in one's inherently individual interest. Among our centrally important, inherently individual interests is that we be physically normal for the species, and disfigurement in greater or lesser degree, temporarily or permanently, brings us down below the standard. That we should be at least at this standard is important to us in part because falling below it may issue in impairment, but meeting the standard is important to us quite apart from its connection with human capacities for action: our self-image rests on assumptions we make about how we appear to others.

At the end of Chapter 8, I suggested that we might say that people's bodies are their First Property. Among the claims we have in owning First Property are the claims infringed in trespass; so also are the claims infringed in harm-causings that are causings of bodily harm. Not so, I should think, the claims infringed in causing psychological impairment or non-belief-mediated distress.

In Chapter 10, we looked at claims to not be caused non-belief-mediated distress. We do have such claims, as (once again) is shown by our being subject to the special behavioral constraint. These claims too issue directly from the source of claims. A centrally important, inherently individual interest is that we not suffer. We dislike belief-mediated distress as much as we dislike non-belief-mediated distress, but we do not have claims against its being caused us—except insofar as by the causing of it we are caused non-belief-mediated distress or harm.

Chapter 11

Liberty

1. We have so far in Part II been asking which claims people have. We need to ask now which privileges people have.

A person X has a privilege as regards Y of doing alpha just in case Y lacks a claim against X that X not do alpha. That follows from a thesis we met in Chapter 2:

(H_5) $P_{X, Y}\ p$ is equivalent to Not-($C_{Y, X}$ Not-p).

For example, I have a privilege as regards you of getting on the next subway to Kendall Square, in that you lack a claim against me that I not do so. So asking what privileges we have is equivalent to asking what claims other people lack.

The question which claims people lack is just as important for our purposes as the question which claims people have. On the one hand, a theory of rights should tell us not only which claims people have but what are the limits to the claims people have. On the other hand, the question which claims people lack is crucial to a question we will shortly turn to—whether we have a right to liberty and, if so, what it includes.

2. If I commit trespass on you, I infringe a claim of yours. If I cause you harm or non-belief-mediated distress, I infringe a claim of yours. But if I get on the next subway to Kendall Square, I do not infringe a claim of yours—your claims do not extend so far. Why?

Well, you might have had that claim. For example, (a) I might have promised you that I would not get on the next subway to Kendall Square. In the following chapter we will begin looking at ways in which one person can acquire claims from another person; meanwhile let us ask whether it can be supposed that you have the claim and did not acquire it from me or, for that matter, from any other individual person.

For another example, (b), if your name is Hilary and today is Tuesday, and our community has a law that assigns to people named Hilary a claim against others that they not take subways to Kendall Square on Tuesdays, then you do have a claim against me that I not get on the next subway to Kendall Square. Or at least you have a legal claim against me that I not do this. Let us bypass the question whether that would give you not merely a legal claim but also (all simply) a claim against me that I not do it.

A third example comes out as follows. My getting on the next subway to Kendall Square is not itself my committing trespass on you, or causing you harm or non-belief-mediated distress, but it might be that (c) I would do one or another of these things *by* getting on the next subway to Kendall Square. If that were the case, then it would follow that you do have a claim against me that I not get on the next subway, by

The Means Principle for Claims:
If
(i) X has a claim against Y that Y not do beta, and
(ii) If Y does alpha then he or she will thereby do beta,
then X has a claim against Y that Y not do alpha, that claim being at least as stringent as X's claim that Y not do beta.

Is there anything else that could have made it be the case that you have a claim against me that I not get on the next subway to Kendall Square? I suggest that there is not. In short, given (a) you did not acquire that claim from me or anyone else and (b) you do not have the claim by virtue of prevailing law, then you have the claim if and only if (c) by getting on the next subway to Kendall Square I would commit trespass on you or cause you harm or non-belief-mediated distress. There is a strong thesis in the offing here, but it is one I think will seem *prima facie* plausible. Let us say that a claim is a *pure social claim* just in case it is had *only* because of private commitments or law. Then the strong thesis can be stated as follows:

The Limits Thesis: X has a claim against Y that Y not do alpha if and only if either

(i) X's claim is a pure social claim, or

(ii) Y's doing alpha either

(a) itself would be Y's committing trespass on X, or causing X harm or non-belief-mediated distress, or

(b) is a means by which Y would be committing trespass on X, or causing X harm or non-belief-mediated distress.

What the Limits Thesis tells us is that—pure social claims apart—we have surveyed all of the claims we have.

As I have stressed several times, a claim can have multiple sources: it could, for example, be had both by virtue of prevailing law and by nature. Let us say that a claim is a *natural claim* just in case it is not a pure social claim. This leaves open that some natural claims have social as well as nonsocial sources: your claim against me that I not kill you counts as a natural claim for, although prevailing law assigns you that claim against me, you do not have it only for that reason. We will be looking at the social sources of claims later. What we are concerned to do here is to attend to the nonsocial sources of claims. And the Limits Thesis tells us that the nonsocial sources of claims extend no further than we have so far looked: a putative claim that is not purely social is not possessed at all unless the putative claim infringer would be committing trespass, or causing harm or non-belief-mediated distress, in or by proceeding. I have no general argument for this strong thesis; I suggest, however, that putative countercases to it turn out, on examination, not to be real countercases.

One putative class of countercases is the class of property claims (more precisely, claims to Second Property). If the Limits Thesis is true, then most property claims are purely social. How so? I own a certain cherry tree and therefore have a claim against you that you not cut it down without my permission. But would you be committing trespass, or causing me harm or non-belief-mediated distress, in or by cutting down the tree? No. The Limits Thesis therefore tells us that if we are to suppose I do have a claim against you that you not cut down the tree, that claim must be purely social. Now some people think that property claims generally, and my claim against you that you not cut down my tree in particular, are what I am here calling natural claims, and if they are right, then the Limits Thesis is false. I will argue in Chapter 13 that most property claims really are purely social.

I say only "most", however. It might be that if you cut down that tree it will fall on me, so that by cutting down the tree you will cause me harm. Then my claim against you that you not cut it down is not purely social: I have the claim against you in part by virtue of law, but in part also by virtue of the fact that you will cause me harm by cutting the tree down. But (as I will argue) a property claim that is not purely social is a relatively rare animal.

A second putative class of countercases issues from consideration of what some people think of as the right to 'noninterference' (compare 'the right to be let alone'). Another way to put the point is this: if the Limits Thesis is true, then the right to noninterference is more limited than one might have thought. I have a privilege of boarding the subway and want to do so, but you get in my way. Do you infringe a claim of mine? Well, do I have a claim that you not interfere with my boarding the subway by virtue of private commitments or law? Let us suppose not. Then the Limits Thesis says that you infringe a claim of mine only if you commit trespass on me (as by shoving me), or cause me harm or non-belief-mediated distress. The mere fact that you get in my way—the mere fact that I cannot board the subway without committing trespass on you (as by shoving you)—does not mean that you infringe a claim of mine, if the Limits Thesis is true.

Again, I have a privilege of making a speech in Harvard Square and want to do so, but you interfere. Do you infringe a claim of mine? Well, do I have a claim that you not interfere with my giving the speech by virtue of private commitments or law? Let us suppose not. Then the Limits Thesis says that you infringe a claim of mine only if you commit trespass on me (as by hitting me with a tomato), or cause me harm or non-belief-mediated distress. The mere fact that you interfere—as by shouting so loud that I cannot be heard—does not mean that you infringe a claim of mine, if the Limits Thesis is true.

In passing, if what you do is merely to shout so loud that I cannot be heard, then, if the Limits Thesis is true, you not only infringe no claim of mine, you infringe no claim of anyone else's, private commitments and law apart. Thus suppose that Bloggs would have liked to hear my speech. His hearing it is interfered with by your shouting, but the Limits Thesis says that you infringe no claim of his by shouting.

But I think that on reflection we will not find these consequences of the Limits Thesis objectionable. There are very many occasions when one ought not interfere with the actions of others—for example, where it would be rude, insulting, annoying, frustrating to do so—

and yet when they have no claim to noninterference. Insult and annoyance are not things we have a *claim* that others not cause us.

What is worth emphasis is that, whether or not we accept the Limits Thesis, we must in any case grant that the mere fact that X has a privilege as regards Y of doing a thing does not by itself give X a claim to Y's not interfering with X's doing of it. Compare D, to whom C had given the privilege of eating C's salad (Chapter 1, section 7). D's having that privilege does not by itself give D a claim against C (or anyone else) to noninterference with his eating of the salad. We may (I hope perspicuously) express the point here in our symbolism as follows:

$P_{X, Y}$X does alpha

does not entail

$C_{X, Y}$Y does not interfere with X's doing alpha.

A more general point, from which this one follows, is a thesis of Hohfeld's:

(H₃) No privilege entails any claim.

That, as I said in Chapter 1, seems entirely plausible.

Yet there are cases that seem more troublesome for the Limits Thesis than your getting in my way when I want to board a subway or shouting when I want to give a speech. Those are cases in which you prevent me from doing what I wish, but by means that are (as I think, plainly) no infringement of a claim of mine; but what if you prevent me from boarding a subway, or giving a speech, by threatening to kill me if I do? That is not merely rude, insulting, annoying, frustrating; it is markedly worse. What we should ask, in other words, is whether coercion is an infringement of a claim. I think we are inclined *prima facie* to think it is and, if it is, then the Limits Thesis needs revision.

But where, exactly, is the claim infringement? I am about to give my speech and you say to me "DON'T GIVE THAT SPEECH OR I'LL KILL YOU!" Can your saying those words to me constitute an infringement of a claim of mine? Your saying those words is your making a threat; is making a threat an infringement of a claim? By making the threat you may cause me fear. But causing fear is causing belief-mediated distress and is not itself an infringement of a claim, private commitments and law apart. By making the threat, you may cause me to not do what I had wanted to do. But causing a person to not do what he or she had wanted to do is not itself an infringement of a claim of that person's: we may do this and have infringed no claim at all. If you infringe a claim of mine in making me not give my speech, that had better be because the means you used were themselves an infringement of a claim of mine. But where is the claim infringement in making threats?

Consider the fact that attempts at coercion do not always succeed. Suppose you say to me "DON'T GIVE THAT SPEECH OR I'LL KILL YOU!" and I merely giggle and give my speech. Why? Perhaps because I think you don't mean what you say. Perhaps because I think that, although you do mean what you say, you are not capable of doing what you say. If you did mean what you said, and are capable of doing what you said, and so proceed to shoot me in mid-speech, you certainly do infringe a claim of mine. But what if you do not in fact do what you threatened to do? Is there some claim of mine that you have infringed anyway? I cannot see any reason to think that there is.

Perhaps it is not the mere attempt at coercion that is a claim infringement but rather the successful attempt at coercion? In other words, perhaps my claim is not that you not threaten-me-with-a-dire-consequence-if-I-do-such-and-such, but rather that you not make-me-refrain-from-doing-such-and-such-by-threatening-me-with-a-dire-consequence-if-I-do? If so, we have to suppose that while issuing the threat is not itself a claim infringement, and making me refrain is not itself a claim infringement, the compound that consists in doing-the-latter-by-doing-the-former is a claim infringement. It is hard to get a grip on this thought.

Moreover, it is hard to see how adding that the attempt at coercion succeeds could make it be the case that a claim is infringed, though no claim would have been infringed if the attempt had not succeeded. Suppose what you say to me is "DON'T GIVE THAT SPEECH OR I'LL PINCH YOU!" and I straightway wilt. Does adding the fact that I wilt to the fact that you threatened mean that you have infringed a claim of mine?

What this case reminds us of is that whether an attempt at coercion succeeds depends on the attempted coercee as well as on the attempted coercer. Sometimes it is sensible and rational to accede to a threat, but sometimes not. Indeed, sometimes it is morally unacceptable to accede to a threat. Here is a reminder of the details of a case we looked at in Chapter 5:

> MAFIA: The Mafia tell the surgeon that they will kill five unless the surgeon cuts a young man up and kills him.

It might be said that the Mafia issue no *threat* in this case since the dire consequence they say they will bring about if the surgeon refuses is not a dire consequence *to the surgeon*. Is that right? Or does the idea merely show something about human attitudes? (The neighborhood loan shark with whom you do your banking displays an assumption about you in choosing to say "PAY UP OR I'LL BREAK YOUR LEGS!" instead of "PAY UP OR I'LL CHOOSE A MAN AT RANDOM FROM THE PHONE BOOK AND BREAK *HIS* LEGS!") In any case, let us set this aside: let us suppose that the five the Mafia tell the surgeon they will kill if the surgeon refuses are the surgeon's five children. (On any view, the dire consequence projected in a threat need not be to the person of the threatened person.) Children or not, the surgeon must not accede to this threat: it would be wrong to do so. Suppose, however, that the surgeon does accede to the threat. Does that mean that the Mafia have infringed a claim of the surgeon's though they would not have done so had the surgeon not acceded? Hardly.

In short, it really won't do to think that adding that an attempt at coercion succeeds makes it be the case that a claim is infringed, though no claim would have been infringed if the attempt had not succeeded.

But then one who wants to locate a claim infringement in coercion has to find it in the attempt itself, that is, in the very issuing of the threat. The trouble is that there does not seem to be a claim infringement there to be found.

We might usefully contrast coercion with murder. If you fire a gun at a man to kill him but your aim is bad, and you therefore cause him no harm, you have infringed no claim of his; you may have imposed a risk of harm on him, but doing that is not itself an infringement of a claim of his. (We rejected the Risk Thesis in Chapter 9.) Similarly, if you threaten a man to get him to refrain from doing something he wants to do, but he does not accede to the threat, you have infringed no claim of his. If you fire a gun at a man to kill him and your aim is good, and you therefore do kill him, you have infringed a claim of his: more than one in fact, for your firing the gun at him was the means by which you killed him and inherits the status of claim infringement from your killing him. (Remember the Means Principle for Claims.) By contrast, if you threaten a man to get him to refrain from doing something he wants to do, and he accedes to the threat, then you still have infringed no claim of his. Mere attempted coercion, like mere attempted murder, is not a claim infringement; successful murder, unlike successful coercion, is.

This of course leaves it open for us to say that mere attempted coercion, like mere attempted murder, is wrongful. It might be worth saying, however, that attempts at coercion are not always wrongful. If the threatened person was about to do something he or she had no privilege of doing (say kill some third party), then an attempt at coercion might not only be morally permissible but morally required. By contrast, the use of "murder" being what it is, attempted murders are always wrongful.

To go back. We were looking at

> The Limits Thesis: X has a claim against Y that Y not do alpha only if and only if either
>   (i) X's claim is a pure social claim, or
>   (ii) Y's doing alpha either
>   (a) itself would be Y's committing trespass on X, or causing X harm or non-belief-mediated distress, or
>   (b) is a means by which Y would be committing trespass on X, or causing X harm or non-belief-mediated distress.

I drew attention to the fact that one consequence of accepting it is that we must suppose that property claims are in large measure purely social, but I said that I will argue in Chapter 13 that this is exactly what we should say. I drew attention to the fact that a second consequence of accepting it is that we must suppose that what people think of as the right to noninterference is more limited than one might have thought. Getting in my way when I want to board a subway, shouting when I want to make a speech, these—if the Limits Thesis is true—are not themselves infringements of claims of mine, private commitments and law apart. Similarly for coercion: if the Limits Thesis is true, coercion too is no infringement of a claim, private commitments and law apart. But I have suggested that we should not be troubled by these consequences of the Limits Thesis.

It pays to stress, moreover, that the Limits Thesis does not conflict with our having a right to noninterference. If X is in process of trying to defend life or limb, for example, then Y does infringe a claim of X's if Y interferes: if Y interferes, Y causes X's efforts to fail, and thus Y himself or herself causes X to lose life or limb, and that the Limits Thesis tells us is an infringement of a claim. More generally, any interference with another's actions that itself involves trespass or harm-causing is an infringement of a claim according to the Limits Thesis. Presumably what we think of as the right to noninterference also includes claims to noninterference with our uses of our own property.

Does the Limits Thesis have other unwanted consequences? There are other kinds of interference than interference with action that some people think we have claims to: what I have in mind are breaches of privacy. (The literature on the right to privacy is one of the prime workshops of the right to be let alone.) I train my long-range listening device on your house and record all the sounds, so I can replay the recordings for my own private pleasure. (If I were going to sell them, other considerations than privacy would be relevant.) Suppose you have no claim against me that I not do that by virtue of private commitments or law. Do you all the same have a claim against me that I not do it? Well, do I commit trespass, or cause you harm or non-belief-mediated distress, by doing it? No. According to the Limits Thesis, it follows that I infringe no claim of yours in doing it. But this seems to me right. That it is wrongful to do a thing in that it is grubby in the way in which pryings for the sake of prurient interest are grubby, does not by itself make doing the thing an infringement of a claim.[1]

So I think we have now covered the territory. I know of no way of proving the Limits Thesis. What could make X have a claim against Y that Y not do alpha? The claim might be a pure social claim. Suppose it is not. Then what could make X have it? Suppose Y's doing alpha neither is nor is a means to Y's committing a bodily intrusion on X. Well, Y's doing alpha might all the same be, or be a means to, Y's causing X something unwanted. What unwanted something? Not just any: for example, the fact that Y would cause X belief-mediated

---

1. I think that my earlier remarks on this topic—in "The Right to Privacy," *Rights, Restitution, and Risk*—would have been less open to criticism if I had seen the implausibility in the supposition that pryings of the kind mentioned above are infringements of claims.

distress by doing alpha does not give X a claim to Y's not doing alpha. Similarly for status worsening and financial loss. I know of no way of proving that harm and non-belief-mediated distress are the only unwanted outcomes that make claims to not causing them, but that seems right. But if X's putative claim that Y not do alpha does not fall under any of these headings, it is hard to see what could be thought to make X have it. Private commitments and law apart, it seems right to think that the space inside the limits set by clause (ii) of the Limits Thesis is Y's own: X's claims do not extend into it.

In sum, it seems to me that the Limits Thesis is very plausible indeed, and I suggest we accept it. Given it is true, our claims are more limited than we might have thought. But the other side of this coin is that our privileges are more extensive than we might have thought, in light of

$$(H_5) \quad P_{X, Y} \, p \text{ is equivalent to Not-}(C_{Y, X} \text{ Not-}p).$$

3. Do we have a right to liberty? Of course we do, since at a minimum we have privileges. The interesting question about the right to liberty is not whether we have it, but what it contains.

The right to liberty is a cluster-right, which includes privileges. Does it include all of our privileges? I suspect that what most people think of as the right to liberty includes only what might be called natural privileges, by analogy with what we have been calling natural claims. Let us say that a privilege is a *pure social privilege* just in case it is had *only* because of private releasings or law. My privilege as regards you of eating your salad (supposing I have that privilege) is a pure social privilege since I have it only because you gave it to me. Then a privilege is a *natural privilege* just in case it is not a pure social privilege. This leaves open that some natural privileges have social as well as nonsocial sources: my privilege as regards you of defending my life against threats to it counts as a natural privilege for, although prevailing law assigns me that privilege, I do not have it only for that reason. Now, as I said, I suspect that what most people think of as the right to liberty includes only the natural privileges. That is anyway true of people who say that all men are endowed by their creator with rights to life, liberty, and the pursuit of happiness: if God endowed us with the right to liberty, then my right to liberty does not include my privilege of eating your salad, for it was not God but you who endowed me with that privilege.

On the other hand, there is some reason to think we should suppose that the right to liberty includes all privileges. When people say "Give me liberty or give me death!" they are indicating how great they take the value of liberty to be, and I think they do not merely mean the value of being unimpeded in exercising one's natural privileges. I think they mean to include the value of being unimpeded in exercising all of one's privileges, including those one has only by virtue of private releasings or law, thus in particular those one has in owning property.

No matter. The boundaries of a cluster-right are on any view fuzzy, and I will suppose that our right to liberty does include all of our privileges, but that for simplicity only.

What else does the right to liberty include? I should think it includes claims as well as privileges, for I should think it includes the right to noninterference, and *that* includes claims. Which? I suggested that the right to noninterference includes such claims as the claim to non-interference with actions taken to defend life or limb, and presumably also claims to noninterference with our uses of our own property. But I fancy we do not think of the right to liberty as including any others of our claims than those that are included in the right to noninterference.

At the heart of the right to liberty, however, is not privileges and claims, but *immunities*. (And perhaps we think of those immunities as included not only in the right to liberty, but in that part of the right to liberty occupied by the right to noninterference.) By way of reminder, Y has a power as regards X just in case Y has the ability to make alteration in X's rights, and an immunity in X is equivalent to a lack of a power in Y. (See Chapter 1, section 8.) Now at the heart of the right to liberty are our rights to a voice in what action will be taken by government, in who shall govern, indeed in what form of government we will be governed by; and it is very plausible to suppose that what we mean in ascribing such rights to ourselves is that government lacks the power to make alterations in our rights unless certain conditions were met—in particular, that we had a voice in the process that issued in the government action that putatively alters our rights. A man who says "Give me liberty or give me death!" is very likely not *just* telling us how high a value he places on his privilege of getting on the next subway to Kendall Square or his claim to noninterference with his eating of his salad: his main point is likely to be the high value he places on his immunity to state action in the absence of a voice in it.

We will have a closer look at immunities later, but there is one matter it might be in place to mention here, in connection with the right to liberty.

To say that X has a certain immunity against Y is to say that Y lacks the power to make the relevant alterations in X's rights. I think that on all views *some* among our rights are rights that others cannot make us cease to have; those rights, whichever they may be, are rights others lack the power to make us cease to have, and thus are rights over which we have immunities against others. Arguably at least some rights in the right to life are among them; it is plausible to think, for example, that Y lacks the ability to make X cease to have the privilege of defending his life against threats to it. Arguably at least some rights in the right to liberty are also among them; it is plausible to think, for example, that Y lacks the ability to make X be a slave. Now people often express their view that others cannot make us cease to have this or that right in the words: "Others cannot take the right away from us". Equally often, they express the view in the words: "The right is *inalienable*". For a right to be inalienable in this sense, then, is for others to lack the power to make us cease to have it, and thus for us to have an immunity against them in respect of it. If the right is one included in the right to liberty, then so presumably is the immunity included in the right to liberty.

But that is only one of the three ways in which the word "inalienable" is used in the literature on rights. In a second sense of "inalienable", an inalienable right is one that a person cannot make himself or herself cease to have by sale or other form of trade. If any of our rights are inalienable in this second sense, then we have immunities against ourselves in respect of those rights—or anyway, our powers to make ourselves cease to have the rights are limited to other means than sale. Property rights are certainly not inalienable in this second sense. Are any of the natural privileges and natural claims in the right-to-liberty cluster inalienable in this second sense? Can one sell one's privilege of self-defense? Or one's claim to noninterference with one's defense of oneself? Can one sell oneself into slavery? My own view is that the answer is yes and, more generally, that no right is inalienable in this second sense. I have no argument for this view; on the other hand, I see no good argument against it. No doubt we would not believe about a person that he or she had really, freely and wittingly, sold centrally important rights, but so far as I can see, it is enough to explain that fact that the rights *are* centrally important, and therefore that a person who seems to be selling such a right is likely to be either not doing so freely or not doing so wittingly or both.

The third way in which the word "inalienable" is used is a strengthened version of the second. In this third sense an inalienable right is one that a person cannot make himself or herself cease to have by any means at all, whether sale or anything else. A right that is inalienable in this third sense is one that not only cannot be sold, it also cannot be forfeited. If any of our rights are inalienable in this third sense, then we have strong immunities against ourselves in respect of those rights—nothing at all that we can do would make us cease to have them. I said my own view is that any right can be sold; it seems to me even more obvious that any right can be forfeited. But that is certainly not universally agreed to. Hobbes, for example, thought that the privilege of self-defense is inalienable in this third sense. Indeed, he thought that the privilege of self-defense is inalienable in all three senses.

What is of interest for present purposes is that while the inalienability of a right in the first sense—others cannot take the right away from us—surely figures centrally in the right to liberty, I doubt that anyone thinks of the inalienability of a right in the second or third senses (if any of our rights are inalienable in those senses) as figuring in the right to liberty. Immunities against others are at the heart of the right to liberty; immunities against ourselves, being lacks of power in ourselves, are thought of, not as parts of the right to liberty, but rather as setting limits to it.

A mildly interesting question that remains is whether the right to liberty includes powers as well as immunities. I think it does not. I have the power to divest myself of some of my property, and if I exercise that ability I will cease to have some of the claims to noninterference that we think of as included in the right to liberty. If I give my salad to D, then I no longer have a claim against D to his not interfering with my eating of the salad. But I think we do not think of that power as itself included in the right to liberty. An exercise of that power—my saying to D "Here, it's yours"—is an act like any other, and the right to liberty includes the privilege of performing it. But I think we do not suppose that the power, the ability by virtue of which I am able to make D have claims and privileges he formerly lacked (as by saying "Here, it's yours"), is *itself* among the rights in the right to liberty. In this respect the right to liberty differs from property rights: powers are at the heart of property rights.

4. The right to liberty is a cluster-right that contains our privileges, our claims to noninterference with our actions, and certain immunities. What makes those rights hang together to form a cluster? Many of the most familiar rights—those we think of first when we are invited to think about which rights we have—are clusters of rights, picked out and marked off by mention of a positive value, the rights in the cluster being those that in one or another way 'protect' the value. The right to liberty is only one among many. We value liberty; and what we think of as the right to liberty is a cluster of rights that protect it.

The right to life is another example. We value life, and what we think of as the right to life is a cluster of rights that protect it. Like the right to liberty, the right to life contains both privileges and claims: the privileges are those of preserving our lives against (human and nonhuman) threats to them; the claims are those against other people that they not deprive us of life. It arguably also contains certain immunities, such as the immunity to being deprived by others of the privilege of self-defense and the immunity to being deprived by others of the claim to noninterference with efforts at self-defense. It is of interest that the right to life is nowadays often said to include powers, for example, powers of making oneself cease to have claims to not be killed, as where a terminally ill patient asks to have the life-support machinery disconnected and is thought to have thereby made himself or herself no longer have a claim to not be killed.

Another of the rights we think of first when we are invited to say what rights we have is the right to property. Did I just mention a positive value, property? Well, property ownership is of great value to us, in a variety of ways; we have already looked at why we value First Property and will be looking at Second Property in Chapter 13.

The right to privacy is another example. We value privacy; and what we think of as the right to privacy is a cluster of rights that protect it. But here it seems to me there is much slithering in the literature: not only is the scope of this right unclear, it is unclear what is even at the heart of it.

But there are no sharp boundaries around any of the cluster-rights, even those whose heart is clearer than is that of the right to privacy.

The right to life and the right to liberty centrally protect life and liberty, but what precisely falls into those cluster-rights, and what precisely falls outside them, is not clear. On the other hand, what precisely falls into and outside them is surely neither an important nor an interesting question.

Moreover, not only are there no sharp boundaries around any of the cluster-rights, but they overlap. If, as I suggested we might as well suppose, the right to liberty includes all privileges, then every other cluster-right that contains privileges overlaps the right to liberty. The right to life, for example, contains the privilege of preserving one's life against threats to it; even if not all privileges are of sufficient moral moment to be thought of as included in the right to liberty, that one surely is. Again, interfering with a man's attempt to protect his life may cause his death; his claim to noninterference with such an attempt is thus presumably included in both his right to life and his right to liberty. Indeed, I think there is at least one cluster-right that is entirely overlapped by other cluster-rights: the right to privacy.[2]

An example of overlap between rights that it pays to single out for special mention is that between other rights and the cluster of rights we have in owning First Property. I said at the end of Chapter 8 that, however odd it may sound to say so, we may well say that we own our bodies—if it should turn out that we have rights over our bodies sufficiently similar to the rights we have over the things (such as typewriters and shoes) that we are more accustomed to saying we own. We have looked at some of the rights we have over our bodies that are similar to rights we have over the things we ordinarily say we own: they were the claims infringed in trespass and in causing harm. (Our claims against being caused non-belief-mediated distress are presumably not similar to claims we have over the things we ordinarily say we own.) The right to liberty includes privileges of action and claims to noninterference with action, and those rights too are similar to rights we have over the things we ordinarily say we own. Presumably the right to liberty too, then, overlaps the rights we have in owning First Property.

---

2. I argued for this thesis in "The Right to Privacy". As I said in note 1, I think the argument would have been sounder if I had not thought that arguing for the thesis required finding room for claims against pryings. For criticism of the thesis, see among others T. M. Scanlon's and J. Reisman's rebuttals in *Philosophy and Public Affairs*, 4 (1975).

But I think that overlaps between rights are not of any particular theoretical interest. Their interest is, rather, practical. What overlapping means is this: in the case of a claim that falls into two clusters, we have two grounds for complaint in case it is violated, and in the case of a privilege that falls into two clusters, we have two grounds on which to argue that we have it. Which ground we will argue from turns on the context, and in particular on which argument is more likely to succeed in the circumstances.

It should be kept in mind also that the contents of the various different cluster-rights can vary across time and person. I have been speaking of *the* right to life, *the* right to liberty, and so on, but there is no such thing, no single determinate cluster that every person has at all times through which he or she has a right to life or liberty. A man might have a right to life that does not include a certain particular claim that you have in having a right to life, in that he has divested himself of it, or forfeited it, whereas you have not. So long as he still has enough of the most central rights protective of life, we will want to say he still does have a right to life, even if the rights in his right-to-life-cluster are not the same as the rights in your right-to-life-cluster.

And as we saw earlier, even where the same rights are possessed by two people, the stringency of the claims among them may vary, according as it is more or less bad for the claim holder that his or her claims be infringed.

What we have taken a brief look at here are some of the grand rights of political theory, but it might pay to draw attention to the fact that cluster-rights also serve us well at a much less lofty level. "I have a right to that green one, the one with the walnut on top," I say, pointing to one of the small cakes on a plate. It may be that what I say is true: I do have a right to the cake I point to. What is that right? Not a claim, surely, for what claim could it be? And against whom could it be thought to be had? I might have a right to the cake I point to without having a claim against you that you not eat the cake, for I might have a right to the cake I point to and yet have given you permission to eat it. (What I want is just that nobody else should eat it.) Nor is the right the privilege of eating the cake. I might have a right to the cake I point to without having the privilege of eating it, for I might have a right to the cake and yet have promised you I would not eat it. (What I want is just to feed it to my dog.) I should think the right includes a power: if I have a right to the cake I point to, then I am able to give that right to someone else. What seems to be in the offing here is a cluster-right, one with *very* fuzzy boundaries, whose contents are different from context to context. There is a central value protected by whatever rights are in the cluster, however, namely the green cake with the walnut on top.

5. To return to the more lofty, there is one issue that calls for brief discussion in connection with the right to liberty: abortion. Many people think that among the rights a woman has is the right to end an unwanted pregnancy. If women have this right, it is presumably among the rights they have in having a right to liberty. It is presumably also among the rights they have in owning their own bodies. Thus the putative right, if a real right, is presumably in the overlap between those two clusters of rights. Do women have this right?[3]

The putative right to end a pregnancy, if a real right, is surely a privilege. This means that a woman lacks this right if and only if someone has a claim against her that she not end the pregnancy. Whose claims are infringed if she does this? In recent years some people have argued that the father of the embryo has a claim that

---

3. Moved by Carol Gilligan's *In a Different Voice: Psychological Theory and Women's Development* (Cambridge: Harvard University Press, 1982), some feminists have come to the view that rights are a male invention and that the true morality does not incorporate them: on their view, the true morality rests moral prescriptions on care, trust, and personal relationships, and does not assign rights. Since, as is plain, I think people do have rights, it seems to me a philosophical error for anyone to say that people do not have rights. In some ways more important, however, is that it is, as I think, a political error for women to say that people do not have rights. In the first place, and more generally, what has oppressed women in the past is precisely the socially engendered expectation that they will melt into their personal relationships; the women's movement succeeded in bringing home to many that women, like men, have inherently individual interests, and for women now to turn their backs on that crucial fact about human beings would be a most unfortunate instance of turning the clock back. In the second place, and more particularly, women's ability to control their own reproductive lives is currently at risk, and it is not a happy idea that a state legislature can be moved to stand firm in support of women's legal rights to contraception and abortion by an argument that appeals to care, trust, and personal relationships. What women surely need now is not less talk of rights, but more. An interesting recent effort to ground women's legal rights to control their reproductive lives in the fourteenth amendment's equal-protection clause is Silvia A. Law, "Rethinking Sex and the Constitution", *University of Pennsylvania Law Review*, 132 (1984). See also Ronald Dworkin, "The Great Abortion Case", *New York Review of Books*, 36 (June 29, 1989).

she not end the pregnancy without his consent, but that can hardly be right. If your mother kills you, it is not your father's claims she infringes, and why should things be thought different in this respect where it is an embryo in question as opposed to someone fully grown?

Obviously enough, if a woman infringes anyone's claims in ending a pregnancy, it is the claims of the embryo. (I throughout say "embryo" since the conceptus, in its very early stages, is not properly called a fetus; but "embryo" throughout is merely an abbreviation for "embryo or fetus".) And it is precisely the claims of the embryo that are said to make ending the pregnancy impermissible. So *a* central moral question here is this: does the embryo have claims against the woman that she not end the pregnancy?

I say only that that is *a* central moral question here, and not that it is the sole central moral question. Even supposing that the embryo has a claim against the woman that she not end the pregnancy, it does not follow that she may not end the pregnancy. It does not even follow that she may not end the pregnancy for any reason less grave than its constituting a threat to her life or health. As I hope we are agreed, it is not true to say that all claims are absolute. To get from the premise that the embryo has the claim to a conclusion about what the woman may do, more argument has to be supplied, perhaps argument to the effect that, although not all claims are absolute, this claim is absolute, or perhaps instead argument to the effect that although this claim is not absolute, still the circumstances are never such as to make it permissible for the woman to infringe it, or are only such as to make it permissible for the woman to infringe it where it constitutes a threat to her life or health. But let us bypass the question how opponents of abortion are to get from the embryo's claim to the impermissibility of ending a pregnancy.

What I think is of more interest from the point of view of the theory of rights is the question whether the embryo does have a claim against the woman that she not end the pregnancy. Why should we think it does? A familiar kind of argument proceeds as follows. (i) A human embryo is a human person. (ii) All human persons have a claim against all others to not be killed by them. The conjunction of those two premises yields that a human embryo has a claim against all others that those others not kill it. A third premise says that (iii) a woman's ending her pregnancy requires killing the embryo, so that it now follows that the embryo has a claim against her that she not end her pregnancy.

Premise (ii) strikes us all, I think, as *prima facie* very plausible. But what of premise (i)? We all have a grip on why many people believe that the conceptus in its late stages, an eight-month fetus, for example, is a human person: it looks like a baby and has much of the internal physiological development of a baby. But a fertilized egg? A one-week-old clump of cells attached to the wall of the uterus? No doubt a fertilized egg if left to itself inside the woman *will become* a human person; how can it be thought to be one *now*? In a recent television interview, the plaintiff who had just won custody of seven fertilized eggs (her ex-husband wished them destroyed) said, "Those are my children."[4] That is easily understood if we take it to be exaggeration indulged in for a purpose—but have we a grip on how someone could really believe it literally true? (If the plaintiff decides against having all seven eggs implanted, so that some are destroyed, will she really think of herself as having killed some of her children? There is surely a failure to connect at work here.)

It seems plain that it is the oddity in these ideas that has in recent years led most opponents of abortion to make a certain interesting shift in premises. Instead of (i) and (ii) we are nowadays offered: (i') A human embryo is human life, and (ii') All human life has a claim against others that those others not kill it. Well, a fertilized human egg is human (not, for example, feline) and is life, since it is alive, so (i') is obviously true. But now it is (ii') that surely needs defense. Once the concession is made that a bit of human life need not necessarily be a human person, then in consistency the concession should also be made that something needs doing to make out that a bit of human life, just by virtue of being a bit of human life, has a claim against all others that those others not kill it. Indeed, is there any good reason to think a fertilized egg has any claims at all? (Would it be permissible to kill one fertilized egg to save five? I cannot see why not, other things being equal of course.)

What is most puzzling, however, is how it can be thought acceptable to discuss this issue as if the woman in whom the embryo is lodged is a mere bystander. Or as if she and the embryo were in competition

4. The Court said it "concludes that it is to the manifest best interest of the children, in vitro, that they be made available for implantation to assure their opportunity for live birth". For discussion of the case, see George J. Annas, "At Law—A French Homunculus in a Tennessee Court", *Hastings Center Report*, 19 (1989).

for the use of a publicly owned resource. And yet the antiabortion argument does proceed in just this way.

It is, after all, the woman's body—her First Property—in which the embryo is lodged. When we remember this, we must surely regard the quite general premise (ii') with suspicion. A bit of human life is lodged inside the woman, and she wants it out. How can anyone think it has a claim against her that it stay?

And what of the *prima facie* very plausible premise (ii)? If you have been invited to take root in someone's innards, and accept the invitation, then we may well suppose that your host bears a considerable responsibility for you and indeed that you have claims against him. But what if your presence there comes to constitute a threat to your host? What is to be said here is a function of a great many things, such as the nature, gravity, and source of the threat, what your host has to do to defend against it, and what were the circumstances of the original invitation. (For example, did your host know, or ought he to have known, or did you know, or ought you to have known, at the time at which the invitation was issued, of the fact that your presence was likely to come to constitute a threat? Or: of the fact that your accepting the invitation would foreclose your choice of other alternatives that would have been markedly better for you?) In some such cases it will seem right to say that your host may not put you out. In others it will seem right to say that your host may put you out. In some of them it will seem right to say not merely that your host may put you out, but that you have no claim that he not do so. But even that would constitute no difficulty for premise (ii): as I will suggest in Chapter 14, we could say that you *had* had the claim, but that—whether innocently or by fault—you have forfeited it.

But becoming pregnant is not like inviting someone to visit for the weekend: the embryo is already in the woman's body when it comes into existence, and if it were not there it would not be anywhere, for it would not exist at all. Engaging in an activity that is an important part of (if I may borrow the expression) human life, the woman and her partner have caused an embryo to come into existence inside her. They may even have taken precautions against an embryo's coming into existence inside her. If you had come into existence in that way inside a person, and are there now, would you have a claim to not be put out? If we think not, we think that premise (ii) is too strong.

But in any case a fertilized egg, a very early embryo, is not a person at all, so premise (ii) is irrelevant to it.

What many people find worrisome is that if nature is left to take its course, then a fertilized egg may very well become a baby. So how can one say that a fertilized egg has no claims, whereas the baby does? ("Where do you draw the line?" is the expression of this worry.) I think it an attractive feature of the account of claims set out in Part I that continuity of development from egg to baby constitutes no theoretical difficulty for the idea that the egg has no claims, whereas the baby does. If, as I suggested, X's having a claim against Y is Y's being under the complex behavioral constraint we looked at in Part I, then there is no theoretical difficulty in the supposition that something could lack claims at one time and gradually come to acquire them later, for there is no theoretical difficulty in the supposition that something in respect of which Y is not yet under that complex behavioral constraint could gradually develop into something in respect of which Y will be under it.

It should be stressed, however, that the supposition that a fertilized egg has no claims is compatible with its being the case that we ought to treat it with a certain respect. It is a bit of human life, after all, and if nature is left to take its course or if, while in vitro now, the egg is later implanted, it may very well become a baby. (What if we discovered in some way, which I leave you to supply the details of, that fertilized human eggs are particularly tasty? Would we think it acceptable that a caviar bottler seek human donors and develop this new marketing sideline?) At the other end of human life is the human corpse. It too has no claims, yet we think it too ought to be treated with a certain respect.

Moreover, the supposition that a fertilized egg has no claims is compatible with its being the case that the later fetus has claims, if not the claim to stay inside the woman's body, then anyway the claim to not be caused pain. An important point lurks in this difference, and it has a bearing on other issues besides abortion. My own view is that animals do not have claims to not be killed and, in particular, that it is not an infringement of any claim of a chicken's to kill it for dinner. (Would it be permissible to kill one chicken to save five chickens? I think it would.) Causing an animal pain, however, is surely a different matter. It seems to me, in fact, that other things being equal it is worse to cause an animal pain than to cause an adult human being pain. An adult human being can, as it were, think his or her way around the pain to what lies beyond it in the future; an animal— like a human baby—cannot do this, so that there is nothing for the animal but the pain itself. But I will not assume you agree with me about animals, or even begin on the wide range of considerations that require attention if one is to engage properly with the question whether they have claims.

I will also not assume that you agree with me about the moral issues raised by abortion, for many people disagree, and vehemently so. The prospects of convincing them seem dim.[5] (Anyone who can say of a batch of fertilized eggs "Those are children", and believe it to be a literal truth, must surely be immune to argument.)

6. What we have looked at so far in Part II are rights with nonsocial sources. What we now turn to are the social sources of rights.

---

5. Kristin Luker says that "While on the surface it is the embryo's fate that seems to be at stake, the abortion debate is actually about the meanings of *women's* lives". The activists on both sides are predominantly women, and for them, she says, "the abortion debate is a conflict between two different social worlds and the hopes and beliefs those worlds support". See her *Abortion and the Politics of Motherhood* (Berkeley: University of California Press, 1984), p. 194. In short, what fuels the antiabortion movement is passionate opposition to the model for women's lives that is advocated by women's liberation.

Chapter 12

Giving One's Word

1. One social source of claims is the making of private commitments, in particular, giving one's word. What is it to give one's word? Well, a person Bloggs gives his word if and only if Bloggs gives his word *to* something (say to a person) *that* something (say that he paid the grocery bill). To give one's word *that* something is to give one's word that a certain state of affairs obtains—equivalently, that a certain proposition is true. The following seems obvious:

> The Preliminary Analysis: Y gives his or her word if and only if for some X and some proposition, Y gives X his or her word that the proposition is true.

I might, for example, give you my word and, in particular, give you my word that I put the car keys on the bureau last night. I do this if and only if I give you my word that the proposition "JJT put the car keys on the bureau last night" is true.

But what is it to give one's word that a proposition is true? I think the following is also obvious:

> The Weak Assertion Thesis: Y gives X his or her word that a proposition is true only if Y asserts the proposition to X.

For example, I give you my word that "JJT put the car keys on the bureau last night" is true only if I assert the proposition "JJT put the car keys on the bureau last night" to you. For me to give you my word that the proposition is true, it is not enough for me to draw attention to that proposition or idly mention it in passing; I have to assert it and, indeed, assert it to you.

The conjunction of those two theses yields that a person gives his or her word only if he or she asserts a proposition, and it is perhaps called for, then, that I stress that it is propositions that are in question here, not words. Although I call the activity we are looking at "giving one's word", it is surely plain that one can give one's word without words. Suppose you ask me "Did you put the car keys on the bureau last night?" and I by way of reply merely nod my head. Then I give my word, in particular, I give you my word that I put the car keys on the bureau last night, and I do so without uttering any words. Giving one's word without uttering any words is possible because it is possible to assert a proposition without uttering any words. By nodding my head in the circumstances, I do assert the proposition "JJT put the car keys on the bureau last night" to you.

Of course we very often do give our word with words; but since it is propositions that are in question here, not words, the exact form of words we use does not matter—so long as we assert a proposition. I may assert the proposition "JJT put the car keys on the bureau last night" by use of any number of different forms of words, such as

> I give you my word that I put the car keys on the bureau last night
> I guarantee that I put the car keys on the bureau last night
> I swear to you that I put the car keys on the bureau last night
> Please believe me! I really and truly did put the car keys on the bureau last night!

as well as by use of the less melodramatic

> I put the car keys on the bureau last night.

I said that the Weak Assertion Thesis is obvious. The following thesis is markedly stronger:

> The Strong Assertion Thesis: Y gives X his or her word that a proposition is true if and only if Y asserts the proposition to X.

Unfortunately this rather attractive (because so simple and straightforward) thesis is not obvious—indeed, there are two reasons for thinking it false.

2. In the first place, giving one's word seems to be in some way a more or less solemn affair, and it is certainly arguable that not just any asserting of a proposition is solemn in the required way. What seems to be required for a word-giving is that the word-giver be positively inviting the word-receiver to rely on the word given, and

it is intuitively wrong to think that just any asserting of a proposition is an invitation to rely. Suppose we are walking through the park, and you say idly, "I wonder how often they mow the lawns here". I then reply, equally idly, "Once a week". I asserted to you the proposition "They mow the lawns here once a week", but did I give you my word that they do? Well, did I invite you to rely on their doing so? It is certainly arguable that I did not. After all, your wonderment was by hypothesis idle, and I knew that it was idle: nothing turns for you on how often they mow the lawns in the park.

The morally fussy may say that I ought not have replied "Once a week" unless I was certain that they do mow the lawns in the park once a week. Why? Just in case, just on the off chance that it might later come to be an important matter for you how often they mow the lawns in the park. (The morally fussy may say that if I was not certain, I ought to have said instead, "Once a week, I think." If I had instead said that, then the proposition I asserted would have been the weaker "JJT thinks that they mow the lawns here once a week".) On their view, every asserting of a proposition is a giving of one's word. I feel considerable sympathy with this idea, but it really won't do: it is overstrong. In the give-and-take of ordinary life there is too much asserting that cannot plausibly be viewed as the giving of one's word— since it cannot plausibly be viewed as the issuing of an invitation to rely. So we do well to weaken the thesis we are looking at so it will read:

> The Less Strong Assertion Thesis: Y gives X his or her word that a proposition is true if and only if Y asserts the proposition to X, and in so doing is inviting X to rely on its truth.

This tells us that every word-giving is an asserting of a proposition, but allows that some assertings of propositions are not word-givings: it says that only assertings that are invitations to rely are word-givings.

3. But that thesis is still too strong. Suppose I take out an ad in the *Boston Globe* that reads: "I hereby assert, and moreover invite all residents of the Boston area to rely on the truth of, the proposition that I, JJT, will go to bed before midnight every night this coming October".[1] Do I thereby give my word to all Bostonians that I will

---

1. This example is adapted from one of Charles Fried's in *Contract as Promise*.

go to bed before midnight every night this coming October? I think we feel uncomfortable about the idea that I do.

In the first place, some readers of the newspaper may just not see my ad at all. (I may send out invitations to a party and some get lost in the mail.) Second, and more important, the readers who do see my ad may think "Who cares when she goes to bed?" (I may send out invitations to a party and some recipients think "Who the hell is she?")

The metaphor "give one's word" itself suggests that issuing an invitation is not enough: the invitation has to be received, and indeed accepted. I might run around town after you, trying to give you a photograph of my children; I do not actually give it to you unless I can get you to stand still and accept it from me. The point lurking in the metaphor might be put: there is no giving one's word unless there is 'uptake', which includes accepting as well as receiving.

If we take the metaphor seriously, then, I do not give all Bostonians my word in taking out that ad, for the truth is that there is no uptake. And it does seem right to think we should take the metaphor seriously. If I assert a proposition to a person, and thereby invite the person to rely on its truth, it does seem right to think I have given the person my word only if there is uptake.

What constitutes uptake may vary from case to case. It is clear, however, that though typically there is uptake when and only when the recipient of the invitation to rely cares whether the proposition asserted is true, there can be uptake without caring and caring without uptake. Suppose I telephone you and say "I swear I will eat my spinach at dinner tonight!" Very probably (i) you couldn't care less, but as a courtesy you say "Okay, fine". If so, there is uptake, without caring. Alternatively, it just might be the case that (ii) you greatly care (I leave open why you do) but you do not trust me, and so you reply "I don't believe a word you say!" Here there is caring but no uptake. What word-giving requires is the uptake, whether or not the recipient of the invitation cares, for if (i) is true I have given you my word, whereas if (ii) is true I have not.

This point needs stress. If (i) is true, then I am bound to eat my spinach at dinner tonight, even though you don't care whether I do. I invited you to rely and you accepted the invitation, so I did give you my word and you are now entitled to rely on it—even if in fact you will not rely on it. By contrast, if (ii) is true, I am not bound to eat my spinach at dinner tonight, even though you do care whether

I do. I invited you to rely but you did not accept the invitation, so I did not succeed in giving you my word and you are not now entitled to rely on the word I offered you. (If you place a bet on my eating my spinach at dinner tonight, you do so your own risk.)

Since there can be uptake without caring, it follows that there can be word-giving without any actual reliance on the part of the word-receiver. So uptake is not the same as, does not include, and need not issue in reliance. But once there has been uptake, the word-giver is morally at risk, for the word-receiver might at any time start to rely.

So we need to weaken our 'assertion thesis' still further. I suggest we should accept the following:

> The Assertion Thesis: Y gives X his or her word that a proposition is true if and only if Y asserts that proposition to X, and
> (i) in so doing, Y is inviting X to rely on its truth, and
> (ii) X receives and accepts the invitation (there is uptake).

4. We can think of word-giving as a genus. Promising has for a number of reasons attracted more attention from philosophers than the other species of word-giving; I think we are helped to understand it if we take seriously the fact that promising is merely one among the many species of word-giving.

Promisings differ from other word-givings in four ways.

First, however, a way in which promisings do *not* differ from other word-givings. Suppose A was concerned about where B would leave the car keys tonight: it was very important to A where B would leave them. Suppose, moreover, that B knew this. And suppose, last, that B said to A, firmly, the words

> I promise you I will put the car keys on the bureau tonight,

and that A said "Okay, I'll count on it." Then B has asserted the proposition "B will put the car keys on the bureau tonight," and (i) in so doing, B was inviting A to rely on its truth, and (ii) A received and accepted the invitation (there was uptake). It follows from the Assertion Thesis that B gave A his word that he will put the car keys on the bureau tonight. Moreover, B did not merely give A his word that he will, B promised A that he will. Suppose B had, in those very same circumstances and just as firmly, said to A instead one or other of the following strings of words:

> I give you my word that I will put the car keys on the bureau tonight
>
> I guarantee that I will put the car keys on the bureau tonight
>
> I swear to you that I will put the car keys on the bureau tonight
>
> Please believe me! I really and truly will put the car keys on the bureau tonight!

or even the less melodramatic

> I will put the car keys on the bureau tonight.

If B had instead said any of these other strings of words in those circumstances, he would also have given B his word that he will put the car keys on the bureau tonight; would he have promised B that he will? Certainly. We very often make promises by use of the special locution "I promise", but use of that locution is not necessary for promising. So it cannot be supposed that promisings differ from other word-givings in that a word-giver makes a promise only if he or she uses the locution "I promise".

Indeed, a word-giver can make a promise without words. If A had asked B "Do you promise to (swear to, guarantee that you will) leave the car keys on the bureau tonight?" and B had nodded, B would have given his word, and moreover promised, that he will.

In circumstances such as we have been imagining, it is sufficient for B's word-giving to have been a promising that B gave his word by use of "I promise". If B had used "I swear", he would have sworn. If B had used "I guarantee", he would have guaranteed. Promising is a species of word-giving, and so also is swearing, and guaranteeing. Though in light of what has just come out, we have to keep in mind that there are interspecific hybrids in this genus—that is, an instance of swearing, or of guaranteeing, can also be an instance of promising.

But there are instances of swearing, and of guaranteeing, that are not instances of promising: promisings (as I said) have four features that make them distinctive among word-givings.

As we know, Y gives Y's word only if Y asserts a proposition to X. The first three distinctive features of promisings lie in constraints on the nature of the proposition asserted in a promising.

First, a word-giving is a promising only if the proposition asserted is in the future tense. If B asserts to A the proposition

> (1) B did put the car keys on the bureau last night,

then B may give A his word that (1) is true; but the word-giving he does in asserting (1) is not an instance of promising.

Second, a word-giving is a promising only if the proposition asserted has the asserter as its subject. If B asserts to the family dentist, A, about B's son Charlie

   (2) Charlie will be in A's office tomorrow at 4:00,

then B may give A his word that (2) is true, and (2) is in the future tense; but the word-giving B does in asserting (2) is not an instance of promising. Notice that in asserting (2) to A, B does not give A his word that he, B, will be in A's office tomorrow at 4:00. Nor does he give A his word that he, B, will bring Charlie there then, or that he will nag Charlie into being there then. *All* B gives A his word of is that Charlie will be there then. For what B gives A his word of is true even if B need do nothing at all to get Charlie there then, because (for a wonder) Charlie decides he wants to be there then and goes by himself, off his own bat. Though of course it may be that Charlie does not want to be there then, in which case what B gives A his word of is true only if B will bring Charlie there himself, or will nag Charlie into going, or will do whatever is required to get Charlie to be there then.

Third, a word-giving is a promising only if the proposition ascribes an act ("B will go to A's office at 4:00"), or a refraining from acting ("B will not go to A's office at 4:00"), or a limited range of states ("B will be in A's office at 4:00"). If B asserts to A

   (3) B will be remembered by many after his death,

then B gives A his word that (3) is true, and (3) is in the future tense and has B as subject; but the word-giving B does in asserting (3) is not an instance of promising.

A fourth distinctive feature of promisings is a matter not of the proposition asserted, but of the promisee's desires. If B asserts to A

   (4) B will break A's legs tonight,

or

   (5) B will go to bed before midnight every night this coming
        October,

then on the assumption that A wants B to not break A's legs tonight, or that A does not care one way or the other what time B goes to bed, then B has not promised A that he will break A's legs or that he will go to bed at the times he mentioned.

This fourth feature of promising should remind us of the uptake required for a word-giving. There is no word-giving at all unless there is uptake (that is, unless the word-receiver receives and accepts the word-giver's invitation to rely),[2] and typically there is uptake only where the word-receiver cares whether the proposition asserted is true. As we saw, there can be uptake without caring, and hence there can be word-giving without caring. The point here, however, is that unless the word-receiver cares whether the proposition asserted is true, and indeed wants it to be true, then even if there is uptake, so that a word-giving does take place, what takes place is not an instance of promising.

In short, we reserve the term "promise" for a word-giving in which the word given is that the word-giver himself or herself (person-condition) will (tense-condition) do, or not do, or be such and such (act-refraining-state-condition) that the word-receiver wants him or her to do or not do or be (desire-condition). If in the situation we imagined, B had asserted to A the proposition

B will put the car keys on the bureau tonight,

then all four conditions would have been met, and B would have given his word, indeed promised, that he will put the car keys on the bureau tonight.

I do not myself think these conditions are anywhere near as firm as I have been implying. For example, if B tells the dentist that Charlie will be in the dentist's office at 4:00 tomorrow, then would it plainly, clearly, flatly be *false* if B later said he had promised the dentist that Charlie would be there then? I think not. Nevertheless, most people do reserve the term "promise" for a word-giving that meets those conditions and do at a minimum feel uncomfortable at hearing it used of word-givings that do not meet them.

In fact, the question whether the conditions are as firm as I have been implying does not really matter for our purposes, since what concerns us is the moral import of a promise and, as I will suggest,

---

2. The requirement of uptake for a word-giving, and *a fortiori* for a promising, is at any rate among the sources of the legal principle that there is no contract without 'consideration'—that is, something offered in exchange for the promise. Consideration assures uptake.

the moral import of all word-givings (whether or not they are prom-isings) is the same.

5. What is the moral import of a word-giving? I suggest that we should accept the following thesis:

> The Word-Giving Thesis: If Y gives X his or her word that a certain proposition is true, then X thereby acquires a claim against Y to its being true.

That it is true seems to me to emerge from what we have already seen in arriving at

> The Assertion Thesis: Y gives X his or her word that a proposition is true if and only if Y asserts the proposition to X, and
> (i) in so doing, Y is inviting X to rely on its truth, and
> (ii) X receives and accepts the invitation (there is uptake).

For Y to give X his or her word that a certain proposition is true is for Y to invite X to rely on its truth, which invitation X accepts; and if you issue an invitation to a person to rely on the truth of a prop-osition, which invitation the person accepts, then surely the person thereby acquires a claim against you to its truth.

Suppose, for example, that B promised A that B will give A a banana at 5:00. Doesn't A have a claim against B that B will do this? The fact that B would generate more good by not giving A a banana at 5:00 than by doing so does not make it permissible for B to not do so—we looked at a number of examples of this kind earlier. Only a considerable increment of good to be got by breaking a promise justifies breaking it, and that is a mark of the presence of a claim.

Something wants stress here. I spoke in earlier chapters of the one who makes a promise as *giving* a claim, but in light of the requirement of uptake, we can see that this won't quite do. A promise takes two parties for completion, a promisor who offers to give his or her word and a promisee who accepts the offer. In that uptake is required, it is not the promisor alone who makes the promisee have a claim: the promisor alone does not give the promisee a claim. What the promisor does is to alter the world in such a way that uptake by the promisee makes the promisee have a claim. In other words, what the promisor does is to give the promisee, not a claim, but a power—a power by the exercise of which the promisee makes himself or herself have the claim. Similarly for word-givings generally.

There is nothing deeper that either needs to be or can be said about how word-givings generally and promisings in particular generate claims. Their moral force lies in their generating claims; and the fact that they do generate claims is explained by the fact that issuing an invitation is offering to bind oneself, so that when the invitation is accepted, the offer is accepted, and one therefore *is* bound.

In particular, explaining the moral import of word-givings does not require appeal to the presence in the word-giver's and word-receiver's background of social understandings. It is a widely received view that social understandings of one or another kind are crucially involved in the fact that promises have moral force.[3] I think this a mistake, on two counts.

In the first place, background assumptions or agreements about what people who make promises will or ought to do cannot in themselves make promises have moral force. That people expect a promisor Y to do what he or she promised X to do, or agree that Y ought to do it, is not what makes it the case that Y ought to do it; what makes this the case is what Y did in making the promise and the uptake in the promisee X. If Y and X did not between them, and by themselves, make it the case that Y ought to do the thing, then nobody else can have made that the case.

Second, though it is certainly true that more than one person is required if a bit of promising is to be carried out, no more than two are required. It is not necessary that there be hordes of others in the background, engaged in the 'practice' of making and keeping promises. No doubt X has to understand that an invitation to rely has been issued, or else there could be no such thing as X's accepting the invitation; no doubt also Y has to understand that X has accepted the invitation, or else Y could not be supposed to know that Y is bound. Typically people indicate these things to each other by use of language, and language is a social product. Moreover, it is unlikely that people would make promises to each other if they had no reason to expect that promisors will do what they promise—more generally, if there were no general background of trust in the word of others. Suppose you and I live in a society in which people do not trust each

3. See, for example, H. A. Prichard, "The Obligation to Keep a Promise", in *Moral Obligation* (Oxford: Clarendon Press, 1957), and John Searle, "How to Derive 'Ought' from 'Is' ". For criticism of these ideas, see T. M. Scanlon, "Promises and Practices", forthcoming in *Philosophy and Public Affairs;* my own account of the moral force of promises is in some ways like his.

other. Then we live in a society in which people do not make promises (what would be the point of making them if no one would trust them?), and probably that society is one whose language contains no linguistic device by means of which to make promises (what would be the point of having a linguistic device if no one ever used it?). But all of this is compatible with its being the case that I make you the first promise our society has ever known—for it is compatible with my being able to communicate to you (by some means other than words if we lack appropriate words) an invitation to rely, and with your then being able to do something that constitutes accepting the invitation, and with your thereby acquiring a claim. If we could not be the first pair to generate a claim in this way, how could any pair become the eighth?

The idea that promises have no moral force unless there is a background of general trust makes it hard to see how the people in Hobbes' state of nature could have got out of it by signing a social contract. It *is* hard to see how they could have got out of the state of nature by signing a joint social contract. But that is not because of a difficulty about the idea of a first promise; it is because of what Hobbes tells us about their motives.

But saying that social understandings are not what make promises binding is compatible with saying that social understandings do figure in what goes on in and around a promise. In the first place, it may be unclear from a promisor's words exactly what is promised, and here an appeal to social understandings may be made in order to settle the matter. Courts often make appeal to current assumptions about behavior, in the community of widget buyers and sellers as it might be, in order to settle what widget maker A is bound to do for widget buyer B by virtue of the more or less unclear contract between them. Again, there may well be constraints imposed by prevailing law on what can be contracted to, who will be liable for what outcomes, whether penalties, fines, or taxes must be paid in what circumstances, and so on. And of course law does enforce (some) contracts. The fact remains, however, that if Y promises X to do something, then other things being equal Y ought to do it; and while law may (or may not) enforce Y's promise, it is not law alone (if at all) that makes Y bound to do it—what makes Y bound is what Y did in making the promise and what X did in accepting it.

6. I am sure that a great many objections to

> The Word-Giving Thesis: If Y gives X his or her word that a
> certain proposition is true, then X thereby acquires a claim
> against Y to its being true

will have occurred to you. I hope that this and the following sections
will speak to the most serious of them.

First, however, a possible objection that I do not think is serious.

Suppose A phoned B to say A wants to give B a manuscript for a
journal B edits, but there is a difficulty: A is extremely busy and must
leave town this evening. Would B be in front of the drugstore at 7:00
so A can give him the manuscript? B said yes. Thus B gave A his
word that the following proposition is true:

(6) B will be in front of the drugstore at 7:00.

Indeed, B surely promised A that (6) is true. The Word-Giving Thesis
tells us that A now has a claim against B to the truth of (6). B infringes
that claim if and only if (6) is not true; so B does *not* infringe that
claim if (6) is true. Are we to say that B keeps his promise to A if (6)
is true?

If we do say this, there may seem to be trouble. For suppose we
add the following details to the story. B acted wrongly in making the
promise: B had every intention of breaking it and wanted merely that
A should rely on the promise and then be disappointed when B breaks
it. But later in the day B forgot the whole episode. B went out to buy
cigarettes at 6:30, and lo and behold just happened to be standing in
front of the drugstore at 7:00 when A arrived. Then (6) turns out to
have been true. But I think that many people would say that if this
is why (6) turns out to have been true, then B does not—does not
really—*keep* his promise. It is arguable, that is, that we so use the
expression "keep a promise" that a person does not keep a promise
unless he or she makes the promised proposition true for the reason
that he or she promised it would be true. If that is correct, then B
did not keep his promise to A.

But whether or not B kept his promise to A, B infringed no claim
of A's. I say that because there is nothing in the story that tells us
that B promised A to be-in-front-of-the-drugstore-for-the-reason-that-
B-promised-A-to-be-there-then. If we had been told that B asserted
to A not merely   •

(6) B will be in front of the drugstore at 7:00

but also

> B will be in front of the drugstore at 7:00 for the reason that B
> promised A to be there then,

then—according to the Word-Giving Thesis—A would have had a
claim to the truth of that proposition as well as to the truth of (6).
But nothing in the story told us this. *All* the story told us that B
promised is that (6) would be true. As it turns out, (6) was true. If
A finds out what made (6) true, he will certainly think ill of B, for B
has acted very badly indeed. But A cannot complain that B has infringed any claim of A's.

A similar point holds of word-givings generally. If B asserted to the
family dentist, A, about B's son Charlie

> (2) Charlie will be in A's office tomorrow at 4:00,

then—according to the Word-Giving Thesis—A has a claim to the
truth of that proposition. *That* proposition. Not also the propositions

> B will bring Charlie to A's office tomorrow at 4:00

or

> B will nag Charlie into going to A's office tomorrow at 4:00.

And if B later forgot all about the word he gave A, but Charlie did
turn up at A's office at the required time, without having to be brought
or nagged, then while if A finds out about B's forgetting, A will
certainly think ill of B, A cannot complain that B has infringed any
claim of A's.

It is for this reason that I said in Chapter 1 (see note 3) that we
should take the claim X has against Y to be that a state of affairs
obtain, and not that Y make it obtain. We were going to need our
notion 'claim' to allow for the possibility of X's having a claim against
Y that some third party will do a thing—and not just for the possibility
of X's having a claim against Y that Y will do a thing.

7. A more serious objection to

> The Word-Giving Thesis: If Y gives X his or her word that a
> certain proposition is true, then X thereby acquires a claim
> against Y to its being true

comes out as follows. What I have in mind is the objection that issues from the possibility that although Y gives X his or her word that a certain proposition is true, Y cannot make it true.

We met some cases that fall under this heading in Chapter 3. I promised to deliver 100 widgets to C and then promised to deliver 100 widgets to D, and it turned out that I could not do both. It pays to stop to remind ourselves of why (as I suggested) we should say I nevertheless did give each of them a claim against me that I deliver 100 widgets. In short, if I cannot deliver to both, then, other things being equal, I have to try to get a release in advance or compensate whichever I do not deliver to for losses he suffers in consequence of his reliance, on the one hand, and my nonperformance on the other. As I put it earlier, promising is a liability-shouldering device.

We will find the same moral phenomena present when we turn to more troublesome cases. In the case I just reminded you of, I cannot keep both promises, but of each of the two promises I made it is true that I can keep it. What of a case in which I make a single promise and simply cannot keep *it?* I promise to give Charles a banana at 5:00 this afternoon, and there just are no bananas to be got in the time available. Here we meet the same moral phenomena, and they do strongly suggest that there is good reason to think that, despite the fact that I cannot keep my promise to Charles, he nevertheless does have a claim against me that I do so.

Suppose I promise you that I will square the circle next month. Do you have a claim against me that I will do it? Here it is not mere facts that make it impossible for me to keep my promise, but logic. Does that make a difference?

Moreover, the Word-Giving Thesis is quite general, not restricted to word-givings that are promisings. Suppose you are worried about whether a certain theorem is provable from a certain set of axioms, and I assure you that it is and you accept my assurance. Then I have given you my word that it is. Have I given you a claim against me that it is? Even if, as a matter of logic, it is not?

Let us focus on the following case. You are rushing to the station. You stop me and say "Look, I need to catch the 10:30 train to New York. Have I got time to get to the station?" I look at my watch and say reassuringly,

(7) It's ten o'clock.

That *is* reassuring since the station is visible down the road, and it can hardly take you more than five minutes to get there; you are reassured and slacken your pace. Do I give you my word that it is ten o'clock? I think I do, for I invite you to rely on its being ten o'clock and you accept my invitation. Do I therefore give you a claim against me that it is ten o'clock?

One thing that is obvious is that if it is ten o'clock, I have infringed no claim of yours. But what if it is not ten o'clock?

What calls for attention is what happens if I myself discover that it is not ten o'clock. Suppose that shortly after you pass on toward the station, I discover that it is actually 10:23. (I catch sight of the town clock, which I know to be very reliable.) What do I do? If you are still within sight, I must not do nothing, I must not say to myself "Well, it's not my problem": I have to warn you that the time I gave you was incorrect. Indeed, I have to do this even at some cost to myself. I have to shout or run to catch you if you are not yet far off. I do not have to go to immense lengths to warn you: if I have a sprained ankle and you are a block away, I am off the moral hook. But there is *a* moral hook. I have to take reasonable steps to see to it that you do not suffer for my mistake. Just as, where I discover that I will be unable to keep a promise (such as a promise to deliver 100 widgets to C on Friday), I must give my promisee warning of that fact in advance if I can, so that he or she does not suffer for my inability.

In some cases of word-giving, the word-giver will have to compensate the word-receiver for his or her losses if the word-given proposition is not true, just as a promisor might have to do when he or she breaks the promise. That is not likely to be so in the case we are looking at. Suppose you needed to catch the 10:30 train in order to get to New York to sign a million-dollar contract. You then miss your train because of my mistake. It can hardly be expected that I reimburse you for the lost million dollars. (And it is certainly in place to ask what on earth you were doing, with a million-dollar contract in the offing, to rely on a passerby for the time.) Still, there are cases in which I do have to compensate. If I assert to you

(8) Charlie will deliver 100 widgets to you on Friday,

Charlie being my employee, and you say "Fine", then I have not made a promise, since (8) does not meet the conditions we laid down for promises. But I have given you my word. And if (8) turns out to be false and you suffer a loss for lack of widgets, then I owe compensation just as I would if what I had asserted was that *I* (and not Charlie) would deliver the 100 widgets on Friday. It is not merely promising that is a liability-shouldering device, word-giving generally is.

The need to give warning in advance that a word-given proposition is false, and where appropriate to compensate for losses caused by its being false, issues from the fact that—as the Assertion Thesis tells us—in giving one's word one invites reliance on the word-given proposition, whether the word-giving is promissory or nonpromissory.

Indeed, it is because one is inviting reliance that one has to be careful in advance of a word-giving to be sure that the word-given proposition really is true. If C needs 100 widgets on Friday, I ought not promise to provide him with them unless I have taken reasonable precautions to be sure I will be able to deliver them. Similarly, if you ask me for the time, I ought not assert (7) on the basis of a mere guess that it is true: I should look at my watch, and if I have reason to suspect my watch may be slow, I should assert not (7), but instead "Well, my watch says ten o'clock, but it may be slow".

There is a similarity in the possible sins here. In the case of a person A who makes a promise with no intention of keeping it, we say that he made a 'false promise'. In the case of a person B who gives his word, believing the word-given proposition is false, we say that he lied. The two phenomena are much alike, however. In both cases the speaker invites reliance, while believing that the world will make the reliance sheer loss. Again, in the case of a person who makes a promise, or gives his or her word, without taking reasonable precautions to be sure the word-given proposition is true, there is negligence.

We could, if we wished, mark the differences between, on the one hand, propositions such as

(7) It's ten o'clock,

whose truth or falsity is out of one's control, and, on the other hand, propositions such as

(8) Charlie will deliver 100 widgets to you on Friday

and

(9) JJT will put the car keys on the bureau tonight,

whose truth or falsity (we may suppose) are in my control, by saying that for me to give my word of the truth of (8) or (9) is to give a claim to the truth of the proposition, whereas for anyone (me or anyone else) to give his or her word of the truth of (7) is to give a claim only to warning of falsehood, if the proposition turns out to be false, and compensation for losses suffered later, if that is called for. But so far as I can see, there is no good reason to introduce this complication into our account of word-giving—just as there was no good reason to introduce a similar complication into our account of claims in Chapter 3. The Word-Giving Thesis is attractively simple, and I suggest we accept it. There is no need for one who accepts it to be misled into overlooking the differences among word-given propositions, and failing to remember that the truth-values of some are not in the word-giver's control.

8. There are three more possible objections to

> The Word-Giving Thesis: If Y gives X his or her word that a certain proposition is true, then X thereby acquires a claim against Y to its being true

that we need to take a look at.

The first issues from the possibility that a word-giving may have its source in coercion or fraud. B is not among the more efficient extortionists: he holds a gun to A's head and says "GIVE ME YOUR WORD THAT YOU WILL GO TO YOUR BANK AND FETCH ME BACK A THOUSAND DOLLARS OR I'LL SHOOT YOU!" A says "Yessir." Did A give B his word that he would fetch the money? Again, D tells C he is in dire financial straights and must therefore part with his favorite Van Gogh for the grotesquely low price of a thousand dollars. C says "Sold!—I'll go to my bank straightway". Did C give D his word that he would fetch the money?

> The Assertion Thesis: Y gives X his or her word that a proposition is true if and only if Y asserts that proposition to X, and
>> (i) in so doing, Y is inviting X to rely on its truth, and
>> (ii) X receives and accepts the invitation (there is uptake)

tells us A gave B his word, and C gave D his word, and that seems right: I think we should agree that even if one's assertion issued from coercion or fraud, one *has* nevertheless given one's word.

But did A give B a claim that he would fetch the money? Did C give D a claim that he would fetch the money? It is of interest that some people would say A and C did give claims—I have Hobbes in mind, in particular. I am sure that none of them would say morality requires that A and C accord the claims: on their view, these are claims it is permissible for A and C to infringe. But should we agree with them that A and C gave claims?

I fancy that anyone who thinks a word-giving whose source is coercion or fraud does nevertheless give a claim is *excessively* respectful of what goes on in a word-giving. Inviting reliance is admittedly a morally serious business. All the same, it is hard to swallow the idea that the word-giver is bound in such cases.

We could simply insert exceptions into the Word-Giving Thesis to limit word-givings that give claims to word-givings that do not issue from coercion or fraud. But I think we should stop for a moment to take note of the fact that something more general is at work here.

What I have in mind is this. For B to attempt to coerce A into doing a thing is for B to try to make A think he lacks eligible alternatives to doing the thing; and B succeeds in coercing A into doing the thing if B succeeds in making A think he lacks eligible alternatives to doing the thing. It may be that B succeeds, not merely in making A think he lacks eligible alternatives to doing the thing, but also in making it actually be the case that A lacks eligible alternatives to doing the thing. Or he may not. No matter. If B succeeds in making A *think* he lacks eligible alternatives to doing the thing, then A will do the thing, and B will therefore have succeeded in coercing A into doing it. In particular, if B succeeds in making A think he lacks eligible alternatives to giving B his word that he will go to the bank and fetch back a thousand dollars, then A will give his word, and B will therefore have succeeded in coercing A into giving his word.

Now there are other ways than coercion in which a person can come to think he or she lacks eligible alternatives to doing a thing. Suppose the barn in which A′ stores his widgets burned down last night—unbeknownst to A′, B′ had villainously burned it down. A′ is now in dire need of 100 widgets. It may be that A′ therefore concludes that he lacks eligible alternatives to offering to pay B′ $1000 if B′ will give A′ the 100 widgets B′ happens to have on hand, $1000 being the going market price for 100 widgets. If A′ does give B′ his word to this effect, A′ does so out of what he thinks is a lack of eligible alternatives; but what made A′ think he lacked eligible alternatives is not coercion, but the villainous act of barn burning by B′ that caused A′ to need 100 widgets.

In the case of A′ and B′, as in the case of A and B, a word is given; but it is excessively respectful of what goes on in a word-giving to suppose that the word-giver gives a claim in either of these cases. The condition of (as I will call it) diminished eligible alternatives that issued in the word-giving was produced by fault in the word-receiver, and it is plausible to think it is for *that* reason that the word-receiver, while receiving the word, receives no claim.

Cases in which a word-giving that issues from diminished eligible alternatives gives no claim are, I think, limited to cases in which the word-receiver is at fault for the word-giver's diminished eligible alternatives. For compare A″ and B″. The barn in which A″ stores his widgets burned down last night. No one was at fault: the barn was hit by lightning. Nevertheless A″ is now in dire need of 100 widgets. It may be that A″ therefore concludes he lacks eligible alternatives to offering to pay B″ $1000 if B″ will give A″ the 100 widgets B″ happens to have on hand, $1000 being the going market price for 100 widgets. Here the word-giving surely does give a claim. It would be kind in B″ to make A″ a gift of the 100 widgets A″ needs; but if B″ does do this, he divests himself of a claim for payment that A″ gave B″ in giving B″ his word that he would pay.

What if B″ charges A″ for the 100 widgets not the going price, but some wildly extortionate price? (What if you are lost in the desert, dying of thirst, and Smith comes along and offers you water for $1000 a mouthful?) Here we may feel that if A″ gives B″ his word to pay the price, he nevertheless gives B″ no claim to be paid the full amount. But if so, isn't that because there is fault in the word-receiver here? B″ did not cause A″ to need 100 widgets and *a fortiori* is not at fault for the fact that A″ now needs 100 widgets. But B″ is at fault for causing A″ to have no eligible alternative to giving his word to pay the extortionate price, for B″ could have, and ought to have, caused A″ to have yet another alternative, namely that of paying a reasonable price. Or anyway I suggest we will think A″ failed to give B″ a claim to be paid the price B″ charged only if we think that B″ ought to have charged less.

So I think that cases in which a word-giving that issues from diminished eligible alternatives gives no claim really are limited to cases in which the word-receiver is at fault, in one or another way, for the word-giver's diminished eligible alternatives.

Something similar seems to me true in the case of what we may call diminished information—where that covers misinformation as well as lack of information. We imagined that D tells C he is in dire financial straights and must therefore part with his favorite Van Gogh for the grotesquely low price of $1000. C says "Sold!—I'll go to my bank straightway." Did C give D his word that he would fetch the money? Suppose C finds out while on his way to the bank that the painting was actually painted not by Van Gogh but (as it might be) by Marvin Witherspoon. Does D all the same have a claim against C for the $1000 in exchange for the painting? No, we think. But this is because D is at fault for the misinformation that issued in C's giving D his word.[4]

A word-receiver who is at fault for the word-giver's lack of information (as opposed to misinformation) also does not receive a claim from the word-giver. If D' has villainously hidden a thing C' is in search of, then C' gives no claim when he gives D' his word to pay him for information as to its whereabouts. But if D' had not been at fault, either for hiding the thing or for charging an extortionate price, C' would have given a claim in giving his word.

If these ideas are right, and I think they are, then we can say that a word-giving that issues from a condition of diminished eligible alternatives or diminished information fails to give a claim only if the condition is due to fault in the word-receiver. Where the condition *is* due to fault in the word-receiver, we can think of the claim as stillborn, forfeit from conception. We can revise the Word-Giving Thesis, inserting explicit exceptions for word-givings that issue from fault in the word-receiver, but I suggest that we not trouble to do so. It is a familiar enough fact that claims can be forfeited, and we need merely keep in mind that these are cases in which a claim would have been given had there not been fault, but is not given because there was.

9. The second of the three remaining objections to the Word-Giving Thesis that I mentioned at the beginning of the last section arises not from consideration of the sources of a word-giving, but from the content of the word given. What I have in mind is that one may give one's word to do something morally impermissible. The Assertion Thesis does not restrict word-givings to assertions of propositions it would be morally acceptable to make true, and that seems right. Suppose we are villains, planning a coup. I volunteer to assassinate the President. (You, in return, volunteer to assassinate both the Vice-President and the Speaker of the House.) I think it right to say, as the Assertion Thesis says, that I thereby give you my word that I will

4. Static is produced here by the fact that C too was at fault in this case. The successful con man is the one with a sharp eye for the sleazy in a potential mark.

assassinate the President. But do I give you a claim that I will? Once again, I am sure that some people would say I do—though they would of course say that it is permissible for me to infringe the claim, indeed, that it is impermissible for me to not infringe it. Should we agree with them?

I think we should disagree with them. (They show excessive respect for what goes on in a word-giving.) It really is intuitively implausible to think I gave you a claim that I will assassinate the President in giving you my word that I will. And there is reason to think I did not give you that claim. Suppose I come to repent of my evil ways, and I therefore do not assassinate the President. This may leave you out on a limb and cause you a harm. All the same, I think I owe you nothing by way of compensation for the harm you suffer.

It might be thought that there is a quite general reason to think I did not give you the claim, and it might pay to look at it. Consider the following thesis:

(T$_1$') If there is an X such that $C_{X,Y}p$, then it is permissible for Y to let it be the case that p.

If this thesis is true, then in particular if X has a claim against Y that Y do alpha, then it is permissible for Y to do alpha; so if it is *not* permissible for Y to do alpha, then no matter who X may be, X has no claim against Y that Y do alpha. It follows that if it is *not* permissible for Y to do alpha, then even if Y gave X his or her word that Y will do alpha, Y did not give X a claim that Y would do it. It is impermissible for me to assassinate the President. If (T$_1$') is true, then it is no wonder that I did not give you a claim that I will in giving you my word that I will.

I gave the thesis the name "(T$_1$')" by way of reminder of a thesis we spent time over in Part I, namely

(T$_1$) If there is an X such that $C_{X,Y}p$, then Y ought not let it fail to be the case that p.

Thesis (T$_1$) says that all claims ought to be accorded, and we rephrased it as the thesis that all claims are absolute. The weaker thesis (T$_1$') says only that all claims may permissibly be accorded, and we could, if we liked, rephrase it as the thesis that all claims are morally accordable. I think that (T$_1$') strikes us as intuitively plausible.

But should we accept it? Suppose you need a copy of Moore's *Ethics* tomorrow morning. I volunteer to get one for you. You say a lot turns on your having the book tomorrow morning, so am I *sure* I can get it for you? I guarantee you that I can and that I will. I then find that the only copy I can lay my hands on is Smith's and, as Smith is out of town, I would have to break into his house to get it. It is not permissible for me to break into Smith's house to get it, and I get it for you if and only if I break into his house. The Sole Means Principle for Permissibility (of Chapter 4, section 2) tells us that it is not permissible for me to get it for you. Should we conclude that you therefore have no claim against me? Really? Is it really in place for me simply to wash my hands of the harm you then suffer for lack of the book? Even if I am not at fault for my inability to do what I guaranteed I would do, still I have shouldered a responsibility in giving the guarantee.

I suggest, in other words, that we should distinguish. We should say that in some cases in which Y gives X his or her word that Y will do alpha, where it is impermissible for Y to do alpha, Y does thereby give X a claim that Y will do it—and thus that thesis (T_1') is false—but that in other cases of this kind Y does not thereby give X the claim. I do give a claim in the case of giving you my word that I will get you a copy of Moore's *Ethics* tomorrow morning; I do not give a claim in the case of giving you my word that I will assassinate the President.

I suggest, moreover, that we can account for this difference if we remind ourselves that a word-giving requires uptake on the part of the word-receiver. For what were you doing in accepting my offer to assassinate the President? I was at fault for making the offer, but you were also at fault for accepting it. Whether or not I was at fault for offering to get you a copy of Moore's *Ethics* tomorrow morning (whether or not I ought to have been more careful about my chances of being able to do what I offered), you were not at fault for accepting my offer. Or at any rate I suggest that we should say I did give you the claim only if you were not at fault for accepting my offer.

In short, I suggest that we can deal with these cases just as we dealt with those under consideration in the preceding section. We can say that if a word-giver would have to act impermissibly to make his or her word-given proposition true, then he or she does all the same give a claim—unless the word-receiver was at fault for accepting the word-giver's word. Where the uptake is a fault in the word-receiver, we can think of the claim as stillborn, forfeit from conception. As I said, we can revise the Word-Giving Thesis, inserting explicit exceptions for word-givings that issue from fault in the word-receiver, but I suggest that we not trouble to do so. It is a familiar enough fact that claims can be forfeited, and we need merely keep in mind that these are cases in which a claim would have been given had there not been fault, but is not given because there was.

10. The last of the three objections to the Word-Giving Thesis is the deepest.

How stringent is the claim one gives by a word-giving? The Aggravation Principle tells us that it must be of at most zero stringency unless one would make things bad for the word-receiver if one broke one's word.[5] Let us look again at a case I drew attention to in section 3 above. I invited you to suppose that I telephone you and say "I swear I will eat my spinach at dinner tonight!" You couldn't care less, but as a courtesy you say "Okay, fine." There is uptake in this case, even if there is no caring. So I have given you my word that I will eat my spinach at dinner tonight. The Word-Giving Thesis tells us that I have thereby given you a claim that I will. How stringent is that claim? If you do not care whether or not I eat my spinach, there will be no such thing as your relying on my eating it, and hence I will cause you no harm, or anything else untoward, if I decline to eat it; that being so, the claim must be of zero stringency.

This is not by itself an objection to the Word-Giving Thesis, for it is not conclusive against the supposition that a person has a claim that the claim—if he or she has it—is of zero stringency. We have already met claims with no stringency. I have David (of Chapter 7) in mind here. David's leg was crushed; to save his life we must cut his leg off; but David is in a coma and cannot be asked for permission to proceed. How stringent is the claim we infringe if we proceed? The claim is of negative stringency, since it is on balance good for David that we proceed. Yet David does have the claim.

But the cases do seem to be different. There is reason to think David does have the claim, lying in the fact that if David *were* conscious then, other things being equal, morality would require us to ask his permission before proceeding. I sit down to dinner, see the spinach,

5. Arnold Isenberg draws attention to the weakness of what (following Ross) he calls the *prima facie* duty to not tell lies in "Deontology and the Ethics of Lying", *Philosophy and Phenomenological Research*, 24 (1964). The article is reprinted in Thomson and Dworkin, eds., *Ethics*.

and feel a welling-up of revulsion. You are not unconscious, I presume. Does morality require me to telephone you again to ask your permission to decline to eat the spinach? I would only annoy you further if I did.

What is supposed to make us think that you do have a claim against me that I eat the spinach? Do I have to produce an increment of good for it to be permissible not to eat it? May I not do exactly as I please about the spinach?

The possibility that emerges then is this. Perhaps we should say that you do not have a claim against me that I eat the spinach. Perhaps we should say, more generally, that the word-receiver has a claim against the word-giver where and only where, and due and only due to the fact that, by breaking his or her word the word-giver would infringe some *independently establishable claim* of the word-receiver. That is, where one infringes no other claim by breaking one's word, one infringes no claim at all when one breaks it; and where one infringes a claim when one breaks one's word, this is because by breaking it one infringes some other claim.[6] (Remember the Means Principle for Claims.) It would follow from this, of course, that you have no claim against me that I eat the spinach—for I infringe no other claim of yours by declining to eat it—and that the Word-Giving Thesis is therefore false. It would follow also that, for all the attention theorists have paid to them, word-givings are not *themselves* of moral interest.

Friends of this idea might draw attention to the contrast between the putative claims given by word-givings and the claims infringed in trespass. It might be that I will not only cause you no harm if I pinch your nose, but that you will not even find out that I did, since you are currently in a coma. Still, you have a claim against me that I not do this; I really do have to produce an increment of good by doing so if it is to be permissible for me to proceed. My deciding "The hell with the spinach tonight!" seems to be different.

Let us call this idea Reductionism about Word-Givings. Is it a plausible idea that one who breaks his or her word infringes a claim if and only if by breaking it he or she infringes some other claim?

What, we may wonder, is a Reductionist about Word-Givings to say about deathbed promises? Suppose we promised Bloggs on his

6. This idea is argued for by P. S. Atiyah, in *Promises, Morals, and Law* (Oxford: Clarendon Press, 1981).

deathbed that we would do alpha after his death. Now he is dead, and we do think ourselves bound to do alpha. Indeed, we think that failing to do alpha would be infringing a rather stringent claim of his. We do think quite generally that we ought to keep promises we make to the dying, even at a considerable cost to ourselves. Can the claim Bloggs now has against us be explained as issuing (by way of the Means Principle for Claims) from some other claim of his that we would infringe by breaking our promise to him?

One possible reply is that our respect for deathbed promises is mere irrationality. That is a very unattractive idea, one I am sure we would prefer to avoid unless driven to it.

But deathbed promises do seem puzzling, on any view about word-givings. In the first place, I said that Bloggs is now dead and then went on to talk of "the claim Bloggs now has against us". A number of philosophers have worried about how the dead can be thought to have any claims at all against the living: how can it be that one who no longer exists now has claims against others? This source of concern *we* are in a position to bypass. I argued in Part I that X's having a claim against Y just is Y's behavior's being constrained in a complex set of ways; if that is right, then there is no difficulty in the supposition that those no longer alive have claims now, for there is no difficulty in the supposition that the behavior of the living is now constrained in the appropriate ways. (Similarly, I might add, for the supposition that those not yet alive have claims now.[7]) It is in fact among the attractions of this account of claims that it enables us to think of the no-longer-alive (as also the not-yet-alive) as now having claims against us.

A second source of puzzlement about deathbed promises does remain, however. Here is our principle governing stringency:

> The Aggravation Principle: If X has a claim against Y that Y do alpha, then the worse Y makes things for X if Y fails to do alpha, the more stringent X's claim against Y that Y do alpha—but for 'worsenings' that consist in X's being caused belief-mediated distress.

We think that the claims given by deathbed promises are very stringent; how can that be so, if the Aggravation Principle is true? One possibility is to revise the Aggravation Principle to make an exception

7. I am indebted to Hugh Sansom for drawing my attention to the symmetry here.

for the claims of the dead. Another, which I prefer, is to recognize that there is such a thing as making things worse for the dead. The notion 'good for a person' that I have been using throughout is not restricted to things the person is aware of; a particular instance of trespass or harm-causing might be very bad for its victim, and thus be an infringement of a very stringent claim, even if the victim never finds out it was committed. So too, I should think we can say, for the dead.[8] Still, it seems to me a real possibility that the claims of the dead, and in particular the claims we gave them when they were dying, are more stringent than can be accounted for in this way. If so, can the stringency of claims given by deathbed promises issue from there being no such thing as making amends to the dead for an infringement of their claims? And if so, should we revise the Aggravation Principle to make a quite general exception for claims it is impossible to make amends for infringements of? (But exactly how one would make this exception is unclear, since it can hardly be thought that all claims given by deathbed promises are maximally stringent. Indeed, are *any* of them maximally stringent?) I will have to leave it an open question whether the Aggravation Principle needs revision to accommodate the stringency of claims given by deathbed promises.

For present purposes what matters is only that if deathbed promises do give claims, then—however we are to accommodate the stringency of the claims they give—Reductionism about Word-Givings is in trouble, because it is hard to believe that by breaking such a promise we are always infringing some other, independently establishable, claim of the dead person.

A second and, I think, even more powerful objection to Reductionism about Word-Givings seems to me to issue from what I pointed to in connection with the spinach in section 3 above. I said to you "I swear I will eat my spinach at dinner tonight!" and you as a courtesy said "Okay, fine." I said that you are now entitled to rely on my eating my spinach. It may be that you not only don't care now whether I eat it, but also never come to care; if so, you not only don't rely now on my eating it, but also never start to rely. As I said, however, once there has been uptake, I am now morally at risk, for you might at

8. There is an interesting discussion of these matters in Thomas Nagel, "Death", *Nous,* 4 (1970), reprinted in his *Moral Questions* (Cambridge: Cambridge University Press, 1979).

any time start to rely. Whether or not you do, you are entitled to, and that entitlement is what your having the claim against me consists in.

A third reason for rejecting Reductionism about Word-Givings lies in the fact that, if we can accept the Word-Giving Thesis, we can secure a rather attractive symmetry for our theory of rights. (I will return to this in Chapter 14.)

In short, I suggest that we should say you do have a claim against me that I eat my spinach at dinner tonight. If you are not going to come to care whether I do, then the claim might well be thought of as a degenerate case, for it is of zero stringency, and I neither need to produce an increment of good by infringing it nor ask you for a release from it. But I suggest that we should be willing to accept that you have it.

11. In sum, a word-giver B alters the world in such a way that an act of the word-receiver A (uptake) makes A have a claim against B to the truth of the word-given proposition. In other words, the word-giver B gives the word-receiver A a power by the exercise of which A makes himself have a claim against B. The word-giver sets the stage; the word-receiver then walks onto it.

But this means that the word-giver B himself had to have had a power, a metapower, a power to give powers, a power to set the stage.

What is the source of that power in the word-giver? It issues from two features possessed by human beings. One I pointed to in Chapter 8: our capacity to conform our conduct to moral law. Only a creature that can conform its conduct to moral law is subject to moral law, and only a creature that is subject to moral law is a creature that others can have claims against. An animal Y cannot alter the world in such a way that an act of another (human or animal) will give that other a claim against the animal Y, since no one and nothing can have claims against an animal.

The other feature is all simply the ability to communicate with others, in particular, the ability to issue invitations to rely. Issuing the invitation *is* doing the stage setting. Animals lack that ability too, but human slaves have it, even if they lack the privilege of exercising it.

We have allowed ourselves to call powers rights. If we do, then something I may have been thought to imply is false. I said in Chapter 1, section 6, that what Hobbes had in mind in the passages I quoted there is this: what the inhabitants of the state of nature have is privileges, and their privileges are natural rights and *a fortiori* are rights. I may have been thought to imply that, on his view, *all* of their natural rights are privileges. But Hobbes said that people could come out of the state of nature into the state of society by contracting with each other. Contracting requires having a power; therefore if powers are rights, and the inhabitants of Hobbes' state of nature are to come out of it in the way he thought they could, we must suppose Hobbes to have thought they have other natural rights than merely privileges. We must suppose he thought that certain powers—in particular, powers to give powers—are also among their natural rights.

I have suggested that two alone can make a word-giving; what I will now argue is that it takes a society to make property.

Chapter 13

Second Property

1. If I said to you "Henceforth this banana is yours" and you replied "Okay, fine", then—given that my assertion was an invitation to rely and yours an acceptance of the invitation—I have given you my word that from then on the banana is yours, and thus have given you a claim against me to its being yours from then on. By asserting a proposition, we exercise a power: we alter the world in such a way that uptake on the part of the word-receiver triggers his or her having a claim against us to the truth of the proposition we asserted. So much we saw in the preceding chapter.

We have other powers too, and in saying what I said I may also have exercised one of those others. When I said to you "Henceforth this banana is yours" and you replied "Okay, fine", I may not merely have given you a claim to its being yours from then on; I may have made it *be* yours. That is, I may have given you a whole host of claims (against myself and others that they not do certain things to the banana) and privileges (as regards myself and others of doing certain things to the banana), and a battery of powers (to make still others acquire claims, privileges, and powers).

Let us look at this a little more closely. Suppose (i) that I owned the banana. Then I had the power to alter the world in such a way that uptake on the part of the word-receiver triggers his or her having that host of claims and privileges, and that battery of powers; and in saying to you "Henceforth this banana is yours" I exercised the power. I think it right to suppose that my saying what I said does not by itself make you have that host of claims and privileges, and that battery of powers. That is, I think it right to suppose that uptake is required for a transfer of property just as it is required for a word-giving. One reason is that property brings duties in its train, and I cannot, for example, make you liable for the taxes I owe on my farm in Indiana just by asserting to you "It's yours"—if you do not accept the gift, my words alone cannot cause the gift to have been made. A second reason is that until there is uptake on your part I am surely free to proceed to find another person to transfer the property to instead. The power of transfer that I have in owning a piece of property is merely that of altering the world in such a way that uptake triggers the transfer.

In short, if I owned the banana, then when I said to you "Henceforth this banana is yours" and you replied "Okay, fine", I gave you a claim to its being yours *and,* moreover, accorded you that claim, for the exchange of words between us made you at one and the same time both acquire the claim and acquire the banana.

Owning a banana is not required for having the power to make someone else have the host of claims and privileges, and battery of powers, that ownership consists in. It might be (ii) that I did not own the banana but had been given the power to dispose of it by its owner. Here again, when I said to you "Henceforth this banana is yours" and you replied "Okay, fine", I have given you a claim to its being yours and, moreover, accorded you the claim.

Of course it might instead have been (iii) that I did not own the banana and moreover lacked the power to dispose of it. Then I gave you a claim against me to your from then on owning the banana and, at one and the same time, infringed the claim.

Transfers of property that go on when one person says "It's yours" and the other person says "Fine", or "Thanks", are among the many ways in which people can come to acquire and cease to have property. Our central question is this: which property rights do we have and what is their source? The question how property can be acquired has a direct bearing on it.

I should perhaps stress, however, that it is Second Property I mean by "property" throughout this chapter. We looked earlier at the sources of First Property; it is Second Property that concerns us here.

2. Current discussions of the sources of property rights tend to focus on 'initial acquisition'. I think the following thesis is accepted by most philosophers nowadays:

> The Ownership-Has-Origins Thesis: X owns a thing if and only if something happened that made X own it.

That is, the world was not created with its contents already owned: ownership has to be *acquired* in some or other way. (This is of course among the many differences between Second and First Property.)

What might happen to make X become owner of a thing? One possibility is (i) transfer of ownership: X might acquire the thing from Y, who had formerly owned it, by gift or sale or other voluntary act. A second possibility is (ii) manufacture: X might make the thing out of a certain stuff, which stuff X had formerly owned. But both (i) and (ii) require prior ownership: X comes to own a thing by (i) transfer only if someone else formerly owned it, and X comes to own a thing by (ii) manufacture only if X formerly owned the stuff of which X made the thing. Since as the Ownership-Has-Origins Thesis tells us, ownership has to be acquired, someone must have been able to acquire ownership in a way that does not require prior ownership. The following thesis-schema suggests itself:

> The Acquisition Schema: If a thing is unowned, then if X does alpha to it, X thereby comes to own it.

This is merely a schema: different theses result from different replacements for "does alpha". What it does tell us, however, is that if a thing is unowned, then something involving X—X's doing alpha, whatever it may be—is sufficient for X's coming to own the thing.

A stronger schema is:

> If a thing is unowned, then if X does alpha to it, X thereby comes to own it *and* X comes to own it only by doing alpha to it.

This tells us that if a thing is unowned, then X's doing alpha is both sufficient *and* necessary for X's coming to own it. If this is correct, then given the Ownership-Has-Origins Thesis, we can conclude also that all ownership of anything has its origin in someone's having done alpha to something unowned. What will interest us here, however, is the Acquisition Schema, which tells us merely that X's doing alpha is sufficient.

What can we plausibly take doing alpha to consist in? Not surprisingly, attempts to answer this question have required hard work. Ownership is a cluster of claims, privileges, and powers, and it is (to say the least) not easy to see what we can suppose a person to do to something unowned that would thereby make him or her have all of those rights in the thing.

This point deserves emphasis. It is plausible to think that if something is unowned, then each of us has a privilege as regards all others of making such uses of it as he or she pleases, for it is plausible to think that if something is unowned, then no one has a claim against anyone that he or she not make use of it. No doubt there are constraints on those uses set by considerations we have already attended to: thus, for example, if my making a certain use of the thing would cause you harm, then it follows by the Means Principle for Claims that you have a claim against me that I not make that use of it. Again, if I have given you my word that I would not make that use of it, then you have a claim against me that I not. But in the absence of such constraints, it is plausible to think that I infringe no claim of yours if I use the thing as I please. We will return to this in the following section.

Yet it is not at all plausible to think that if something is unowned, then each of us has claims against others to noninterference with our uses of it. Having a claim to noninterference is very different from having a privilege; and it is not at all clear what I could do to an unowned thing that would generate in me a claim to noninterference with my uses of it.

Ownership includes not merely privileges, not merely claims, but powers as well, such as the power to make other people have powers. What could I do to an unowned thing that would generate in me the power to make other people have powers in respect of it?

So friends of the Acquisition Schema have their work cut out for them.

A Lockean idea is that X might come to own a formerly unowned thing by 'mixing his or her labor with' the thing—working on it in some way. (In the hands of some writers, mere taking possession of the thing in some way seems to be thought sufficient for mixing one's labor with it.[1]) But how could one's mixing one's labor with an unowned thing make one have all of the rights over it that ownership consists in? On some views (perhaps Locke's own), mixing one's labor with a thing increases its value, it being for *that* reason that the labor-mixing generates ownership. But why conclude that the labor-mixer

---

1. Locke himself thought that one's merely picking up an acorn constitutes one's mixing one's labor with it. See John Locke, *Second Treatise of Government*, ch. 5. But something in the way of positive taking of possession is surely required. I surely do not acquire ownership of the moon by merely pointing to it and saying "I take that!".

now owns the more valuable thing? Why not instead conclude that, thanks to the labor-mixer, something still unowned now has more value than it formerly did?

The idea that mixing one's labor with an unowned thing makes one own it is the idea that engaging in a certain activity in respect of an unowned thing makes one own it. We have to notice, however, that a further condition is presupposed. Suppose that X mixes his or her labor with an unowned thing and then sets it aside for a moment. During that moment Y comes along and mixes his or her labor with it. X has made the thing X's own; not so Y. Why does X's labor-mixing make the thing X's own whereas Y's does not make it Y's own? It will be replied, "At the time at which X's labor-mixing took place, the thing was unowned, whereas by the time at which Y's labor-mixing took place, the thing was already owned, for X's labor-mixing had by then made it belong to X." What this brings out is that on these views it is not the fact that X mixed his or her labor with the thing that made it belong to X: it is the fact that X was the first to mix his or her labor with the thing that made it belong to X.

But we might well ask why this should be thought true. Here is something unowned. X is the first to mix labor with it. Then Y mixes labor with it. Then Z does. Why is it the first labor-mixing that generates ownership? Why not the third? I know of only two kinds of argument for the conclusion that it is the first labor-mixing that generates ownership.

In the first place, there is the kind of argument that appeals to desert: it says that the first labor-mixer has earned ownership of the thing, that he or she merits ownership as a reward. But this will not seem plausible to us when we remember that there are cases in which it was just a matter of luck for the first labor-mixer to come first. One cannot really appeal to desert to explain why, quite generally, the first labor-mixer acquires ownership.

Moreover, an appeal to desert does not even suffice in cases in which it was not just a matter of luck for the first labor-mixer to come first. Suppose that Bloggs has been in search of a source of oil for years, expending much time, energy, and money in the search. Lo, he is first to find a certain source of oil just off the coast of Rhode Island. No doubt he deserves a reward, since oil is important to us. But why should it be thought that the reward he deserves is ownership of the oil source? Why not instead a medal and a handshake from the President?

The second kind of argument for the conclusion that the first labor-mixing generates ownership appeals to considerations of efficiency—it appeals, in particular, to the efficiency of adopting a 'first come first served' rule. Suppose I take out an ad in the newspaper that says: "I, JJT, will give out a million dollars each to ten people tomorrow morning, third come first served". There will be people lurking in doorways up and down my street all day, waiting for the first two to have come and gone—a highly inefficient outcome.

Now it is currently common in philosophical writing on these matters to use the term "efficiency" in such a way that considerations of efficiency are contrasted with considerations of equity. Suppose you think that the end a group should aim at in adopting a certain rule is the on-balance good of all; then you would be said to think that the end a group should aim at is efficiency. Suppose you think instead that the end a group should aim at in adopting a certain rule is the good of each (or the equal good of each or the good of the least well off, etc.); then you would be said to think that the end a group should aim at is equity in some form or other. For our purposes, the differences between these different ends do not matter. I will therefore use the term "efficiency" as I think ordinary speakers of English use it: I will say that adoption of a certain rule would be most efficient if adoption of it would bring the group more of the end—whether on-balance-good or equitably-distributed-good or whatever else is your favorite end—than any other available rule. In short, I will use the term in such a way that efficiency is relative to the end to be accomplished, leaving aside which end is to be chosen.

For example, if you think that the end a group should aim at in adopting a certain rule is the on-balance good of all, then you will think it should adopt whatever rule maximizes the on-balance good of all. And you might then wish to argue for the conclusion that what makes first labor-mixing generate ownership is the truth of

(1) Adopting a rule according to which first labor-mixing always generates ownership would be on balance better than adopting any incompatible rule—

that is, better than adopting a rule according to which first labor-mixing never generates ownership, and better than adopting any of the possible rules according to which first labor-mixing sometimes generates ownership and sometimes does not. For a particular example, consider oil sources. It might be thought better to adopt a rule according to which the first to locate and develop an oil source is always the owner than to adopt any incompatible rule, on the ground that adoption of this rule gives explorers the best possible reason for trying to come first, and oil resources are therefore more quickly developed.

Alternatively, you might think that the end a group should aim at in adopting a certain rule is the good of each; then you will think it should adopt whatever rule maximizes the good of each. Then you might wish to argue for the conclusion that what makes first labor-mixing generate ownership is the truth of

> (2) Adopting a rule according to which first labor-mixing always generates ownership would be to the greater good of each than adopting any incompatible rule.

It might be thought that adoption of 'first come first served' for oil sources is not merely on balance better than adopting any incompatible rule, but to the greatest good of each, on the ground of the benefits to each of quick development of oil resources.

There are obviously any number of other possible arguments here, according as one chooses one or another end. We might summarize them in the words,

> Adopting a rule according to which first labor-mixing always generates ownership would be most efficient,

having in mind that efficiency here is relative to chosen end.

So far so good. But the fact is that friends of the efficiency-based arguments we are looking at do not think these premises are true. I am sure that if they thought them true they would think that first labor-mixing generates ownership; but they do not actually think that that is *in general* true or that first labor-mixing *always* generates ownership.

Consider the moon and its contents, which I presume are currently unowned. Last week all of the oil on earth dried up. Disaster! But quick as a flash I went to the moon over the weekend and located (and mixed my labor with) all of the moon's oil sources. If first labor-mixing generates ownership, I own all the moon's oil sources. But no one of sound mind would say I do.[2] And certainly anyone for whom

2. Even the most devoted friends of these ideas would say I do not. Compare Nozick: "a person may not appropriate the only water hole in a desert and charge what he will". *Anarchy, State, and Utopia*, p. 180.

considerations of efficiency are determinative here would say I do not. That oil should have been discovered on the moon is, in the circumstances, a splendid thing, potentially of great good to all; but that I be the owner of it is not to the good of each, and not even on balance good. It is greatly to the disadvantage of everyone other than me if I own all of the moon's oil sources.

It might be said that if I hadn't thought I would become owner of the moon's oil sources, I would not have expended effort to discover and work them. That can hardly be right. There are many possible arrangements under which I would profit enough to make expending the effort worth my while, but which fall far short of my owning the oil sources outright.

Indeed, it emerges from this very fact that

(1) Adopting a rule according to which first labor-mixing always generates ownership would be on balance better than adopting any incompatible rule

is false. Adopting a rule according to which some first labor-mixings generate ownership, but my first labor-mixing with the moon's oil does not generate ownership, would certainly be on balance better than adopting a rule according to which all first labor-mixings (and *a fortiori* mine) generate ownership. Similarly for

(2) Adopting a rule according to which first labor-mixing always generates ownership would be to the greater good of each than adopting any incompatible rule—

it too is false. And similarly, I should think, for any plausible version of

Adopting a rule according to which first labor-mixing always generates ownership would be most efficient.

Friends of efficiency-based arguments therefore do not believe it *in general* true that first labor-mixing generates ownership. They would agree that the fact that I was first to mix my labor with the moon's oil sources does not make me owner of them.

What they believe is that the first labor-mixer must meet a further condition if the labor-mixing is to generate ownership. (For the purposes of

The Acquisition Schema: If a thing is unowned, then if X does alpha to it, X thereby comes to own it, then, we are to understand 'doing alpha' to be, not merely engaging in some activity, not merely being first to engage in that activity, but rather: being-first-to-engage-in-that-activity-given-a-certain-further-condition-is-met.) What further condition? We have taken note of their appeal to one Lockean idea already: the relevant activity is 'mixing one's labor with'. A second Lockean idea turns up here: the further condition is that the first labor-mixer must leave 'as much and as good' for others who come along later. When I went to the moon and mixed my labor with all of the moon's oil sources, I did not leave as much and as good for others, and that is why my being first to mix labor with the moon's oil sources did not make me owner of them.

And then the argument to ownership should be understood to proceed not from premises (1) or (2), but rather from premises

   (1′) Adopting a rule according to which first labor-mixings that leave as much and as good for others always generate ownership would be on balance better than adopting any incompatible rule

or

   (2′) Adopting a rule according to which first labor-mixings that leave as much and as good for others always generate ownership would be to the greater good of each than adopting any incompatible rule

or some similar efficiency-based premise.

But how exactly is that Lockean phrase to be understood? Ingenuity is required in its interpretation, since the phrase cannot be read literally. If the first labor-mixer must literally leave as much and as good for others who come along later, then no one can come to own anything, for there are only finitely many things in the world so that every taking leaves less for others. But how then are we to understand the phrase? What is to replace F in "A first labor-mixer leaves enough and as good for others just in case that particular labor-mixing has feature F"?

One might think to appeal to considerations of efficiency here. Thus one might try: "A first labor-mixer leaves as much and as good for others just in case that particular labor-mixing is on balance good, or is to the good of each". That won't do. My locating and developing the moon's oil sources is on balance good, indeed, is to the good of each, for in the circumstances (the earth's oil sources having dried up) it is on balance good, indeed it is to the good of each, that oil become available. According to the proposal we are looking at, we may conclude that my locating and developing the moon's oil sources does leave as much and as good for others. But adopting a rule under which I own the moon's oil sources would not be on balance better, or to the greater good of each, than adopting a rule under which I do not own them. In short, if my mixing my labor with the moon's oil sources counts as a first labor-mixing that leaves as much and as good for others, then (1') and (2') are not true.

The following proposal makes a more subtle appeal to considerations of efficiency: "A first labor-mixer leaves as much and as good for others just in case it is on balance good, or it is to the good of each, that that particular labor-mixing *generate ownership*". My being owner of the moon's oil sources is not on balance good, is not to the good of each, and so far so good: my mixing my labor with the moon's oil sources does not (as it should not) count as a labor-mixing that leaves as much and as good for others.

But is it plausible to think that each particular first labor-mixing has to be such that *its* generating ownership would be efficient in order for it to satisfy the 'as much and as good' condition, and thereby generate ownership? Mightn't the general rule it would be most efficient to adopt be one that allows of some particular ownership assignments that would be inefficient? And isn't it precisely considerations of efficient *rule* adoption that motivate the entire line of argument we have been looking at?

It is arguable, in fact, that it was a mistake from the start to search for a replacement for F in "A first labor-mixer leaves enough and as good for others just in case that particular labor-mixing has feature F", and that we do well to suppose that the idea behind that Lockean phrase is best understood as pointing to a requirement on the character of a set of general rules—that adopting the set should be efficient—rather than as a condition on particular labor-mixings.

Indeed, it is arguable that concentration on first labor-mixings was itself a mistake, the crucial point about them not being that they are first, but rather that the adoption of a 'total' *set* of rules, among which is a rule that assigns ownership to anyway some first labor-mixings, is efficient. (By contrast with accounts that appeal to desert, in which it is crucial to a first labor-mixing that it is first.)

What suggests itself is that the idea behind this entire line of argument is, all simply, the following thesis:

> The Efficient-System Thesis: People own what they would own under the 'total' set of rules, the adoption of which would be most efficient.

Since efficiency is, as we are supposing, relative to an end, we should keep in mind that the thesis might be understood to say

> (i) People own what they would own under the 'total' set of rules, the adoption of which would be on balance best,

and that it might instead be understood to say

> (ii) People own what they would own under the 'total' set of rules, the adoption of which would be to the greatest good of each,

and so on, for other possible ends. If in the case of formerly unowned things, the set of rules it would be most efficient to adopt contains one that requires one to mix one's labor with an unowned thing in order to come to own it, if the rule requires one to be first labor-mixer with the thing in order to come to own it, if the rule imposes further constraints on a first labor-mixing, then fine: whatever that rule does require is what we are to take 'doing alpha' to be in

> The Acquisition Schema: If a thing is unowned, then if X does alpha to it, X thereby comes to own it.

Now I think it very helpful to see that it is the Efficient-System Thesis that lies behind this entire line of argument because we can now see that behind this talk of labor-mixing, and leaving as much and as good for others, there lie some familiar ideas. People who accept the Efficient-System Thesis interpreted as (i) above have at work in them one or other of the moral theories that go by the name RULE UTILITARIANISM. People who accept the Efficient-System Thesis interpreted as (ii) above have at work in them one or other of the moral theories that go by the name CONTRACTUALISM.

It is not necessary for our purposes that we ask what is to be thought about those theories as general moral theories: what we need is only to ask how plausible it is to think that property rights are distributed—are *in fact* distributed—as (i) or (ii) say they are. Is it so much as within reason to suppose that the fact that adopting a certain set of rules would be efficient in one or another of the ways I indicated, or in any way at all, makes it be the case that those rules among them that govern property rights are *already* in force? It might be most efficient to adopt a set of rules for our club that includes the rule "Any member who comes in on a Saturday and works in the clubhouse garden will thereby come to own the mug of his/her choice from among the mugs on the shelf over the bar". But if we have not in fact adopted that particular rule, then it is not in force. It just is not the case that if I go in next Saturday and work in the clubhouse garden, then I will in fact own the mug of my choice from among the mugs on the shelf over the bar.

If it would be efficient to adopt a certain set of rules, then that is at least some reason to adopt them. Arguably (more or less well, depending on the end that would be most efficiently accomplished by adoption of the set of rules) it would be just or fair to adopt them; arguably we positively ought to adopt them. That much can be conceded to friends of RULE UTILITARIANISM and CONTRACTUALISM. But even if it is true that we ought to adopt a certain set of rules containing rules governing property rights, it does not for a moment follow that those rules governing property rights do already govern them.

What does govern property rights? We will come back to that question in section 4. First, however, a detour worth making.

3. I said at the beginning of the preceding section that most philosophers nowadays accept the following:

> The Ownership-Has-Origins Thesis: X owns a thing if and only if something happened that made X own it.

That is, the world was not created with its contents already owned: ownership has to be *acquired* in some way. But should we accept this thesis?

Well, what alternative do we have? Locke said at the outset of his chapter on property that God *"has given the Earth to the Children of Men,* given it to Mankind in common". Why not take this literally? We could suppose that in creating the world, God was creating things that were already, as of the time of their creation, owned by all mankind in common. Thus that in the beginning, everything was already owned: I owned it, you owned it, and people not yet born owned it. Of course this view does not yield, indeed denies, that any of us had 'private property' in it: of none of us could it be said that he or she alone owned any of it—on this view, we were only joint owners of it. But on this view we none of us needed, or now need, to do anything to have acquired ownership rights in it. Let us call this view the Jointly-Owned-from-the-Outset Thesis. (I do not attribute it to Locke; I merely say that his words can be so taken.)

What difference does it make whether one accepts the Ownership-Has-Origins Thesis or the Jointly-Owned-from-the-Outset Thesis? The question is an interesting one.

Accepting the Ownership-Has-Origins Thesis leaves us with a problem: what could make X come to own a thing that was formerly unowned? Accepting the Jointly-Owned-from-the-Outset Thesis leaves us with a similar problem: what could make X alone come to own a thing that was formerly owned by all mankind? And the second problem, though not the same as the first, is no less hard to solve. In particular, appeal to labor-mixing will no more easily serve the purposes of those for whom the Jointly-Owned-from-the-Outset Thesis sets the problem than of those for whom the Ownership-Has-Origins Thesis sets the problem.

Indeed, appeal to labor-mixing will even less easily serve those purposes. I said in the preceding section: it is plausible to think that if something is unowned, then each of us has a privilege as regards all others of making such uses of it as he or she pleases, for it is plausible to think that if something is unowned, then no one has a claim against anyone that he or she not make use of it. But if something is owned by a group of people in common, then it is not at all plausible to think that each member has a privilege as regards each other member of the group of making such uses of it as he or she pleases. If you and I jointly own a house, then it is not at all plausible to think that I have a privilege as regards you of painting it red, of tearing down its chimney, of doing what I please to it. If we jointly own a house, then I must surely have your consent (tacit if not explicit) to my doing these things to it if I am to have the privilege as regards you of doing them. Now as we saw, those who accept the Ownership-Has-Origins Thesis have trouble if they try to explain coming to own the formerly unowned by appeal to labor-mixing; those who accept the Jointly-Owned-from-the-Outset Thesis, and who would like to appeal to labor-mixing to explain private ownership, have the prior problem of explaining what could make labor-mixing with the jointly owned permissible in the first place—in the absence of consent (tacit if not explicit) by all the other owners, past, present, and future. (Is their hypothetical consent supposed to suffice?)

This does nevertheless point to one reason why a person might prefer the Jointly-Owned-from-the-Outset Thesis to the Ownership-Has-Origins Thesis. Consider the moon again. Suppose (i) the moon is unowned. Then it is plausible to think that I have a privilege as regards you of going there and making such uses of it as I please. Dig up oil and burn it, break such rocks as I please, do whatever I like, no matter what damage to the moon issues from my doing of it. Of course we cannot conclude that I thereby acquire ownership over the things I use, unless the kind of argument we looked at in the preceding section goes through; and I have argued that it does not. All the same, I infringe no claim of yours in making those uses of the moon's contents. Suppose instead (ii) the moon is owned by all mankind in common. Then it is no more plausible to think I have privileges as regards everyone of damaging the moon's contents than it is to think I have a privilege as regards you of painting our jointly owned house red. But doesn't this give us reason to prefer (ii) to (i)? For who can plausibly suppose I have a privilege as regards everyone of making such uses of the moon as I please?

Still, the Jointly-Owned-from-the-Outset Thesis is not a happy idea. As I said, it is no clearer how private property can have arisen from the jointly owned by all mankind than it is how private property can have arisen from the unowned, and even less clear if labor-mixing is to do the explanatory work. Moreover, it is hard to see what could have made the Jointly-Owned-from-the-Outset Thesis true. An account of the sources of property rights which rests on the theological supposition that God made a gift of the world to all mankind is not likely to be found attractive by many people nowadays; but if God did not create the world, if there is no God, then what could be thought to have made it the case that all mankind in common owned the earth at the outset, and currently own everything that is not now privately owned?

But if we reject the Jointly-Owned-from-the-Outset Thesis, and then accept that (i) the moon is unowned, how are we to avoid the conclusion that I have a privilege as regards everyone of making such uses of the moon as I please? Well, does it really follow from the fact that a thing is unowned that no one has a claim against anyone that he or she not make use of it? Perhaps, in particular, we can accept

that (i) the moon is unowned, while saying that others nevertheless
do have claims against me that I not dig up its oil and burn it, that
I not break such rocks as I please, that I not do whatever damage I
like to it.

But what could these claims of others issue from if the moon is
unowned? There is no problem if I would commit trespass on them,
or do them harm, or cause them non-belief-mediated distress by damaging the moon, for then it would follow by the Means Principle for
Claims that they have claims against me that I not damage the moon.
But what if I would not do these things to them by damaging the
moon? What claims of theirs would I infringe if I proceeded? It may
be true that if I proceed, others will later not have benefits they would
have had if I had not proceeded, and other things being equal, that
makes it wrong for me to proceed. But people do not have *claims*
against a person that the person not do a thing just on the ground
that they would be better off if he or she did not do it. (We do not
even have a claim that our lives be saved, much less a claim that we
be made better off.)

There is a possibility I have not mentioned, however. Consider

> The Limits Thesis: X has a claim against Y that Y not do alpha
> if and only if either
>> (i) X's claim is a pure social claim, or
>> (ii) Y's doing alpha either
>>> (a) itself would be Y's committing trespass on X, or
>>> causing X harm or non-belief-mediated distress, or
>>> (b) is a means by which Y would be committing tres-
>>> pass on X, or causing X harm or non-belief-mediated
>>> distress.

This thesis tells us that others may have a claim against me that I not
damage the moon even if I would commit no trespass and cause no
harm or non-belief-mediated distress in or by doing so: it explicitly
says they do have a claim against me that I not damage the moon *if*
they have a pure social claim that I not do so. That they do is a
possibility we will return to later.

Meanwhile, I will myself suppose that the Jointly-Owned-from-the-
Outset Thesis is false and that the Ownership-Has-Origins Thesis is
true. I will also suppose that if a thing is unowned, then everyone
does have a privilege as regards all others of making use of it, subject
only to the constraints set out in the Limits Thesis.

4. Friends of the ideas we have been looking at think people have, or anyway can acquire, pure natural rights to property. Locke himself thought that people could acquire property rights in the state of nature. That, I suggest, is a mistake. Property rights are less deep than these ideas presuppose.

What makes property? Law. I own the house I now live in. How come? I bought it from someone else who had owned it, the transaction having proceeded in accordance with prevailing law. That is, we live under a set of legal rules according to which if Y meets conditions C, and X does such and such, then X thereby acquires ownership of so and so; and it is because a certain woman met those conditions C, and I did the such and such, that I acquired ownership over the house I now live in.

Is the set of legal rules we live under the most efficient set? Is there an alternative possible set of legal rules that would be better on balance or to the greater good of each? So far as current ownership is concerned, *it does not matter whether there is.* On some views it is perfectly obvious that there is a more efficient possible set of legal rules than the one we live under. Well and good: it is then arguable that we ought to alter our own legal rules to bring them into accord with the more efficient rules. If that alteration of our rules would make me not own the house I now live in, then if we ought to make that alteration in our rules, we ought to make it be the case, among other things, that I do not own the house. But if I am right in thinking that prevailing law made me owner of the house I now live in, then I do now own it.

A proviso is in order, however, for considerations of efficiency are very plausibly thought to enter into the question what exactly a society's legal system *is.* That this is so has been argued by writers with widely different conceptions of the aim of law. Some legal writers think our law ultimately aims at the end of on-balance-good; others think our law ultimately aims at the end of good-to-each, or some other notion of equity. Written law obviously requires interpretation, and both groups have argued that, in case of doubt between possible interpretations of a legal provision, the interpretation should be supplied such that, if the provision is so interpreted, the system as a whole is most efficient relative to the favored end. This does seem plausible: if there is such a thing as the purpose of the legal system, and if that purpose is to bring about such and such a state of affairs, then surely the system's provisions are best interpreted in such a way as to make the system most efficient at bringing that state of affairs about. In particular, then, if a group of people complain of an inefficiency in the legal system under which they live, then that may mean, not that the system is inefficient, but rather that it has been incorrectly interpreted.

The efficiency I refer to here is of course the efficiency of the legal system, and not of any system of natural rights prior to law. It is of interest that those who think we have natural property rights prior to law do address themselves to the efficiency or inefficiency of this or that set of natural property rights prior to law; but this must surely be a confusion. Consider again an example I gave earlier: first labor-mixing with oil sources. I imagined it said that adopting a rule that assigns ownership rights to the first labor-mixer would be efficient in that it would give explorers a good reason to try to come first, and oil resources would therefore be more quickly developed. But it cannot be thought that assigning natural ownership rights in the absence of law would have this effect: the effects would not follow unless those ownership rights were embodied in law. Coming first to an oil source is costly, after all, and it is not likely to seem to a person worth paying those costs unless he or she would not only thereby acquire ownership rights but also would be legally protected in the enjoyment of them.

And it should, I think, be even more obvious that "Adopting legal system L would be efficient" does not yield that we already live under L than it is that "Adopting a set of rules assigning natural rights N would be efficient" does not yield that we already have N.

A number of points call for further discussion.

5. The first point is familiar but worth repeating, namely that ownership is a cluster-right: to own a thing is to have a cluster of claims, privileges, and powers in respect of it, and ownership clusters may differ. If my house is in a historic district and yours is not, then though we each own our houses, you have privileges in respect of yours that I do not have in respect of mine: you have the privilege of painting your house red, whereas I must get permission from the appropriate agency in order to have the privilege of painting my house red. Indeed, you have claims and powers that I lack: you have a claim against others to noninterference with your painting your house red and I do not, you have the power to make a house painter have the privilege of painting your house red and I do not. Which rights are in a particular ownership cluster? Those that the law says are in it. If I buy

a house in a historic district, then I acquire only those rights in respect of its appearance that the statute governing the district says I acquire.

What if I buy a house and then the district is later made a historic district? More generally, the second point we need to attend to is change of law.

The set of legal rules we live under does not contain merely what might be called object-level rules, such as rules that say who acquires what property from whom under this or that condition; it also contains metarules, rules that prescribe procedures for addition of new rules and alteration or deletion of old rules.[3] And among those metarules are rules that prescribe procedures for addition of new metarules and alteration or deletion of old metarules, so that among the metarules in the legal regime we live under are rules governing procedures for amending the procedures by means of which we amend laws.

What this means is that much of what might have appeared to be deprivation of rights by change of law *can* also be described as not a deprivation of rights. Suppose I buy a house in a part of town that is not a historic district. Then a statute is passed that declares that part of town a historic district and imposes a set of constraints on houseowners' activities in respect of the appearance of their houses; and let us suppose that the statute is passed in full accordance with the metarules governing change of law. Have I been deprived of property rights by the statute? For example, the privilege of painting the house red? We can say yes, for we can say that I did have the privilege before passage of the statute, and because of passage of the statute I now lack it. But we can also say no, for we can say that I never did have the privilege, all simply, of painting the house red: I had only the complex privilege of painting-the-house-red-unless-and-until-the-object-level-rules-governing-house-appearance-are-altered-in-accordance-with-the-legal-regime's-metarules.

Which should we say? Saying no, the statute did not deprive me of any rights, might seem preferable for one of the following two reasons. It might be said (i) that if the statute did deprive me of rights then the legislature did me a wrong, for don't you do a person a wrong whenever you deprive him or her of a right? But other things being equal, the legislature did not do me a wrong in passing that statute. (I will return to that "other things being equal" in the following section.) Second, it might be said, more strongly, (ii) that the

3. See H. L. A. Hart, *The Concept of Law* (Oxford: Clarendon Press, 1961).

legislature *cannot* have deprived me of any rights. What I have in mind here is that infringing a right is one thing, and on any view possible; depriving someone of a right—making that person not have the right at all—is quite another, and on some views impossible. The views I have in mind are those according to which one can cease to have a right only if one voluntarily divests oneself of it; and if (as we may suppose) I did not vote for the statute declaring the area a historic district, I did not voluntarily divest myself of the right to paint the house red.

But neither of these two reasons is an obvious truth. Why should we believe (i) that depriving a person of a right is *always* doing the person a wrong? By hypothesis, the statute was passed in accordance with the legal regime's metarules; why should we not therefore say that the statute does deprive me of a right, but—other things being equal—without doing me a wrong? Why should we believe (ii) that one can cease to have a right only if one voluntarily divests oneself of it? It may be *prima facie* plausible to think that one can cease to have rights over First Property only if one voluntarily divests oneself of them, but why should one think this true of rights over Second Property? And isn't that independently implausible, for if it is, as I am suggesting, law that makes property, then how could it fail to be the case that law can also unmake property?

Moreover, there is reason to think it better to say yes, the statute did deprive me of rights, in particular of the privilege of painting my house red. The account of what happened according to which I had the privilege of painting the house red, and then the statute made me cease to have it, just is simpler than the account according to which I had only the complex privilege mentioned above. And that simplicity mirrors the legislature's record, for in fact there was no constraint governing house appearance on the record (nothing that said a house-owner may do such and such unless and until we change the law), and there now is such a constraint on the record.

So I suggest that we say yes, the statute did deprive me of rights, in particular of the privilege of painting my house red. And that it was not merely possible for it to do this, but also that—other things being equal—it did me no wrong in doing so. These are matters we will return to in the following chapter. Meanwhile, however, I think them intuitively very plausible.

Regulations of a variety of other kinds can also be plausibly de-scribed in this way. Suppose that while each widget manufacturer emits a certain amount of smoke, not enough to cause any harm to anyone, they jointly emit a considerable amount of smoke, enough to cause harm to the community at large. One way to deal with this problem is to require them to use a certain screening device in their smokestacks. We can say that widget manufacturers never had the privilege of operating without a screening device, and that what they had was only the complex privilege of so-operating-unless-and-until-the-object-level-rules-governing-procedures-of-operation-are-altered-in-accordance-with-the-legal-regime's-metarules. But it is simpler to say that they did have the privilege of operating without a screening device and that the regulation deprives them of it.

A different way of dealing with this kind of problem is a 'buyout': the legislature *could* choose to pay the manufacturers to install screening devices in their smokestacks. If the legislature chooses not merely to pay the manufacturers, but to pay them whatever price they ask, then the legislature does not deprive the manufacturers of any right at all in dealing with the problem in this way. (On the assumption that the manufacturers are willing to sell at some price or other.) However, the probability that any sane legislature would choose to pay whatever price the manufacturers ask is vanishingly small, so what is paid is better seen as compensation for the deprivation of the right rather than a buying of the right.

Regulation is deprivation of rights without compensation, and a society's metarules might themselves include constraints on the legislature's use of that device: the metarules might prescribe, everywhere or in some selected areas, that the legislature compensate for the deprivation. Our legal regime, for example, characterizes some possible legislative deprivations of property rights as 'takings', for which compensation must be paid.[4] One kind of taking under our regime is where the legislature would be making the owner cease to have rights that are centrally of interest to owners of property of that kind, rights buyers of that kind of property buy it precisely in order to acquire. A more extreme kind is that in which the legislature would be depriving the owner of all rights over the property, literally taking the property away, as where the legislature takes the property by eminent domain. Compensation must be paid in these cases under our legal regime's metarules, but since the metarules do not require

---

4. The eminent-domain (or 'takings') clause of the U.S. Constitution says: "nor shall private property be taken for public use without just compensation".

payment of whatever price the owner asks, what goes on *is* deprivation of rights.[5] I am at liberty to charge what I like to one who wants me to cease to own my typewriter; not so for my house, if the legislature decides to build a highway through it.

If money is thought of as property, then the imposition of a new tax, or even the increase in the rate of an old tax, is a deprivation of rights too. But taxation is presumably best seen as a matter of duties rather than rights. When I bought my house I acquired duties as well as rights, and in particular I acquired the duty to pay real-estate taxes on it; I could not under our law have acquired ownership rights over the house without acquiring that duty along with them. What if I live in a state that up to year 2000 imposes no real-estate tax and then adopts one? I could not under our law have acquired ownership rights over the house without being subject to imposition of the duty to pay taxes if and when the object-level rules governing real estate are altered in such a way as to require payment of them.

Other things being equal, none of these steps in which government deprives one of property rights, or attaches duties to property ownership, is a wrong to those affected, if the step is taken in accordance with the legal system's metarules. But of course other things may not be equal.

6. Law makes—and unmakes—property: and mightn't it do so unjustly? Suppose the legislature decides to impose a special additional real-estate tax on land owned by Jews. Suppose the legislature chooses to run its projected new highway through my house for no better reason than that doing so will increase the value of property owned by the legislators. We will certainly feel under pressure to interpret

5. Richard A. Epstein has argued that all *morally* acceptable deprivations of property rights by government action are takings, for which compensation is therefore owed, though he says that the compensation may be indirect. (What he has in mind by indirect compensation is that a property owner might be compensated by way of the benefits of community action in providing defense against aggression from abroad, police protection against aggression from within, and so on.) His argument goes through only if there are natural rights to property. He argues in addition for the different conclusion that under our legal regime all *legally* acceptable deprivations of property rights by government action are takings, for which compensation is therefore owed, though the compensation may be indirect. This conclusion about our law looks to me very implausible, but I am not competent to assess it. See his *Takings* (Cambridge: Harvard University Press, 1985).

the legal system's metarules in such a way as to make these actions be violations of them, and in the case of our society, or any other at least moderately just society, we would surely be right in so interpreting them. But what of a society in which, with the best will in the world, there is no metarule we can plausibly interpret as violated by such legislative actions? Consider an extreme example, a society whose legal rules really do—on any plausible interpretation of them—assign ownership of everything to a very few people, all the others being assigned ownership of nothing at all in the way of Second Property, not even the clothes they wear.

I think it is clear enough that and why we will feel inclined to say that the rich in this society do not really own the things assigned to them by the society's legal rules: if the rich really do own those things, then the rich have rights in respect of them. In particular, the rich have claims in respect of them. Not merely legal claims, but (all simply) claims, for to say that law makes property is not merely to say that law makes legal rights to property, it is to say that law makes property rights. But didn't we agree that having a claim is having a certain moral status? Didn't we agree that for X to have a claim against Y is for Y's behavior to be constrained in certain ways?—in particular, that other things being equal, Y ought to accord X what X has a claim to? But it cannot at all plausibly be thought that morality requires the poor of that society to accede to so unjust a distribution of goods.

On the other hand, we *can* say that the rich in that society do not really own those things without resting our case on an appeal to a system of natural property rights independent of law. I suggest that the gravamen of the charge against that society is not that its legal system assigns rights to property that are out of accord with the system of property rights generated by natural law, for (I have suggested) there is no such thing. I suggest that the gravamen of the charge against that society is a failing we can express in two different ways. We can say (i) the society has no legal system at all, but merely a set of rules backed by force. Or we can say (ii) in that the society has a set of rules backed by force, it does have a legal system, but one lacking in legitimacy. Which of these you will prefer depends on the extent of your leanings toward legal positivism: strict legal positivists would plainly prefer (ii) to (i). We should say one or the other, however, since by hypothesis the rich in that society are few and have everything, whereas the poor are many and have nothing, and the set of rules from which that distribution flows are such as the poor cannot be thought to have freely consented to, on any plausible construal of the kind and nature of the consent required to make a set of rules have legitimacy as law for a society. Morality no more requires the poor in that society to accede to the distribution of goods current in their society than it requires the citizens of a conquered country to accede to the redistribution of goods imposed by the victors.

I will leave open (as I did in Chapter 2) what we should think of positivistic accounts of law. But in light of their availability, I should have said, not simply that law makes property, but rather that a legitimate legal system makes property. Antipositivists will regard that phrase as a pleonasm.

7. Let us go back to the unowned. It should really be clear that there are unowned things under our law. You buy a chocolate bar and eagerly tear off the foil. Then you have a shock: "Almonds, hell!" you think, and you throw the thing in the nearest trash bin. I then come along and see it; I think "Almonds, heaven!" and remove the thing from the trash bin and eat it. During its residence in the trash bin, that chocolate bar was unowned under our law.

Does anybody think the chocolate bar was owned by all mankind in common during that time? I hope not. Certainly no one had a claim against me that I not remove it from the trash bin; I had a privilege as regards everyone of doing so. So did everyone else have that privilege, but I got there first, and under our law, first labor-mixings with abandoned chocolate bars make property.

We might have lived under a legal system according to which that was not so. We might have had a rule according to which abandoned chocolate bars, perhaps even abandoned things generally, are the property of the state. We might have had a rule according to which abandonment has no legal effect, so that a person who abandons a thing still is owner of it. There are any number of possibilities. But, no doubt for good reasons, our legal system does not incorporate them.

What are we to say about the moon? Isn't it unowned? And do I therefore have a privilege as regards everyone of going there and doing as I please, whatever damage I may cause to the moon's contents?

Moreover, if the moon is unowned, why can't I acquire ownership over it? I can acquire ownership over an unowned chocolate bar; why not over an unowned moon?

The question that needs an answer is whether there is any legal system that is *sovereign* over the moon. If there is, then the question whether I have a privilege of going there and making use of its contents, and the further question whether I can thereby, or in some other way, become owner of it, are to be answered by appeal to it.

That notion 'sovereignty over a territory' is crucial to the account of property rights I have been offering here, for not just any legal system can make just anything *be* property, even if the rules of the system have legitimacy as law for the members of the society governed by it. Suppose our club, which has its own system of laws, decides to acquire certain parts of Manhattan. We think it would be too expensive to buy them, so we choose the cheaper route: we unanimously vote for certain additions to our legal system, namely that henceforth A owns Central Park, B owns Madison Avenue, C owns Broadway, and so on. Do we now own those parts of Manhattan?

There are two ways of describing what goes wrong here. It could be said (i) that our club did not acquire ownership over those parts of Manhattan because they are already owned. By whom? If there is an answer to that question, it would have to be very complex. One can't after all reply that the residents of Manhattan own Manhattan: for example, they can't sell Central Park to Japan or to Donald Trump. (Or so, at least, I assume.) Moreover, we would also be owed an answer to the question how the owners of Manhattan (whoever exactly they may be, whether residents of New York City or New York State or Americans generally) came to own it. (Remember the Ownership-Has-Origins Thesis.) I should imagine therefore that offering description (i) would in the end require making appeal to some notion other than that of ownership—the very notion that is appealed to if it is instead said (ii) that our club did not acquire ownership over those parts of Manhattan since some other legal system than our club's is sovereign over Manhattan. Which? Presumably the complex legal system that includes New York city, state, and federal law.

For a particular legal system to be sovereign over a territory is for that legal system to be the law of the territory, governing not merely the behavior of people in it, including those who merely visit or pass through it, but also what uses can be made of, and what ownership rights can be acquired over, the very stuff of the territory, including the land itself and whatever is under or on it. What makes a legal system L be the law of a certain territory? Here again there are a number of different possible answers, more or less positivistic. My own leanings here are relatively positivistic: for my part, what is necessary and sufficient is that the society whose legal system L is be in settled control over the territory. *Settled* control. Suppose a society S moves into a territory that is not at the time under the control of any other people, and S comes to have control over it. Is S in settled control over it? Well, what happens next? Is S driven out by another society? Then we may say that S never was in settled control over the territory (and its law never was the law of the territory). But we may prefer to say that S was for a time in settled control of the territory. Which we will prefer to say depends on such matters as how long S was in control over the territory, how rich the life S had developed on it, how deeply involved with it S's culture had been, and so on.

Others may prefer a less positivistic account of the matter, focusing on the fact that sovereignty over a territory had better be sufficient for a second kind of legitimacy. What I have in mind is this. I said in the preceding section that a set of rules does not have legitimacy as law for a society, governing the behavior of the members vis-à-vis each other, unless the rules were consented to by the members, on some plausible construal of the kind and nature of the consent required. Suppose a set of rules does have legitimacy as law for a society. There remains the question whether that society's law has legitimacy as law for the territory the society lives on, governing the behavior of the society vis-à-vis other societies that might like to possess the territory—subsocieties (such as our club) or, more important, other states currently established elsewhere. My own view, as I said, is that the law of a society S does have that second kind of legitimacy as law for a territory if S is in settled control over the territory; others may think something further is required, some analogue among nations of the consent by individuals required to secure legitimacy of the first kind. I leave this open.

To return to the moon. Is it unowned? Of course. (It is even clearer that the moon is unowned than that Central Park is unowned. Contrast our town dump, which is straightforwardly owned by the town.) But this is compatible with there being a legal system sovereign over the moon. Is there such a legal system? No, on my view, since no society is in settled control over the moon, not even the supersociety that consists of the nations on earth. (Contrast the floor of the oceans, which arguably the nations are in settled control over.) On my view, then, I really do have a privilege of doing as I please on the moon—subject, of course, to the constraint that I not thereby commit trespass on others or cause them harm or non-belief-mediated distress—for there being no legal system sovereign over the moon means that others have no pure social claim against me that I not proceed, and as the Limits Thesis therefore tells us, others have no claim at all against me that I not proceed. But my having those privileges does not mean I can come to own the moon or any of its contents. There being no legal system sovereign over the moon means that I have privileges in respect of the moon; by the same token it also means that I cannot come to own the moon, since it means that there is no legal system under which I could come to own it. (Though there might in future be one.)

Others would give a different answer to the question whether there is any legal system that is sovereign over the moon. Some, for example, would say that existing public international common law is sovereign over the moon. On such views, while the moon is unowned, I nevertheless have only such privileges of action on the moon as that law assigns me, the legal system itself being what gives others pure social claims, and therefore claims, against me. (Here is the possibility I mentioned at the end of section 3 above. Central Park is surely unowned too, but I have only such privileges of action there as prevailing law assigns me.) By the same token, however, there being a legal system sovereign over the moon means that acquiring ownership rights over it is possible—if the legal system assigns ownership rights over it to those who do this or that.

I leave open whether there is a legal system that is sovereign over the moon. My concern throughout has been only to make it seem plausible to think that it is law, and not nature, that makes property.

Chapter 14

Ceasing To Have a Right

1. We can make ourselves cease to have rights. Can anyone or anything other than ourselves make us cease to have rights? I drew attention in the preceding chapter to the idea some people have—typically they are libertarians—that it is not possible to take a right away from a person; on that view, only right holders themselves can make themselves cease to have rights. Let us call this the Libertarian Thesis. We will want to ask whether it is true.

2. But let us look first at some of the ways in which right holders can make themselves cease to have rights. Word-givings can be thought of as one way in which right holders do this, for the outcome of a word-giving is that the word-receiver has acquired a claim, and thus that the word-giver has ceased to have a privilege. The privilege no longer possessed may be social: you might have given me a (social) privilege of eating your salad, which I then cease to have when I give you my word that I will not eat it. Alternatively, the privilege no longer possessed may be natural: I have the (natural) privilege of singing the *Marseillaise* today, which I then cease to have when I give you my word that I will not sing it.

   A second way in which right holders can be thought of as making themselves cease to have rights is consent. The outcome of consent is that the consent-receiver has acquired a privilege, and thus that the consent-giver has ceased to have a claim. (This is actually only one of the two kinds of consent; I will ignore the second kind here and return to it in the next section.) And here similarly, the claim no longer had may be either social or natural. When I consent to your eating my salad, I cease to have a social claim; when I consent to your pinching my nose, I cease to have a natural claim.

Now it is a very attractive idea that consent is just the obverse of word-giving. They are at a minimum analogous. In word-giving one gives one's word that a certain proposition is true: if I assert to you the words "I will eat a banana" I give you my word that the proposition that I will eat a banana is true. In consent one consents to a person's letting a certain proposition be true: if I assert to you the words "You may pinch my nose" I consent to your letting the proposition that you will pinch my nose be true.

Again, word-giving is a more or less solemn affair: the word-giver must not be speaking idly, but must really be inviting reliance. Consent is also a more or less solemn affair: the consent-giver also must not be speaking idly, but must really be giving permission.

But now we may be struck by a difference. Uptake on the part of the word-receiver is required for a completed word-giving, so word-givers do not strictly speaking make themselves cease to have privileges. What a word-giver A does is only to give the word-receiver B a power to make A cease to have the privilege; A does not, by himself, make A cease to have the privilege—A merely so alters the world that uptake on B's part makes A cease to have the privilege. Is uptake required for a consent-giving? That certainly seems *prima facie* dubious. Suppose I say to you in my coy way "You may stroke my knee any time you like". You think "Who on earth wants to stroke her knee?" Perhaps (i) out of mere courtesy you say "That's kind of you, thank you very much". Then you have accepted my offer of the privilege, and we can think of your doing so as like uptake in the case of a word-giving; on any view, you now have the privilege of stroking my knee any time you like. Suppose instead (ii) you simply stare and say nothing at all, or (iii) you say "I can't think why you'd suppose I want to!" Then there is nothing you do that is like uptake in the case of a word-giving. But haven't I all the same given you the privilege of stroking my knee any time you like? We could say yes, and therefore that there is at least this difference between word-giving and consent-giving: the former requires uptake whereas the latter does not. But it is arguable, I think, that this is not so. For suppose you responded to my offer of the privilege as in (ii) or (iii). And suppose it later sweeps over you that it would pay you to stroke my knee. Mightn't I object to your doing so on the ground that although I offered the privilege, you did not accept it and therefore do not now have it? I think it a plausible idea that I can make this objection and, more generally, that where A says "You may", what A does is merely to offer a privilege, and that B does not acquire the privilege unless he accepts the offer—though no doubt acceptance of an offer of a privilege can be as informal as you like. Compare my saying to Bloggs "It's yours" of my farm in Indiana. If there is no uptake on Bloggs' part, ownership of the farm does not transfer from me to him, and in particular Bloggs acquires no privileges of use of the farm (I am still free to offer the farm to someone else or to no one)—though no doubt acceptance of an offer of a bit of property can be as informal as you like.

If we accept this idea, then we must say that in giving consent, as in giving one's word, *what* one gives is strictly speaking only a power, it being the ensuing uptake that makes the right formerly had no longer be had. If we reject the idea, if we say that, although word-givers themselves give only powers, consent-givers themselves give privileges, then we must say that consent is in this respect unlike word-giving. Despite a preference for accepting the idea, I leave open whether we should. I will say that a word-giver B gives a word-receiver A a claim, though strictly speaking B gives A only a power to make himself have the claim against B; I will say that a consent-giver B gives a consent-receiver A a privilege, leaving open whether strictly speaking B gives A only a power to make himself have the privilege as regards B.

The important similarity between consent and word-giving, however, lies in their moral import. The moral import of a word-giving is expressed in

> The Word-Giving Thesis: If Y gives X his or her word that a certain proposition is true, then X thereby acquires a claim against Y to its being true.

Similarly, the moral import of a consent-giving is expressed in

> The Consent-Giving Thesis: If Y consents to X's letting a certain proposition be true, then X thereby acquires a privilege as regards Y of letting it be true.

And there is no more reason to think that a background of social understandings is required if consent is to be given than there is to think that a background of social understandings is required if a word is to be given. (Also no less reason to think this. It is puzzling that, although many philosophers say that social practices are required if a word-giving is to give a claim, they do not also say that social practices are required if a consent-giving is to give a privilege—it seems to be widely thought that word-giving is fundamentally a social matter, whereas consent is entirely a private matter, brought off by two people in their private relations with each other. This *is* puzzling, in light of the analogies we can now see between these acts.)

There were three objections to the Word-Giving Thesis that we looked at in sections 8, 9, and 10 of Chapter 12; let us look at analogous objections to the Consent-Giving Thesis.

In the first place (section 8), there was the objection to the Word-Giving Thesis that a word-giving may have its source in coercion or fraud, and if it does, then it does not give a claim. (It is excessively respectful of what goes on in a word-giving to suppose such a word-giving gives a claim.) So also may a consent-giving have its source in coercion or fraud, as where I elicit your consent to my doing a thing by holding a gun to your head or by lying to you about the condition of your children's health, and if it does, it does not give a privilege. (It is excessively respectful of what goes on in a consent-giving to suppose such a consent-giving gives a privilege.) I suggested that we should say in the case of word-givings: word-givings under coercion or fraud are special cases of word-giving under diminished eligible alternatives or diminished information, and word-givings that have their source in those conditions give a claim if and only if it is *not* the case that the word-receiver is at fault for the condition. It is equally plausible to say that consent-givings that have their source in conditions of diminished eligible alternatives or diminished information give a privilege if and only if it is *not* the case that the consent-receiver is at fault for the condition. Where the condition is due to fault in the word-receiver or consent-receiver, we can think of the claim or privilege as stillborn, forfeit from conception.

Second (section 9), there was the objection to the Word-Giving Thesis that it allows that a word-giving may give to the word-receiver a claim to the word-giver's doing something moral impermissible. Similarly, the Consent-Giving Thesis allows that a consent-giving may give to the consent-receiver a privilege of doing something morally impermissible. I said it is implausible to say that a word-giver who gives his or her word to do something morally impermissible does everywhere give a claim, and that we should say he or she does give a claim if and only if the word-receiver is *not* at fault for accepting the offer of the word. Perhaps a difference between word-giving and consent-giving emerges here, for it is not implausible to say that a consent-giver who gives consent to the consent-receiver's doing something morally impermissible does everywhere give a privilege. ("For my part", I say to you, "you're free to assassinate the President". Don't I thereby give you a privilege, anyway as regards *me*, of doing so?) But perhaps not. Perhaps the consent-giver gives the privilege only if the consent-receiver is *not* at fault for accepting the offer of the consent. Taking this line would, of course, presuppose a willingness to accept the idea that completed consent, like completed word-giving, requires uptake in the consent-receiver.

Third (section 10), there was the objection to the Word-Giving Thesis that accepting it requires us to suppose that a claim is given by a word-giver even if the word-receiver does not care whether the word is kept, and therefore does not rely on its being kept. This may well seem puzzling. A difference between word-giving and consent-giving really does emerge here, for it is not at all puzzling that a consent-giver gives a privilege even if the consent-receiver does not care to do what the consent-giver consents to his or her doing. (If I say to you "You may stroke my knee any time you like" and you reply "That's kind of you, thank you very much", then on any view you now have the privilege of stroking my knee, even if you said what you said out of mere courtesy and have not now, and never will have, any desire to exercise this privilege.) Securing the attractive symmetry between word-giving and consent-giving was among my reasons for suggesting that we should say, after all, that the word-giver does give a claim even if the word-receiver does not care, and therefore does not rely.

3. There are acts by which we give both privileges and claims, and they can be seen as a complex of consent-giving and word-giving. For example, there is giving permission. As I suggested in Chapter 1, giving permission is typically giving both privileges and claims. When Y says to X of Y's salad "Feel free to eat it", Y is typically consenting to X's eating it, and thus giving X the privilege of eating it, *and also* giving X his or her word not to interfere with X's eating of it, and thus giving X a claim against Y to noninterference with X's eating of it.

What is more interesting is that there is a second kind of consent, by which one gives rights of a kind other than privileges: what I have in mind is the consent by which one gives powers. Well, as we saw in the preceding section, it can be said that consent of the kind we were looking at there is strictly speaking itself just the giving of a power. Whether or not we accept that idea, there is a second kind of consent that is on any view the giving of powers—it may even include the giving of large-scale powers and metapowers. If Y says to X of Y's salad "I leave it to you to dispose of it as you like", Y gives X the power of altering the rights of others, for among the many things X is now able to do is to give the salad to Z: X can now so change the world that uptake on Z's part will make Z owner of the salad. Perhaps I should have said powers as well as privileges, for if Y does say this to X, then Y thereby gives X powers *and also* the privileges of exercising them. But it is the fact that one who says such things gives powers that is of particular interest; and I think one's doing this would very naturally be called consent.

In consent of the kind we looked at in the preceding section, one gives privileges and thus makes oneself cease to have claims; in consent of this second kind, one gives powers and thus makes oneself cease to have immunities. So both kinds of consent are ways in which one can make oneself cease to have rights. I should imagine also that the same kinds of constraints hold for both kinds of consent, as, for example, that consent of either kind gives no rights at all if elicited by coercion or fraud.

It is the very naturalness of calling the giving of powers "consent" that explains the central role that many political theorists assign to consent in their accounts of what makes for legitimacy in government. Some actions by a legitimate government deprive the governed of rights, and a government's actions can do this only if the government has powers to alter the rights of the governed. How could government have acquired those powers? Consent of the governed, we say, and only consent of the governed. I said in Chapter 11 that at the heart of the right to liberty are our rights to a voice in what action will be taken by government, in who shall govern, indeed in what form of government we will be governed by; it is very plausible to suppose that what we mean in ascribing such rights to ourselves is that government lacks the power to make alterations in our rights unless certain conditions were met—in particular, that we had a voice in the process that issued in the government action that (putatively) alters our rights. On a very natural way of construing the matter, the requirement of having had that voice just consists in the requirement of consent.

Let us look a little more closely at government action that deprives the governed of rights.

4. Some government action does deprive of rights. I suggested in the preceding chapter that we should take the allocation of property rights as an example: it is simplest and most plausible to suppose that government action can and often does take property rights away from the property owner.

Property rights are social rights, however. Can government action take natural rights away from the right holder? Government action can remove the social sources of a natural right; can government action remove a natural right altogether? Surely yes.

Consider behavior that causes offense. Offense is an instance of belief-mediated distress, and therefore, as I argued in Chapter 10, we have no claim to not be caused it in the absence of private commitments and law. So let us suppose that our society has no law prohibiting offense-causing behavior, and let us for simplicity suppose that no one has made anyone any private commitment not to engage in it. Things go well for a time (everybody behaves with great concern for the feelings of others); then things start to not go well—some people begin to behave in ways that greatly offend others. Suppose, for example, that some young people take it into their heads to engage in sexual relations in public places. (If that would not cause you offense, feel free to choose another example.[1]) By hypothesis, there is no law against doing so, and no private commitments stand in the way. The young people therefore have a privilege, a natural privilege, of acting as they do. But the rest of us feel offended, angry, morally indignant, resentful at what we see as a form of bullying on their part, what you will, and we therefore approach our legislature with a request that their behavior be made illegal. There being many of us and few of them, our legislature responds as we wish it to. Now there is a law prohibiting the behavior. Since there formerly was no law against engaging in sexual relations in public places, the young people then had a legal privilege of doing so; there now being a law, they now lack a legal privilege of doing so. That much is clear. Moreover, the young people formerly had (all simply) a privilege of engaging in sexual relations in public places. That much is also clear. Do they

1. For a dazzling list of possibilities, see Joel Feinberg, *Offense to Others,* vol. 2 of *The Moral Limits of the Criminal Law,* ch. 7.

now lack not merely a legal privilege of doing so, but also (all simply) a privilege of doing so? Legal privileges, after all, are not the same as privileges,[2] so saying they now lack the legal privilege is not the same as saying they lack the privilege. Well, *did* the legislative action deprive them of the privilege by depriving them of the legal privilege? If so, then the legislature made them cease to have a natural right.

It is trivially true to say: the lawmaker deprived them of the privilege by depriving them of the legal privilege if and only if the lawmaker had the power to do so. Did the lawmaker have that power? Only if it was legitimately lawmaker for our society.

It is arguable that something more is required, namely that the deprivation of the legal privilege was morally permissible. Let us suppose that our legislature is legitimately lawmaker for our society. Then the first condition I mentioned is met. I should think we may suppose also that the second condition is met too, for it seems to have been permissible for our legislature to deprive of the legal privilege of engaging in sexual relations in public places. It does seem right to think, then, that the legislature did have the power to deprive of the privilege by depriving of the legal privilege, and did do exactly that.

But that might very well not seem to be the case for other examples. Suppose that no blacks and whites in our society have ever walked hand in hand in public because they never wished to. Now some begin to wish to. That gives offense to many people: they feel offended, angry, morally indignant, resentful at what they see as a form of bullying by blacks and whites, what you will, and they approach our legislature with a request that the behavior be made illegal. There being many of them and few of the rest of us, our legislature responds as they wish it to. Now there is a law prohibiting the behavior. Was it permissible for our legislature to pass that law? I am sure that you and I and our friends would say that the legislature ought not have passed it. I am myself inclined to conclude that our legislature did not deprive of the privilege by depriving of the legal privilege: the concept 'privilege', after all, is a moral concept and, morally speaking, I should think, blacks and whites are at liberty to walk hand and hand in public, despite the fact that the law now makes it illegal for them to do so. If so, then the lawmaker's having the power to deprive of a privilege by depriving of a legal privilege requires more than

---

2. Extreme antipositivism apart. I ignore that view of law here.

merely legitimacy as lawmaker: it requires in addition that the deprivation of the legal privilege is a morally permissible act.

Or should it be said that the fact that our legislature acted impermissibly in depriving blacks and whites of their legal privilege of walking hand and hand in public shows that the legislature was not really, fully, the legitimate lawmaker for our society? I think this a very dubious idea,[3] but there is no need for us to decide the matter. If we adopt

> The Government Power Principle for Natural Privileges: the lawmaker has the power to deprive of the natural privilege of doing alpha by depriving of the legal privilege of doing alpha if and only if
>> (i) the lawmaker is legitimately the lawmaker of the society, and
>> (ii) the lawmaker acts permissibly in depriving of the legal privilege,

then we can just leave open whether if condition (i) is met so also is (ii)—as also whether if condition (ii) is met so also is (i).

A similar principle for government power to deprive of natural claims is equally plausible. So also for similar principles for government power to deprive of social privileges and claims.

But I should stress that these ideas are plausible only if we allow that the 'permissibility requirement' in clause (ii) can be met even if the choice of law made by the legislature is not the best choice it could have made. Perhaps it would have been better for the legislature to tailor its deprivation of the legal privilege of engaging in sexual relations in public places more narrowly—as it might be, exempting Central Park between midnight and dawn. Let us suppose that would have been better. The legislature did not tailor its deprivation of the legal privilege in this way, and I should think nevertheless did deprive of the privilege by depriving of the legal privilege: the young not only now lack a legal privilege, they now lack a privilege of engaging in sexual relations in Central Park between midnight and dawn. This is compatible with the Government Power Principle for Natural Privileges only if we can suppose that the lawmaker's failure to tailor its law more narrowly was permissible. But surely this failure was not

---

3. It is the analogue for legitimacy in government of extreme antipositivism in law.

impermissible. The fact that a better alternative was available does not make the choice actually made impermissible.

Gross injustices in lawmaking are one thing, failures to reach the best are quite another. Consider property rights again. As I said in the preceding chapter, a government makes property rights (as opposed to merely making legal property rights) only if it is itself the legitimate government of the society over which it governs; and a government that makes grossly unjust property law is not plausibly viewable as legitimate. What of unjust property law that is less than grossly unjust? These are matters of degree. In the case of some degrees of injustice, we may feel inclined to say that passage of the law does show that the lawmaker is not legitimate, even if the law is not *grossly* unjust; in the case of lesser degrees of injustice, we may feel inclined to say that, although the lawmaker is legitimate, passage of the law was impermissible. But a mere failure to reach the best does not mean the choice was impermissible, and so does generate property rights in generating legal property rights. Under our law, I have the legal right to arrange for my house to pass at my death to my cat, and I think I have (all simply) a right to do so. Perhaps a system of property law like ours except in not allowing one to will anything to an animal would be better than ours is; let us suppose that is so. It does not follow that I lack the right—because it does not follow that our lawmaker acted impermissibly in giving me that legal right.

I said in the preceding chapter that this much can be conceded to friends of RULE UTILITARIANISM and CONTRACTUALISM: if adopting a set of rules governing property rights would be efficient (to the on-balance good of all, or to the greatest good of each, or whatever your favorite end), then it is arguable that we ought to adopt them. But two things need to be noticed. In the first place, the fact that a choice of law was not the most efficient does not by itself make the choice have been impermissible. There are other things relevant to a choice of law than the efficiency of adopting it. Second, that its having been permissible at an earlier time to make a choice of law is compatible with its now being the case that we ought to alter it. I don't say that we ought to change our law so as to deprive of the legal right to will one's house to one's cat; but even if we ought to do so, that is compatible with its having been permissible for the lawmaker to give that legal right.

I hope it will not be thought that I underestimate the difficulties that confront one who tries to supply a general account of the conditions under which it is permissible for a legislature to deprive of legal rights; fortunately (because the issues are so hard to see through[4]) it is not necessary for our purposes that we arrive at a general account of this matter. What concerns us here is only the fact that permissible legislative deprivation of legal rights does in fact deprive of rights, whatever precisely it may be that makes legislative deprivation of legal rights permissible. My two examples have been legislative deprivations of legal rights that cause deprivations of property rights, and legislative deprivations of legal rights that cause deprivations of natural rights to engage in certain kinds of offense-causing behavior; among other examples of legislative deprivations of legal rights that cause deprivations of rights are some paternalistically motivated legislative deprivations of legal rights and some legislative deprivations of legal rights that issue from the need to decide on a convention, such as where what needs deciding is the side of the road people should be permitted to drive on.

In light of all this, what is to be said about the Libertarian Thesis, which, it will be remembered, says that only right holders themselves can cause themselves to cease to have rights?

Friends of that thesis might, of course, simply deny that government action can deprive of rights. Perhaps an anarchist is by definition one who denies this. But can it plausibly be thought that *no* government action deprives of rights? Consider adopting a rule governing the side of the road people are to drive on. Should we say that the English *really* have a right to drive on either side, though a legal right only to drive on the left? That Americans *really* have a right to drive on either side, though a legal right only to drive on the right?

The better option for friends of the Libertarian Thesis is to appeal to that second kind of consent we looked at in the preceding section. If a lawmaker's power to deprive of rights rests on its being legitimately lawmaker, and if its being legitimately lawmaker rests on consent, then by transitivity the lawmaker's power rests on consent, the governed themselves having given the lawmaker its powers. And it could then be said that where a lawmaker does deprive of rights, then—ultimately—the governed themselves are depriving themselves of rights; and the Libertarian Thesis therefore remains a truth in face

4. A splendid account of the moral constraints on making conduct a crime appears in the four volumes of Feinberg's *The Moral Limits of the Criminal Law*. A caveat, however: Feinberg thinks the realm of rights is larger than I have said it is.

of government action that deprives of rights. This is in fact a very common idea in libertarian writings.

It is, quite generally, an attractive idea. As I said, the attractiveness of the idea that consent is what makes a lawmaker legitimate issues from the fact that the lawmaker can deprive of rights, for how could a lawmaker have acquired that power if not by having been given it by the governed? Hobbes thought that the natural state of mankind is one in which everyone has privileges as regards everyone else: thus in Hobbes' state of nature, no action on the part of Y infringes any claim of X's. That view seems implausible to us to the extent that we think people have natural claims, such as the claim to not be caused harm. It seems to us very much more plausible to think that the natural state of mankind is one in which everyone has immunities against everyone else: thus in what we take to be a more plausible conception of the state of nature, no action on the part of Y deprives X of any right. But if the natural state of mankind is one of immunities, then how else could a legitimate government arise than by a process of the kind of consent-giving that consists in giving powers?

The deep, and I hasten to say very familiar, difficulty for this idea is whether consent can play the role it is asked to play here. There certainly is such a thing as the giving of powers, and it is natural to call it consent. If Y says to X of Y's salad "I leave it to you to dispose of it as you like", Y gives X the power of altering the rights of others, for among the many things X is now able to do is to give the salad to Z. Again, if Y says to X "I hereby give you the power to act for me at next week's auction", Y gives X the power of altering the rights of others, in particular of altering Y's rights, for X is now empowered to commit Y to pay for such goods as X chooses to bid for. Is it to be supposed we have each of us explicitly given government powers to alter our rights? I cannot myself remember having done so.

Consent of the first kind we looked at, which consists in the giving of privileges, can be tacit as well as explicit. If you look questioningly at me as you get ready to pick one of my roses, and I see you and do not say no, it is plausible to think I have tacitly consented to your picking the rose and thereby (tacitly) given you the privilege of picking it. Can the consent that consists in the giving of powers be tacit as well as explicit? Perhaps. But the idea that it is tacit consent that gives government powers to deprive of rights is not obviously acceptable. (Can a man's remaining in a country constitute the required tacit consent? It depends on why he remains.)

Many contemporary political theorists who think the difficulty of locating actual consent (even actual tacit consent) to government appeal instead to hypothetical consent, thereby displaying the strength in us of the feeling that it is only by consent that we can cease to be immune to deprivations of rights. But as I suggested in Chapter 7, what does the moral work in appeals to a person's hypothetical consent to a thing—a course of action, a form of government, what you will—is not that the person would consent to it, but rather whatever it is about the thing that makes it worthy of consent by the person. Thus appeals to hypothetical consent to a government to justify its legitimacy are really appeals to the goodness of that government for the governed. But we will find the fact (supposing it a fact) that a particular government is good for the governed insufficient to make it legitimately their government to the extent that we feel, as most of us do feel, that it is only by consent that we can cease to be immune to deprivations of rights. (Mightn't a usurper impose a better government on a people than the one they had formerly been subject to? Would its being the case that the new government is good for them itself make it legitimately their government?)

To some extent this consideration turns up in the case of appeals to actual consent as well as in appeals to hypothetical consent. I said that if you look questioningly at me as you get ready to pick one of my roses, and I see you and do not say no, it is plausible to think I have tacitly consented to your picking the rose and thereby (tacitly) given you the privilege of picking it. But we have to remember that it may well be that I have not given the privilege. To give the privilege, my refraining from saying no has to have a certain kind of source. If I refrained from saying no because you had just said "DON'T SAY NO OR I'LL BREAK YOUR LEGS!" then my refraining from saying no did not give a privilege. Similarly for explicit consent: explicit consent that issues from coercion also gives no privilege. And it would certainly be good reason to think X's consent had not really given Y a power if Y's getting that power would be bad for X. But *only* good reason, for after all X just might want what is in one or another way bad for himself or herself.

These questions lie at the heart of political theory and call for much closer attention than I can give them here. Our concern is the ways in which people can come to lack rights they formerly had. People can divest themselves of rights in several ways. In the first place they can give their word, which is giving a claim and thus divesting oneself of a privilege, and (its obverse) they can give consent of the kind which is giving a privilege and thus divesting oneself of a claim. In the second place, they can give consent of the kind which is giving a power and thus divesting oneself of an immunity. (A love of symmetry might incline us to ask whether there isn't also such a phenomenon as giving an immunity and thus divesting oneself of a power; the answer surely is yes, and it seems to be natural enough to call this phenomenon too a kind of consent.) We have also seen one way in which people can be made by others to lack rights they had formerly had, namely government action. Let us leave open the question whether when government action deprives of rights what has happened is that the governed themselves have, by transitivity, divested themselves of the rights. It seems to me intuitively right to think that consent in some form must be understood to be the source of government power to deprive of rights, but I do not offer an account of what form—much less of whether that consent can be thought of as transitive. I thus leave open whether deprivation of rights by government constitutes a fatal objection to the Libertarian Thesis.

Let us instead attend to some other ways by which people can divest themselves of rights.

5. Consider waiving a right, for example. By waiver, we can divest ourselves of a claim, a privilege, a power, or an immunity.

More interesting still is forfeiting a right. This category of rights divestiture overlaps waiver, for some waivings of rights might as well be called forfeitings of rights. We can waive a right by an act intended to do exactly that; but we can also waive a right by just 'letting it lie' and in that case might as well be said to have forfeited the right.

It is useful to take note of the possibility of forfeiting a right by just 'letting it lie' because this keeps before our minds the fact that there can be forfeiting of rights without fault. If the prize in the lottery is the privilege of dining on an evening of my choice with the Vice-President, I may simply make no choice, I may forfeit the privilege, and without fault.

Despite the possibility of forfeit without fault, however, the most salient examples of forfeit are those that do involve fault. Suppose that B villainously acts in a way that, if no one interferes, will constitute a violation of a claim of A's. Then it is *prima facie* plausible to think that four consequences for B's rights follow.

In the first place, it seems to follow from B's acting as he does (i) that if A can defend himself against B's violation of his claim only by causing B harm, then A has a privilege as regards B of doing so. That is, by acting as he does, B conditionally divests himself of a claim against A. A further requirement of proportionality must surely also be met: if the claim of A's that B threatens to violate is very weak, and the only way in which A can defend himself against it is by causing B a grave harm, then we may well think that A does not have the privilege of causing B the harm. (If A can defend his garden ornament from an attack on it by B only by shooting B, then even so, A lacks the privilege of shooting B. See Chapter 4, section 3.) So let us put the point as follows. By acting as he did, B made the following true: if A can defend himself against B's violation of his claim only by causing B harm, *and* the harm to B would not be out of proportion with the stringency of A's claim, then A has the privilege of causing B the harm.

What if A can defend himself by means other than causing B harm? (What if A can defend himself either by causing B harm *or* by shouting "STOP, OR I'LL SUE!") Then I should think A lacks the privilege of causing B harm. If so, we could strengthen (i), so as to have it supply a necessary as well as sufficient condition for A's having the privilege. The point here is of interest, and we will return to it. For the moment, however, let us focus on the sufficient condition supplied by (i).

Second, it seems to follow (ii) that if A can be defended against B's violation of his claim only by C's causing B harm, then C has a privilege as regards B of doing so—subject, of course, to the same proportionality requirement. We have a privilege of other-defense as well as of self-defense.

It is worth stress that in these two kinds of cases, B does (conditionally) divest himself of a claim. That is, we should not say that while B retains the claim, A may permissibly infringe it, for it is permissible for A to cause B the harm despite the fact that the conditions on permissible infringement of a claim are not met. If A can be defended against being villainously blinded by B only by A's killing B, then A may kill B, despite the fact that A's being sighted is not better for A than B's being alive is for B. Similarly for C: if A can be defended against being villainously blinded by B only by C's killing B, then C may kill B. So in these two kinds of cases we have to suppose that B (conditionally) divests himself of claims he had formerly had: here there is not permissible infringement of claims, but the forfeiting of them.

For our purposes, the question is: why does forfeiture work? I don't think it is fault in B that makes it work, so let us postpone this question until we get to forfeit without fault.

We were supposing that B villainously acts in a way that, if no one interferes, will constitute a violation of a claim of A's. Then, I said, it is *prima facie* plausible to think that four consequences for B's rights follow. It seems to follow (i) that if A can be defended only by A's causing B harm, then A has a privilege of doing so, and it seems to follow (ii) that if A can be defended only by C's causing B harm, then C has a privilege of doing so—given the meeting of a proportionality requirement. These two consequences do seem to me to follow from our supposition.

Let us now turn to the third and fourth. It seems to follow from our supposition also (iii) that if A's (or C's) causing B a harm would forestall B's (and perhaps others') launching similar attacks in the future, then A (or C) has the privilege as regards B of causing B that harm—subject, presumably, to some similar proportionality requirement. And it seems to follow from our supposition also (iv) that A (or C) has a privilege as regards B of causing B a harm by way of punishment for his acts—again subject to some similar proportionality requirement.

I divide the third and fourth since on my view, as I think on most, they are different. Punishment may forestall wrongful acts in the future, and we would probably engage in it less (and perhaps less severely) if it did not have this consequence; but on most views the central point of punishment is retribution for a wrong and not the forestalling of future wrongs.

Let us begin with (iii). I am standing in a crowded subway, and a pickpocket tries to pick my pocket. I slap his hand away, and he gives up on me. So far so good. But what if I then think "That's not good enough", so I break his arm, thinking "That'll teach him!" (Perhaps it will also teach other pickpockets as well.) Did I have a privilege of breaking his arm?

A similar question arises about (iv). What if I break his arm, thinking not "That'll teach him!" but "Serves him right!" Did I have a privilege as regards him of doing so?

Is the trouble here that the proportionality requirements are not met? Perhaps the point in connection with (iii) is that there are ways of deterring potential pickpockets less severe than arm breaking, *that* being why the pickpocket's act did not give me the privilege of acting as I did. Perhaps the point in connection with (iv) is that arm breaking is an inappropriately severe punishment for pocket picking, *that* being why the pickpocket's act did not give me the privilege of acting as I did. There may well be a failure to meet the proportionality requirements here, but what goes wrong surely has a deeper source. Harm-causing with a view to deterrence or punishment is something that under our law—and I should think under the law of any organized society—is arrogated to government and not to the private person.

It is surely right to think, not merely that under our law a private person lacks the privilege as regards government of causing harm to deter or punish a wrongdoer, but that under our law a private person lacks that privilege as regards anyone, including the wrongdoer. The pickpocket's act did not give me the privilege as regards him, or anyone or anything else, of breaking his arm to deter or punish. And would not have done so even if arm breaking met the proportionality requirements on deterrence of or punishment for pocket picking.

Some political theorists believe that government's privilege of causing harm to deter or punish is a privilege possessed by people in a state of nature, and that the formation of a government is a process in which people come to lack the privilege. If you think that government has no rights not given it by the governed, and think also that government has the privilege of causing harm to deter or punish, then it would be no wonder if you thought that the governed did have that privilege prior to formation of their government. Is it plausible to think that people in a state of nature have a privilege of causing harm to deter or punish?[5] Deterrence seems to me one thing, punishment quite another. For my own part, it seems right to think that if we are in the state of nature, and you are about to cut my throat, then I have a privilege of causing you more harm than is necessary to defend my throat against your current assault on it: I have a privilege of causing you as much harm as is necessary to defend my throat against not merely your current but your otherwise likely future assaults on it. But punishment strikes me as different. Who am *I* to arrange for *you*

5. It will be clear that the notion 'state of nature' at work here is not Hobbes'. In Hobbes' state of nature, it will be remembered, everyone has a privilege of doing everything, and hence *a fortiori* a privilege of causing any harm at all, and hence *a fortiori* a privilege of causing harm sufficient to deter and punish. It is Locke I have in mind here, and his best-known modern friend, Nozick. For Locke on punishment in the state of nature, see *Second Treatise of Government*, secs. 7–13; for Nozick, see *Anarchy, State, and Utopia,* ch. 5.

to get your comeuppance? No matter for our purposes. In arrogating to itself the privilege of causing harm to deter or punish, government does deprive people anyway of the natural privilege of causing harm to deter; and we have in hand yet another instance in which government makes the governed lack natural rights.

In any case, I suggest we should agree that though (i) and (ii) are consequences of B's villainously acting in a way that, if no one interferes, will constitute a violation of a claim of A's, (iii) and (iv) are not—at any rate where A and B are in a state of society rather than in the state of nature. In short, B's acts make A (and C) have a privilege of causing B such harm as is necessary for immediate defense of A; but B's acts do not make A (or any other private person) have a privilege of causing B more harm than that, even if causing B more harm than that would be necessary to deter B or others, or would be suitable punishment of B.

A brief aside on government's privilege of causing unwanted outcomes to deter or punish is in order, since the considerations dealt with in this and the preceding sections have a bearing on it. Suppose B succeeded in his villainous assault on A: B broke A's arm. Government then sentenced B to jail. Due process having been followed, and other things being equal, government may now permissibly jail B. How so? Many accounts of the justification of punishment appeal to B's having forfeited a right in order to explain it. But we should ask: *which* right has B forfeited, his forfeiting of which makes it permissible for government to jail B? Presumably we must suppose that the right B forfeited was his natural claim against government that government not jail him; and presumably it was by his violation of A's claim that B did forfeit this claim against government. But how could B's violation of A's claim make B have forfeited B's claim against government? In the absence of a penal code under which those who violate claims like A's earn jail, B's violation of A's claim would not have made B have forfeited B's claim against government to not be jailed. Imagine a society whose penal code does not attach jail as a penalty for arm breaking. (Perhaps its code instead attaches a fine, community service, or what you will.) In that society, B would not have forfeited his claim against government to not jail him by his violation of A's claim, and it would be impermissible for government to jail him. What emerges is that it is the fact (supposing it a fact) that government has adopted a penal code under which those who violate claims like A's do earn jail that makes B's violation of A's claim make B have forfeited his claim against government to not be jailed. That is, government action in adopting its penal code has made the following conditional true: if Y villainously breaks X's arm, then Y thereby forfeits Y's natural claim against government to not be jailed. B of course is the one who forfeited the claim against government; but it is government itself that made it be the case that, by acting as he did, B would forfeit the claim. I stress: this is something government made true, and it would not have been true if government had not made it true. (We could therefore say that what punishment by government involves is pure social forfeiture of claims.) So though there is nothing wrong with an account of the justification of punishment that justifies the punishment by appeal to the wrongdoer's forfeiting of a right, it has to be remembered that such a justification can only succeed against a background that supplies a justification for adoption of the penal code itself. For as I said, government action deprives of a natural right (as opposed to merely depriving of a legal right) only if the action is one that government may permissibly take; *a fortiori,* government's adoption of a penal code under which a person who does alpha ceases to have a *legal* claim to not be jailed does make it be the case that a person who does alpha ceases to have a *natural* claim to not be jailed only if government acted permissibly in adopting that particular penal code. And it might be well to add that the permissibility of adopting a particular penal code turns not merely on what is in it, but also on what is not in it. That it should not attach disproportionately large penalties to violations of weak rights is only one consideration among many; that it should not fail to attach penalties to violations of stringent rights is another.

6. There can be forfeiture of rights without fault. We can waive a right by just 'letting it lie' and in that case might as well be said to have forfeited the right. There need have been no fault in our doing so.

But just how far does forfeiture without fault extend? Consider

> INNOCENT AGGRESSOR: D and E are in an elevator. E suffers a temporary fit of insanity and goes for D's throat to kill him. D can save his life only by killing E.[6]

---

6. This example comes from George P. Fletcher, "Proportionality and the Psychotic Aggressor", *Israel Law Review,* 8 (1973).

Does D have a privilege as regards E of killing E in INNOCENT AGGRES-SOR? It is surely permissible for D to kill E, and therefore we had better agree that D has the privilege of doing so, for the conditions in which it would be permissible to infringe a claim are absent in this case: in particular, we cannot suppose that D's living is a greater good to D than E's is to E. But how could D have acquired the privilege of killing E? Can we plausibly say that E has forfeited his claim against D to not be killed by D? E is aggressing against D, but he is not at fault for doing so; doesn't it seem an odd idea that he has forfeited a claim against D? One is reluctant to say that he did, since insanity is the source of his aggression.

On the other hand, one's reluctance to say that E forfeited his claim against D may issue from nothing better than our inclination to forget that there can be forfeiture of rights without fault.

The English word "forfeit" is really too soft an affair to rest any great weight on. I think we had better agree that E no longer has the claim against D; we can then just leave open whether or not it would be right to say also that E forfeited the claim.

If E no longer has the claim against D, then it is surely his aggression against D that makes him lack it. And then isn't it plausible to think that it is B's aggression against A in the range of cases of the preceding section that made B lack his claim against A? Compare INNOCENT AGGRESSOR with

> VILLAINOUS AGGRESSOR: B and A are in an elevator. B has always hated A and takes this opportunity to get rid of him: B goes for A's throat to kill him. A can save his life only by killing B.

We might have thought it was the fact that B is at fault for his aggression that makes B now lack a claim against A. (It is because B is at fault for his aggression that it strikes us as entirely right to say B has forfeited his claim against A.) But E is not at fault for his aggression and yet E too now lacks a claim against D. If fault is not necessary, then it is not fault that does the moral work in VILLAINOUS AGGRESSOR. And I think we should say, quite generally, that aggres-sors—whether or not at fault for their aggression—cease to have the claims, it being their aggression itself that makes this happen.

For consider again a point I mentioned earlier. If you can defend yourself against a man who will otherwise cause you harm by less drastic means than causing him harm (if, for example, shouting "STOP, OR I'LL SUE!" would quite adequately stop him), then you had better not choose to cause him harm, and this whether or not he is at fault for his aggression. Thus it is the fact that you *need* to cause harm to defend yourself—and not fault in the aggressor—that makes it permissible to cause the harm. Can it at all plausibly be thought permissible to use more drastic means where the aggressor is at fault than where he is not? (Would using more drastic means than is necessary be arranging for the villainous aggressor to get his comeuppance?) And it is certainly not permissible to go on using those means after the aggression ends. (Kicking a man when he is already down is a dismal business, however nasty a character he may be.)

Moreover, consider third-party interventions. If A were unable to defend himself in VILLAINOUS AGGRESSOR, but C could defend A, though only by killing the aggressor B, then it would be permissible for C to do so. So much we agreed to in the preceding section. What if D were unable to defend himself in INNOCENT AGGRESSOR? What if we could defend D, though only by killing E? My own view is that the answer is plainly yes. E is not at fault for his aggression against D, and this may make some people feel uncomfortable at the thought of our choosing between them who shall live. But we would not here simply be making a choice as to which of two people shall live: E is aggressing against D—E will kill D if we do not kill E.

After all, if it were not permissible for us to defend D where D cannot defend himself, why would it be permissible for D to defend himself where he can? On some views, a self-defender may take an innocent life that threatens his or her own in virtue of having a special 'agent-centered permission', a permission not possessed by an other-defender, who therefore may not intervene.[7] I think this must be a mistake. What I may do to defend my own life I may surely do to defend the life of someone I love; and it is an odd idea that I may kill an innocent to save the life of someone I love but not to save the life of a mere acquaintance or a stranger. (Can it plausibly be thought

7. For interesting discussion of the matters dealt with throughout this section—and of their bearing on the problem of abortion—see Nancy Davis, "Abortion and Self-Defense", *Philosophy and Public Affairs,* 13 (1984). Fletcher also attends to third-party interventions in "Proportionality and the Psychotic Aggressor"; and see his *Rethinking Criminal Law* (Boston: Little, Brown, 1978), ch. 10, sec. 5.

that a man's being rather a bore is going to make him not defendable in circumstances in which he would have been defendable had he only been more charming?) The fact that it is my own life, or the life of someone I love, that I save—as opposed to the life of a mere acquaintance or a stranger—might be thought to make an otherwise inexcusable wrongful act be excusable, but it cannot be thought to make an otherwise wrongful act be permissible.

I should perhaps stress: I am not suggesting that other-defense is permissible wherever self-defense is. For example, as I said in Chapter 4, it might be important for Bloggs to learn to fight his own battles, even at the cost of losing some, and there might be cases, then, in which it would not be permissible for us to barge in to defend him. I suggest here only that the guilt or innocence of an aggressor makes no difference.

In short, I suggest that it is B's aggression against A in VILLAINOUS AGGRESSOR, and E's against D in INNOCENT AGGRESSOR, that make it permissible for A and D to defend themselves by killing, and that would make it permissible for third parties to defend them if they could not defend themselves. The fault in B is irrelevant.

But for the aggression to make the self- and other-defense permissible, the aggression has to make the aggressor lack claims, and we stand in need of an account of why it does. I think it an attractive idea that the answer is simply this: if the aggressor is not stopped, he will violate a claim of the victim's. On any view, B will violate a claim of A's if not stopped; but E too will violate a claim of D's if not stopped—for it should be remembered that fault is not a necessary condition for infringing a claim, so that the fact that E is innocent does not mean that he infringes no claim of D's if he proceeds. The fact that the aggressor will violate a claim of the victim's if not stopped makes him lack a claim against the victim, *and* lack a claim against third parties if the victim cannot stop the aggressor but third parties can. (The same fact also makes the aggressor lack a privilege of defending himself against the victim's, or a third party's, defense of the victim.)

This is unfortunately not the end of the matter, however. An aggressor constitutes a threat to the one aggressed against. What if there is threat without aggression? Consider

INNOCENT THREAT: A sudden gust of wind blew E' down a well. D' is at the bottom. If D' does nothing, E' will survive the fall but D' will die; D' can use his ray gun to disintegrate E', in which case E' dies but D' lives.[8]

It is permissible for D' to kill E' in INNOCENT THREAT, just as it is permissible for D to kill E in INNOCENT AGGRESSOR. So here too we have to say that E' has ceased to have his claim against D'. But though E' is a threat to D', he is not aggressing against D', and we cannot plausibly say that E' will have violated a claim of D''s if not stopped. E is about to throttle D in INNOCENT AGGRESSOR; E' is merely falling toward D' in INNOCENT THREAT.

More puzzling still is

> INNOCENT SHIELD OF A THREAT: F strapped the innocent E'' onto the front of a computer-controlled tank that he now directs toward D'' to kill him. D'' has only one weapon, an antitank gun. If D'' does nothing, the tank will reach and kill D'' and E'' will have time to escape. D'' can use his antitank gun on the tank, in which case he destroys E'' along with the tank but D'' lives.

Here again it is permissible for D'' to kill E''. (Wouldn't it have been permissible for the Belgians to defend themselves against the German tanks if the Germans had been so inventive as to strap a baby onto the front of each tank?) But E'' is not even a threat to D'': the tank is the threat to D'', and E'' merely 'shields' it.

Moreover, third-party intervention would be permissible in both these cases if it were impossible for D' and D'' to defend themselves. (Wouldn't it have been permissible for the British to shoot down the baby-laden German tanks if the Belgians had been unable to do so themselves?) For here again, as in INNOCENT AGGRESSOR, the third party would not simply be making a choice as to which of two people shall live: E' constitutes a threat to D', and E'' shields a threat to D''.

Nevertheless the question remains: *why* have E' and E'' ceased to have their claims against D' and D'' or against third parties if D' and D'' cannot defend themselves? We had a grip on why E had ceased to have his claims in INNOCENT AGGRESSOR: if not stopped, E will

---

8. This and the next example, and their names, are adapted from Nozick's: see *Anarchy, State, and Utopia*, pp. 34–35. Interesting discussion of real (as opposed to merely hypothetical) cases like some of those dealt with here may be found in Michael Walzer, *Just and Unjust Wars* (New York: Basic Books, 1977), esp. pp. 172–175.

violate a claim of D's. That explanation is not available to us in the cases of E′ and E″.

The puzzling fact seems to be that nature (the wind in INNOCENT THREAT) and other people (F in INNOCENT SHIELD OF A THREAT) can make us cease to have claims. We *can* be unlucky enough to find ourselves in a situation in which something other than ourselves, something other even than government, has made us cease to have rights we formerly had. So much, therefore, for the Libertarian Thesis. But just what the conditions are in which this can happen, and why it happens, seems to me a deep and difficult question.

The only thing that does seem clear is that the phenomenon is limited to cases in which Y is, or shields, a threat to X, for X may not kill Y just on the ground that doing so is necessary for X to save his or her life. If X and Y are shipwrecked, and now cling to a life preserver that will support only one, that does not justify X's shoving Y off. If X is starving, and will otherwise die, that does not justify X's eating Y. If X is in need of a new heart, that does not justify X's taking Y's. (The patient's need of a heart certainly does not make the young man cease to have claims in TRANSPLANT.) But exactly what constitutes being, or shielding, a threat that it should make this difference is very hard to see.

7. One final point about consent and forfeiture. A principle we made use of earlier is this:

> The Aggravation Principle: If X has a claim against Y that Y do alpha, then the worse Y makes things for X if Y fails to do alpha, the more stringent X's claim against Y that Y do alpha—but for 'worsenings' that consist in X's being caused belief-mediated distress.

Consideration of consent and forfeiture brings out that this principle really does require emendation. Suppose, for example, that B in a fit of pique smashed A's pink plastic garden flamingo. Terrible business! B has infringed a claim of A's. How stringent was that claim? Well, the principle tells us we are to ask how bad B makes things for A by doing so. But it might be that A, expecting B's assault on the flamingo, has so arranged things that B's assault on it would destroy not only the flamingo but also much more of A's property, so that B's assault on the flamingo makes things very bad indeed for A. (Why did A so arrange things? Resentment, perhaps. A's actions might be thought to fall under the genus Martyrdom in the Name of Making Grief for Others.) In light of A's contribution to the worsening he suffers in consequence of B's smashing of the flamingo, it seems wrong to think that B has infringed a very stringent claim of A's. The point is not merely that B did not know he would be making things so bad for A in smashing the flamingo: as we saw in Chapter 9, there is good reason to say that the stringency of a claim does not rest on the claim infringer's knowledge of how bad the claim infringement would be for the claim holder. The point is rather that the claim holder here has himself made the claim infringement worse for him than it would otherwise have been.

There is room for much discussion as to how, exactly, the Aggravation Principle should be emended to avoid yielding implausible results in such cases. I suggest we not undertake it and instead merely add the rough qualification I have inserted in

> The Aggravation Principle: If X has a claim against Y that Y do alpha, then the worse Y makes things for X if Y fails to do alpha, the more stringent X's claim against Y that Y do alpha—but for 'worsenings' that consist in X's being caused belief-mediated distress, and 'worsenings' that X consents to,

keeping in mind that consent that issues from coercion or fraud, for example, does not have the moral import it would otherwise have had.

And of course there may be no claim infringed at all, for X might have divested himself or herself of it. If A throws his plastic garden flamingo into the path of B's car, then B infringes no claim of A's when he drives over it, however much harm B may thereby cause A. Assumption of risk is a form of consent to it.

8. I think we have now surveyed the most important ways in which one can come to lack a right one formerly had. I have no argument to the effect that we have surveyed all the ways in which this can happen, but then again I have no argument to the effect that in the earlier chapters of Part II we had surveyed all the rights we have prior to ceasing to have them. If the Limits Thesis of Chapter 11 is true, then we had surveyed all our claims; if the powers and immunities we have taken note of are all our powers and immunities, and if also it is correct to think that all rights are either claims, privileges, powers, or immunities, or clusters of them, then we really had surveyed all

our rights. But I have no argument to the effect that these things are so.

What we have done is two things. In the first place we looked at what having a right *is*. To have a right is to have a kind of moral status, so working out what a right is comes to the same as working out what people ought or ought not do, may or may not do, given a person has a right. I have had very little to say about the areas of morality outside the realm of rights. My concern has only been, first: where within morality does the realm of rights lie?

My concern has been, second: what is in that realm? I have tried to bring out that and why the rights we take to be most important are in it, but there may be others I have overlooked. I think that the account of rights presented in Part I showed itself to be useful when brought to bear in Part II on the rights we did look at; I hope it would show itself to be equally useful when brought to bear on such other rights as people may say we have, helping us to decide whether they are right to say so.

And I have tried to bring out that although the realm of rights does not exhaust all of morality, it is deep inside it, imposing constraints on the contours of all the rest.

Index

Abortion, 288–293

Absolute rights, 3–4; and fault, 80, 121; argument for, from ought, 82–87; rejection of, 85–86, 98–100, 103–104, 118–122, 178; argument for, from enforcing, 107–117, 118; explanatory uses of, 120. *See also* Claims; Rights

Acquisition Schema, 324, 329, 332

Action: parts and consequences of, 125–126, 129–130, 134; in Reductive Theory of Action, 125–127, 133–134, 139–140, 141; and failure to act, 126n3, 237–239, 241; and Consequentialist Act Utilitarianism, 127, 130–131, 133–141, 146–148; and Non-Consequentialist Act Utilitarianism, 130–131, 134–141, 142; intrinsic value of, 131–134, 135–141, 143–145; intentional and unintentional, 133; and Transplant case, 134–146; temporal order of, 139–141, 142–143; and fault, 229–231, 234–239; and causation, 234–235, 237–239. *See also* Reductive Theory of Action

Action on the case, 206. *See also* Trespass, right against

Acts and Other Events (Thomson), 140n10, 239n3

Act Utilitarianism, 124–148, 217; individual interests in, 218–220; and ethical egoism, 220–221. *See also* Consequentialist Act Utilitarianism; Non-Consequentialist Act Utilitarianism

Advantage: defined, 170; increments of, 174–175, 198; and Trolley Problem, 191–196, 198; and risk, 244–247

Agent regret, 97n11, 240–242. *See also* Nondoer's regret without fault

Aggravation Principle: and stringency, 153–158, 161–163, 164; and infringement of claims, 154–158, 161–163, 164, 175, 198, 253–257; and distress, 251–252, 253–257; qualifications of, 255–256, 267, 371–372; and word-giving, 318–319

Aggression: innocent and villainous, 366–369; and threats, 369–370

Animals, 42, 49, 217, 292–293

Annas, George J., 290n4

Aristotle, 213

Assertion Thesis, 298, 310; Strong, 295–296; Less Strong, 296–298; and word-giving, 302–304, 313

Atiyah, P. S., *Promises, Morals, and Law,* 317n6

Ayer, A. J., 6n4

Bad for a person, 151. *See also* Good

Bennett, Jonathan, *Events and Their Names,* 126n3, 140n10

Bodily harm, 209; and belief-mediated distress, 264; disfigurement, 265–266, 270. *See also* Harm

Bodily intrusion: and consent, 208–209, 234; and trespass, 208–211, 225–226; and fault, 229–230, 231; disfigurement, 265–266, 270

Body: ownership right over, 225–226; as first property, 226, 270–271. *See also* Bodily harm; Bodily intrusion; Disfigurement; Trespass

Bork, Robert, 257–258

Capital punishment, 9, 10, 27–28; deterrent effect of, 7–8, 21, 22, 23–24; permissibility of, 21–24

375

Care: and word-giving, 297–298, 300–
  301, 319–320; and consent-giving, 352
Case. *See* Action on the case
Causal verbs, 207
Causation: and fault, 229–231, 234–239;
  freakishness of, 230, 236–237; and
  action, 234–239; transitivity of, 235;
  overdetermination of, 235–236; and
  randomness, 236–237
Causal Theory of Intention, 133–134, 144
Central Utilitarian Idea, 124, 129, 196;
  and Transplant case, 134–148; and
  Trolley Problem, 177. *See also* Act Utilitarianism; Consequentialist Act Utilitarianism; Non-Consequentialist Act
  Utilitarianism; Rule Utilitarianism
Claims: and ought, 2, 3, 79–104, 116,
  120; and privileges, 40, 46–47, 49–53,
  64, 66–67, 272; and powers, 40, 57–
  59, 67, 287–288; and rights, 40–43,
  46–47, 50–51, 61, 62, 77–78; defined,
  41; as behavioral constraint, 64, 65–67,
  77–78, 175, 197, 200–202, 208, 214,
  270; and promises, 85–98, 107–116,
  118–120, 302–310, 350; and not-
  ought, 116–117; stringency of, 153–
  169, 175, 197–200, 252, 255–256,
  316–320; in state of nature, 213–218;
  and inherently individual interest, 222–
  224, 269–270; and harm, 227–247;
  and fault, 233–234; and Limits Thesis,
  273–276, 336; waiving, 361. *See also*
  Absolute rights; Conflict of claims; Enforcing of claims; Infringement of
  claims; Natural claims; Pure social
  claims; Stringency of claims
Classical Utilitarianism, 124. *See also* Act
  Utilitarianism; Central Utilitarian Idea;
  Consequentialist Act Utilitarianism;
  Non-Consequentialist Act Utilitarianism; Rule Utilitarianism
Cluster rights: defined, 55; liberty, 55,
  281–283, 285–286; and duties, 56, 67;
  and privileges, 56, 67, 281; and claims,
  56, 67, 282; ownership, 57–58, 98,
  285, 324–325, 338; boundary vagueness in, 282, 285–288; life, 285–286;
  privacy, 285–286
Coercion: and infringement of claims,
  276–279; and word-giving, 310–313;
  and consent-giving, 351. *See also* Fraud
Communitarianism, 223

Comparison Principle, 154, 158, 161–
  162, 169
Compensation, 93–96, 123, 201, 233,
  307–310; legal, 100–103
Conee, Earl, 84n3
Conflict of claims: and absolute claims,
  82–91; Denial Reply to, 87–88; External-Condition Reply to, 89–90, 91, 92–
  93, 93n7; Internal-Condition Reply to,
  90–91, 93n7, 99; ownership, 98–100;
  and Tradeoff Idea, 158–166; and Mafia
  case, 160–163; and Transplant case,
  160–163
Connect, failure to, 24–27, 28, 225
Consent-giving: hypothetical, 187–188,
  192–194, 360; informed, 198; and bodily intrusion, 208–209, 234; and rights
  divestment, 348–352, 360, 361; and
  word-giving, 348–350; and privileges,
  349–350, 352, 359; and powers, 350,
  352–353, 359, 361; and social understandings, 350–351; and coercion, 351;
  and fraud, 351; for impermissible acts,
  351–352; and care, 352; and immunities, 353, 361; and governmental legitimacy, 353–354, 358–361; actual and
  tacit, 360; and forfeiting rights, 371–
  373. *See also* Consent-Giving Thesis;
  Hypothetical consent
Consent-Giving Thesis, 350, 351–352
Consequence: ambiguities in, 125–129;
  and cause, 127–128
Consequentialism. *See* Central Utilitarian
  Idea; Classical Utilitarianism; Consequentialist Act Utilitarianism; Non-
  Consequentialist Act Utilitarianism;
  Rule Utilitarianism
Consequentialist Act Utilitarianism: as
  moral theory, 124n2; action and, 127,
  130–131, 133, 146–148; hedonistic,
  131; and Transplant (Natural Causes)
  case, 134–136, 141; Transplant (5 Villain Causes) case, 137–139, 144–145,
  147, 151; and Transplant (Surgeon
  Cause) case, 139–141; as explanatory
  theory, 142n11
Contracts: renegotiation of, 92–93; a liability-shouldering device, 94–95; and
  promises, 94–95. *See also* Compensation; Promises; Release
Contractualism: and ownership, 332–333;
  and property rights, 357

Davidson, Donald, *Essays on Actions and Events*, 126n3

Davis, Nancy, 368n7

Day's End case, 229, 232–234, 235, 240, 241–242, 243

Day's End (No Harm) case, 246, 247

Death, 184, 185–186, 263, 264

Deathbed promises, 317–319

Death penalty. *See* Capital punishment; Punishment

Denial Reply, 87–88

Deprivation of rights, 339–342, 361

Desert, appeal to, 326–327

Deterrence: and capital punishment, 7–8, 21, 22, 23–24; and other punishment, 363–365

Diminished eligible alternatives: and word-giving, 312, 313; and consent-giving, 351. *See also* Coercion; Fraud

Diminished information: and word-giving, 312–313; and consent-giving, 351. *See also* Coercion; Fraud

Disadvantage, 244–247

Disfigurement, 265–266, 270. *See also* Bodily harm

Distress: and Aggravation Principle, 251–252; and trespass, 252; and stringency, 255–256; and harm, 259–262, 264; and psychological impairment, 265–266

Distress Thesis, 251–253

Distress, belief-mediated, 253–257; and law, 257–259, 354–356; and bodily harm, 264; and property damage, 268; and claim infringement, 276–277; offense as, 354–356. *See also* Harm; Impairment

Distress, non-belief-mediated, 250–253, 258–259, 271, 272; and Limits-Thesis, 273, 280, 281; and natural claims, 274. *See also* Disfigurement; Harm

Distress, right against: non-belief-mediated, 251–253, 258–260, 273; belief-mediated, 253–257

Distribution, 166–169, 198

Divestment of rights: and consent-giving, 348–352, 360, 361; and governmental action, 354–358; and word-giving, 360–361; waiving, 361; forfeiting, without fault, 361, 366–367; forfeiting, with fault, 361–366. *See also* Forfeiting of rights

Doer's regret without fault, 241–242

Doings, 237–239. *See also* Action

Duty: and correlative right, 39–43, 56, 61, 62, 69; and privilege, 44–48, 66; and ought, 61–65, 79–82, 103; a two-hat concept, 62–63; and commitment, 63, 68–70, 83–84; as behavioral constraint, 64–65; legal, 70–73; and moral dilemmas, 83–85; and act of omission, 238. *See also* Obligation; Ought

Dworkin, Gerald, 269n8

Dworkin, Ronald, 288n3, 316n5; *Taking Rights Seriously*, 71n3, 153n2

Efficient System Thesis, 332

Efficiency: and equity, 327; and ownership, 327–332; of law, 337–338, 357

Embryo, rights of, 289–292

Eminent domain, 341

Ends Principle for Claims, 227–228

Enforcing of claims: and permissibility, 105–116; and means, 106–113; principles of, 107–116; and absolute claims, 107–117, 118–122; legal reading of, 113; and consequences, 113–116. *See also* Absolute rights; Permissibility

Epstein, Richard, 103n14; *Takings*, 342n5

Equity, 327

Ethical Egoism, 216, 218, 220–221

External-Condition Reply, 89–90, 91, 92–93

Fact-Value Thesis, 29; and No-Reason Thesis, 6–9, 24; falsity of, 10–19

Fault: and absolute claims, 80, 121; and infringement of claims, 163, 229–234; relieving of, 171; and permissibility, 171–172; and harm, 229; and bodily intrusion, 229–230, 231; and causation, 229–231, 234–239; and ought, 233–234; and forfeiting rights, 365–369. *See also* Requirement-of-Fault Thesis for Claim Infringement; Requirement-of-Fault Thesis for Ought-Not

Feinberg, Joel, 358n4; *Harm to Others*, 160n4, 260n4; *Offense to Others*, 354n1

Feldman, Fred, *Doing the Best We Can*, 130n5

Feminism, 288n3

Fine-Grain Conception of Stringency, 155–156. *See also* Large-Grain Conception of Stringency; Stringency

First property, 225–226, 266, 340. *See also* Bodily intrusion; Body; Distress; Harm
First property, right to, 225–226, 270–271, 286–287. *See also* Trespass
Fletcher, George P., 366n6; *Rethinking Criminal Law*, 368n7
Foot, Philippa, 10–11, 84n3, 100n12; *Virtues and Vices*, 176n1
Forfeiting of rights: without fault, 361, 366–367; with fault, 361–366; and harm, 362–363; and insanity, 366–367, 369; and consent, 371–373. *See also* Divestment of rights
Forster, E. M., *Howard's End*, 25n17
Fraud: and word-giving, 310, 311; and consent-giving, 351. *See also* Coercion
Fried, Charles, *Contract as Promise*, 94n8, 269n1

Genovese, Eugene, *Roll, Jordan, Roll*, 224nn9,10
Gilligan, Carol, *In A Different Voice*, 288n3
Giving one's word. *See* Word-giving
Goldman, Alvin, *A Theory of Human Action*, 126n4
Good: and Consequentialist Act Utilitarianism, 123–124, 130–131; and Non-Consequentialist Act Utilitarianism, 129–131; and value, 150–152; for a person, 151–152, 189–190; nonsubjective, 152, 189–190; and claim stringency, 152–158; increment of, 153–158, 163, 164–166, 168, 174, 198, 199; distribution of, 166–169, 198
Government: rights against, 42; legitimacy of, 353–354, 358–361; and social rights, 354; and property rights, 339–340, 342–344, 354, 357–358; and natural rights, 354–358; and deprivation of rights, 361; punishment privileges of, 363–365
Government Power Principle for Natural Privileges, 356
Guilt, 96–97

Happiness, right to, 37n1
Hare, R. M., *The Language of Morals*, 19n12
Harm: and compensation, 159; and trespass, 209, 227–229, 242–243; and

fault, 229–234; and freakish causation, 230; without fault, 231, 239; and agent regret, 240–242; and risk, 243–247; and distress, 259–266; as damage, 260–262; counterfactual analysis of, 261–262; psychological, 265; disfigurement, 265–266, 270; and status, 266–267; and financial loss, 267–268; and property damage, 268; and moral corruption, 268–269; and impairment, 270; and natural claims, 270–271, 274; and right to noninterference, 280; and Limits Thesis, 280–281; and forfeiting of rights, 362–363; and punishment, 363–365. *See also* Bodily harm; Distress
Harm Thesis, 228, 237, 239, 250, 252–253, 266–267, 269
Harm, right against, 211, 228; and fault, 229–234; and causing harm, 234–239; and risk, 243–247
Hart, H.L.A.: *The Concept of Law*, 71n3, 339n3; *Causation in The Law*, 230n1
Hedonism. *See* Consequentialist Act Utilitarianism; Non-Consequentialist Act Utilitarianism
High-Risk Thesis, 245–246. *See also* Risk Thesis
High-Threshold Thesis, 167–169, 174, 175, 176
Hobbes, Thomas, 304, 310, 320–321; state of nature in, 49–50, 109, 213–218, 359, 364n5
Hohfeld, Wesley Newcomb, 39–60, 62, 68, 76, 200, 276
Honoré, A. M., *Causation in The Law*, 230n1
Hume, David, 5, 10, 20n14
Hypothetical consent: in Trolley Problem, 181–187, 192–194; an epiphenomenon, 187–188, 360

Immunities: and rights, 40, 59, 67; and powers, 40, 282; and liberty, 282–285; and inalienability, 283–285; and consent-giving, 353, 361; waiving, 361. *See also* Powers
Impairment: physical, 264–265; psychological, 265–266, 270. *See also* Distress; Harm
Impermissibility, and ought, 86. *See also* Permissibility

Inalienable rights, 37n1, 59; ambiguities in, 283–285
Increment of good, 153–158, 163, 164–166, 174, 198, 199
Indignation, moral, 250–251, 257–259
Informed consent. *See* Consent-giving
Infringement of claims: permissibility of, 106, 107–116, 118, 123–124, 149–153, 158, 164–175, 197; and ought, 117, 122, 123–124, 232–234; and violation, 122; and release, 123; and Tradeoff Idea, 123–124, 149–175, 197; and Transplant cases, 146–148; and stringency, 153–158, 161–170, 197–200, 267; and aggravation, 154–158, 161–163, 164, 175, 198, 253–257; and fault, 163, 229–234; circumstantial constraints on, 165–166; distribution constraints on, 166–169; and Trolley Problem, 178–179, 197–200; and agent regret, 240–242; and distress, 249–271, 276–277; and status, 266–267; and threats, 276–278; and coercion, 276–279; and word-giving, 306–310, 317; and deprivation of rights, 339–342. *See also* Conflict of claims
Inherently individual interests, 222–224, 269–270, 271
Innocent Aggressor case, 366–367, 369
Innocent Shield of a Threat case, 370–371
Innocent Threat case, 369–370, 371
Insanity, 366–367, 369
Instrumental value, 132n6
Interference. *See* Noninterference, right to
Internal-Condition Reply, 90–91, 93n7, 99
Intrinsic value. *See* Value
Isenberg, Arnold, 316n5

Johnston, Mark, 190n6
Jointly-Owned-from-the-Outset Thesis, 333–337; and labor mixing, 334, 336; rejection of, 335–336

Kant, Immanuel, 108, 215
Katz, Jerrold, *Cogitations*, 19n13
Keeton, Robert E., 103n15
Kripke, Saul, *Naming and Necessity*, 19n13, 20n14

Labor: and ownership, 325–333; and desert, 326–327; and Jointly-Owned-from-the-Outset Thesis, 334–336
Large-Grain Conception of Stringency, 156, 158. *See also* Fine-Grain Conception of Stringency; Stringency
Law: and claims, 1–3, 70–76, 102, 212, 214, 273; positivism in, 71, 74–75, 102, 344, 346; and violent self-help, 109–110; and risk, 247; and morality, 257–259; and belief-mediated distress, 257–259, 354–356; and coercion, 278–279; and privacy, 280; and pure social privileges, 281, 282; and basis of property, 337–338; efficiency of, 337–338, 357; and ownership, 339–340; illegitimate, 342–344; sovereignty over a territory in, 345–347; unjust, 357. *See also* Legal rights
Law, Silvia A., 288n3
Legal rights: and moral rights, 70–76, 113; positivistic account of, 71–72; and Two-Species Thesis, 73–74; and Three-Species Thesis, 74–76; absolute, 100–103
Legitimacy: and consent-giving, 353–354; and Libertarian Thesis, 358–361
Less Strong Assertion Thesis, 296–298. *See also* Assertion Thesis
Liability, 94–95, 307
Liberalism, 223
Libertarian Thesis, 358–361
Liberty, right to, 37–38, 54–56, 272–273, 281–285; privileges in, 53–54, 281–285; and right to noninterference, 53–56, 281–285; a cluster right, 55, 281–286; claims in, 282; and immunities, 282–285; and powers, 284–285; and right to first property, 286–287; and abortion, 288–293
Life, right to, 37–38, 73, 83, 283, 285–286
Limits Thesis: and pure social claims, 273–274; and privileges, 273–281; and property claims, 274–275, 336; and noninterference rights, 275–276; and non-belief-mediated distress, 273, 280, 281; and privacy, 280; and harm, 280–281; no proof of, 280–281
Lindley, Lord, 54n10, 55n11
Locke, John: state of nature in, 109–110; ownership in, 325, 330, 333; proviso

Locke, John (*continued*)
 of, 330–331; *Second Treatise of
 Government*, 325n1, 364n5
Log case: and harm, 228, 243; and risk,
 243, 245, 247
Log (No Harm) case, 243, 245, 247
Luker, Kristin, *Abortion and the Politics
 of Motherhood*, 293n5
Lying 11, 21, 25, 69

Maclagan, W. G., 269n8
Mafia case, 144–145, 147, 153, 178, 278;
 and Non-Consequentialist Act Utilitarianism, 141, 142; and good, 150–152;
 and conflict of claims, 160–163
Marcus, Ruth, 83n1, 84n2, 97n10
Means Principle for Claims, 156–158,
 175, 211, 228; and distress, 270; and
 liberty, 273, 279; and property, 325,
 333, 336, 337
Means Principle for Permissibility, 112–
 113, 157–158, 164
Moore, G. E., 130n5, 173n7; *Ethics*,
 124n1, 173n7; *Principia Ethica*, 6n4
Moral codes, personal, 25, 26–27
Moral corruption, 268–269
Moral dilemmas, 83–85
Moral disputes: empirical judgments in,
 7–8; pure, 8, 24, 27; stalemating of,
 29; and object-level moral judgments,
 30–31
Moral hazard, 184
Morality: skepticism toward, 16–17; and
 law, 257–259
Moral judgments: truth value of, 5–20,
 21; and statements of fact, 6–9, 11–17,
 21–22, 28; thick ethical concepts in,
 11–13, 16, 17; explanatory, 30–33;
 object-level, 30–33
Moral progress, 27–29
Moral residue, 84, 85, 86, 93, 96
Moral rights, and legal rights, 70–76. *See
 also* Rights
Murder, 278–279

Nagel, Thomas, *Mortal Questions*, 319n8
Natural claims: and trespass, 270–271,
 274; inalienability of, 283–284; and
 governmental action, 354–358. *See also*
 Claims; Rights
Natural privileges, 281–282, 320–321.
 See also Privileges

Non-Consequentialist Act Utilitarianism,
 143–145, 147; as moral theory, 124n2;
 action in, 130–131, 139–141; hedonistic, 131; and Transplant (Natural
 Causes) case, 134–136, 142; and Transplant (5 Villain Causes) case, 137–138,
 142; and Transplant (Surgeon Cause)
 case, 139–141; and Mafia case, 141,
 142; as explanatory theory, 142n11
Non-Counterfactual Condition for Harm-
 Causing, 262
Non-Counterfactual Necessary and Sufficient Condition for Harm-Causing, 262
Nondoer's regret without fault, 241–242
Noninterference, right to, 38, 50–52, 53–
 56, 116, 275–280, 281–285. *See also*
 Liberty, right to; Privacy, right to
No-Reason Thesis, 4–9, 10, 24, 29, 32;
 and Fact-Value Thesis, 6–9, 24
No-Value Thesis, 133–134, 144
Nozick, Robert, *Anarchy, State, and Uto-
 pia*, 153n2, 328n2, 364n5, 370n8

Oakes, James, *The Ruling Race*, 225n11
Obligation, 63, 83–84. *See also* Duty;
 Ought
Offense, 209–210, 354
Other-defense, 115–116; privilege of,
 362–363; and self-defense, 368–369
Other things being equal, 13–16
Ought: and rights, 2, 3, 33, 79–104, 116,
 120, 121; and duty, 61–65, 79–82,
 103; a one-hat concept, 62; and conflict
 of claims, 82–91; and wrongness, 87,
 122; and infringement of claims, 117,
 122, 123–124, 232–234; and permissibility, 123–124; subjective and objective senses of, 172–173, 232, 241–242;
 and fault, 233–234; and doer's regret
 without fault, 241–242. *See also* Duty
Ownership rights, 105–107, 118, 119,
 268; powers in, 38, 57–58, 324–325,
 338; a cluster right, 57–58, 98, 285,
 324–325, 338; and right against trespass, 98–100, 207–208, 336; of body,
 225–226; pure social, 274–275, 279,
 337–338, 357; and Limits Thesis, 274–
 275, 336; acquisition of, 323–333;
 claims in, 324–325; privileges in, 324–
 325, 334–335, 338; and labor mixing,
 325–333, 334–335; and efficiency,
 327–332; and Contractualism, 332–

333, 357; and Rule Utilitarianism, 332–
333, 357; joint, 333–337; and Means
Principle for Claims, 336; governmental
action, 339–342, 354, 357–358; and
proportionality, 362, 363–364. *See also*
Jointly-Owned-from-the-Outset Thesis;
Property
Ownership-Has-Origins Thesis, 323–333

Parfit, Derek, 167n5; *Reasons and
Persons*, 262n7
Penalties, legal, 71–73, 74–75, 77
Permissibility: of capital punishment, 21–
24; and infringement of claims, 107–
116, 118, 123–124, 149–153, 158,
164–165, 174–175, 197–200; Sole-
Means Principle for, 108–111, 315;
Means Principle of, 112–113, 157–158,
164; and moral value, 147–148; and
fault, 171–172; and stringency, 197–
200; of law, 357
Positivism, legal, 71, 74–75, 102, 344,
346
Powers, 78, 200; and immunities, 40,
282; defined, 57; large-scale and meta-,
58; and rights, 40, 57–59, 67, 287–
288; and ownership, 57–58, 324–325,
338; and liberty, 284–285; and word-
giving, 320–321; and consent, 350,
352–353, 359, 361; waiving, 361
Prichard, H. A., *Moral Obligation*,
303n3
Prima Facie Plausible Analysis of Harm-
Causing, 261
Prima facie rights, 118–120
Prior, Arthur N., 10n6
Privacy, right to, 280; a cluster right,
285–286
Privileges: and rights, 2, 39–40, 44, 66–
67, 320–321; and claims, 40, 46–47,
49–53, 64, 66–67, 200, 272; defined,
44–45; extensivity of, 45–46; weakness
of, 46–47, 49–50; strength of, 48; 49–
50, 51–53, 67, 272; and noninterference, 51–52, 276; and liberty, 53–54,
281–285; and trespass, 211–212; of action, 212; pure social, 281–282, 294–
321; in right to life, 285, 286; and
abortion, 288; in ownership, 324–325,
334–335, 338; and natural rights, 320–
321; divestment of, 348; and consent,
349–350, 352, 359; and impermissibil-

ity, 352; waiving of, 361; and other-
defense, 362–363; and self-defense,
362–363; in Innocent Aggressor case,
366–367, 369. *See also* Privileges, legal;
Privileges, natural
Privileges, legal, 75; and natural privileges, 354–358
Privileges, natural, 281, 283–284; and
legal privileges, 354–358
Probabilities, 145–146, 170–174
Promises, 59–60, 70, 212, 272–273; a
thick ethical concept, 11–13, 16; breaking of, 83–98, 108–116, 305, 306–310;
and claims, 85–98, 107–116, 118–120,
302–310, 350; priority of, 89, 109n1;
release from, 92–95, 307; compensation
for, 93–96, 201, 307–310; and contracts, 94–95; a liability-shouldering
device, 94–95, 307; and *prima facie*
rights, 118, 119; stringency of, 154,
267, 316–320; and other word-givings,
298–302; and social understandings,
303–304; 'false', 309; deathbed, 317–
319. *See also* Word-giving
Property, 37–38, 73; body as first, 226,
270–271, 323; damage to, 268–269;
transfer of, 322, 324; initial acquisition
of, 323–333; abandoned and unowned,
324–325, 334, 335–336, 344–347; legal basis of, 337–338; and governmental action, 339–340, 342–344, 354,
357–358. *See also* Ownership rights
Prosser, William L., *Law of Torts*, 205n2,
209n6
Punishment: capital, 7–9, 10, 21–23, 27–
28; deterrent effect of, 7–8, 21, 22,
23–24, 363–365; and harm-causing,
363–365; and retribution, 363–365,
366; governmental privilege of, 363–
366; justification of, 365–366
Pure social claims: and Limits Thesis,
273–274; and property rights, 274–
275, 279, 337–338, 357
Pure social privileges, 281–282, 294–321;
and Limits Thesis, 273–274

Rawls, John, *A Theory of Justice*, 32n20
Reductionism about Word-Givings, 317–
320
Reductive Theory of Action, 125–127;
and value of act, 133–134, 139–140,
144

Regulation, governmental, 340–342
Reisman, J., 286n2
Release from claims, 92–95, 98, 123, 201, 232–233, 307
Remorse, 96–97
Requirement-of-Fault Thesis for Claim Infringement, 229, 231–234
Requirement-of-Fault Thesis for Ought-Not, 171–173, 231–232, 246
Respect, 210–211
Revised Tradeoff Idea, 197–200
Rights: and ought, 2, 3, 33, 79–104, 116, 120, 121; ascription of, 4, 33; inalienable, 37n1, 59, 283–285; and correlative duty, 39–43, 56, 61, 69; of animals, 42; as behavioral constraint, 64, 65–67, 77–78, 175, 197, 200–202, 208, 214, 270; stringency of, 153–169, 175, 197–200, 252, 255–256, 316–320; in state of nature, 213–218; and inherently individual interests, 222–224, 269–270; feminist rejection of, 288n3; and abortion, 288–293. *See also* Absolute rights; Claims; Cluster rights; Distress, right against; Divestment of rights; First property, right to; Forfeiting of rights; Harm, right against; Immunities; Infringement of claims; Liberty, right to; Life, right to; Natural rights; Noninterference, right to; Ownership rights; Powers; Privacy, right to; Privileges; Saved, right to be; Trespass, right against
Rights, Restitution, and Risk (Thomson), 96, 179n2, 280n1
Risk: and harm, 243–247; and advantage, 244–247
Risk imposer's regret without fault, 246n5
Risk Thesis, 243–247, 278. *See also* High-Risk Thesis
Ross, W. D., *The Right and the Good*, 14n11
Ruffin, Justice, 224n9
Rule Utilitarianism, 332–333, 357

Sansom, Hugh, 318n7
Saved, right to be, 160–163
Scanlon, T. M., 20n15, 30n19, 188n5, 268n2, 303n3
Schilpp, Paul Arthur, 130n5
Searle, John, 13n9, 363n3
Second property. *See* Property

Self-defense, 115–116, 217–218; privilege of, 362–363; and other-defense, 368–369; and intervention, 368–369
Self-help, 109–110
Self-respect, 80, 121
Sen, Amartya, 20n15
Simplifying Idea, 80–81, 84–85; rejection of, 86–87, 117, 120
Slavery, 224–225
Social rights. *See* Pure social claims; Pure social privileges
Social understandings: and word-givings, 303–304; and consent, 350–351
Socrates, 31
Sole-Means Principle for Permissibility, 108–111, 315; qualification of, 110–111
Statements of fact, 11–17, 21
State of nature, 359, 364n5; and self-help, 109–110; indifference in, 213–216, 222; claims in, 213–218; moral law in, 215; ethical egoism in, 216; and Act Utilitarianism, 217–218
State v. Mann, 224n9
Stringency of claims: and good, 153–158; and infringement of claims, 153–158, 161–170, 197–200, 267; and promises, 154, 267; and aggravation, 153–158, 161–163, 164; Fine-Grain Conception of, 155–156; Large-Grain Conception of, 156, 158; and Means Principle for Claims, 156–158; maximal, 168–169; and Trolley Problem, 197–200; negative, 198–199; and distress, 255–256; and word-giving, 316–320
Strong Assertion Thesis, 295–296. *See also* Assertion Thesis

Taurek, John, 138n9, 167n5, 196n7
Taxation, 342
Thick ethical concepts, 11–13, 16, 17
Threats: and claim infringement, 276–278; and aggression, 369–370
Three-species Thesis, 74, 76
Torture, 17–20, 169
Tradeoff Idea, 146, 151; and infringement of claims, 123–124, 146–148, 149–175, 197–200; vagueness of, 153, 158; and conflict of claims, 158–166; and probabilities, 170–174
Transplant cases, 153, 168, 218–219,

220, 252; and Central Utilitarian Idea, 134–148; and conflict of claims, 160–163; and Trolley Problem, 176–179, 183, 185, 195, 197–200

Transplant (Natural Causes) case, 134–136, 141, 144–145, 147, 151

Transplant (5 Villain Causes) case, 137–139, 144–145, 147, 151

Transplant (Surgeon Cause) case, 139–141

Trespass, right against: and ownership, 98–100, 336; legal, 100–103, 205–207; and property, 207–208; and bodily intrusion, 208–211, 225–226, 229; and infringement of claims, 208–211; and harm, 209, 227–229, 242–243; and insult, 209–210; and privileges, 211–212; source of, 211–224; and distress, 252, 254–256; a natural right, 270–271, 273, 274, 317; and noninterference, 280

Trespass on the case, 206

Trolley Problem, 176–202; and Transplant case, 176–179, 183, 185, 195, 200; and Central Utilitarian Idea, 177; and permissibility, 177, 181–187, 191–196, 197–200; infringement-of-claims solution to, 178–179; and advantage, 191–196; and ought, 196–197; and Revised Tradeoff Idea, 197–200; and fault, 231

Two-Species Thesis, 74–76

Utilitarianism. *See* Central Utilitarian Idea; Classical Utilitarianism; Consequentialist Act Utilitarianism; Non-Consequentialist Act Utilitarianism; Rule Utilitarianism

Value, 131–134, 135–141, 143–145; and good, 150–152

Villanous Aggressor case, 367–369

Vincent v. Lake Erie Transp. Co., 101–103, 113

Violation of claims, 122

Waiving, 361

Washington, George, 225

Walzer, Michael, *Just and Unjust Wars,* 370n8

Weak Assertion Thesis, 294

Westen, Peter, 103n17

Williams, Bernard, 11, 20n15, 84n2, 97n10; *Ethics and the Limits of Philosophy,* 85n5; *Moral Luck,* 240; *Problems of the Self,* 83n1

Wills, Garry, *Inventing America,* 37n1

Word-giving: and Assertion Thesis, 294–298, 302–304, 313; uptake in, 297–298, 301, 301n2, 315, 319–320, 349–350; promises, 298–304, 316–320; and claim acquisition, 302–304, 350; and infringement of claims, 306–310, 317; release in, 307; compensation in, 307–310; and fraud, 310–311; and coercion, 310–313; and diminished eligible alternatives, 312, 313; and diminished information, 312–313; for morally impermissible acts, 313–316; stringency of, 316–320; and Aggravation Principle, 318–319; and powers, 320–321; and consent, 348–350; and rights divestment, 360–361

Word-Giving Thesis, 310, 313, 350; and claim acquisition, 302–304; criticism of, 304–320

Wrongness, 7, 15–16; and ought, 87, 122